THE
SOCCER
TRIBE

Desmond Morris

THE
SOCCER
TRIBE

JONATHAN CAPE
THIRTY BEDFORD SQUARE LONDON

For Jason

by the same author

THE BIOLOGY OF ART (METHUEN)
MEN AND SNAKES, *with Ramona Morris*
(HUTCHINSON)
MEN AND APES, *with Ramona Morris*
(HUTCHINSON)
MEN AND PANDAS, *with Ramona Morris*
(HUTCHINSON)
THE MAMMALS; A GUIDE TO THE LIVING
SPECIES (HODDER)
PRIMATE ETHOLOGY, *editor* (WEIDENFELD)
THE NAKED APE (CAPE)
THE HUMAN ZOO (CAPE)
PATTERNS OF REPRODUCTIVE BEHAVIOUR
(CAPE)
INTIMATE BEHAVIOUR (CAPE)
MANWATCHING (CAPE)
GESTURES, *with Peter Collett, Peter Marsh
and Marie O'Shaughnessy* (CAPE)
ANIMAL DAYS (CAPE)

First published 1981
Text copyright © 1981 by
Desmond Morris
Jonathan Cape Ltd, 30 Bedford Square,
London WC1

British Library Cataloguing in
Publication Data
Morris, Desmond
    The soccer tribe.
    1. Soccer
    I. Title
    796.334   GV943
ISBN 0–224–01935–X

Filmset by Keyspools Ltd, Golborne,
Lancashire
Printed in Italy by New Interlitho, SpA,
Milan

Contents

The Tribal Trappings

The Tribal Elders

The Tribal Followers

The Tribal Tongue

1 Introduction

The human animal is an extraordinary species. Of all the events in human history, the one to attract the largest audience was not a great political occasion, nor a special celebration of some complex achievement in the arts or sciences, but a simple ball-game – a soccer match. On a June day in 1978, it is claimed that more than a thousand million people tuned in to the World Cup Final between Argentina and Holland. This means that something like one-quarter of the entire world population stopped whatever they were doing and focused their attention on a small patch of grass in South America where twenty-two brightly clad figures were kicking a ball about in a frenzy of effort and concentration.

If this occurrence was monitored by aliens on a cruising UFO, how would they explain it? What would they record in their ship's log? A sacred dance of some kind? A ritual battle? A religious ceremony, perhaps? If their curiosity was aroused and they carried out a survey of human cities around the globe, they would quickly discover that almost every major settlement boasted at least one large, hollow building with a green hole in the middle on which similar ball-kicking rituals could be observed at regular intervals. Clearly, ball-kicking has some special significance for the human species – a unique obsession not shared by any of the hundreds of thousands of other life forms visible on the planet earth.

The biggest problem for the puzzled aliens would be discovering the function of this strange activity. Why do thousands of people do it and why do millions of other people watch them doing it? What possible fulfilment can it bring? On the surface it appears to be little more than a child's playground game, a harmless pleasure gained from the realization that striking a spherical object produces a much more spectacular movement than hitting any other shape. For children, this is merely an amusing pastime, part of the business of

The worldwide appeal of soccer. Matches in progress in Brazil (below), Singapore (below right) and, overleaf, in the Andes (top left), Bahrain (below left) and Bali (right).

exploring the physical properties of the environment, like skipping, jumping, rolling a hoop or spinning a top. But unlike these other juvenile actions, ball-kicking, for some strange reason, persists into adulthood and acquires the trappings of a major industry. It is no longer accompanied by high-pitched laughter, but by deep groans, shouts and roars from manly throats. It is now a serious endeavour, with every move dissected and debated in earnest tones, the whole ritual elevated to the level of a dramatic social event. There must be more to it than meets the eye. Since the actions themselves are so simple, the true explanation must be that they have somehow become loaded with a symbolic significance.

Hardly anyone seems to query the importance attached to the game. For those who do the kicking and those who watch it so avidly, the whole matter is taken for granted. Football is football, and of course it is fascinating, so what is there to question? For those who ignore it, it is plainly a stupid waste of time, so why bother with it? It is not worth discussing. Both sides overlook the fact that, viewed objectively, it is one of the strangest patterns of human behaviour to be seen in the whole of modern society.

With this in mind I decided to carry out my own investigation. It soon became clear that each centre of football activity – each football club – was organized like a small tribe, complete with a tribal territory, tribal elders, witch-doctors, heroes, camp-followers, and other assorted tribesmen. Entering their domain I felt like an early explorer penetrating for the first time some remote native culture. I understood little of their echoing war-chants or their colourful displays, their primitive superstitions or their weird customs. It occurred to me that the best course of action was to behave as if I really *were* an anthropologist making an unbiased field-study, and I set about a systematic analysis of this strange and often savage 'Soccer Tribe'.

It is some years now since I began my field-trips, ranging far and wide, from Blackpool to Bali, from Sheffield to Singapore, from Manchester to Malta, from France to Fiji, and from Aston Villa to Avellino. This book is my report on what I have seen and what I have learned of the Soccer Tribe's unusual way of life.

The Tribal Roots

2 The Tribal Origins

The roots of the Soccer Tribe lie deep in our primeval past, when our early ancestors lived and died as hunters of wild beasts. Almost the whole of man's evolutionary history belongs to that hunting period, when the pursuit of prey was not a sport, but a matter of survival. It moulded us and made us, genetically, what we are today. And it changed us dramatically from our nearest relatives, the monkeys and apes. To be good hunters we had to acquire a whole new set of qualities, both physical and mental.

Our bodies had to change from tree-climbing machines to running machines. We had to rear up on our hind limbs and stay there, our longer legs pounding the ground as we sped after our quarry. If we were to catch our prey, we not only had to be nimble and fast – good sprinters – we also had to be endurance athletes – good long-distance runners – which meant better breathing, with larger, deeper chests. Then, at the kill, we required a superior aiming ability, calling for stronger arms, and hands better designed for gripping and throwing weapons.

These changes took place in both sexes, but were more marked in the males. The heavy maternal demands put upon the females of the tribe meant that there had to be some division of labour, with the young adult males playing the major role in the hunt.

Our mental attitudes also had to change. The switch from fruit-picking to prey-hunting demanded greater intelligence and cunning. It also required the ability to concentrate on a long-term project, to avoid distractions and to keep doggedly after the main objective until a successful climax had been reached and the kill made. There was a greater need for courage in the face of serious physical threats, from cornered or desperate prey. Above all, the tribesman had to improve his ability to communicate and cooperate with his fellow-hunters, as a way of increasing the efficiency of the hunt. Without active cooperation, the human predator could not hope to compete with the larger and more highly specialized carnivores, such as lions and hunting dogs.

So our early hunting ancestors became gradually more athletic and, at the same time, more intelligent. Using these advantages and working together as a team – a hunting pack – they were able to plan strategies, devise tactics, take risks, set traps and, finally, aim to kill. Already, you will admit, they are beginning to sound like the perfect prototype for a soccer team. And it is my contention that this is no accident. But how did they make the transition from prey-killers to goal-scorers? The answer is embodied in a single word: farming.

After more than a million years of hunting and gathering, we discovered that it was more efficient to capture, enclose, breed and domesticate our prey, and to sow special crops rather than search for wild fruits and grains. About ten thousand years ago, our brave hunters settled down to become responsible farmers. The rewards were great – food was always readily available and could even be stored when there was a surplus – but there were penalties, too. The revolution came too quickly and the quieter way of life did not altogether suit our ancient, hunting spirit. We still needed the challenge of the chase, the exciting tactical moves, the risks, the dangers, and the great climax of the kill. This was something that careful farming routines failed to provide.

The solution was simple enough: to keep the hunt going. It had ceased to be a question of life and death, but no matter. There were still open hunting grounds and plenty of wild game for the taking. The world had not yet

In ancient Rome the Colosseum provided a huge arena where blood sports could be brought to the teeming urban population.

become too crowded, too boxed in. So the hunt continued and flourished, not as a survival mechanism, but as a recreation. The era of blood sports was upon us.

Following the agricultural revolution came the urban explosion. Great towns and cities sprang up and their teeming hordes had no space for field sports and little hope of enjoying the excitements of the hunt. The ancient Romans solved the problem in a way that was to be immensely important for the later development of the Soccer Tribe: they undertook the formidable task of building a vast arena, the Colosseum, and, in effect, brought the hunt to the people. If the city-dweller could not rush out into the countryside to hunt, then the animals would be brought into the centre of the city and challenged there in an enclosed space, watched by thousands of frustrated hunters.

Wild beasts were shipped in from all over the known world. To satisfy the crowd, the slaughter in the arena was immense. On its opening day, 1,900 years ago, no fewer than 5,000 animals perished. In the hundred days that followed this massacre, 9,000 more were slain. The slaughter continued, at intervals, for roughly the next 500 years, until it was finally abolished. During this period more than seventy similar arenas were built in Roman territories, although none was as great as the original Colosseum. This gigantic building housed an audience of between 45,000 and 50,000 spectators – about the same number as one of today's major soccer clubs. Its arena (at roughly 100 yards by 60 yards) was somewhat smaller than a modern soccer pitch, so that the impact of the slaughter must have been acute.

There have been several legacies from this Roman institution. The most obvious is bull-fighting which, after gaining popularity at the Roman Games, lives on in the modern bullrings of Spain and elsewhere. This ritual is the only major survival of the ancient arena blood sports and there are signs that even this may eventually succumb to the rival popularity of Spanish soccer matches. Less obvious is the lion-taming in the modern circus-ring and other similar animal acts. These too are now dwindling and under constant attack. Despite the fact that blood-letting no longer occurs, they are viewed unfavourably by large sections of the population. The third legacy was animal-baiting, especially bull-baiting, a more cowardly version of bull-fighting, in which the tethered animal was set upon by dogs as a local entertainment. This spread all over Europe in medieval times and persisted in England until the early part of the nineteenth century. Although bull-baiting has since vanished, the closely related practice of bull-running still survives in the now famous annual event at Pamplona in northern Spain. This is as close as one can come to an 'urban hunt' and, if we now tend to think of it as essentially Spanish, it is worth recalling that, as late as 1825, bull-running was a regular spectacle in the English Midlands, at the city of Birmingham.

It was in the 1820s that a new and more humane attitude to animals gained strength, culminating in the formation of the Royal Society for the Protection of Animals. The RSPCA and other animal protection societies grew and flourished as the nineteenth century wore on and, before long, most of the animal abuses showed a sharp decline. Viewed on a world scale, the epoch of arena blood sports was virtually over. This coincided with a new social trend – the movement of huge populations from the fields to the factories as the industrial revolution gathered momentum. The combination of these two trends created a great vacuum in terms of dramatic entertainment for hordes of ordinary, wage-earning city-dwellers. The stage was set for a new era in the history of pseudo-hunting. A new form of sport was about to explode across the globe – the bloodless, animal-free arena sport: the ball-game.

Ball-games were not new. They had existed in classical times in both

Il Calcio (opposite, above), a medieval ball-game, has been played in the Piazza della Signoria in Florence for centuries. As with nearly all ancient ball-games the ball was rarely kicked, although this was permitted. It was a violent game with few rules, but unlike other early forms of folk football it was played between specified teams in a controlled space, and it has been suggested that it is the true forerunner of the modern game. This is unlikely, however, because Calcio had dropped out of favour in the eighteenth century and was not revived until after modern Association Football had been fully established in the late nineteenth century. Today it has become a great tourist attraction in Florence, where it is presented with all the pomp and colour of its antique heritage (right and opposite, below).

During classical times ball-games were largely used for exercise and were not given great significance. The ball was bounced and thrown rather than kicked.

Greece and Rome, but they had not then been taken seriously. True, they were given a boost when Alexander the Great took up ball-play. Being fast on his feet, he had preferred athletics, but was forced to abandon running because his competitors always allowed him to win. When he turned to throwing a ball about as a form of exercise, he was quickly imitated and before long special ball-courts were built, first in Greece, then in Rome.

One of these Roman ball-courts was warmed by a hypocaust (under-floor heating) for winter play, and it is a shaming thought that, 2,000 years later in Europe, many winter soccer matches have to be cancelled because of freezing pitches. The ancients did have one technical problem, however, and that was the production of a perfectly spherical ball that bounced well. Light-weight balls were made out of inflated pig or ox bladders, but they were easily burst. Heavier balls were made by using a stuffing of hair or feathers. Neither type was suitable for fast, kicking games and this may well be the reason why ancient ball-play remained an informal, non-competitive affair, something like the throwing games seen today on the beaches of holiday resorts. There is a line in one of Martial's poems that sums up the classical attitude to ball-play: 'The prancing pansy snatches at this ball ... trying to make his neck muscular by this useless exercise.'

Some modern writers have placed great emphasis on the ancient game called Episkuros, in which two teams opposed one another. Superficially it sounds like the perfect precursor of today's football games, but scholars now reject this view. Closer scrutiny has revealed that Episkuros was a ball-throwing game of a very different kind.

As non-competitive exercises or warm-up routines, these ancient ball-games attracted few spectators. By contrast, the main enclosure for Roman chariot races held crowds of up to 250,000, more than even the biggest of our modern-day football stadia.

In the centuries that followed, ball-games remained rough and ready, rowdily informal sports of little importance and with virtually no

In England, a rough and tumble form of folk football has survived for nearly a thousand years despite repeated attempts to suppress it. It was this game that became transformed into the seven, standardized, modern forms of football during the nineteenth century. The ancient style of play still persists in a few places, such as Ashbourne in northern England (above), where there are two annual games, on Shrove Tuesday and Ash Wednesday. Hundreds of players take part, trying to carry the ball, through fields, rivers and streets, to one of two traditional goals set several miles apart. The contrast between the robust chaos of this old-style game and the formal grandeur of modern international soccer (below) is striking.

organization. But they never died out. It was as if they were lying fallow, waiting for their day to dawn. With the eventual decline of blood sports, their moment had arrived. English public schools, with the dictum 'a healthy mind in a healthy body', began to encourage various forms of football among their pupils. The wildly uncontrolled and highly variable types of popular football, raucously played in villages across the land, were made more systematic in the school games. But there was more than one system. At Harrow and certain other schools, a kicking game was played that was to grow into modern Association Football, first called 'Socker' and then 'Soccer'. At Rugby school and elsewhere a different form of play was used, in which handling the ball dominated the kicking element. This grew into modern Rugby Union Football. The two games were formalized at about the same time, the Football Association being established in 1863 and the Rugby Union in 1871.

In Ireland, a game that was a blend of soccer and rugger, called Gaelic Football, was becoming popular and was formalized in 1884. In Australia a mixture of Gaelic Football and rugger was being played on cricket pitches. It developed rapidly into the modern game of Australian Rules Football, known affectionately as 'The Footy'. In the 1860s, soccer of a sort was spreading in the United States, but under the influence of rugger-playing Canadians from Montreal, the Americans switched from the kicking game to the handling, run-with-the-ball game and, in 1874, American Football was born. As time passed, this diverged slightly from Canadian Football, so that today they are two distinct games, although both remain clearly derived from Rugby Union. Back in England, in 1895, Rugby Union suffered a split from which it has never recovered, when a large splinter group formed the Rugby League, with slightly different rules again, and with professional players in contrast to Rugby Union's amateurs.

In a few short decades in the second half of the nineteenth century, the foundations were laid for all seven of the modern games of football. All established fixed rules and were systematically controlled by official organizations. Football had come of age. Five of the games (Rugby Union, Rugby League, American, Canadian and Australian) used an ovoid ball, its shape reflecting the early use of inflated bladders, while the other two (Association Football and Gaelic Football) employed a spherical ball. Six of the seven variants followed the original Rugby style in allowing the ball to be handled. Only one rejected this: Association Football, and it is this form, the soccer game, that has come to dominate the world. Clearly, soccer has special qualities that the other variants lack. American, Canadian, Australian and Gaelic Football have remained largely restricted to their countries of origin. For some reason, they lack wide appeal. Rugger has fared a little better, taking a hold not only in the British Isles but also in Australia, New Zealand, South Africa and France. But that is as far as it goes. Soccer, in dramatic contrast, is now being played by 146 different nations – virtually the whole world – and when the World Cup is staged, FIFA, the organizing body, can proudly boast that it flies more flags than the United Nations Organization.

So there are Soccer Tribes everywhere, in every remote corner of the globe, making the game of Association Football the most all-embracing and most successful sport of all time. More cultures have adopted it, more people play it and far more people watch it than any other sport in the history of mankind. It is the sport phenomenon of the twentieth century, and its raging popularity shows not the slightest sign of abating. If fewer people are attending soccer matches in certain countries than they used to do, this is because they are watching more of it on television. The obsession with the game remains just as high. And in some countries, such as the United States of America, Japan and China, the sport is showing a rapid increase in popularity.

3 The Many Faces of Soccer

Soccer today presents many faces to the analytical eye. Some are obvious, some are masked, and others are false. To understand the enormous, worldwide interest in this rather simple ball-kicking activity, it is important to reject at the outset the naive idea that it is 'only a game'. This phrase is often heard, uttered in exasperated tones by angry anti-sportsmen, whose outrage usually focuses on the fact that more column-inches in the newspapers are devoted to the sport than to other major social preoccupations such as the arts, the sciences, education, or even politics. 'How can people waste so much time on something which is, after all, only a game?' they ask, failing to appreciate that it is much more than that. If they examined it more carefully they would soon realize that each soccer match is a symbolic event of some complexity. To recognize its many faces more clearly, it will help if we isolate them and examine them one at a time, starting with the image of the ritual hunt.

Survival Hunters

Sport Hunters

Arena Blood-Sportsmen

Arena Ball-Sportsmen

The Soccer Match as a Ritual Hunt

This is one of the masked faces of soccer, concealed by the fact that two teams confront each other in their effort to score goals. Although on the surface the players appear to be doing battle, in reality they are not attempting to destroy one another, but only to get past their opponents in order to make the symbolic kill by shooting at the goalmouth.

We have already seen the way in which football filled the gap left by the decline of the more obvious hunting activities. In tracing the roots of the Soccer Tribe we passed through four main phases. First, there were the *Survival Hunters* – our primeval ancestors for whom the chase and the kill were matters of life and death. Second, there were the *Sport Hunters* – men who remained active in the hunting field even after hunting for food ceased to be a necessity. Third, there were the *Arena Blood-Sportsmen*, who brought the hunt from the field into the city. And finally, fourth, there were the *Arena Ball-Sportsmen* who converted the ancient blood sports into modern ball-games.

In this sequence, the final transformation saw the hunters become the football players, the weapon become the ball and the prey become the goalmouth. We now speak of the players 'attacking' the goal and of the ball being 'shot' into the goalmouth. The use of such words is an important clue revealing the true nature of soccer as a disguised hunt.

Many other elements of the primeval hunting sequence are also retained in the soccer ritual. There is the STRATEGY to be discussed before the event and the TACTICS to be employed during it. Active COOPERATION is required between the participants if the symbolic kill is to be made successfully. There is DANGER involved and the risk of serious physical injury. The CHASE after the ball requires supreme fitness. The speed of the game demands a high level of CONCENTRATION and the non-stop running over a long period of time requires great STAMINA. Control of the ball is perfected by the development of special SKILLS and the unpredictability of the action-sequence fosters IMAGINATION of a kind that can be transformed instantly into physical movements. Considerable STRENGTH is required to carry out these movements effectively and a COOL HEAD is needed at moments of acute tension. Above all, each individual must have excellent VISION and the ability to AIM accurately, especially in the climactic moments when shooting at the goalmouth. Finally, there must be a high degree of assertive MOTIVATION and the capacity to act with BRAVERY when threatened by strong opposition.

All the words emphasized here relate to elements shared by the activities of the primeval hunter and the soccer player. When expressed in this way, the parallel between the two is striking, and the soccer player is revealed in his true light as a modern pseudo-hunter. In some ways he is also playing the role of a pseudo-warrior, but if that were entirely the case he would be attacking his opponents rather than the goalmouth.

One of the problems of holding a pseudo-hunt in a confined space is that the 'prey' cannot run away (as in field blood sports) and this makes the kill too easy. In the bull-fighting arena this difficulty is overcome by pitting an extremely powerful and fierce animal against an almost unprotected man. In the soccer arena the prey has become a static goalmouth attacked by a whole band of pseudo-hunters and so some other form of complication has to be added to make the hunt more challenging. The answer, obviously, is to defend the inanimate prey with a group of opponents whose task it is to make aiming and 'killing' as hard as possible.

In this way it is possible to devise a 'reciprocal hunt' in which both teams have a double role. As defenders of a goal they become part of the 'prey's skill' at avoiding a symbolic death, and as attackers they become hunters themselves, assaulting their opponents' elusive 'prey'. Of all the players on the field, the two goalkeepers are least like symbolic hunters. They resemble more the claws of the cornered prey, lashing out to protect its vulnerable surface. Only when they kick the ball down the field do they become part of the attacking force hunting goals at the other end of the pitch.

Earlier it was emphasized that soccer has outstripped all other forms of sport in global appeal. Part of the explanation for this seems to be the way in which it manages to retain so many of the ancient hunting elements. Other sports retain some elements, but omit others, and therefore provide a less perfect parallel. Archery, darts, bowling, billiards, snooker, skeet, skittles, curling, croquet and golf all concentrate on the climax of the ancestral hunting pattern – the AIM at a target. They also require the development of great SKILLS, but they are sadly lacking in physical risks and dangers and the massive exertions of the headlong chase, not to mention the complexity of the relationships and active cooperation of the members of the hunting pack. Other sports such as tennis and squash are more physical but still lack the group structure typical of the ancient hunting pattern. Many forms of racing, especially motor-racing, are extremely dangerous and have the necessary risk factor, but lack other features such as the vital aiming element. Motor-racing

To triumph in the hunt, our ancestors had to cooperate actively with one another. Large prey could not be carried back to the tribal home without mutual aid. In the same way, the great football trophies can only be won by cooperative team action on the part of the modern pseudo-hunters of the Soccer Tribe.

is little more than a mechanized version of the 'chase' element of hunting.

Of the more closely related sports, such as basketball, netball, volleyball, hockey, cricket, baseball, lacrosse, and the rugger-based forms of football, all seem to be weak in at least one aspect of the hunting sequence. Some, such as basketball and netball, involve a great deal of fast-flowing movement and also the climactic aiming at a target, but there is too little threat of physical danger and the aiming itself is far from 'ballistic'. Cricket and baseball use a much more savage aiming element, but there are too many static features and they lack the thrill of the hunting pack in full chase. The handling, run-with-the-ball forms of football are violent enough and involve perhaps the maximum amount of physical risk and danger, but are weak on free-flowing movements leading directly to a climax of aiming at a target. None appears to have the magic mixture of the elements of the primeval hunt that are seen in the game of soccer, although it must be admitted that a few, such as Australian Rules Football and the different forms of hockey, do come very close indeed. It is something of a mystery why these particular sports have been dominated globally to such an extent by soccer. Perhaps the Australian game has been too isolated geographically, but this cannot be said of hockey. Ice hockey suffers presumably because of the complexity of its specialized arena and all forms of hockey are hindered to some degree, it seems, by the small size of their 'weapon' – the puck or ball – which makes it difficult for spectators to follow during fast play. Also the hitting action with the hockey-stick requires a 'bent posture' on the part of the players which may work against them psychologically in their role as brave hunters going into the attack with 'heads held high'. Making them look rather like frenzied road-sweepers, it has the curious effect of limiting their action to one plane and eliminating the leaping and jumping element so exciting in the typical soccer match.

For the spectator, soccer has a unique appeal. For the participants, all forms of sport have the potential for an intense degree of involvement, even if, as with archery, they are limited to a single element. But for the onlookers, who can only enjoy the event by proxy, the more hunting elements there are on display the more satisfying the sporting ritual becomes. This is the only way in which it is possible to explain the domination of soccer over all other sports.

The Soccer Match as a Stylized Battle

The pseudo-hunting quality of soccer is only one of its many faces. Another, more obvious way of seeing a match is as a kind of miniature war. This is misleading, as already explained, because the two teams are not (officially) trying to destroy one another. The opponents are merely an interference placed between the hunters and their prey, the goalmouth. They are to be avoided or robbed of the ball, but not deliberately injured or incapacitated. The main task of the referee is to penalize any slight tendency towards man-to-man aggression and to prevent, at all costs, the degeneration of the ritual hunt into a stylized battle.

Yet it cannot be denied that there *is* a warlike element in every soccer encounter and that this, too, adds inevitably to the excitement of the occasion. It has to be recognized that, at the end of the match, there is a winner and a loser and that this is not a feature which can be related to the symbolism of the pseudo-hunt. If the soccer match was nothing more than a ritual hunt, all that would matter to a team and their followers would be how many goals (that is, kills) *they* had scored, regardless of how many their opponents had achieved. But obviously this is not the case. It is the difference between the number of goals scored that is all-important, and it is far better to win 1–0 than to lose 3–4. So, although the sequence of the game and its

'ritual aim at a pseudo-prey' are based on the hunting analogy, the final outcome relates instead to the symbolism of a battle. Both facets are active and contribute to the excitement felt by the spectators.

Judging by their comments during the matches, certain onlookers would like to see a greater swing away from the hunting sequence towards the direct confrontation of a pitched battle. 'Get stuck into them', 'Take him out' and 'Cut him down' are screamed from the terraces with alarming frequency. If an obviously savage tackle perpetrated by one of their own team is penalized by the referee, the more vociferous onlookers jeer the decision and hurl abuse. Occasionally they may even cheer an injury, as a member of the opposing team lies writhing on the ground. Soccer, it must be said, often stirs up great waves of violent emotions among its spectators. Soothe them, it does not.

This warlike aspect of soccer and the aggression it arouses has been the subject of much debate. One view has it that, by playing or watching the sport, feelings of violence will be satisfied and dissipated in a harmless way. The idea here is that we all suffer frustrations in our everyday lives and that we carry these with us all the time in the form of pent-up anger. We store this anger up and it seethes away inside us, waiting for an opportunity to explode in some visible form. If no such opportunity arises, we may turn the anger inwards, giving ourselves stress diseases, growing ulcers, or even, in extreme cases, causing suicides. If an opportunity does arise and someone irritates us

The soccer field sometimes looks alarmingly like a medieval battle scene, with proud standards held high, shining shields, explosions and rallying cries, and dense clouds of smoke.

enough to trigger an outburst, then we overreact savagely, the pent-up anger forcing us to lose control. It is argued that if, through participation in a soccer match, either as players or as spectators, we can channel this internal aggression through a harmless outlet, then we will have spent our anger in an acceptable way and avoided more serious incidents at other times.

This is the 'safety-valve theory' of competitive sport. It is based on the tradition that it is socially permissible to shout and snarl and curse at a soccer match and that 'offenders' will not be taken to court for doing so. The spectator who yells abuse is, in a sense, 'licensed' to do so by the context of the sporting event. His anger is no longer pent up, it is unleashed. His aggression is therefore supposedly dissipated and the tension inside him is reduced, making him feel cleansed of his ill-nature and ultimately more relaxed and socially non-violent.

It is certainly true that if the yelling soccer spectator were to behave in a similar way in his place of work or amongst his family or friends, he might quickly find himself in serious trouble. The abuse he directs so freely at officials, players, managers and directors during a soccer match would soon lead to retaliation in a business or social context. So the match does allow him a *release* from social controls, but is it truly therapeutic? Does he really benefit from shouting his head off? Does he, as the saying goes, 'get it out of his system'? Some authorities believe that this is, indeed, the case. They see the mass explosion of verbal and gestural aggression that takes place at every soccer match as the equivalent to taking a time-bomb out of the city and detonating it in a safe place. But there are critics of this view.

Other authorities feel that, at competitive sporting events such as soccer matches, our aggressive feelings are *aroused*, not assuaged. Their argument runs as follows. Aggression is a reactive urge – it is the way we react when we find ourselves under attack. We are all potentially aggressive and we all have an inborn pattern of defensive behaviour if we, our loved ones, our territories, or our possessions are threatened. Because an essential ingredient of the soccer ritual is the risk of being beaten by a group of opponents, we are immediately threatened by them. While the battle on the pitch continues to rage, the tension mounts. There is no relief until the whistle blows to end the contest. Only if our team wins do we finally enjoy the sensation of triumph and the exhaustion of our aggressive urges. But since these are urges that the soccer match itself inflamed, we are really no better off. We may enjoy the glow of victory, but that is not the same as saying that we have found a safety-valve for a backlog of pent-up angers caused by the frustrations of everyday life. We have simply added a new anxiety (will they beat us?) which we have then successfully resolved.

If our team loses, that is another matter. The aggressive tension built up by the contest is not then resolved. For the defeated spectators, the anger aroused during the match remains after the final whistle has blown. In most cases this anger is contained and short-lived. Turned inward, it gives rise to no more than a brief period of dejection. For some, however, it lingers on as a seething need for revenge, and for the explosive few it can lead to actual violence with brawling and vandalism after the match.

These two views appear to be incompatible but in reality they are probably both correct. Both processes seem to be at work. If I take my frustrations with me to a soccer match and vent my spleen on an unfortunate referee or player, the chances are that I will come away feeling slightly the better for it. Equally, if I see something occur in the match itself which adds a new outrage to my store of frustrations, or if my team loses, I will feel worse than I did before I went. Together, the two processes more or less cancel each other out.

Suppose, for example, a man is criticized unfairly by his boss. He wants to strike back, but dare not do so. That afternoon he goes to watch his local soccer team playing in an important match. He storms and shouts at their

A fanatical Scottish supporter, with colours flying, charges across the no-man's-land of the field in a sudden pitch invasion. To the authorities he is nothing but an unruly nuisance, but in his imagination he is no doubt a young warrior running bravely through enemy fire on some historic battlefield.

opponents and gradually his anger towards his boss is used up. His team scores and now he feels on top of the world, his hated boss forgiven and forgotten. Then, just before the final whistle, the opponents score twice and win the match. He goes home furious. Back at work, he sees his boss again and all the pent-up anger he felt against the soccer opponents wells up inside him. He wants to strike back at them by shouting at his boss, but he dare not do so.

In other words, angers and frustrations shifted from work or social life on to the soccer scene can just as easily be shifted in the opposite direction. Both movements undoubtedly occur and who can say what the final balance will be? It is so easy to redirect aggression. It can go either way, and probably does so at every sporting event. Every soccer match, it would seem, is therapeutic and inflammatory in roughly equal proportions. The soccer fanatics and the social puritans would do well to call it a draw.

The Soccer Match as a Status Display

If the home team wins a match, the victorious local supporters can boast an important psychological improvement, namely an increased sense of social status. Since, in every case, there is a strong identification of the local soccer team with the local community, a victory in the stadium acts as a victory for the town. Because most Soccer Tribes grew up in close conjunction with local industrial developments, this means that a soccer victory becomes, in effect, a victory for the local industries. The remarkable testimony to this is the discovery that success for the local soccer team actually increases the efficiency and output of nearby factories. The high status felt by the local workers, who make up the bulk of soccer supporters, becomes translated into a better work-rate and a more buoyant local economy. This has been proved over and over again and yet, in many instances, local industries are too short-sighted to put their weight – and their financial backing – behind the local teams.

The other side of this coin, of course, is that if the local team has a disastrous season (and somewhere, someone has to lose), then the local industries will also suffer.

The status of each Soccer Tribe is measured in the short term by the result of its last match and, more importantly, in the long term, by the position it holds in the League tables. These tables are scrutinized eagerly each week by all the Tribal Followers and discussed at length. In most countries the football clubs are divided up into different grades. In England there are four 'divisions', presenting a parody of the social class system. The First Division is upper class; the Second Division, upper-middle class; the Third Division, lower-middle class; and the Fourth Division, lower class. This does not mean that the tribesmen come from these social classes. It means simply that the official, player or follower of a club in a particular division will look UP to the official, player or follower of a club from a higher division, and DOWN upon those from a lower division, regardless of their social positions outside the clubs. Outwardly, they will often deny this, claiming that their own, lowly club is the best in the country and is merely going through a 'bad patch' or an 'unlucky spell' and will soon be 'back up where it belongs' in the soccer status race. But secretly they will envy the higher-placed clubs and will long for the day when their own local club gains promotion to a more senior division.

When a local team achieves a great victory it dramatically raises the status of the club followers and leads to joyous pitch invasions and wild celebrations at the close of the vital match.

Each season is a formalized status battle to gain promotion or avoid relegation and at its close the top clubs in each division are elevated to the division above while the bottom ones are banished to the one below. This is the greatest status-crisis the members of each Soccer Tribe encounter and the threat of it acts as one of the principal motivating forces in every contest. There is no tribal disgrace greater than relegation, and so severe is the loss of status when this occurs that some kind of tribal sacrifice has to be made – usually in the form of the ritual dismissal of the club's manager.

The Soccer Match as a Religious Ceremony

Many people – some jokingly, some seriously – have likened soccer to a religious order, and have caricatured soccer supporters as modern equivalents of religious fanatics. The grass that grows on the soccer pitch is often referred to as 'the sacred turf', and the stadium is called 'the shrine'. Star players are 'worshipped' by their adoring fans and looked upon as 'young gods'. The directors' board-room becomes 'the Holy of Holies'. Superstitions and magical practices are rife and, on the terraces, the crowded ranks of so-called hooligans sing songs in unison which, despite their often

For many Tribal Followers, regular attendance at home matches has taken over the social role of weekly visits to church (below). Among the fanatics of the tribe, belief in the power of God has been replaced by belief in the invincibility of the local team.

Some of the greatest figures in the Soccer Tribe have become almost 'holy men'. Here (above) revered Liverpool manager Bill Shankly is honoured by one of his faithful followers, who attempts to kneel and kiss his feet.

obscene words, sound for all the world like the hymns of massed choirboys. Indeed, some of them *are* hymns, borrowed directly from the church hymn-book. Perhaps the comparisons that have been made between a soccer match and a church service are not so far-fetched after all.

In one important respect, there can be no doubt about the religious significance of soccer events. They have, in a very real way, replaced the church services and festivals of yesterday, for a large slice of the population. As the churches of many Western countries have emptied with the weakening of religious faith, the communities of large towns and cities have lost an important social occasion. The regular coming together of large congregations on Sunday mornings was more than a matter of communal prayer, it was also a statement of group identity. It gave the pious churchgoers of yesterday a sense of belonging. The crowded church service was a social as well as a theological event. Now, with its passing, and with the fading also of the public dancehalls and cinemas, and the rise of that great social isolator, the television set, the urban dweller is increasingly starved of large community gatherings at which he or she can see and be seen as part of a local population. The soccer match has somehow survived these changes and now takes on a more significant role as a means of displaying a local allegiance.

Like a religious gathering, the soccer match not only brings a large group of local people together in a visible crowd, it also associates them with a commonly and strongly held belief: no longer a belief in a deity, but a belief in a team. Some may feel this is a poor substitute and in terms of group philosophy it may be so, but in other ways it is not. For the young enthusiasts, many of whom lead a drab and repetitive existence in factories and stores, the match is an 'acute' moment in a 'chronic' week. For them it is a peak

In moments of agony and triumph, players are sometimes moved to adopt the postures of devout worship, as if offering prayers to some unseen soccer deity.

experience, giving them a unique opportunity to display, with colours and emblems, chants and cheers, their presence in the community and their shared belief in a common cause. The fact that this cause is no more than the success of their local team, rather than some loftier, more grandiose pursuit of political or religious ideals, in no way robs the occasion of its psychological significance.

There is no escaping the fact that, as a quasi-religious service, the soccer match has an important role to play in modern society.

The Soccer Match as a Social Drug

A political view of the soccer match, expressed by some writers, sees it in the unlikely guise of a drug peddled by capitalist exploiters. Early communists looked upon religion as 'the opium of the masses' and certain modern socialists have interpreted soccer in a similar way.

According to the German political theorist Gerhard Vinnai, the dissatisfaction caused by the social conditions under advanced capitalism demands some kind of emotional outlet. He goes on: 'If this is not to lead to the overthrow of bourgeois society, it must be guided along "safe" channels. Football provides an opportunity for emotional release of this kind ... the pseudoactivity of football canalizes the energies which could shatter the existing power structures.' In Victorian times, he explains, 'English entrepreneurs promoted the new sport, hoping it would keep the workers away from political and trade union activity.'

It is hard to resist the urge to reject this approach as nothing more than political claptrap. To see something as globally popular as soccer in this one-sided way is almost laughable. There is, however, a small grain of truth in the argument. Because this grain has been unfairly magnified, it should not be ignored, and it is worth examining briefly the route by which the left-wing extremists have arrived at their conclusions.

They focus their attention on the way in which large-scale, organized soccer first began. When the factory bosses of nineteenth-century England were forced to shorten the working hours of their employees, a problem arose as to how the men could be occupied during their new-found leisure. At the time when this happened, the elite public schools were in the process of formalizing soccer and the early FA Cup Winners included such teams as the Old Etonians, the Old Carthusians and Oxford University. When these young gentlemen completed their education they often took their enthusiasm for soccer with them to their new lives as members of their family business empires. Teams of workers were encouraged to play one another as a way of spending their newly freed Saturday afternoons.

According to the socialist view, this development had the double advantage for the factory bosses of keeping the idle males out of mischief (and the pubs) and at the same time making them physically fitter for their work in the factories. In 1885, such was the success of this 'capitalist plot' that some of the football-playing workers turned professional. In no time at all, professional soccer was the rule rather than the exception and the old amateur clubs of the elite schools were swept to one side and finally eliminated. Now vast numbers of other workers clamoured to see their ex-worker idols, the new professionals, performing on the soccer pitch. The era of the soccer supporter was born. Terraces were built. Entrance fees were charged. The spectators might not gain physical fitness from their watching in the way the players did, but if the soccer match could keep the workers engrossed on Saturday afternoons and give them pride in their local teams, then this too suited the capitalists' aims. Contented workers work harder.

So the factory bosses became the soccer club directors and encouraged the new trend as much as they could. Huge stadia were erected and great club traditions were fostered in all the major industrial centres of England. The new, professional soccer explosion was a gift on a golden platter – say the socialist writers – to the bourgeois manipulators. While they appeared to be giving intense pleasure to their workers by organizing the new sport, they were in reality exploiting them. They were turning them into automatons, with the soccer match no more than a cleverly disguised play-version of the work-style in the factories and businesses.

The clue to this, it is claimed, lay in the words used to praise a soccer player. He was congratulated for his tremendous effort and his high work-rate. But how could a 'player' have a 'work-rate'? A player must surely have a 'play-rate', but no such thing was ever considered. It was always a 'work-rate'. Which means, of course, that the member of a professional soccer team was not a player but a disguised worker. The socialist critics see this as the bosses' cunning way of promoting the capitalist work-ethic, even during the leisure hours of the workers when, supposedly, they were resting and relaxing.

This is the soccer scenario as they depict it. Their view can be summed up as interpreting the development of modern soccer as a bourgeois-capitalist plot to keep the workers' minds *on* the glory of hard labour and *off* political revolt. The competitive, energetic nature of soccer takes care of the first, and the moments of shared excitement, coupled with club loyalty, take care of the second.

It is entirely possible that such thoughts did pass through the minds of some of the more unscrupulous factory bosses in Victorian times, but to see

Soccer's early industrial background, with hordes of factory workers streaming into their local stadium, is perfectly captured in L.S. Lowry's painting 'Going to the Match'.

this as the whole basis for the development of the sport is a gross distortion. Many factory owners were deeply concerned about the welfare of their workers and welcomed soccer as a way of providing genuine entertainment for them. Furthermore, the workers hardly had the game foisted on them – they clamoured for it – and were themselves soon actively involved in organizing and promoting it. Nor did it stop them becoming politically active or making progress with trade unionism. As their conditions improved over the years, they became sufficiently well paid to choose from a whole variety of Saturday afternoon entertainments and occupations, yet they still flocked to the soccer stadium every week in their thousands. And, incidentally, so did their communist equivalents in Eastern Europe, despite the absence there of the 'repressive conditions of advanced capitalism' which are claimed to be so essential to the growth of soccer enthusiasm.

Perhaps the grain of truth in the argument that sees soccer as a social drug is not political after all, but rather has to do with human nature. If it is possible to find some social event which is exciting, entertaining and keeps large groups of people fascinated, then yes, they will indeed be less likely to occupy themselves with political terrorism and bloody rebellion. There is a much greater chance that they will influence political and other changes in a less destructive fashion. This is bad news for political extremists, but not particularly distressing for those who foster professional soccer.

The Soccer Match as Big Business

One face of soccer that is often mentioned is its financial aspect. The taunt is familiar enough: 'The players don't take part for the fun of it and they don't behave like true sportsmen – they are simply in it for the money. Soccer is an industry, not a sport.'

Again, this is an exaggeration. To say that soccer is merely a business is to overlook one of its most important features. The vast majority of people involved in the sport, from chairmen and directors to players and ballboys, are there because they happen to love the sport. Money is a secondary factor. If they are among those who *are* paid for their involvement, the chances are that in most cases the money will be less than they could obtain outside the sport. The huge transfer fees and top wages of the star players are rarities. Most players earn a moderate wage for a high-risk occupation where serious injury is commonplace and where 'old age' starts at thirty.

The 2½-million-pound handshake. Transfer fees for star players like these are now in excess of a million pounds, as top clubs vie with one another to improve the composition of their teams.

In England, the men who run the soccer clubs – the directors – are not allowed to take any fees for their activities and frequently have to make a large financial loan to the club to obtain a seat on the board. Far from making a profit out of their soccer involvement, they usually incur a loss. And when their team matches this with a loss on the pitch, they can often be heard to question the sanity of their role in the sport.

Shareholders in soccer clubs in England have their dividends restricted to a level that usually means they would be far better off to switch to other types of investment. The only reason for not doing so is a wish to retain a voice in the running of their local club. Furthermore, the vast majority of the ninety-two League clubs run at an annual loss and many are heavily in debt. Among the few super-clubs, where the large crowds do bring profits, any surplus money is rapidly eaten up by paying huge transfer fees for star players.

Apart from a handful of star players and managers, nobody could truthfully be said to be in English football 'for the money'. If modern players appear, from the sports pages of the newspapers, to be increasingly mercenary in their attitude and less 'loyal' to their local clubs than was once the case, it must be remembered that until recent years the clubs have treated them almost as slave labour. All they are asking for now is to be given

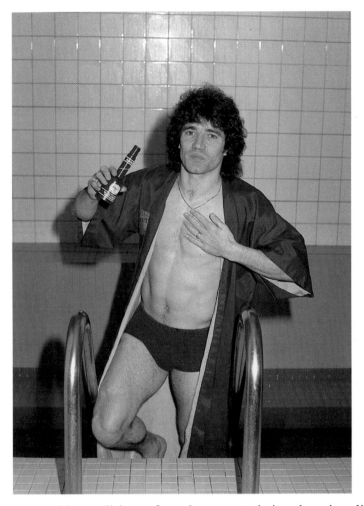

The soccer player as a star celebrity in the world of big business: Kevin Keegan advertising Brut (above left) and Franz Beckenbauer book-promoting (above).

reasonable conditions of employment to bring them into line with workers in other fields, a request that has produced near hysteria among the more reactionary members of the soccer hierarchy. This response reflects as clearly as anything else the difference between the soccer world and ordinary business.

It must be said, though, that these comments do not apply globally. In North America, for instance, where professional soccer on a grand scale has only taken a hold during the 1970s, there is a much greater commercial factor involved. Each soccer match is a 'hard sell', with massive advertising and television sales, high-profit catering and expensive seat tickets. The players, who are expected to take part in a great deal of promotional work, are much more highly paid, and the men who run the clubs are experienced business executives who make no apology for organizing the sport as a major commercial venture, with even greater profits looming on the horizon as the North American population discovers the magic of the event they now sell as 'a kick in the grass'.

The Soccer Match as a Theatrical Performance

Whatever else it may be, modern soccer is certainly mass entertainment, with all the trappings of showbiz. It boasts great stars, virtuoso performances, gala occasions, fan clubs and groupies, and yet it has a very ambivalent attitude to this, its most glamorous face. The sterner elements in the game view the encroaching theatricality as somehow degrading. In England there are many things that are decidedly 'not cricket'; in Europe as a whole there are also

The idea of the traditional soccer match as a spartan ordeal, to be bravely suffered in appalling weather conditions, is under attack from the more progressive elements in the tribe. They wish to see it packaged as family entertainment, with the razzmatazz approach of show business.

some things, it seems, which are definitely 'not football'. Their more progressive opponents view their cautious clucking as fossilized Victorianism and accuse them of treating soccer like a trembling virgin in need of a chastity belt.

There is a great gulf here between the European and the North American approach to the soccer event. In the United States every effort is made to keep the spectators amused and entertained, both before and during the match. There is a colourful parade with marching bands and dancers; there are seductively underclad cheer-leaders; there is elaborate music and an ample supply of food and drink for the onlookers in their comfortable seats. The players make a theatrical entrance to fanfares and personal acclaim, and during the game the giant electronic scoreboard provides running information on each stage of the contest. The members of the team are treated very much like stars, with reporters crowding their dressing room and with many public appearances away from the stadium to boost their glamour images. To the puritan, the American soccer match looks like a musical spectacular, with intervals for a little sport.

The contrast with the typical English soccer match is striking. In England there is hardly any advertising of matches and little publicity about future events. The grounds are universally drab, cold and damp. Even in the appalling English climate, where the game is perversely played throughout the worst months of the winter, many of the spectators must stand on wet concrete with no shelter from the rain. Those who stand under cover must huddle together in what appear to be overgrown cow-sheds and those who are feeble enough to insist on sitting down must do so on seats that are old, hard and cramped. Outside the grounds there are poor parking facilities and inside, poor catering. Struggling into their places long before the start of the game, the spectators must wait patiently while being assailed by recorded music on harshly distorting loudspeakers and faced with a glumly empty pitch. During the half-time interval they will be regaled with little more than a few crackling announcements over the loudspeakers and at the close of play they will trudge stoically out of the ground again to the sound of more shrilly irrelevant pop songs.

Despite these terrible conditions, hundreds of thousands attend the matches, week in and week out, with rarely a complaint. A few clubs attempt to improve the situation with minor entertainments – a raffle or a local brass band – but serious face-lifting of the ancient soccer ritual is virtually non-existent in Europe today. This is not entirely a matter of laziness or complacency. To many stalwarts, spartan conditions actually seem preferable. Any move to introduce improvements would be viewed as 'soft'. It would mean tampering with the traditional hardness of the game. 'It wouldn't be football, would it?' is the usual answer.

In a sense what these traditionalists are saying is that, since there is an ordeal taking place out on the pitch, we, the spectators, must also suffer a little in order to be more a part of it. If we have a 'hard' afternoon, it will

The spectators at a soccer match may be loyal supporters but, like a theatre audience, they are also paying customers without whom the Soccer Tribe would perish, and some clubs are wise enough to acknowledge this fact from time to time with public gestures.

Traditionalists view the showbiz approach to soccer as threatening a sad decline in tribal dignity. For them, the sight of a great star like Johan Cruyff posing with a cuddly mascot would be an embarrassment rather than an entertainment. They fear that modern trends may reduce the Tribal Heroes to the level of circus clowns, and their reaction is neatly summed up in Mike Gorman's 1976 painting (right) entitled 'Coach'.

remain a hard sport – it will retain its ritual quality, as a test of manhood, not only for the players who represent us, but also for ourselves. If it is softened by comfortable seats and modern amenities, the strength of the ritual will suffer. It will deteriorate from a sacred male gathering in the tribal long-house to a cosy family outing.

Undoubtedly, it is this hardline attitude that has sustained the intensely tribal atmosphere of European soccer matches and given them their special ceremonial mood. It will be interesting to see how long it survives in the face of the new American developments and whether it manages to resist all forms of progress in the years ahead.

These, then, are the seven faces of soccer, which together make it much more than 'just a game'. They explain why it is so passionately loved by some and so fervently hated by others. They demonstrate its strengths and its weaknesses. And they indicate the danger of identifying soccer by any one of its faces alone. Every visit to a soccer match is a rich encounter with all its many tribal aspects at once. There, inevitably, are the harassed managers yelling tactical advice in their desperate hunt for goals; there, the triumphant players leaping to hug and embrace one another after a successful attack on the enemy; there, the elderly directors fussing over their League tables and dreaming of the status boost of promotion to a higher division; there, the choir-like chanting of the massed supporters as their idols reappear on the sacred turf; there, the muttering experts who have seen it all before and know with a deep pessimism that the good old days of true sportsmanship are gone for ever; and there, the thinly clad young fans clustered on the icy terraces in a display of manliness, ready to cheer themselves hoarse for the soccer stars that they themselves can never be; the Soccer Tribe in all its curiously isolated and yet intensely public glory. Having looked at its faces, we must now dissect its body.

The Tribal Rituals

4 The Tribal Laws

One of soccer's greatest strengths is its simplicity. At its crudest level, all that is needed is a ball and an open space, with something to act as goalposts. For schoolboys, the space may be no more than a garden, the corner of a field, a back alley, a side-street, or a piece of waste land. The goalposts may be marked out with rough sticks, piles of clothes, old boxes, or lines painted on brick walls. With these primitive preparations a game can be played that is just as satisfying and exciting, to the participants, as that undertaken by the great stars in the super-stadium of the capital city.

This simplicity, and the fact that the game can be engrossing at all levels of sophistication, helps to boost its worldwide popularity. Its breeding grounds are everywhere, from the slums of Rio to the playgrounds of expensive private schools in Switzerland. For the twelve-year-old boy twisting past an opponent, with the ball running at his feet, and with dreams of becoming a future Pelé firing his imagination, the excitement of the game momentarily blots out the cares of the rest of the world and turns him, for a while, into a Tribal Hero. No other sport is so easily available or so immediately inspiring.

As if to guard this simplicity and to preserve the global understanding of the game, the Tribal Laws have remained largely unchanged over the years. Each season there are clever suggestions for 'improvements' and modifications and each season these are stubbornly resisted by the tribal powers. Even in a case where an alteration would truly improve the game, it may be rejected in order to retain the traditional qualities of the sport. This fossilization of soccer has sometimes infuriated experts, but it is clearly an essential part of keeping the game as a fixed ritual comprehensible to all.

If one compares the official Tribal Laws as they were applied at the end of the last century with those of the present day, the almost sacred rigidity of the game soon becomes obvious. Not one major new law has been added during the twentieth century. There were seventeen laws in operation at the end of the nineteenth century and today there are still only seventeen. It is true that they were rewritten in 1938, to rearrange them into a more sensible order, but this was no more than a reshuffling of existing rules. Nothing of importance was added and frequently the wording was identical. Modernizations have consisted merely of trivial adjustments to the main laws.

The laws themselves say practically nothing about the tactics of the game. Only one, the offside law, has any influence on the mode of play. All the rest are concerned with setting up the game and the measures to be taken when something goes wrong:

1 The Field of Play
This establishes the size, shape and markings of the pitch and the goals.

2 The Ball
This details the shape, size, construction, weight and inflation of the ball.

3 Number of Players
This requires that each team shall be of eleven players, including one goalkeeper, and provides for the use of substitutes.

4 Players' Equipment
This states only that players shall not wear anything that may endanger their opponents and restricts the kind of studs which may be worn on the boots. Surprisingly, there is no regulation for the clothing worn, other than that the

Soccer's great advantage over most other sports is its essential simplicity, making it possible for players to enjoy it fully at all levels, from the most sophisticated to the most primitive. All it needs is an open space and a ball, and the contest can begin.

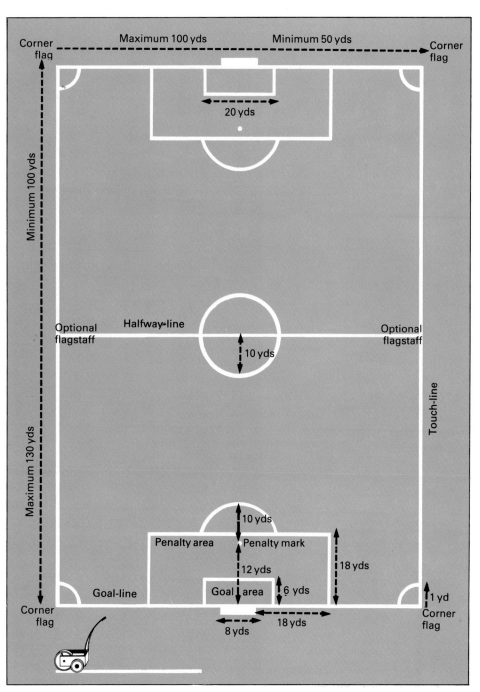

Corner flag

Maximum 100 yds   Minimum 50 yds

Corner flag

20 yds

Minimum 100 yds

Optional flagstaff

Halfway-line

Optional flagstaff

10 yds

Touch-line

Maximum 130 yds

10 yds

Penalty area   Penalty mark

12 yds

18 yds

Goal-line

Goal area

6 yds

1 yd

Corner flag

8 yds   18 yds

Corner flag

The dimensions of a soccer field, as laid down in the official laws, are only approximate. Newcomers to the game are surprised to learn that different pitches have quite different lengths and widths. This is one of the factors that make playing on the home ground an advantage, because the home team can judge distances slightly more accurately than their visitors. To give some idea of the variations that exist today, the dimensions of ten randomly selected English League clubs are tabulated here.

Variations in the Size of the Pitch		
Club	Width (in yards)	Length (in yards)
Hereford United	80	111
Manchester City	79	119
Carlisle United	78	117
Hartlepool United	77	113
Northampton Town	75	120
Exeter City	73	114
Mansfield Town	72	115
Arsenal	71	110
West Bromwich Albion	76	116
Leicester City	65	112

Play on

Indirect free-kick

Direct free-kick

Penalty

Booking

Sending-off

Offside

Offside near
to linesman

Offside far from linesman

Throw-in

Foul near to linesman

Match nearing end
(Two fingers
equals two minutes)

Time up

Foul is in penalty area

New ball

Stop the clock

Originally the linesmen (then called umpires) were more important than the referee, but today they play a subordinate role. One of their specific tasks is to examine the studs of a substitute before he runs out on to the pitch, to ensure that they conform to the required safety regulations.

The Signals of the Referee and Linesmen

Most of these signals (opposite) are understood by the regular spectators, but some are less familiar and go almost unnoticed by the crowd. One that is unknown outside North America is the crossed hands signal for 'Stop the clock', used at electronically timed matches. There, the referee has the help of an official timekeeper who halts the stadium clocks (which count down each half of the game from 45 to 0 minutes) when there is an injury stoppage. The referee's restarting whistle acts as the automatic sign to switch the clocks on again. Other countries have not adopted this timing system because of the absence of accurate stadium clocks at many grounds and because of the difficulty of calculating 'seconds added on' for time-wasting.

goalkeeper must wear different colours from the other players and from the referee. So, in theory, the players could appear in evening dress or bathing suits without breaking this law.

5 Referees
This requires that a single referee shall be appointed to control the game and to enforce the seventeen laws. It also makes the important point that his decision is final. The Soccer Tribe allows for no court of appeal and no 'steward's inquiry' after the game is over. Even though we now have the technology (through television replay) to detect blatant refereeing errors, no post-mortem alterations in any match result are permitted.

6 Linesmen
The referee is to be assisted by two linesmen equipped with flags to signal when the ball is out of play or when infringements have taken place. But the referee may ignore their signals if he wishes.

7 Duration of the Game
This states that the game shall be of two periods of forty-five minutes, separated by an interval, and with extra time added on for stoppages.

8 The Start of Play
This requires that a coin shall be tossed to decide the choice of ends. The winner of the toss can choose ends or can choose to kick off. On the starting whistle, the ball is kicked off from the centre spot, with both teams in their own halves, and this is repeated whenever a goal is scored and after half-time. After a goal has been scored, the team that has conceded the goal takes the kick-off. After half-time, the teams change ends and the kick-off is taken by the team which did not start the game at the beginning of the first half.

9 Ball In and Out of Play
This states that the ball is only out of play if it passes completely over the boundary line of the pitch or if the referee stops the game for some reason.

10 Method of Scoring
This establishes that a goal is scored whenever the whole of the ball enters the goalmouth, without any infringement having occurred. If one team scores more goals than the other, they are declared the winner. If not, the game is a draw.

11 Offside
This is the one tactical law and is designed to prevent players from waiting near their opponents' goal for the ball. It states that when a player is in his opponents' half of the field, and he himself is not playing the ball, he must have at least two opponents between him and their goal. When this rule is broken, the referee must stop the game and award a free-kick to the opposing team, to be taken from the spot where the infringement occurred. However, if he feels that the player's position is accidental and that he is neither interfering with play, nor seeking to gain an advantage, then he will allow play to continue.

12 Fouls and Misconduct
This is the law which lists the offences a player may commit and the punishments inflicted for them. Briefly, they include violent actions, handling the ball (except for the goalkeeper in his own penalty area), entering or leaving the field of play without permission, arguing with the referee, or

ungentlemanly conduct. The punishments include a direct free-kick, an indirect free-kick, a penalty kick, a caution and, ultimately, a sending-off.

13 Free-kick
When a free-kick has been awarded, the opposing players must stand at least ten yards away from the kicker until he has struck the ball. The kicker must not touch the ball a second time until it has been played by someone else. In a direct free-kick, the kicker himself may score a goal from his initial kick, but in an indirect free-kick the ball must be played by someone else before a goal attempt can be made.

14 Penalty Kick
When an offence has been committed by a defender in his own penalty area, a penalty kick is awarded, the ball being placed on the penalty spot and the kicker aiming directly at goal, with the penalty area cleared of all players except the goalkeeper who must remain on his goal-line and must not move until the ball has been struck.

15 Throw-in
When a player drives the ball over the touch-line a throw-in is awarded to the opposing team, at the spot where it left the field of play. The thrower must have both feet on the ground, just outside the touch-line, and must have both hands on the ball, throwing it from behind and over his head.

16 Goal-kick
If a member of the attacking team drives the ball over the goal-line on either side of the goal, the defenders are awarded a goal-kick to be taken from inside their goal area. As with free-kicks and penalty kicks, the kicker is not allowed to touch the ball a second time until it has been played by someone else.

17 Corner-kick
If a member of the defending team drives the ball over his own goal-line, on either side of the goal, the attackers are awarded a corner-kick from the nearest corner of the field. The ball must be placed inside the small quarter-circle marked in the corner of the field and the opposing players must stand at least ten yards away from the kicker. The kicker must not touch the ball a second time until it has been played by someone else. It is permissible (though not easy) to score a goal direct from a corner-kick.

These, briefly stated, are the Tribal Laws. Reading through them, it is clear that they are concerned mainly with what must be done before the game starts and what must *not* be done after it has started. What *must* be done after the game has started – in other words, how the team sets about achieving the object of the game, the scoring of goals – is barely mentioned. Apart from the offside rule, the tactics and strategy of play are left entirely to the players and their advisers. As far as the Tribal Laws are concerned, all eleven team members could, if they wished, form a tight circle around the ball and shuffle it up to their opponents' goalmouth. Or they could all run back and stand in a solid row across their own goalmouth. There is nothing in the laws to prevent them from taking up almost any clustering or spacing out over the field of play, or to require them to play in any fixed pattern, position or sequence. As a result, in the very early days of the game some extremely odd movements were employed, but as time passed orthodox patterns emerged and tactics became rather predictable. Without being forced to do so, players adopted set formations and fixed positions. New variations were tried, with the general shift being from stronger attack to stronger defence. But none of these changes had anything to do with the laws themselves. They took place *within* the laws because these were so simple and so unconstraining.

Progress of the Tribal Laws

1815 Eton College has the earliest known set of rules for football.

1848 Each major public school having now developed its own set of rules, a meeting is held at Trinity College, Cambridge, to standardize these.

1856 Sheffield, the oldest football club, founded in 1855, adopts a set of Sheffield Club Rules, based largely on the Cambridge decisions.

1863 The Football Association is formed in London and, after some disputes, establishes its own set of 14 laws on December 1st.

1865 It is agreed that a tape must be stretched across the goal at a height of eight feet.

1866 The offside rule states that there must be at least three opponents between attacker and goal.

1869 Goal-kicks are introduced.

1871 In this, the first year of the FA Cup, goalkeepers are mentioned in the laws for the first time.

1872 The size of the ball is fixed for the first time.

1874 Shinguards are introduced and umpires are mentioned in the laws.

1875 The crossbar, a Sheffield innovation, replaces the goal-tape.

1877 The FA and the Sheffield Association agree to one uniform code of the Laws of the Game.

1878 First use of a whistle to control the game.

1882 The two-handed throw-in is introduced.

1885 Professionals allowed for the first time.

1888 The Football League formed.

1890 Goal-nets used for the first time.

In 1890 the earliest goal-netting stood as a separate screen behind the goal posts.

1891 The penalty kick introduced, and a referee and two linesmen replace the umpires.

1898 The number of official laws now reaches the modern figure of 17.

1899 Promotion and relegation introduced into the League.

1905 Goalkeepers are ordered to stay on their goal-line for penalties.

1912 Goalkeeper's use of hands is restricted to his penalty area.

1913 Distance of opponents at free-kicks is extended from 8 to 10 yards.

1914 Distance of opponents at corner-kicks is also extended to 10 yards.

1920 Players cannot be offside at a throw-in.

1924 A goal may be scored direct from a corner-kick.

1925 A player must have both feet on the touch-line for a throw-in.

1925 The offside rule is modified from 3 to 2 defenders between attacker and goal.

1929 Goalkeepers are ordered to stand still on their goal-line for the taking of a penalty kick.

1931 The goalkeeper can take 4 instead of only 2 steps while carrying the ball.

1935 Two-referee trials carried out, but the idea is abandoned.

1938 The 17 Laws of the Game are redrafted into their modern form by Stanley Rous, Secretary of the Football Association.

1939 The numbering of players is made compulsory.

1951 The use of a white football is permitted.

1955 Floodlighting is used for the first time at an international.

Modern floodlighting arrived in the 1950s, but an early attempt was made as long ago as 1878.

1956 Floodlighting is used for the first time at a League match (at Portsmouth).

1965 One substitute is allowed to replace an injured player in League matches.

1966 One substitute is allowed to replace a player for any reason in League matches.

1976 Yellow (warning) cards and red (sending-off) cards introduced for display by referees.

5 The Tribal Territories

FROM PLAYING-FIELD TO SUPER-STADIUM

At the heart of each Soccer Tribe lies its great temple, the stadium. So strong is its magic that, for a tribesman to approach it, even on a day when no match is being played, creates a strange feeling of mounting excitement and anticipation. Although it is deserted he can sense the buzz of the crowd and hear again the roar of the fans as the ball hits the back of the enemy net. To a devoted tribesman it is a holy place, with a significance that it is hard for an outsider to appreciate.

Soaring into the sky at the four corners of the stadium are the huge tribal totem poles, the floodlight pylons. Sometimes these are gracefully tapering concrete pillars, but more often they are open metalwork towers, looking like oil-field derricks surmounted by batteries of powerful lamps. Rising high above the surrounding buildings, they are visible for great distances, a constant reminder of the hallowed ground that lies between them.

In the very centre of the Tribal Territory lies the sacred turf of the pitch itself, the green focus of all tribal activities. Known technically as 'the field of play', it is often referred to, by the players and managers, as 'the park'. What matters, they say, is what happens 'out on the park'. Like so many football words and phrases, this has an antique quality, dating back to the time when most matches were played on a marked-out section of public parklands, before the great crowds gathered to watch.

The sacred turf at the centre of the territory of each Soccer Tribe is surrounded by soaring terraces (left) and dominated by great floodlight pylons which, like Indian totem poles (above), jut into the night sky as constant reminders of the tribal presence (opposite). Some carry specially arranged batteries of lights, spelling out the initials of the home club. In this case (below, left and centre) the letters A and V proclaim the home ground of Aston Villa.

Going back further still, to the folk football of medieval times, there were no special arenas. The game was played through the village streets, across fields and meadows, and even along the beds of rivers and streams, anywhere the force of movement took the struggling crowds of players. The goals were often far apart, as much as several miles in some cases, and there were no rules and no boundaries. When the English public schools took up the game, the school playgrounds, often flagstoned and walled in, became the centres of activity and automatically limited the area of play. With such hard surfaces, injuries were all too frequent, but the passion for the game was so great that even the impact of flesh on stone could not halt its progress. In order to protect the limbs of their pupils, the schools were driven to provide softer substitutes for these playground yards. They did this by marking out special areas on nearby fields, imitating the rectangular shapes of the old playgrounds. The football pitch was born.

Later, when the factories took over the game from the schools, patches of waste land were bought up cheaply, usually near the local railway station. Crude sheds and terraces were erected around the edge of the playing areas, often only a few feet from the perimeter lines. The local crowds arrived on foot or by bicycle; the visitors chugged in by steam train. Most had to stand, often out in the rain and with little protection from the cold winter winds. Again, the passion for the game was so intense that few complained.

One of the most imaginative of modern stadia is the Munich Olympiastadion (above), with its curving weather-shields looking like dismembered sections of a vast Arab tent. Few existing grounds can boast such advanced architectural features.

Since it first opened in 1923, Wembley Stadium in London (right) has remained the Mecca of English soccer. Despite its huge size, it cannot fulfil the demand for tickets at important matches. In England, as elsewhere, even larger super-stadia are needed to house the hordes of followers attracted by soccer's greatest occasions.

Attending the match became a shared 'ordeal by climate', almost a test of manhood. This pride in the toughness of the event lingers on even today, and many young fans still resist the idea of being seated in comfort to watch their Tribal Heroes.

Others did not share this spartan view. Gradually, bigger and better tiers of seats were constructed, eating up the strips of land bordering the field of play. The crowds were growing larger and more space was needed, but the Tribal Territories were already finding themselves hemmed in by the spread of urban housing. As the industrial towns flourished, the open areas around the football grounds suddenly blossomed into densely packed rows of terraced houses. Although this kept the tribal centres in the very heart of their communities, it also meant that they were becoming increasingly cramped and congested. Then, with the advance of the twentieth century, came greater affluence. Motor cars replaced the bicycles and on match-days long streams of vehicles converged on each stadium. Huge car-parks were needed, but there was no space available for them and the neighbouring side-streets became choked with traffic.

This problem still exists today at most of the ninety-two professional soccer grounds in England, and it is causing growing concern. A few clubs are lucky and have space for expansion, but most are helpless. Some have constructed impressive new grandstands to house the thousands who turn out for every home match, but most still offer the same old wood and metal sheds that have been towering over the pitches for decades, usually propped up by heavy metal posts that obscure the view of many of the spectators.

Many stadia are hemmed in by tight rows of terraced houses (above), giving the tribal territories no space for expansion or to accommodate the increasing number of cars that converge on the grounds on match-day.

Despite this, the number of complaints is small compared with the degree of discomfort.

All the same, the Tribal Elders are unhappy. They would like to see modernization and improvements on a vast scale. To outsiders, who read of staggering sums of money being paid for the transfer of players, it is hard to understand why more is not spent on updating the facilities. England is the traditional home of soccer and yet no new stadium has been built in living memory.

There are two reasons for this stagnation. In the first place, money spent on a new player has tax advantages in that it can be written off as 'expenses', whereas money spent on stadium modernizations is taxable. Secondly, clubs are biased against moving from their cramped but historically tradition-laden old grounds to sites outside their supporting towns and cities. The new sites would have wide open spaces for car-parking, training grounds and all the other back-up facilities, but would lack the magical aura of the ancestral homes.

The position in other countries is very different. Lacking the antique heritage of the English clubs, they have felt free to strike out with stylishly designed new stadia, often of breathtaking proportions. Great curves of reinforced concrete wrapped in tiers around carefully designed pitches with wide margins, protected by deep trenches and approached by the players through underground tunnels, are the order of the day.

To the English soccer fanatic, these modern stadia in South America and continental Europe are too impersonal, the pitches too remote, and the all-seating facilities too controlled. The Englishman prefers to feel he is breathing down the neck of the player making a throw-in on the touch-line, and to immerse himself in the crowded frenzy of standing body-to-body on the terraces. The oddity of the shapes of the different grandstands gives him a sense of special location and provides each ground with its own characteristic identity. He is wary of architectural elegance that destroys the old tribal idiosyncrasies. As in so many other aspects of the soccer world, the stubbornly traditional and the logically improved modernistic continue to do battle.

Only at the very zenith of territorial display does this conflict fade. In the great stadia of the capital cities, where international matches are fought out before truly vast crowds, there is no place for the quaintly historical. Here the sheer size of the operation demands the most efficient solution that modern architecture can offer.

If an outsider was asked to guess where the most impressive of all the national super-stadia was located, he would probably choose one of the most affluent countries of the Western world. But he would be wrong. Paradoxically, the most gigantic and expensive stadia are to be found in some of the poorer countries. The greatest soccer stadium in the world is in Brazil. Although now over thirty years old, the Maracana Stadium in Rio de Janeiro still holds the record for the largest attendance at any soccer match: 199,854. And those were only the ticket-buying members of the audience; the full total was far in excess of 200,000. No other stadium has ever approached this figure.

Built in the shape of a huge oval, the Maracana is 350 yards long and 305 yards wide. The top of the grandstand is over 100 feet from the ground and it has been estimated that the worst-placed spectators are more than 400 feet away from the centre spot of the pitch. This remoteness would disturb the typical English soccer fan, but for the teeming thousands of Rio, the scale of the arena means that there is a much greater hope of seeing at least something of the action. And there is the added attraction of becoming, for a couple of hours, a member of an enormous and important Tribal Gathering.

The Maracana pitch is defended, like some ancient castle, by a deep, ten-

The passions aroused among the spectators at big matches have become so intense that many pitches now have to be protected from invasion (above) by tall wire fences and deep ditches.

The largest soccer building in the world is Brazil's Maracana Stadium in Rio (right) housing 200,000 spectators. Even the towering giants of Europe such as the Stadio San Paolo at Naples and the Stadio di San Siro at Milan (above left) have a far lower capacity – in this case 81,000 and 83,000 respectively. In the United States the recent rapid growth of soccer interest has been satisfied by the 'borrowing' of huge stadia built for the long-established sport of American Football, like the Rose Bowl in California (above right).

foot-wide moat. Spectators driven to frenzy by the excitement of the game are virtually unable to cross this fierce obstacle and invade the sacred arena.

The three-tiered grandstand, constructed from 435,000 tons of concrete, provides seating for 36,000 people on the ground level, called the 'geral'. On the second level there are seats for 30,000 in the 'cadeiras' and a further 1,500 in 300 five-seater boxes called 'camarotes'. The third and biggest tier, called the 'arquibancada', provides 100,000 seats and standing room for many more. It also houses the journalists, in 438 special press seats, with an additional 20 air-conditioned TV and radio commentary boxes. Finally there is a privileged section holding more than 3,000 'life members' – people who have bought their special seats 'in perpetuity'.

Despite its massive size, the Maracana Stadium can be cleared in a mere fifteen minutes, no matter how packed it may have been. Entrance speeds are also impressive, with no fewer than 120 box-offices selling tickets and 86 turnstiles.

Behind the scenes the extensive facilities include such refinements as a special roadway running beneath the stands and reserved exclusively for ambulances, a 100-bed hotel, a first-class restaurant, six dressing rooms each with a private entrance to the pitch, 330,000-watt floodlighting, a large electronic score-board, and an automatic exchange serving the stadium's 120 telephones.

In a word, the Maracana is a giant. It puts the stadia of all other countries to shame. And it was already in use at the 1950 World Cup contest. Since then there has been little advance, except in one direction, and for that we

The latest development in stadium design is the air-conditioned dome, now found in a number of American cities, such as Dallas (left) and Houston (above). The great curved roof of the Houston Astrodome covers an area of 405,000 square feet, with a playing area of 125,000 feet.

must look northwards from Brazil towards the extraordinary covered stadia of the United States. These huge buildings are the domed cathedrals of sport. They protect players and spectators alike from the elements and create an isolated inner world of arena excitement.

The Astrodome in Houston, Texas, was opened by President Johnson in 1965. It towers over 200 feet into the Texan sky, twice the height of the Maracana Stadium, but it seats far fewer people, having a maximum capacity of only 66,000. Instead of three tiers, it has six. For its many affluent spectators, the Astrodome provides 53 super-luxury, 24-seater 'Sky Boxes' which, even in its early days, cost £5,000 per season to rent.

The greatest feature of the Astrodome is spectator comfort. As you arrive and leave there are no traffic jams. Fifty traffic lanes radiate from the circular stadium building, in all directions. Everyone comes by car, but there is always space to park and at the end of the game the grandstands can be emptied in six minutes, the car-park in fifteen. You are shown to your seat by a gold-lamé-suited hostess. If you are hungry, you can eat in one of five restaurants with a total seating capacity of 3,280, where you are still able to follow events on the pitch via closed-circuit television.

Air-conditioning was one of the biggest problems posed by the Astrodome. Its filtered, temperature-constant, circulated air demanded a control system weighing over 6,500 tons and costing, even back in the 1960s, the staggering sum of £1,500,000. Another task was to provide an electronic scoreboard big enough to do justice to the Astrodome's spectacular interior. The monster that was eventually installed had an 'information space' of half an acre, and required seven men to operate it.

The Super-stadia of the World

Each man represents 5,000 people

Country: Brazil
City: Rio de Janeiro
Stadium: Maracana
Capacity: 200,000

Country: Spain
City: Barcelona
Stadium: Nova Campa
Capacity: 150,000

Country: Chile
City: Santiago
Stadium: Bernabeu
Capacity: 135,000

Country: Scotland
City: Glasgow
Stadium: Hampden Park
Capacity: 134,000

Country: Scotland
City: Glasgow
Stadium: Ibrox Park
Capacity: 118,000

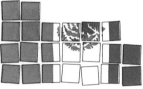

Country: Mexico
City: Mexico City
Stadium: Aztec
Capacity: 112,000

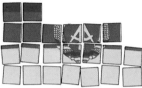

Country: E. Germany
City: Leipzig
Stadium: Central
Capacity: 110,000

Country: Hungary
City: Budapest
Stadium: Nep
Capacity: 105,000

Country: England
City: London
Stadium: Wembley
Capacity: 100,000

Country: W. Germany
City: Berlin
Stadium: Olympic
Capacity: 100,000

Country: Argentina
City: Buenos Aires
Stadium: Huracan
Capacity: 100,000

Country: Brazil
City: Maceio
Stadium: Maceio
Capacity: 100,000

Country: USSR
City: Leningrad
Stadium: Kirov
Capacity: 100,000

Country: USSR
City: Moscow
Stadium: Lenin
Capacity: 100,000

Country: Rumania
City: Bucharest
Stadium: Army
Capacity: 100,000

In its early, trial period, a crisis threatened the giant stadium. Despite the 4,500 skylights in the great dome, the grass on the beautiful pitch gave up the ghost and turned a depressing brown. Hurried research led to the invention of an artificial turf called, inevitably, 'Astroturf'. The great advantage of this development was that it meant the surface could be played on repeatedly without the kind of damage experienced on ordinary turf pitches, where the frequency of games has to be strictly limited to preserve the health of the grass. Also, when Astroturf becomes soiled, it is easy to clean. You simply vacuum it. There is no more surrealist sight in the sporting world than a team of men spread out over a sports field laboriously pushing vacuum cleaners.

The success of the Astrodome has led to other covered stadia, such as the 80,000-seater Pontiac Silverdrome in Michigan, which is roofed over by a vast, balloon-like cover, kept aloft by air pressure. The increase in pressure needed is no more than a quarter of 1 per cent of the outside air, and is indetectable. Again, artificial grass is used and this has, indeed, become the standard surface for North American soccer.

It is sad to report that, after its honeymoon period, Astroturf has come under increasingly heavy fire from the players. True, it never needs sanding, never sinks into muddy, boot-clinging wallows, and always gives an accurate and predictable bounce to the ball, but it has serious shortcomings. The surface it offers is horribly hard for a falling human body moving at speed. Sliding over it produces unpleasant skin-burns. European players who have moved across the Atlantic to find their fortunes in North American soccer have become more and more disillusioned by it and dread the thought that it might spread to European stadia. The Dutch and German stars, Cruyff and Beckenbauer, have made no secret of their hatred for the artificial turf. One North American Soccer League coach commented, 'I am sure I speak for all the coaches in the League when I say that I wish they would rip it all up and make one huge bonfire of it.'

Because of these criticisms, new research is now under way to find a better, more advanced substitute. In particular, it is hoped to discover a type of real grass that will grow and flourish in the indoor conditions of the new, domed stadia. If this research is successful, we may yet see a soccer future in which, eventually, all major stadia round the world are fully covered and climate-controlled, to eliminate once and for all the many frustrating cancellations and abandoned games of the past, not to mention the spartan conditions for the shivering spectators.

A rare sight – the ruins of a derelict soccer stadium. Accrington Stanley Football Club in the north of England, one of the twelve original League clubs in 1888, died in 1962, its ghostly grandstand silent and decaying in the snow.

6 The Tribal Taboos

FOULS AND INFRINGEMENTS, MISTAKES AND MISCONDUCT

The most exciting quality of soccer is that it is a quick-moving, fast-flowing game. Many other sports are for ever stopping and starting, but each half of a soccer game could, in theory, go speeding on for forty-five minutes non-stop. Inevitably there are brief stoppages from time to time, but these only occur when something has gone wrong. They are not *planned* pauses of the kind built into other games, where players 'take turns' in a fixed pattern. This means that each break in play at a soccer match is an irritation, an interference with the graceful rhythm of the game, and together these disruptions constitute the major Tribal Taboo.

Some of these stoppages are mere accidents, but others are the result of the breaking of more specific taboos. If a player is unfairly tackled, for instance, and the punishment is a free-kick, two taboos have been broken – the specific one of the foul tackle and the more general one of the break in the flow of play. The first is punished by the referee. The second, if too many stoppages make the game disjointed, is punished by the disapproval of the spectators.

At their worst these stoppages can lead to the sending-off of a player. At their mildest, they give rise to no more than an inward groan from the crowd. Some are classed as serious offences, while others are merely minor infringements. They fall into six main categories:

1 Violent Actions

These are all punishable fouls and include kicking, tripping, striking, holding, pushing, obstructing or jumping on an opponent. They also include dangerous or unfair charging at an opponent, although shoulder-to-shoulder charging is permitted. In addition there is 'dangerous play', a vague term which covers any other violent action that may occur, such as aiming a very high kick near an opponent's face.

This first category creates a special problem for the referee, because on the one hand he must protect players from being maimed for life and yet, on the other, he cannot allow the game to lose its traditional toughness and manliness. It is his job, of course, and his main reason for existence, to prevent the hunt for goals from turning into a man-to-man battle, in which the main target of the kicking becomes the opponents' bodies rather than the

Tackles directed at the man rather than the ball, whether dangerous tripping (opposite) or the milder but equally effective shirt-pulling (below left) or shorts-pulling (below), are major taboos, but referees are forced to ignore all but the most blatant cases, for fear of unduly disrupting the flow of play and 'softening' the game.

goalmouth. But if he is constantly blowing his whistle at every minor clash, the game soon loses its appeal, not merely because it becomes fragmented, but also because it can rapidly decline from a vigorous sport into a pussyfoot pastime. So for the referee, controlling the game means walking a tightrope between hard and soft play.

2 Insulting Actions

These too are punishable offences and include challenging or ignoring the referee's authority, and the insulting of one player by another. This category embraces such items as spitting in the face, using obscene language, making rude gestures, questioning the referee's parentage or sanity, and arguing with him about his decisions. Throwing or kicking the ball away in a fit of pique when the referee has stopped play is another common misdeed.

Spectators often criticize the lack of emotional control of many professional players. It is in the very nature of the game that all players are going to hate the referee from the moment the kick-off whistle blows, but since they must know this beforehand it is felt that they should be able to control their emotions in at least this one respect. The players' difficulty, however, is that the game takes place at such a high level of emotional tension that they are unable to prevent their feelings from spilling over in this one unfortunate and ultimately futile direction. It is futile, of course, because the referee always wins.

3 Cowardly Actions

The soccer player is cast in the mould of a Tribal Hero and is automatically expected to be brave and courageous. So automatic is this expectation that the rules do not even bother to refer to it, and there are hardly any official

Unfair charging, obstruction, holding and pushing are specific fouls (opposite) but there is also a general category called 'dangerous play' which permits the referee to penalize virtually any violent action if he so wishes. The most common example of dangerous play (left and below) is high kicking near an opponent's body, referred to in players' slang as 'showing studs'.

The emotional tensions of the game are so great that players often lose control and insult the referee, a reaction that is quickly punished unless a team-mate is there to apply a restraining hand (above)

punishments available for cowardly play. The only exception is the offence known as 'time-wasting', which the referee can punish either by awarding a free-kick or by adding on extra time. Time-wasting is achieved by such devices as holding on to the ball after a stoppage, or by a goalkeeper taking a goal-kick at a snail's pace, and is indulged in by the winning side when nearing the end of a match.

Other forms of cowardice are punished not by the referee but by the spectators, who are sometimes driven to hurl mass abuse even at their own team if they are performing poorly. The great advantage for the spectators, at such a moment, is that, unlike the hapless players, they cannot be penalized for their insulting behaviour. One particular action that enrages them and which occurs in almost every match at some point, is the dreaded 'back pass'. In this, a threatened defender plays safe by passing the ball harmlessly backwards to the waiting arms of his goalkeeper, instead of facing up to his attacker and driving the ball forward, past him. True, there are moments when he really has no choice and the crowd recognize this fact. All too often, however, he opts for the easy solution and is rewarded by an outburst of enraged booing. His excuse would be that the modern soccer crowd are more concerned with seeing their team win than with being entertained by an unfaltering display of bravery. But the truth is that the crowd want more than a win, they want a brave win, and they are reluctant to settle for anything less.

In addition to these three 'emotional taboos', there are three 'technical taboos'. They are:

4 Handling

This is the great and ancient taboo that makes soccer the only true game of football. All other so-called football games – Rugby Football, American Football, Canadian Football, Australian Rules Football and Gaelic Football – permit the use of the hands to such an extent that they might just as well be called handball. Except for the goalkeepers in their own penalty areas, the only time when a soccer player can legally handle the ball is at the moment of the throw-in. Throughout the rest of the game his hands and arms are unwanted appendages useful only for keeping his balance and for softening his fall. (In fact a one-armed player has been highly successful on the soccer field. Castro 'The One-armed' came on to play as centre-forward for the victorious Uruguay team in the 1930 World Cup Final, and scored one of the winning goals.)

There are often fierce disputes about whether 'the hand strikes the ball' or 'the ball strikes the hand'. Officially only the former is an offence, but it is not always easy for a referee to decide, in the rush of play, whether the handling was intentional. This gives rise to yet another situation in which the anger of the crowd can vent itself expressively with well-known phrases and sayings.

5 Hitting the Ball off the Field

This is a taboo only in the sense that it breaks the flow of play. Since the perimeter of the pitch is no more than a white line on a flat surface it is inevitable that the ball will stray off the playing area many times during a match and when this happens accidentally it arouses little or no comment. With increasingly defensive play, however, there is a much greater tendency to kick the ball out of play deliberately as a safety precaution, sometimes so frequently that it starts to irritate the spectators. But even when a panicked defender purposely gives away a throw-in or a corner-kick, he rarely receives much abuse.

6 Offside

This, the only tactical taboo, arouses more spectator confusion and disagreement than any other aspect of the game. It is a particularly difficult rule for the referee to enforce fairly and yet it is essential to the game and appears in the very earliest written instructions. Back in the middle of the nineteenth century, when the game was only being played by a few public schools, the rule was already established. It was considered bad form for a

The handling of the ball by an outfield player is forgiven only if it is accidental, but frequently, as in this case (left), it is hard to tell whether the action is intentional or not. So every time the cry of 'handball' goes up, the referee is faced with yet another difficult decision.

player to edge quietly up towards the enemy goal and loiter there waiting for the ball to come his way. The manner of preventing this varied from place to place. At Eton, where the offence was known as 'sneaking', the rule stated that whenever the ball was behind a player he must have at least *four* opponents in front of him. But when the Football Association was formed in 1863 its original offside rule was more strict. Any attacker who was in front of the ball when it was being played by a team-mate was automatically offside, regardless of how many opponents stood between him and the enemy goal. Three years later, in 1866, this law was judged to be too severe. Two other public schools, Charterhouse and Westminster, had gone even further than Eton in allowing a player to be onside when only *three* opponents stood between him and the enemy goal, and the FA wisely adopted this softer version of the offside rule. Much later, in 1925, the rule was softened even more, when the figure was reduced from three opponents to only *two*, and this is the way it has remained ever since. The general effect of this change has been to enable an attacker to come closer to the enemy goal before being offside. In the modern game, since one of the two defenders is nearly always the goalkeeper, an attacker without the ball can approach the goal until there is only one outfield player standing in his way, and still be onside.

In addition he cannot today be offside when he is in his own half of the field, or when he is receiving the ball direct from a goal-kick, a corner-kick, a throw-in, or when it has been dropped by the referee to restart play. All this is straightforward enough; the trouble starts with another 'softening' of the rule. This states that a player shall only be declared offside if, *in the opinion of the referee*, he is 'interfering with play or with an opponent, or seeking to gain an advantage by being in that position'.

This is no longer a matter of fact, but a matter of opinion. The referee is required to read the player's mind and interpret his intentions. In the heat of the game this is asking a great deal of any man, and at first referees repeatedly came unstuck. Their solution, not unreasonably, was more or less to ignore this clause. If a player was signalled offside by a linesman, it was nearly always because he was in an offside position *regardless* of his reason for being there, and the referee was all too ready to accept the linesman's decision at its face value. And who could blame him? If a 'sneaker' is going to 'sneak' upfield, to use the old term, he is obviously going to try to make it look unintentional. So why give him the benefit of the doubt?

As a result, any professional player knows today that even if he finds himself in an accidental offside position, where he does not want to be and where he is not in any way interfering with play, he will nevertheless stand a strong chance of being flagged down and having his side penalized by the award of a free-kick to his opponents. He therefore runs as fast as he can to avoid being caught. This in turn has led to the development of a special defensive tactic known as the 'offside trap', in which all the defenders move swiftly forward in an attempt to leave an opponent stranded. According to the Laws of the Game, such a trap cannot succeed, because the stranded player is in no sense seeking to gain an advantage. No player can have an 'evil intention' forced upon him, yet the offside trap has become a way of life for certain teams and has made a nonsense of the rule as it stands.

On the other hand, no referee can afford to disregard the offside trap because, if he did so, and obeyed the law strictly, a cunning attacker would then *pretend* to find himself stranded. And it is this that exposes the weakness of the rule, because the referee cannot be asked to become a mind-reader.

The outcome is that there exists an unspoken agreement between players and referees largely to ignore this aspect of the offside rule. The fact that it is not ignored in every single case leads, of course, to endless arguments, and makes the offside rule confusing to many of the spectators and a perennial topic for angry debate.

When the linesman's flag is raised for 'offside' (below) the referee should overrule the signal if he feels the player in question is not seeking to gain an advantage and is not interfering with play. In practice, he often ignores such considerations and penalizes the player merely for being in an offside position.

The offside rule: red player no. 1 is offside because he is in front of the ball with only one blue player between him and the blue goal-line. Red player no. 2 is onside even though he is in front of the ball, because there are two blue defenders between him and the blue goal-line.

Further confusion is created by another clause which states that: 'Offside shall not be judged at the moment the player in question receives the ball, but at the moment when the ball is passed to him by one of his own side.' In other words, if he is onside when the ball is kicked by a team-mate and he then rushes madly forward during its flight up the field, gathers it up and rushes on again, he has committed no offence. This is clear enough in theory, but extremely difficult for any linesman or referee to judge accurately in the hurly-burly of fast play, with a number of players moving swiftly in different directions. It even has the damaging effect of penalizing particularly rapid sprinters. If they get to the ball fairly with amazing speed they cannot help giving the false impression that they must have been offside at the moment the ball was passed forward for them. Careful analysis of video recordings of matches reveals that this often happens and it causes great frustration for the players, not to mention the spectators. But the referee cannot be blamed because too much is being asked of him.

There is no obvious solution to this problem and the offside rule will undoubtedly remain one of the great arguing points of soccer for many years to come. Viewed perversely, this could even be seen as an advantage. To have a few taboos that are controversial adds emotional excitement to the game. Human errors creeping in help to stir up the passions of both the players and the crowd. If everything was neat and tidy there would be a danger of the whole ritual becoming too mechanical and too cold. And with the present offside rule, there is no risk of that ever happening.

These, then, are the six major Tribal Taboos and it is the task of the hard-pressed referee to punish those who break them. It is extraordinary that, given such a task, he should be called a 'referee'. By definition, this means someone to whom you refer and yet this is the one thing that players are forbidden to do. They must obey him, but if they refer to him verbally in any way they are soon punished for it. Since they must always defer to him, perhaps the correct name for him should be, not referee, but 'deferee'.

One particular criticism of the referee occurs again and again in the memoirs of ex-players. They all resent the fact that referees frequently punish offenders harder for insults than for violence. If a player attacks an opponent and seriously injures him in a vicious tackle, he is unlikely to be penalized any more severely than if he answers back to the referee in a momentary loss of temper. The reason is thought to be the direction of the foul. In the case of a violent attack the victim is another player, while in the insult the victim is the referee himself. It is only human to respond more aggressively when you yourself are the recipient of the foul, but there does seem to be some justification for these criticisms, especially when most experienced referees are fully alert to the tricks of the 'hard men' in the game.

These tricks include the well-known 'hit him in the first five minutes to let him know you are there' routine. Hard defenders are well aware that referees do not like to book a player or send him off during the opening moments of a game, so that it is fairly safe to assault an eager forward during this period. What is surprising is that referees have not dealt more strictly with this practice.

'Going over the top' is another hated foul. The offender pretends to kick hard at the ball but lets his foot glide just over the top of it on to the victim's ankle or shin. Referees are said to be poor at detecting this, even though it is quite common. 'Following through' is a rather similar foul, in which the ball is kicked but the kicking foot is allowed to follow through and strike the victim's leg as well.

Other tricks include the 'blindside elbow' in which an apparently fair shoulder charge is augmented by a hidden elbow blow to the chest of the victim, and the 'heel flick' in which the heel is jabbed hard against an ankle during a close tackle. All these and many other deliberate fouls are perpetrated in almost every game and most players plead, in their writings, for stronger action by referees to prevent injuries that can and frequently have destroyed a promising career. The argument that severity in dealing with these offences will soften the game is not accepted. The view is that robust tackling and even crude fouling is an inevitable part of the game and will help to retain its manliness, but that the viciously planned and cunningly executed, crippling fouls are another matter altogether. Sadly, the clumsy and unplanned fouls are the more obvious ones and are therefore easily punished, while deliberately brutal play is more difficult to detect.

At a less physical level, many players complain of the attitude of referees to retaliations. Played well, the 'retaliation game' becomes a fine art. The victim is insulted in some way that makes him so angry that he retaliates wildly and is spotted doing so by the referee. He is then penalized, while the true instigator of the incident escapes.

In criticizing referees in this way, for the manner in which they deal with the breaking of the Tribal Taboos, players are sometimes unduly harsh. Jimmy Greaves, one of the greatest players the game has known, was prepared to sum up his attitude to referees with the sentence: 'Some referees, it seems, don't honestly know the difference between "going over the top" and a tap dance.' He went on, 'It takes boldness by a referee to send a player off and too few of them will do it for the right reason. Somebody argues and he'll probably get the finger-waving bit or even be sent off. Yet a fellah can take a diabolical kick at a forward just going into the box and he often gets away with it.' This may be an exaggeration but it sums up what most players feel about most referees. The referees in their turn might well argue that few of the men who complain are themselves angels on the pitch, and that if they did become too strict when taboos were broken, there would be few professionals left to play the game. And so the argument goes on. It is doubtful if it will ever stop. Taboos will be broken and angry debates will continue to rage. Laws will be tightened and loosened, hardened and softened. The referee, as tireless controller of taboos, will always be abused from all quarters and will continue, as ever, in his vital role in the life of the Soccer Tribe, walking his perpetual tightrope.

7 The Tribal Punishments

PENALTIES AND BOOKINGS, FINES AND TRIBUNALS

When the time comes to punish the guilty, the Soccer Tribe is a law unto itself. Star players, with the roar of adoring fans still in their ears, may suddenly find themselves reduced to the status of naughty schoolboys in the headmaster's study, or soldiers facing a court martial. Much has been written about the high-handed manner in which punishments are meted out by the Tribal Elders, and surprise has been expressed at the way the accused accept their sentences, even when these are heavy fines or suspensions. There are moments when the Soccer Tribe begins to look more like the Foreign Legion than a modern entertainment industry.

It is easy to imagine the outrage that would erupt if such brusque treatment was given to one of today's factory workers, and the endless walk-outs, strikes and negotiations that would ensue. But the modern footballer behaves more as if he were under martial law, with no arguments and no challenging of authority. It is as though he sees himself in the front line of a tribal army, with any act of revolt tantamount, not to a strike, but to mutiny.

Since the players are the most important members of the Soccer Tribe and its success or failure lies entirely in their hands, or rather feet, one is forced to ask why they are prepared to submit so humbly to tribal discipline. To understand their attitude, it is first necessary to classify the various forms of punishment inflicted. Minor misdeeds are dealt with on the spot by the referee, but more serious tribal crimes are handled either by the senior members of the local clubs, or by a special committee of one of the parent organizations, such as the Football Association. There are two main kinds of punishment: negative and positive.

Negative punishments are those which are not applied directly to the guilty party, but are given in the form of a reward to his victim. This solution is the favourite way of dealing with minor offences during the game. A player commits a foul and the referee stops play to award a free-kick to his opponents. In such a case, the offender may have hacked down his rival with a savage tackle, but he suffers no direct punishment himself. He is penalized only by the advantage given to the enemy. There are eight negative punishments of this kind available to the referee:

1 The Throw-in
Awarded to the opposing side when a player kicks the ball out of play across the touch-line, this is perhaps the most trivial of punishments, for the smallest of crimes. In the early days of the game it was not even considered a crime worthy of punishment, and when the ball went over the line it was the first player, of either side, who touched it, who was allowed to bring it back into play. This is why the line down the side of the pitch is called the 'touch'-line, yet another soccer term that is a relic of the ancient past. Today, many teams have one player who has developed the art of the 'long throw' and is capable of hurling the ball right into the enemy's penalty area from the nearby touch-line, giving the throw-in a much greater value as a negative punishment.

2 The Goal-kick
Awarded to the opposing side when an attacker kicks the ball out of play across the enemy goal-line, on either side of the goalmouth, this punishment penalizes the attacking team for failing to direct the ball between the goalposts. It gives the defenders the advantage of immediately transferring play to the centre of the field or beyond, away from their own danger zone.

Minor offences are punished by giving an advantage to the enemy. There are eight negative punishments of this kind, including the throw-in (below).

3 The Corner-kick

This punishes the defenders if, in a moment of panic, they drive the ball over their own goal-line, rather than risk its continued presence near to their goalmouth. The kick, taken from the small quadrant at the corner flag, has the great advantage that the attackers cannot be ruled offside during the goalmouth scuffle that follows.

4 The Indirect Free-kick

This is awarded to the opponents of a player who has committed certain types of foul, on the spot where the offence occurred. Although a goal cannot be scored direct from such a kick, the ball has only to be tapped across to a team-mate before an attempt may be made to score, so it is almost as valuable as a direct free-kick. Indeed, some direct free-kicks are taken indirectly in this way, as a tactical device to confuse the enemy. It is doubtful whether, in modern soccer, the distinction between a direct and an indirect free-kick is of any great value.

During the taking of a free-kick, the defenders must stand back at least ten yards (it used to be six yards) from the ball. If the kick is being taken near to their goalmouth, they are in considerable danger and the awarding of this form of negative punishment may often lead to the scoring of a goal.

5 The Direct Free-kick

This differs from the last only in that the kicker himself may score a goal direct from the free-kick. It is awarded against a side that has committed slightly more serious fouls. Many people are confused about which fouls lead

to a direct and which to an indirect free-kick, and it would probably simplify matters to return to the old system where there was only one kind of free-kick. In the meantime, here are the subtle distinctions made between bad fouls and worse fouls:

Bad Fouls for which an Indirect Free-kick is awarded	Worse Fouls for which a Direct Free-kick is awarded
1 Dangerous play.	1 Kicking an opponent.
2 Charging fairly, but off the ball.	2 Tripping an opponent.
3 Obstructing a player intentionally.	3 Jumping at an opponent.
4 Charging a goalkeeper unless he is holding the ball, obstructing an opponent, or has passed outside his goal area.	4 Charging violently.
	5 Charging from behind when not being obstructed.
5 When playing as goalkeeper, taking more than 4 steps while holding or bouncing the ball, or deliberately wasting time.	6 Striking an opponent.
	7 Holding an opponent.
	8 Pushing an opponent.
	9 Handling the ball, unless he is the goalkeeper in his area.

Viewed objectively, the distinction between these two categories of fouls is in some ways decidedly odd, and it is hard to see how it has arisen. To take two examples: if a player takes a wild, high kick at a ball and nearly embeds his studs in the face of an opponent, it is classed as dangerous play and is considered less serious than if he merely pushes an opponent. Similarly, if the offender blatantly obstructs the run of the man on the ball, it is considered to be less serious than if he were to tug at his shirt, which would be called holding. Since the importance of each of these fouls can vary so much in relation to the moment when it occurs, their separation into two categories with different punishments makes little sense.

6 The Penalty Kick

If any of the fouls listed above, in the category that leads to a *direct* free-kick, are committed inside a defender's own penalty area, then the punishment is the much more severe one of the penalty kick. In this, the ball is placed on the penalty spot twelve yards from the centre of the goalmouth and one of the attackers is allowed a direct kick at goal while the goalkeeper remains on his goal-line. All the other players must stay outside the penalty zone until the kick has been taken. It is a punishment that nearly always leads to the conceding of a goal and is therefore the most serious of all the different forms of negative punishment available to the referee. It is so serious, in fact, that many referees apply their own 'severity' rule to make sense of it. In other words, if they see a mild foul inside the penalty box, they ignore it completely because there is no way they can give a suitably mild punishment for it. Sometimes they pretend that they have seen an obstruction instead of a penalty foul and award an indirect free-kick. Famous referee Arthur Ellis considers this to be an 'unforgivable sin', commenting that, 'When they should have awarded a penalty they have taken the easy way out and given, instead, an indirect free-kick, or, worse still, in shirking the main issue they have brought the ball outside the penalty area and ordered a free-kick from there. It happens. Players know it. Managers know it. The fans we might sometimes under-estimate know it and the guilty referees know it.'

Referees who bend the rules must be condemned, of course, although their behaviour is understandable. They are reluctant to give penalties in certain cases because they intuitively feel that the crime committed is not bad enough to warrant the award of a penalty kick. Unfortunately they are faced with an all-or-nothing decision. They cannot award a half-penalty – there are no subtle gradations of punishment.

This dilemma is perhaps the soccer referee's greatest problem and it applies to all fouls, both inside and outside the penalty box. How savage does a foul have to be before he blows his whistle? How mild does it have to be for him to ignore it? This will always be a matter of individual taste and it will always vary slightly from one referee to another. And the supporters on the terraces will always be angered by what they consider to be inconsistencies favouring their opponents. To say that the solution is to change the punishment system so that the referee has a scale of punitive measures which he can apply to any foul, according to its severity, is only to replace an old

One of the defender's most dreaded moments (left) – when he gives away a penalty by fouling an opposing striker 'inside the box'. The penalty, or 'spot-kick', is nearly always successful, as in this case (below), which makes it the most feared of all the negative punishments. Since it almost amounts to the awarding of a goal against the offending team, referees are sometimes reluctant to recognize a mild but unmistakable foul in the penalty zone, an understandable attitude that inevitably leads to howls of protest.

problem with a new one. In some ways it would be an improvement, but it would also create endless confusion and misunderstanding in a game that is so fast-moving that it demands a set of rigid rules, even if these are sometimes unfair. And the unfairness itself, of course, helps to maintain that high level of emotional tension among the spectators which is such a vital part of the Tribal Ritual.

7 Playing the Advantage

The fact that there are rigid punishments for specific fouls has led to a practice known as the 'professional foul'. A defender sees an attacker running full tilt with the ball, straight towards his goal. There is no time to make a fair tackle. In his mind he must calculate the alternative risks of letting the attacker go on and shoot, or of callously bringing him down with a foul so obvious that he knows he must give away a free-kick. If he decides that the free-kick would be the lesser of the two threats, he then blatantly commits his foul. This gives his team-mates time to regroup in defence of the goalmouth.

This device made referees angry because it ridiculed the only negative punishment they were able to inflict. Their answer was to introduce the 'advantage rule'. This meant that if the victim of the foul was able to pick himself up and struggle on, or even while sprawling on the ground was able to pass the ball across to one of his own team-mates to continue the run, the referee was empowered to ignore the foul and wave play on. It punished the offender by refusing to allow him to benefit from his own misconduct.

8 Added Time

If a winning team resorts to time-wasting tactics, the referee can add on extra time to give the losing side a last-minute chance to score. This is why it is difficult to use electronic timing to ensure that the forty-five-minute rule for each half is adhered to precisely. The referee would find it hard to signal his 'added time' to a remote time-keeper, or to indicate adjustments to be made to an electronic clock.

Those, then, are the eight forms of negative punishment. There are also seven positive punishments, in which the offenders are themselves directly disciplined in some way:

1 The Warning

If a player commits a particularly nasty foul, or a long series of ordinary fouls, or if he behaves abusively, he will receive a verbal scolding from the referee.

2 The Booking (Yellow Card)

If the referee feels that a simple warning is not sufficient for these offences, he performs what might be called his 'Traffic Light Display', pulling from his pocket a large yellow card and holding it stiffly aloft in the direction of the offender. The latter then has to perform his own small ritual of turning his back to the referee to display his number, so that it can be written down in the little black book that every referee carries during the game. This event, always immensely popular with the opposing supporters, results in the player being given a number of 'black marks', like a schoolboy who has misbehaved in class. The marks, or 'points' as they are called, are noted on his record and, when he has reached a certain total, he is disciplined in a more serious manner, as we shall see in a moment.

The number of points given to an offender varies in a complicated way according to the seriousness of his misconduct. To give a few examples: one point for entering or re-entering the field of play without the referee's permission; two points for handling the ball or time-wasting; three points for obstruction or refusing to retreat the full ten yards when a free-kick is being taken; four points for dangerous or foul play, or for showing dissent against the referee's decision.

When a player has accumulated twenty of these penalty points he is automatically summoned to appear before the Disciplinary Committee of the Football Association. This body of men, usually elderly and distinguished chairmen of various clubs, is in effect the High Court of the Soccer Tribe. The Tribal Judges examine the evidence in each case and then pronounce judgment, which can vary from a warning about future conduct to a punishment as severe as a three-match suspension. If this maximum penalty is given it means that the offender's team will have to play their next three games without his help and it also means that he will lose the financial benefits of the usual 'match bonuses'.

If a player accumulates another ten penalty points later in the same season, he will find himself up before the Tribal Judges again. The pattern is repeated each time his total gains another ten points, with his judges taking an increasingly severe line. At the end of the season, however, his slate is wiped clean and he begins the new playing year with zero points, like everyone else.

Every team has its 'hard men' or 'bad boys' who are constantly being booked by the referee and make repeated trips to the FA, and by contrast there are usually a few players who adopt a deliberately smiling, friendly approach towards the referees in an attempt to curry favour with them and bias their judgment. In general, however, the punitive points system is a fair one and works well.

(opposite) When a player commits a serious offence, he receives a positive punishment, called a booking (above left), as a result of which he is given a number of punishment points. In earlier days, the referee simply recorded the offence in his little black book, but since 1976 he has had to embellish this action with a conspicuous Traffic Light Display, holding aloft the yellow card to broadcast the offender's shame to all corners of the stadium (above right).

If a second or more villainous offence is committed, the referee performs the final act of the Traffic Light Display: the showing of the bright red card (below) which signals the complete halt of the offender's game. Known in soccer slang as the 'early bath' or 'marching orders', the act of sending off a player is a drastic one and rarely employed because it unbalances the game.
(The English FA and Football League banned the Traffic Light Display from all their domestic matches in January 1981, but it is still widely used elsewhere and will probably never be banished from international matches, where it was originally introduced because of language difficulties. It remains to be seen how long the English ban lasts and whether other countries follow suit.)

The referee's dreaded Yellow Card is a rectangular piece of plastic, 11cm. by 9cm., which he keeps in readiness in his pocket at all times throughout the match. The Red Card, even more hated than the Yellow, is an oval piece of plastic of a similar size. The reason for the difference in shape between the red and the yellow is that it enables a referee to feel for the correct colour without peering in his pocket.

3 The Sending-off (Red Card)

This is 'Act Two' of the referee's Traffic Light Display. When a player has already been shown the Yellow Card and then commits another bad foul, or when he completely loses his temper and starts a fight, or becomes intensely abusive, the referee pulls from his pocket a bright red card and holds this aloft, to the intense delight of the opposing supporters. This means not only that the culprit will receive twelve points to be added to his record, but also that he must leave the field of play for the rest of the game, forcing his team to conclude the contest with only ten men and thereby giving the opposition the distinct advantage of superiority in numbers.

In addition, the red-carded player will automatically be suspended from his team's next game, so that this form of punishment is extremely severe and is comparatively rare.

4 Fines

If a player behaves in a particularly outrageous way, the authorities may go beyond the ordinary points-and-suspension system and impose heavy fines. The dignified phrase employed by the Tribal Judges in such a case is 'bringing the game into disrepute'. If they consider that this has been done, they estimate the degree to which they feel the honour of the Soccer Tribe has been damaged and fix the fine accordingly. As with all their judgments, there is no appeal and no escape from payment. Like the referee's decision during a match, their word is final.

They may also fine players for misconduct that has nothing to do with the matches themselves. Many players write articles in magazines, for example, in which they comment on the state of the game, and if their remarks are viewed by the authorities as 'bringing the game into disrepute', they may be fined for what they have written. One player recently wrote an attack on poor refereeing and was fined for his remarks which were considered to be offensive. As in the army, freedom of speech of this kind is not permitted.

Fines do not stop at players. A manager who makes a savage criticism of a referee during a television interview is also liable to find himself in serious trouble. Whole clubs can be penalized in the same way. If local fans burst on to the field and abuse the referee or the linesmen, it is the club that suffers with a heavy fine, if it can be shown that they did not provide reasonable protection for the officials concerned. Other aspects of club life also come under strict scrutiny. One English club was fined £15,000 for irregularities in its book-keeping.

Perhaps the strangest example of tribal punishment is that meted out by managers to their own players. If players misbehave when travelling with the club, or in some social context, their manager has the power to fine them as if they were soldiers under military law. One of England's top goalkeepers was punished in this way for 'wearing scruffy trousers', another player for failing to wear the club blazer when travelling with the team. This is similar to a soldier being court-martialed for being improperly dressed on parade and it underlines the fact that players are 'on parade' even when they are not playing in a match. Their match-playing clothes are their 'battle-dress', and their travelling clothes are their 'ceremonial dress'. This contrasts strikingly with other professions, where any restrictions on ordinary day-wear would be furiously opposed, and explains why footballers are, in general, much more smartly dressed than other young men of their age group.

Many managers restrict their 'finings' to extreme cases – when, for example, a group of high-spirited players cause havoc at a luxury hotel during a club tour – but others have started to use this type of punishment as a regular form of chastisement, and have gone so far that they have become the subject of press ridicule. One sportswriter commented: 'Begging your pardons, M'luds, but what is it with all these fines? Players are fined for not wearing a blazer, being late for training, back-chatting the bench, kicking the cat and being late for supper. I sometimes think it is borstals we are running here, not football clubs.' As an objective observer, the only answer one can give to such criticism is that it seems to be the most successful managers, such as Brian Clough and Lawrie McMenemy, who impose the most fines.

5 Suspension

As already mentioned, players may be suspended for up to three matches when they have accumulated twenty penalty points, but there are other, more serious forms of suspension available. In theory, a player, manager, or other club official could be banned from the game for life for major offences, but such drastic steps are extremely rare. Rare, but not unknown. Recently, Italian goalkeepers Albertosi and Cacciatori, and Milan president Colombo were all banned from the game for life, following a match-fixing scandal. Other players were banned for periods of up to five years which, in a profession where you are old at thirty, virtually amounts to a 'professional-life' ban.

In such serious cases, where the outside law courts are also involved, appeals are sometimes heard. If the courts were to clear some of the players already suspended, the football authorities would have to review their decisions.

The punishment of suspension may also be applied to managers. Former England manager Don Revie was banned from all English soccer for a period of ten years, but fought the decision by bringing a case in the law courts, accusing the authorities of 'restricting his trade' unfairly. He won his case, which reveals that, when the Soccer Tribe reaches these heights of punitive action, its pseudo-legal posture, although suitable for minor cases, begins to look a little shaky. With 'industrial action' and union activity becoming stronger in other spheres, the near future may see some rather startling clashes between the Tribal Law-makers and those of the world outside.

Major punishments sometimes involve suspensions lasting several years. The 1980 match-fixing scandal in Italy (below left) led to savage bans on leading players and lengthy legal investigations. In England, the FA's ten year suspension of manager Don Revie in 1978 (below) resulted in a prolonged legal battle in which Revie successfully challenged the authority of the Tribal Judges.

One special form of suspension sometimes inflicted is aimed, not at an individual, but at a whole club. When the supporters of a particular club have caused repeated trouble, becoming unduly violent, invading the pitch and generally causing chaos at the home ground, the authorities may impose a ban on home games for a number of weeks, forcing the club to play several of their fixtures on neutral ground. This form of punishment damages the club financially and it also penalizes the supporters, who are robbed of the chance to attend their home games. It further penalizes the players, who lose the psychological advantage always gained by playing 'at home'. In some ways this is an unfair punishment, because the players themselves are in no way to blame, but it is hard to think of an alternative way of chastising the unruly supporters. Even if the games are played at the home ground behind locked doors, as a way of hurting the guilty supporters without forcing the players to move to a neutral ground, the team are still punished by the absence of their cheering followers driving them on.

To date, no satisfactory way of punishing supporter hooliganism has been found, other than the ordinary process of police action and the outside law-courts, and the soccer clubs continue to bear the brunt of the official ruling that sees *them* as guilty for every case of crowd violence. If a bottle is thrown on to the pitch during a game, it is their fault, as far as the Tribal Judges are concerned. This is a punitive problem that remains to be solved.

Finally, there is one form of limited banishment that applies only to managers and their coaching staff. These senior tribesmen usually sit in little buildings that look rather like small bus shelters, at the side of the pitch, while the game is in progress. Referred to in soccerese as the 'dug-out' or the 'bench', these two small structures are seldom peaceful during the match. Shouts, yells and gestures emanate from them for much of the ninety minutes, as the frustrated occupants hurl abuse, encouragement and instructions at their sweating players on the field. Strictly speaking, all such signals from the side-lines are forbidden during play, but referees seldom enforce this rule. On occasion, however, especially when the remarks are aimed at them instead of the players, they will stop the game and rush angrily towards the huddled managerial group. After a forceful exchange of words, a manager or coach may find himself booked and told to remain silent. In extreme cases, he may later be banned from sitting on the bench for a considerable period of time, and is then forced to watch future games from the more remote position of the directors' box.

6 Deduction of League Points

If a club fails to obey the League rules, it may find itself losing precious points in its struggle to gain promotion. If, for example, it fields a team containing an unqualified or unregistered player, it may be penalized by losing the two points it gained for winning the match with that 'illegally composed' team.

7 Relegation

For more serious misdemeanours, a club may even find itself relegated to a lower division for the following season. This has been done on a number of occasions, the most famous recent example being the relegation of Milan, one of the great Italian clubs, to the second division, following the bribery scandal in 1980. Since the whole life of a Soccer Tribe revolves around its success in the League tables, this punishment is viewed as a tribal disaster of major proportions.

These, then, are the punishments inflicted inside the world of soccer and, by and large, they work extremely well. The point has been made several times that although they may seem harsh in comparison with those of other professions, they are generally accepted rather meekly, and this attitude of subservience requires an explanation. Why do the Soccer Tribesmen not rebel, except in rare cases, against the various fines and bans? What is the 'big stick' that keeps them in order?

For the players the answer is simple – it is the threat of the reserves. Each club has a highly trained reserve team full of players bursting to break into the first team squad. The modern manager holds the ace card of team selection, and this is his major weapon of authority. No player has a given right to play in the first team and even a star performer who goes 'off form' may find himself suddenly dropped and thrust into the obscurity of the reserves. There is no way he can object officially to this treatment and, if his replacement shines in his debut, the old star has great cause to worry.

This insecurity means that each first team player must not only always play his hardest, but must also avoid any souring of his relationship with his manager. Playing in the reserves means both a loss of status and a loss of match bonuses, so it is doubly to be avoided. If he is constantly at loggerheads with his manager, or refuses to pay his fines, he runs a much greater risk of losing his treasured place in the team. Even a star player who is performing well may find himself suspended if his behaviour becomes too wayward, because of the bad influence he has on general team discipline. If football glory was less sought after he would be in a stronger position, but somehow there always seems to be a brilliant young seventeen-year-old lurking in the wings ready to snatch his place.

For the clubs themselves and their senior members there is also little room for manoeuvre, because they are up against a monopoly. There is only one parent body in the country and it controls all soccer activities. A Hollywood actor who clashes with his studio can always move to another studio; a television executive can switch channels; a businessman can move companies; but a Soccer Tribesman has nowhere to go if he rebels against his Football Association or Football League. If he fights them he becomes an outcast. This is yet another way in which the soccer world parallels the military. And it is why the higher ranks of soccerdom can enjoy an attitude that is sometimes undeniably autocratic. It is also why the PFA (Professional Footballers' Association) has always had such an uphill struggle in gaining improved conditions of employment for its members, over such matters as freedom of contract.

It would be unfair, however, to paint a picture of the soccer authorities as posturing martinets or stubborn tyrants. Theirs is no easy task. They are not dealing with a bunch of naive, playful kittens. Soccer is a tough, dangerous sport and the lords of the tribe know full well that the tiger they have by the tail needs firmer handling than the pussy cats of other spheres. As the tamers of this beast, they realize that it requires strict discipline, but without breaking its spirit. To beat it into submission would create a soccer world so docile and meek that nobody would pay to watch it perform its tricks. So, although they must always carry a big stick, they must use it sparingly. And this, in general, they do with great skill.

They are aided in their endeavours by a deep, unspoken sympathy at all levels of the Soccer Tribe. Few players or managers would admit it openly, but deep inside they know that the discipline against which they shout and storm so often in private (but always accept so quietly when the official moment arrives) is a vital and necessary part of their professional lives. They realize that their success depends upon intensive, often painful training and on perfect team-sharing on the field of play, and such endeavours in a strongly competitive atmosphere cannot possibly succeed without some degree of enforced regimentation. This knowledge gives added support for the acceptance of the tribal system of punishment which, to the outside world, sometimes seems strangely severe.

Managers are often strict disciplinarians and treat their players as if they are under martial law, imposing fines and bans for misbehaviour – an approach dramatically depicted in this 'Roy of the Rovers' cartoon.

8 The Tribal Strategies

FORMATIONS OF ATTACK AND DEFENCE

There is an old saying in soccer which states that there is only one strategy in the game: when *we* have the ball, we attack, and when *they* have the ball, we defend. All the rest, the complex planning, the theories and the diagrams, are merely an attempt by wily managers and coaches to confuse honest ball-players and keep them in their place.

There is a small element of truth in this, but how small it is can soon be revealed by a glance at the history of soccer strategy. Over the years there have been distinct shifts of emphasis in the deployment of the players on the field, and these changes are clearly the result of careful pre-match scheming rather than on-the-spot improvisations. Whether the simple, honest player likes it or not, he is part of a strategic plan and he ignores this at his peril.

Viewed over a hundred years, the greatest modification in the style of play has been a steady move away from attacking formations to strong defensive ones. In the early days, teams were more concerned with the glory of winning than the fear of losing. They gave away more goals, but they also scored more. Everything was thrown into the attack. But then, as the cult of the manager emerged and grew increasingly entrenched, the old swashbuckling approach began to fade, to be replaced by a siege mentality. The gallant, charging cavalry were converted into sullen palace guards. Both sides fell back to man the barricades, leaving only a few lonely snipers to assault the enemy stronghold. The result, to many eyes, was a spectacle sadly lacking the heady excitements of the old days.

These critics argued that the new breed of all-powerful managers were so scared of losing that they were destroying the game with their cowardly, defensive strategies. They demanded a return to the earlier, more entertaining style of play, and a removal, if necessary, of the managers from their dominant position as tribal strategists. The retort from the managers was blunt and to the point. According to them, it is the supporters themselves who are to blame, for it is they who demand victory above all else. They may call for entertainment, but given the choice between a dour victory and a gallant defeat, they prefer the former. Ideally, of course, they would like a gallant victory, but if this is not to be, then winning at all costs takes priority, whatever they may say in their more reflective moments.

This attitude is borne out by the attendance figures. If a team is winning all its matches and is heading for promotion to a higher division, huge crowds turn out to cheer it on, no matter how it achieves its triumphs. If, on the other hand, a team is losing all its games, but playing elegantly in the process, the crowds dwindle and the club suffers. With no money coming in through the gates, the directors turn on the manager and sack him. If, in his defence, he points out that he has insisted on his players providing entertaining, attacking, skilful football, regardless of the risks involved, there is little chance that this plea will save him. It will not deter the shrinking crowd from jeering his name at each home defeat, nor will it melt the hearts of the harassed directors. He will still be sacrificed, and he and his family will suffer.

This managerial dilemma explains a great deal about the general shift in soccer strategies over the years. It reflects the way in which soccer has become increasingly symbolic and competitive. Even in so-called 'friendly' games, where there are no points or trophies to be won and nothing is at stake, the symbolism of the soccer win as a tribal victory remains. The days when risk-taking strategies could be employed for the sheer fun of it are long departed.

All is not lost, however, and the pessimists are often guilty of wildly

overstating their case. No matter how much they cluck and wag their heads, the game survives as an undeniably exciting event. The reason for this lies in a weakness of the military analogy. In speaking of the game as the attacking and defending of two fortresses by two opposing armies, a vital difference is overlooked. This concerns the presence of the ball. In the military context, it would be possible for two highly defensive armies to sit tight, each in their own fortress, patrolling the battlements, but never lowering the drawbridge. The field of battle between the two strongholds could remain deserted for long periods, until one side decided to venture an assault. This cannot happen in a soccer match because of the existence of the ball. From the moment of the kick-off, the player in possession of the ball must act without delay, or he will be penalized for time-wasting. So no matter how defensively both sides are playing, there is always bound to be *some* action. The drawbridges are always down, even if the attackers that sally forth are few in number and the bulk of the troops stay back in defence.

Because of this difference it is wrong to over-emphasize the damage done to the spectacle by the more wary, more self-protective styles of play seen at modern matches. There may be more defenders than strikers, and the lonely attackers may repeatedly be outnumbered and mercilessly hacked down, but the ball rarely stops moving. The intense activity of the game persists. It could even be argued that, in becoming more strategic, it has become *more* interesting. If the players, under the guidance of their managers, act more like animated chess-pieces than marauding pirates, the result could, in theory, be even more absorbing to watch. The catch here is that this type of

Viewed from above, the pattern of players at the beginning of a match reveals the special formation they are adopting, but within seconds of the kick-off this pattern becomes disrupted and is not always easy to follow. Even so, its influence is always present, creating a more attacking or more defensive deployment. Over the years, formations have become increasingly defensive and cautious.

manoeuvring play only fires the imagination when it operates at the highest level. The old-style, boisterous onslaughts were entertaining at all levels, even when they were rather clumsily executed. Poorly played defensive soccer, on the other hand, can reach depths of boredom unparalleled in the earlier days of the game. This may explain why it is that attendance figures have declined at matches played in the lower divisions, but capacity crowds still turn out for the top clubs and the great international matches.

Having outlined the general trend in soccer strategies, it now remains to trace the sequence of the specific formations employed. In doing this we can ignore the goalkeeper, who has remained a constant feature throughout, and concentrate on the ten outfield players. As a manager, it is possible to rearrange these ten men in any pattern that comes to mind – ten abreast, ten in line, anything that takes the fancy. Many variations have been tried, but they almost all have one thing in common – soccer's holy trinity of attackers, middlemen and defenders, arranged in three ranks across the pitch. At the start of a match, the attackers take up their positions near the centre-line, the middlemen stand behind them, about halfway back to the goal, and the defenders spread out just in front of the goal. Once the whistle blows, these three lines quickly become jumbled and confused in the rush of play, but whenever there is a lull or a stoppage they tend to re-form. It is as if each player is attached to his opening position by a long piece of elastic that pulls him back there whenever the play moves on and leaves him out of the action. For some players this elastic tether is stronger than others. They must remain as much as possible in their designated zone of action. But others are freer to dash hither and thither, pursuing the ball wherever it may go.

The manager's major strategic decision before each match concerns the number of players he allocates to each of his three ranks. Given the ten outfield players to juggle with, he has no fewer than sixty-six possible arrangements. The majority of these are of little use, but as the history of the game has unfolded, fourteen different combinations have been successfully employed. Each in its turn has been a favoured formation and has then been superseded by some new fashion, as the managers have struggled to outwit the enemy.

Although these changes have arisen naturally with the passage of time, in one respect they look almost like a planned progression. The number of defenders at the back of the field has steadily increased. In the very earliest days, there was only one, then two, then three, then four and finally, in the most defensive of modern games, five. This neat growth in the number of backs can be used to divide the history of soccer strategies into five main eras:

1 The One Back Era: The Defiant Dribblers

If it were possible to journey back through time and stand on the touch-line of a match being played in the middle of the nineteenth century, the style of play would be extremely puzzling to modern eyes. To start with, there would be no deliberate passing of the ball from one player to another. Although we think of passing as the very essence of soccer, it had yet to be invented. Instead, each attacker tried to dribble the ball forward until he lost it to an opponent. His team-mates would follow him up the pitch until he was robbed of the ball, when they would try to win it back and start off on a long dribble of their own. There was little true team-work or division of labour.

In this primitive stage of the game, the formation consisted of a goal-minder, a solitary defender to help him out, and *nine* forward attackers (Formation: G–1–0–9).

By the time the Football Association was founded in 1863, a slight change was visible. One of the nine attackers was now brought back to act as a half-back in the middle of the formation. This was done because the tactics of attacking were improving and teams felt the need to fill the gap between the

The Fourteen Favoured Formations

G – 1 – 0 – 9	The Defiant Dribblers of the 1850s
G – 1 – 1 – 8	The Middleman of the 1860s
G – 1 – 2 – 7	The Defended Dribblers of the 1870s
G – 2 – 2 – 6	The Queen's Park Passers of the 1870s
G – 2 – 3 – 5	The Perennial Pyramid of the 1880s
G – 3 – 2 – 5	Chapman's WM of the 1920s
G – 3 – 4 – 3	The Defensive WM
G – 3 – 3 – 4	The Double Spearhead
G – 4 – 2 – 4	The Double Stopper of the 1950s
G – 4 – 3 – 3	The Top Heavy Defence of the 1960s
G – 4 – 4 – 2	The Twin Attackers of the 1960s
G – 4 – 5 – 1	The Lone Ranger
G – 5 – 3 – 2	The Cautious Catenaccio of the 1960s
G – 5 – 4 – 1	The Ultimate Catenaccio of the 1970s

remote defender and the forward line (Formation: G–1–1–8).

During the 1870s, the weaker teams took this trend one step further, pulling back a second attacker and leaving a front line of only seven. This meant that there were now two half-backs positioned between the one full-back and the forward line of three central attackers and four wingers. This arrangement proved highly successful for the dribbling game and soon became widely adopted (Formation: G–1–2–7).

2 The Two Back Era: The Passing Pyramid

Before the 1870s were over, a revolution had occurred. It began at a club called Queen's Park in Scotland, where an inventive brain introduced the novel idea of deliberately passing the ball to one of his team-mates. Instead of having to steal the ball from an enemy after it had been lost, a Queen's Park player would receive it as a gift from a friend. Kicking it back and forth between themselves, they threw the enemy into total confusion. Their opponents rushed this way and that, but wherever they went, the ball had already been moved on somewhere else. This new device, which today we take so much for granted, proved a stunning success and spread like wildfire through the other clubs. The Dribbling Game had become a Passing Game.

The immediate result of this development was to open up the field of play and spread the players out. Before, they had rushed back and forth in clusters, but now they were forced to disperse. The solitary defender looked too lonely and was joined by a second back. There were now two backs, two half-backs and six attackers, the last consisting of two inside-forwards and four wingers (Formation: G–2–2–6).

As passing skills improved, it soon became clear that yet another attacker would have to be dragged back into the middle of the field. The English club of Preston North End had imported a number of Scottish players adept at the 'short pass', and in the early 1880s they invented a new position: the central half-back. This 'centre-half' had previously been one of the two attacking inside-forwards. His abandoned companion now became the centre-forward.

This important shift was to create an enduring Pyramid Formation that was to spread throughout the world of soccer, where it survived as the dominant arrangement for nearly fifty years. The pyramid was formed by the goalkeeper, protected by two full-backs and then three half-backs, with five attackers up front. For the first time there was a balance between attackers and defenders. When the five forwards advanced they found themselves faced by five defenders – the combined force of half-backs and full-backs. Much more efficient man-to-man marking became possible (Formation: G–2–3–5).

The most important player was now the centre-half. He had a double task that required great skill and stamina. When under pressure, he fell back as a defender, but more often he would be rushing up to support an all-out attack. As time went on, and the Preston Pyramid became more and more entrenched, small variations were tried out. The formation was made more flexible, with the new inside-forwards often being pulled back a little way to improve the passing possibilities that were somewhat stifled if the front five formed too rigid a line across the field. But the basic pattern survived from the 1880s right up into the mid-1920s, when a new transformation was to occur.

In 1925, the offside rule was changed. Previously, there had to be three players between an attacker and the goal when the ball was played forward to him, but now this was reduced to only two. The change had been forced on the authorities by the cunning of the defenders at the English club Newcastle United, who had devised the first 'offside trap' in the history of the game, running up the field to strand a hapless attacker in the offside position. When

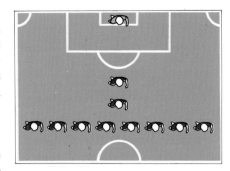

Formation G–1–1–8

Formation G–2–2–6

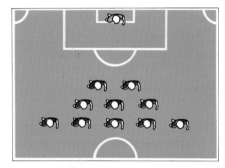

Formation G–2–3–5

other clubs took this up it was clear that the game was suffering. Referees were wearing out their whistles and spectators and players alike were becoming frustrated by the constant stoppages. The new rule gave attackers a much greater chance and the result was a dramatic feast of goals. In the 1925–6 season, immediately following the change in the rule, there was a total of 6,373 goals scored in League matches, compared with only 4,700 in the previous year.

This new development produced entertaining, high-scoring games and many records were broken – but so were the hearts of many defenders, who seemed helpless to stem the flood. The Two Back Era was drawing to a close.

3 The Three Back Era: The Central Stopper

Soccer inventiveness now moved to a London club – the Arsenal, where manager Herbert Chapman met the challenge of the rampant goal-scorers by withdrawing the centre-half and converting him into a centre-back. He was no longer allowed to rush forward into the attack, but had to stay back between the other two defenders and act as a central stopper, or 'policeman', to arrest the advancing centre-forward and patrol the central zone in the very front of the goal.

With this system, Chapman had three full-backs, two half-backs and five forwards, and Arsenal soared to victory after victory (Formation: G–3–2–5).

He did not stop there. He also brought his inside-forwards back behind the front line, creating what was known as the WM Formation. (When seen from above, the positions of the five forwards looked like the letter W and the positions of the combined backs and half-backs looked like the letter M.) Chapman used this WM arrangement in a special way that was to give Arsenal the League Championship five times in eight years, and the FA Cup twice. The main trick was to pull back seven players when the enemy were attacking. The Arsenal half-backs and even the inside-forwards would retreat to form a massive defensive block, which drew the opposition forward in large numbers in an attempt to break through the huge barrier. As soon as they were enticed into this position, with their own defences considerably weakened, the Arsenal sprung their trap. Robbing the enemy of the ball they shot it far and fast up the field to their three waiting forwards, where the fast-raiding wingers, instead of carrying the ball right on down to the corner flag, in the usual winger fashion, for a long cross into the penalty area, charged straight in towards the goal and fired at the target themselves. This is similar to the modern device of 'playing on the break', employed by intensely defensive teams, and it revolutionized English soccer. Strangely, it was not taken up so quickly by continental European or South American teams, who continued to play the old Pyramid Formation for some years.

Some teams took the WM Formation's defensive style to extremes, keeping the inside-forwards back so much that they effectively became extra half-backs, giving a pattern of three defenders, four half-backs and only three forwards (Formation: G–3–4–3).

Other clubs tried to beat Arsenal's triumphant WM with what was called a Double Spearhead Formation. In this, one central attacker was brought back to replace the lost centre-half, giving a pattern of three defenders, three half-backs and four attackers. The two central attackers became a twin assault-force – the Double Spearhead – and if they worked well together could do great damage to the massed defences trying to block their path (Formation G–3–3–4).

4 The Four Back Era: The Double Stopper

The obvious solution to the problems created by the Double Spearhead was the invention of the Double Stopper – two central defenders that brought the

Herbert Chapman, the famous Arsenal manager who revolutionized defensive play by introducing the centre-back, or Central Stopper.

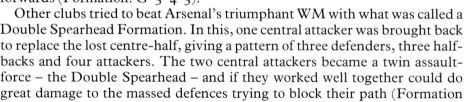

Formation G–3–2–5
(WM version)

Formation G–4–2–4

Formation G–4–3–3

Formation G–4–4–2

line of full-backs up to four in number, yet another step in the long path towards defensive soccer.

In 1958, the Double Stopper technique came of age at the World Cup, when the Brazilians swept to victory with a perfected version of the new Four Back Formation. The essence of the Brazilian strategy was that, with four attackers, two middlemen and four defenders, it was possible to create a six-man attack and a six-man defence, simply by giving the two middlemen a double task. Because they were now as much attackers as defenders, it was no longer suitable to refer to them as 'half-backs', which sounded too biased towards an exclusively defensive role, and a new name was added to the language of soccer, that of the 'midfield player' (Formation: G–4–2–4).

The *strength* of this formation was the speed with which it could be converted from a strong attack to a strong defence, and many other teams began to copy it. They did not always succeed, however, because the *weakness* of the system was that it put enormous pressure on the two midfield players. Their double task meant that they had to be intensely athletic and have great stamina. No soccer player had ever been asked to work so hard, run so far, and switch roles so repeatedly, at any previous point in the history of the game. Without such supermen to fill the midfield gap, the formation could easily lead to disaster.

The answer for many clubs was to bring back yet another attacker, to fill the old centre-half position. This meant that, with four defenders, three midfield linkmen and only three surviving attackers, the game had, for the very first time, reached a condition in which the defence outnumbered the attack. Defensive soccer had now truly arrived. This happened in the early 1960s and the formation is one that is still with us today in the 1980s (Formation: G–4–3–3).

Worse, for the attackers, was yet to come. Some clubs, in the late 1960s, pulled back yet another front-line player, to create a midfield quartet, leaving two lonely attackers to face the might of their opponents' equally swollen defence (Formation: G–4–4–2).

As if this were not defensive enough, certain teams, in later years, created a Lone Ranger pattern, with but a single solitary attacker up front, and his lost companion now playing in midfield as a protector of the four linkmen already there. This midfield barricade has been used on occasions when the opponents happen to have a midfield star of such brilliance that he warrants the extra attention (Formation: G–4–5–1).

5 The Five Back Era: The Safety Sweeper

Driven to defensive extremes by the intensely competitive pressures of the modern soccer world, certain managers have become so fearful of failure that, instead of playing to win, they play *not to lose*. Avoiding defeat is all that matters to them, and to this end they have pushed the defensive barrier up to its maximum level (so far) of five full-back players. Four of them are concerned with zonal defence of particular areas around the goal, or with specific man-to-man marking of opposing attackers, but the fifth has a special role to play – that of the *libero* or sweeper. He is a safety man who is at liberty to move around freely, sweeping up anything that the others fail to stop. Sometimes he sweeps up behind the back four, sometimes in front of them, according to his particular skills. He is the phenomenon of the 1970s, but he began his life long ago in Switzerland, where he was christened 'the bolt', because he slotted into place to secure the defensive wall. He was originally the invention of the Austrian-born coach, Karl Rappan, in the 1930s, but did not become a strategic device of major importance until the 1960s, in Italy. There, the less affluent clubs were being faced with star strikers imported from abroad by the richer teams. To defend themselves against this new onslaught, they took over Rappan's bolt and re-christened it the *catenaccio*.

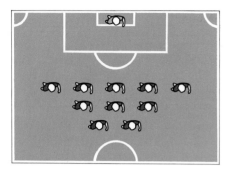

Formation G–5–3–2

They played with a solid wall of four defenders, with the *libero* behind them to sweep up any trouble. This left only three players in midfield and a pair of attackers up front (Formation: G–5–3–2).

Trainer Helenio Herrera was the main instigator of this ultra-defensive formation and was much criticized for it. One famous authority called it 'the infamous *catenaccio*'; another talked of 'Herrera's destructive tactics which infected the whole of Italian football.' These feelings are understandable, but all was not lost. There was much exciting play 'on the break', as the two lonely attackers took the ball upfield at a gallop, towards the enemy goal. And to be fair, the formation was a successful one and spread to other countries, where it was widely used in the 1970s.

There were examples of an even more defensive arrangement at certain clubs, in which a solitary attacker was backed up by four midfield players and the five defenders. This lone ranger was called a 'target man' because, while the others all pulled back in defence, he stayed in an advanced position and acted as a target for any long ball they could kick up to him, from the scrabble around the goal (Formation: G–5–4–1).

These then, are the five eras of soccer strategy with their fourteen increasingly negative formations. In recent years only a few of these arrangements have been used – usually the 4–3–3, the 4–4–2 or the five-back sweeper system. The others have faded into soccer history. But the suggestion made by certain authors, that this shift towards the defensive pattern is stifling soccer, is hardly justified. At any one moment in a soccer match, *someone* has to be attacking, and the excitement survives.

The truth about strategies and formations is that they can never truly dominate or spoil the game because, once the players are in action on the pitch, the carefully laid plans soon become blurred by the rush of play, by the special skills of certain individuals, and by the refusal of many players to become rooted in a rigidly designated role. A few managers, it is true, do try to stifle players' individualities by demanding a blind loyalty to complex, theoretical schemes, but even where such martinets scream and roar at their team, in the end they have no power to control what is taking place out on the field. If players retain their personal touches, their particular flair for the unexpected, and their oddities of movement and sequence, there is little the teeth-gnashing manager or coach can do, sitting frustratedly on the side-lines.

This will always be so and soccer will always be the better for it, because the element of the unexpected is a vital ingredient of the game. Too much planning creates robot players who may avoid a defeat but who also avoid entertaining the spectators.

Some managers in recent years have taken an excitingly different view of strategic problems. They have virtually told their players to forget about rigid formations and fixed positions. This system, which blossomed first in Holland, became known as Total Football. Every one of the ten outfield players was told that he was both an attacker and a defender. Every player is interchangeable in position with every other player. If one moves out of place in pursuit of the ball, another quickly fills the gap. This fluid style of play not only creates great flexibility and mobility around the field, it also helps to confuse the enemy, who find it hard to operate their rigid systems of man-to-man marking. Its only disadvantages are that it requires a tremendous degree of understanding between the different members of the team and also great physical fitness. The total footballer has to be highly intelligent and sensitive to movements all around him, and he has to be as fit as a fully-trained athlete. But if a team of such men can be built and kept together until they react to one another's moves as if by instinct, they will surely be the great threat of the future and may well prove the heralds of the next major era in world soccer.

The latest in a long line of formation variations is Total Football, introduced by Holland to defeat rigid man-to-man marking and to increase overall flexibility. Each outfielder is a 'total' player, expected to move into any position, from deep defence to front-line attack, and to exchange places with a team-mate whenever the run of the ball demands it.

In describing soccer strategies, the main topic has been the decisions taken before a match concerning the dispersal of the players across the playing surface, but there are other planning points that are made concerning the overall style of play. These, too, can be considered as strategic devices, since they are pre-planned and have to do with the game as a whole, rather than small parts of it (in which case they would be *tactical* devices).

Among these strategies of style are such considerations as whether the team shall concentrate more on short passes and possession play, or whether they shall hurl long balls up the field in the hope of finding advancing team-mates to carry them on. This could be called the 'pretty-passing' versus 'boot-and-bash' alternative. Skilled teams are usually encouraged to use the former strategy, while tough teams are advised to follow the latter. There is one phrase employed in this connection that puzzles outsiders. The manager says that he has told his players to 'go out there and play football'. The outsider wonders what else they might play: cricket? baseball? The statement seems ludicrous. But to 'play football' means to play the pretty-passing game, as distinct from booting the ball upfield and bashing the opposition. To an insider – a tribesman – it is a phrase with a quite specific meaning.

Other stylistic instructions may include requests to attack the goal 'up the middle', or from 'bye-line passes'. Or the manager may suggest an aggressive all-out attacking mood, or alternatively a defensive play with goals to be scored 'on the break'. He may demand 'push-and-run', which means a great deal of active off-the-ball movement; or 'slow/fast' play, in which a deliberately slow build-up is followed by suddenly speeded-up dashes to catch the enemy unawares; or he may ask for a tight offside-trap system to be used throughout the game; or he may insist on the use of the 'whirl', a style of movement invented by Dr Willy Meisel, in which there is a constant rotation of players; or he may lay down the law about zonal marking of opponents versus man-to-man marking.

All these devices are essentially strategic since they affect the whole game and can be used as a stylistic bias throughout the ninety minutes. In this way they differ from the tactical devices discussed in Chapter 9, which have to do with ways of handling specific problems at particular moments in the game.

9 The Tribal Tactics

PASSES AND TACKLES, MOVES AND SET-PIECES

The tactics of the tribe have only two aims, to score goals and to stop the enemy scoring goals. Because of this and because there are no complicated sets of tactical rules laid down in the laws of the game, the sequence of play is easy to understand even for an outsider. This contrasts strikingly with, say, American Football, where the extremely complex moves are confusing to a novice spectator and their subtlety is only appreciated by expert eyes. This does not mean that soccer is a crude, predictable game. Its strength lies in the fact that its few tactical moves are so variable and flexible that their style of execution is infinitely fascinating.

When a player has the ball in his possession there are only five things, tactically speaking, that he can do with it:

1 Shoot and Score

His greatest hope is to find the ball at his feet when he is in a position to shoot at goal. This may happen only a few times during a match, but when it does, he must be ready to strike with the speed of a hungry snake. The moment will only last for a fraction of a second and any slight hesitation can be disastrous. Surprisingly, many players below the top class level lack the speed of reaction that is needed at this moment. Sometimes it is almost as if they are mesmerized by the open goalmouth yawning in front of them, or as if they simply cannot believe their luck. They pause for an instant and then it is too late. A defender has come crashing into them, or across their line of vision.

There are, of course, several ways in which the player can strike the ball at the goal. He can gather it up with his feet, take aim and fire off a powerful ballistic shot, or he can tap it in deftly during a scrambled exchange in the very goalmouth itself. He can lob it high into the air so that it falls down into the goal, or he can skim it along the grass. He can butt it into the goal with a spectacular diving header, or a simple nod of the brow. He can volley it in with great force, or he can curve it round an enemy obstacle by putting spin on it in the so-called 'banana shot'.

Spectators often talk about a 'good goal', claiming that they prefer to see the ball fly like a bullet through the air, from a considerable distance. A goal that is scrambled in during a confusion of bodies close to the goalmouth, or one where the ball accidentally trickles over the line and hardly manages to reach the back of the net, is usually referred to as a 'poor goal'. The fact remains, however, that whether a goal is good or bad stylistically, it still counts as a goal. There are no marks out of ten for the manner of its scoring. If a goal scored from outside the penalty area counted as two, there might be far more dazzlingly 'good' goals, of the kind so favoured by the spectators, but this would add a complication to the game and, as we have seen on several occasions, traditional simplicity has always dominated the soccer world.

2 Run and Risk

If a player receives the ball when there is no possibility of shooting, his most positive reaction is to run forward with the ball dribbling at his feet, keeping possession and twisting and turning past opponents until he is near enough to the goal to attempt to score. This was the old attacking game so popular until the post-war period. It produced dribblers of sensational agility and gracefulness, who could go past one opponent, then another, then another, feinting and darting in unexpected directions, until close enough for a shot. Nowadays, this dribbling tactic is a rare and vanishing species, but it still produces an appreciative roar from the crowd whenever it occurs.

The most important tactical move in soccer is the last one before the ball hits the back of the enemy net. All other tactical devices, no matter how complex and clever, fade into insignificance beside the ability to strike like a snake – to *Shoot and Score*.

3 Pinpoint and Pass

If the player with the ball finds his path blocked by an opponent, or several of them, his alternative to dribbling through them is to pass the ball accurately to an unblocked team-mate. Since his possession of the ball will have drawn opponents towards him, it follows that, the longer the pass, the more chance there is of transferring the ball to a team-mate who is uncrowded and free to run forward in a dribbling advance. On the other hand, the shorter the pass, the more precise it will be. So, long passes are more valuable but short passes are safer, and this means that every time a player is faced with an instantaneous decision about which team-mate to give the ball, he is forced to use his footballing intelligence as well as his aiming skill. This is one of the reasons why top class soccer demands more and more imaginative players and why the old cartoon image of the soccer hero as a dim-witted thug is becoming increasingly misleading and out of date.

Although some critics feel that the modern player is too dominated by the doctrine that favours passing over dribbling, it is nevertheless true that a network of quick passes can become an elegant and intricate way of advancing towards the enemy goal. Triangular passing, wall-passing, swerved passing, overlapping passing, reverse passing and one-touch passing are variants employed to outwit the opponents and confuse them. In all types of pass but one the ball is aimed *at* the team-mate. The exception is the through-pass, when the ball is played forward to a position where the team-mate has not yet arrived, but to which he is already speeding. It has the special advantage of beating the offside rule, and in games where repeated and skilfully organized offside traps are being used by the enemy, the 'through ball' becomes a common feature of tactical play.

The weakness of passing, as opposed to dribbling, is that it permits the concealment of cowardly play. An individual who lacks the bravery, or has lost the determination to challenge his opponents by fighting his way through them, is able to hide his fears behind seemingly clever passing. The moment he receives the ball, his one thought is how to get rid of it as quickly as possible, to avoid trouble. He makes an imposingly swift and accurate pass to a team-mate and heaves an inner sigh of relief that the danger is over for the moment. Such a pass might be quite useful, but had he turned and charged forward with the ball, taking on the enemy, the advantage gained might have been much greater. Occasionally, the cowardly pass is not even useful and merely plays his team-mate into trouble. If the latter is surrounded by opponents when he is given the ball, the outcome often favours the enemy. What is unfair in such a case is that it is the team-mate who appears to have played badly, since it is he who is robbed of the ball, and the cowardly passer escapes with the disguise of having been 'let down' by his companion.

4 Hit and Hope

An alternative to running with the ball, or passing it accurately, is to hit it as hard as possible up the field and hope for the best. There is no specific aiming involved, beyond directing the ball crudely into enemy territory, and the obvious risk of such tactics is the loss of the ball to an opposing player. Used repeatedly and boringly, it is a typical device of tough teams lacking in ball skills, but used sparingly and well it can become a valuable solution in moments of panic and near-disaster. The defender who acrobatically hooks the ball away from a goalmouth scramble is performing a vital salvage

The urge to *Run and Risk* – to dribble the ball repeatedly past enemy defenders (left) – has been suppressed to some extent in recent years in favour of a *Pinpoint and Pass* technique (below).

operation for his team. He cares little where the ball lands, or who gains it. All that matters is that the enemy's close-range shooting chance has evaporated.

Apart from the optimistic long ball flying upfield from defenders, there is also an attacker's version of Hit and Hope sometimes seen near the enemy goal. This is a backward kick in which the attacker, finding himself facing away from the goal and with no time to turn, hits the ball backwards in the hope either that it will find a scrambling team-mate in a shooting position, or that it will strike an opponent and be accidentally deflected into the goal, or even that it may find the goalmouth direct. The aim is vague and taken blindly, with a great deal being left to chance, but in the chaos of a goalmouth scramble there is always the possibility of a lucky rebound and the backward kick, adroitly applied, may easily win a game.

There are several forms of the backward kick and they go under a variety of popular names: the bicycle kick, the donkey kick, the overhead kick, the back-flick and the back-heel, but tactically speaking they all amount to the same device, with optimism replacing precision.

If accurate passing is not possible, a player occasionally reverts to the more desperate tactic of *Hit and Hope*. When he does this, he usually drives the ball into a group of players near the enemy goal, but once in a while he may attempt a spectacular overhead kick aimed roughly in the direction of the goalmouth. In the case shown above, this dramatic kick scored the winning goal in a League Cup Final.

The goalkeeper has his own version of Hit and Hope – the long goal-kick up the field. This seems to be the only thought that enters the keeper's head in lower levels of soccer, despite the fact that there is no more than a fifty-fifty hope of one of his own team-mates acquiring the ball as it sails down through the air into the middle of the opposing territory. The chances are that, within seconds, the ball will be scudding back towards his goalmouth, but such keepers never seem to learn from this. It is as if they have no faith in the passing skills of their team-mates and do not feel safe until the ball is as far away from their own penalty area as the human leg can propel it. Top class keepers are much more likely to roll, throw, or gently tap the ball out to one of their defenders and leave it to them to pass it on up the field, rather than risk the fifty-fifty chance of losing possession. They only resort to the long kick when time is running out and their team is in desperate need of a goal before the final whistle.

5 Play It Safe

There are moments when even the bravest player realizes that he must play for safety, or risk giving away a goal. There are three Play It Safe reactions available to him, all unpopular with spectators, and all over-used by inferior teams, but completely justified under extreme conditions. They are the kick-into-touch, the conceding of a corner, and the back pass. They make no attempt to keep the flow of play going and settle instead for a brief moment of security. The back pass is without question the most hated move of the entire game, largely because it has the quality of a cringing retreat, the ball being kicked deliberately away from the enemy goal and back towards the protective hands of the player's own goalkeeper. Any form of backward play is sneered at by the watching crowd, but this particular tactic of taking the ball right back to the keeper is often violently booed. Frequently the critics are justified, but sometimes they are unfair, because there are moments when, through the sudden, unexpected onrush of an enemy striker, a defender finds himself trapped with the ball in a dangerous position. His only sensible solution then is to pass back to the keeper, no matter how unpopular this makes him with the impatient spectators.

These are the five basic tactical moves available to the man with the ball. His team-mates meanwhile will be adopting supporting, positional or distraction tactics to help him. They may run with him to offer support for the moment he is forced into passing, or they may position themselves in such a way as to anticipate what may happen a few moves ahead, or they may preoccupy opponents by making decoy runs, short dashes, or sudden unpredictable shifts which create confusion and divert attention.

The opponents of the man with the ball also have several options open to them. They may:

1 Tackle and Take

This means boldly competing with feet or head for the possession of the ball. Since the laws of the game prohibit almost all forms of powerful body contact except the shoulder-to-shoulder charge, there is always the danger that a referee will consider a strong tackle to be a foul move and will award a free-kick to the enemy. This inhibits would-be tacklers to some extent, but fortunately referees have always interpreted the fouling rule in a practical way and have ignored much of the accidental body-clashing that inevitably occurs. Unless they feel there has been a deliberately foul move, most referees will permit play to continue even though, in theory, they should signal an infringement. If they did not bend the rules in this way, the game would be for ever grinding to a halt and would lose much of its vigour.

There are no special categories of tackling – except perhaps for the sliding

When a team-mate has the ball, a player must adopt positional, distraction or, as here, supporting tactics.

tackle, in which any hope of taking the ball is abandoned and all effort is concentrated on simply dispossessing the enemy. The tackler, seeing his opponent making off and almost free, throws himself forward feet-first, slithering along the ground to a point where his feet strike the ball away from enemy control. It is a desperate last-bid form of tackling because it leaves the slider sprawling on the ground and usually unable to regain the loose ball himself. It can easily run to another member of the opposing team, or roll out of play, but at least the momentum of the attack has been halted.

It has to be said that some players use the sliding tackle to cover up their own deficiencies. It always looks dramatic, especially on a wet, muddy ground, and once they are down, skidding along, if the tactic fails and their opponent races on with the ball and scores, it gives the crowd a feeling that at least their defender did his utmost. Many managers would argue that his utmost should have been to pursue and tackle his opponent in the ordinary way, keeping upright and ready to deal with the ball he might win. Once he is on the ground he can, so to speak, be excused further duty for a few moments while he picks himself up, and can disclaim any responsibility for what happens immediately following his sliding tackle. It is a useful cover-up, therefore, for players who are no longer fast enough on their feet when in pursuit of a sprinting striker. But as with other moves, it can also be used sensibly in moments of impending disaster and frequently saves the day for a struggling team.

2 Intercept and Save

Instead of aiming himself directly at an opponent who is in possession, a player may try to intercept the ball while it is in flight. He may do this by a brilliantly timed run that 'steals a pass', or by flinging himself into the air to divert the flight of the ball with his head. When free-kicks are being taken he may risk a heavy blow by standing directly in the path of the kicker, as a member of a 'wall'. If he is a goalkeeper, his main task, of course, is

interception, as shots are fired at goal. Keepers rarely use their heads or feet to save goals, concentrating primarily on grabbing the ball or, failing that, on punching it clear.

3 Position and Pressure

Opponents will rarely stop applying positional pressure when they are without the ball. They are constantly moving their points of defence, adjusting to the flow of the attack and attempting to harass the men with the ball. The most basic movement is to run into a position that blocks a run or a pass. Fast sprinting has become an essential part of modern soccer and most players today are powerful athletes compared with the often stocky or scrawny stars of the earlier years.

More devious forms of positional play also exist, including the frustrating offside trap, where all defenders rush forward at the same moment to strand an attacker in an offside position and thus break up an assault with the award of a free-kick to the defenders.

Man-to-man marking has also become a fine art, with a key player followed everywhere at almost indecent proximity by his opposing defender. These moving couples, often looking as though they are roped bodily together, sometimes explode into violence when the ball is far away down the pitch. What happens is that the defender hovers so close behind his shadowed enemy that the latter reaches exasperation point and, at a moment when the eyes of the referee (and those of the spectators) are riveted on some dramatic event at the other end of the field, he lunges backward with his elbow or his heel and leaves his 'shadow' writhing on the ground. Alternatively, the shadow himself may use a similar moment to thump his enemy from behind. This may be done at such close quarters that it is almost invisible to the outside world and goes unnoticed until the injured player is seen to be rolling on the ground in pain. By now, of course, he is unmarked and nobody is anywhere near him, so although a foul has obviously been committed, the referee is powerless to act.

Constant man-to-man marking of a star player has sometimes become so extreme that the two opponents appear to be glued together. Taken too far, this form of *Position and Pressure* can lead to frustration and ill-tempered matches, but many top players learn to live with it, as an inevitable price for their brilliance.

Apart from tackling, intercepting and positioning, a player may gain the ball occasionally by sheer accident, when it falls suddenly at his feet or drops from above. He must always be ready to *Accept a Gift* instantly when this happens and must never hesitate in his response.

4 Accept a Gift

If a player does not gain a ball by tackling or intercepting, his only hope is to have it offered to him as a free gift. This happens when a loose ball drops suddenly in his path or when a deflection carries the ball in an unexpected direction. Players have to be on the alert at all times for this possibility. In every game, no matter how beautifully controlled by skilful footwork, there are always occasions when there is a free ball on the loose and when a quick reaction may win a game. Mediocre players can sometimes be seen to be taken by surprise when a ball arrives at their toes as if by magic, and during the fraction of a second when they hesitate, their accidental advantage is wasted.

These are the basic tactical possibilities for the modern soccer player. Apart from special tactics employed during the seven 'set-pieces' (kick-off, throw-in, goal-kick, free-kick, corner-kick, dropped ball and penalty kick), they cover the whole range of situations in which a player is likely to find himself during a match. Clearly, there is nothing too demanding about soccer tactics, and the result is that a group of twenty-two young schoolboys are perfectly capable of playing an efficient, entertaining game, without any detailed coaching. Despite this, the coaching manuals are full of confusing diagrams and charts festooned with dotted lines, arrows and symbols. It is doubtful whether many players bother to study them, preferring to rely more on intuition and general experience on the field. Indeed, there is considerable danger in becoming over-analytical. The soccer player who burdens himself with a mass of technical, theoretical information may well become too clever for his own good, and lose the spontaneous inventiveness that sets the game alight and wins the great matches.

10 The Tribal Gathering

THE PARADES AND THE WARM-UP,
THE COURTESIES AND THE KICK-OFF

On the morning of an important match, the tribesmen awake with the familiar mixture of excited anticipation and mild anxiety. They know that by the end of the afternoon they will be heading for home in glory or in gloom.

When they dress for the match, many of them take care not to forget the special mascot, charm, talisman or lucky garment they always carry to aid their team's success. They may treat their mascots almost as a joke, but they would feel uneasy without them.

Later, as they head for the sacred ground and begin meeting their friends, there are repeated assurances that today they are bound to win, certain to massacre the enemy, sure, quite sure, to see them utterly defeated. Anyone foolish enough to suggest the opposite is quickly silenced, for this is the time when tribal sorcery begins to take a grip. Even to speak of the possibility of losing might bring bad luck. The gods would be angry at such disloyalty.

At the stadium, the groundsmen are examining the turf, the office staff are dealing with countless enquiries, the stewards are arriving. Turnstiles are manned, programme-sellers are organized. Outside the gates the first fans are already beginning to assemble. Not far away, the shiny coach carrying the visiting team is nosing its way into enemy territory, the players on board

As match-time approaches, the area surrounding the stadium starts to come alive. Expectant fans bearing club colours hurry towards the turnstiles (below), the bus carrying the tense visiting players noses its way slowly into the ground (right) and the familiar programme sellers take up their posts (right, below).

gazing from the windows at the alien colours on the scarves and hats of the home supporters, now streaming down the roads. If the visitors are a blue team entering a red territory, the sight of all those flecks of red as the coach nears the stadium entrance reminds them all too vividly that they are a long way from home and that there will be many voices raised against them in an hour or so's time.

Guided carefully into its special place in the car-park, the coach comes to a halt. As the door hisses open, the tension already felt by the visiting players becomes acute. The back-chat and card-playing of the long trip are forgotten. As they walk briskly to the visitors' dressing room they may encounter members of the host team arriving from their homes nearby, but the two sides studiously ignore one another. There is virtually no contact between the opponents before the game, because of an unspoken feeling that to communicate would somehow give the other side an advantage.

Now the supporters are pouring into the ground and filling the stands, already starting up the tribal chants. The loudspeakers are blaring out pop music and the season-ticket holders are taking their familiar routes to their favourite seats, checking the team-lists in their programmes. The directors are assembling in the board-room for their hospitality rituals and the reporters and commentators are fortifying themselves with a last drink in one of the bars before mounting to the press box. At the far end of the ground, the visiting supporters are being herded like wild horses into the special pen allocated to them, watched warily by the police who are trying to assess the likelihood of crowd trouble after the match. Deep inside the grandstand the referee and his linesmen are changing into their sinister black costumes, as if in mourning for some unidentified death.

In the two dressing rooms, the players are preparing themselves for the struggle to come. Before the end of the afternoon several of them, at least, will

have suffered severe cuts and bruises, perhaps even serious injury. Palms are already moist. Superstitious rituals are being faithfully carried out. The extroverts are making a fuss, joking nervously; the introverts are quietly withdrawn, concentrating exaggeratedly on little personal procedures that help to pass the time – bootlacing and bandaging, examining shinpads and studs, checking things that need no checking, doing muscle-exercises, jigging about. The smell of liniment hangs in the air. The manager makes his rounds, doling out words of advice and encouragement, as much to fill the vacuum of waiting as to provide last-minute instruction.

Outside, the terraces are throbbing. The amplified pop music is fighting a losing battle with the rhythmic chants of the opposing fans at the two ends of the ground, who are already hurling massed insults at one another and extolling the great virtues of their own teams. Suddenly the loudspeakers crackle, a voice takes over from the blaring music and the names of the players are read out, each one cheered by his own supporters and jeered by

In some countries teams of girls are used to welcome the Tribal Heroes into the arena and to heighten the excitement of the spectators. Scantily clad cheer-leaders are most commonly seen at American matches (above left), but have also appeared at pre-match ceremonies in Africa (below left), Japan (above) and elsewhere.

(opposite) Since the earliest days of soccer, massed bands have marched and counter-marched on the pitch before kick-off at important matches, giving a distinctly military air to the contest that is about to commence. This form of soccer warm-up display (seen below, in England, and above, left to right, in Argentina, Scotland and Italy) has now spread around the globe.

those of the opponents. Only the directors' box is empty now.

Down below, the sound the players have been waiting for like Pavlovian dogs abruptly fills the air – the referee's buzzer is summoning the teams on to the pitch. It sounds, too, in the board-room and the Tribal Elders pull on their overcoats and mount the stairs to their special seats. In the two dressing rooms, the buzzer triggers a dramatic change of mood. The players move about, shaking hands and wishing one another good luck. They begin to line up at their dressing room doors, the studs on their boots clattering on the hard floor as they exercise their legs, impatient to feel the turf beneath their feet, and the physical freedom of open space. Several are changing position in the group, trying to get themselves into the place that their private superstitions demand. Finally, the door opens and the players advance, moving down the tunnel and out on to the expanse of the arena.

If the match is a modest one, the teams will make their entrance separately, one a few moments after the other, avoiding a meeting even at this stage. For the great matches, however, there is one last patience-testing ritual to be performed – the ceremonial walk-on. For this the two teams line up side by side down in the tunnel and then march out alongside one another. As they stand there below ground, the two columns only a few feet apart, they still do not look one another in the face. They fidget and jig, make little jumps in the air and stretch their bodies, more like exercising ballet dancers than sportsmen about to do battle. If they risk a sidelong glance at the enemy it is not at their faces but down at their legs, legs which suddenly seem alarmingly powerful and muscular and clearly capable of doing terrible damage to ankles

At routine matches the teams make their entrances separately (above) but at important encounters (below) they march on ceremonially, side by side, like gladiators entering the Colosseum. On truly great occasions, their arrival may be heralded by the mass release of coloured balloons (right) or other carefully prepared displays.

and heels, calves and knees. But as the walk-on is signalled, these thoughts are swept aside by the rising roar of the towering ranks of cheering supporters. The players' sense of being part of a great Tribal Gathering rapidly overwhelms their private worries, and they give themselves up to the magical feeling of movement on the open turf.

If it is a very special occasion, some kind of display may still be taking place on the pitch, a gymnastic demonstration, or the marching of massed bands. As the players stretch their legs and kick practice balls back and forth, testing the texture and hardness of the ground, the pre-match displays wind to an end and suddenly the mood changes. The practice balls are being called in. Ball-boys in track-suits are running into their final positions. The referee and linesmen are taking up their places at the centre of the field for the ceremonial spin of the coin.

The coin is tossed and ends chosen. If it is an international game, the captains will not only shake hands with one another, but will also exchange pennants as souvenirs of the occasion, after which they awkwardly dispose of them as quickly as possible and take up their places. With a contradictory mixture of relief that, at last, the game is about to get under way, and a further heightening of physical tension, the players position themselves and the referee settles the ball on the centre spot. He signals to his linesmen, starts his stop-watch, blows a shrill blast on his whistle, the crowd roars, and the Central Ritual of the Soccer Tribe begins.

The pattern of the Tribal Gathering described here is typical, but there are some striking local variations. At the start of North American soccer matches the pitch is graced by groups of nubile cheer-leaders dressed in scanty costumes that seem to label them as something midway between healthily efficient bathing beauties and sexy chorus-girls. They kick and twirl and rouse the crowd with waving pom-poms until an announcement heralds the arrival of the Tribal Heroes. They then form cheering columns to flank the entrance of the stars, who run on to the field one by one, like gladiators, as their names are boomed out over the loudspeakers and their faces are flashed up on the electronic scoreboards.

Outside North America, these razzmatazz showbiz embellishments are viewed with mixed feelings. No red-blooded tribesman would deny that the high-kicking girls are visually appealing. It is not prudery that prompts the criticisms of the All-American Warm-up. It is rather that there is a deep-seated feeling of something 'out of place', as if Rommel and Montgomery had staged strip-tease shows at the front lines before going into battle. To the soccer traditionalists, the Tribal Gathering is more in the nature of a shared, symbolic ordeal, rather than a fun-and-games family outing. It is a time for displays of prowess by heroic hunter-warriors and, while marching military bands are considered appropriate, the cavorting of sex symbols, even healthily energetic ones, seems ill-suited to the aggressive tension of the occasion. The American retort is that the sternly masculine approach pursued elsewhere has gone too far and lies at the root of many of soccer's crowd problems. Turn it into an entertainment, they say, and the mood will be softened beneficially. The violence will recede and the sport will once again offer spectators an attractive game instead of a potential riot-scene.

Above the club level, at international championships, another form of embellishment occurs. The match preliminaries often seem to last longer than the game itself. Great parades are organized, gymnasts weave patterns on the turf, and flags are marched proudly around the arena. During these elaborate ceremonials, the teams become frustrated and impatient, but there is little they can do to complain.

The pomposity of local officials charged with hosting such contests sometimes becomes excessive. To give an example: in one Caribbean championship, the first match was preceded by a beauty contest in which a

'Queen of Football' was elected, her five runners-up being dubbed the 'godmothers' of the competing teams, one per country. Wherever her team went, the godmother was sure to be present, even on the pitch at the opening ceremony. For this, the teams of the five countries had to march on behind a band, with boy scouts bearing their various banners, and with the godmothers gaily stepping out in front of their adopted players. When they reached the main stand there was a special flag-raising ceremony followed by the playing, in full, of each of the five National Anthems. The President of the local FA then made a long speech, to which the Governor of the host island replied at even greater length. By this time the players and officials had been standing on the pitch in the hot sun for more than an hour, without a ball being kicked, giving an entirely new interpretation to the soccer term 'warm-up'. The players' comments on this ornate method of starting a match are not recorded.

On the other side of the world, Russian soccer has its own special form of pre-match ceremony. It was first witnessed in the West shortly after the Second World War, when the famous Moscow Dynamos team made a tour of England, and caused great surprise both to the capacity crowd that turned out for their first match, at Chelsea, and to their opponents. After a ten-minute kick-about, the Russian team, husky athletes all, disappeared into their dressing room. When they reappeared alongside the Chelsea players, the spectators were amazed to see that each of the tough, grizzled visitors was carrying under his arm a large bunch of flowers. They stood holding these pretty bouquets throughout the playing of the National Anthems and then, much to the embarrassment of their Chelsea opponents, stepped smartly forward and, with stiff bows and stern poker-faces, presented their opposite numbers with a posy of friendship. This mission accomplished, they set out across the field to take up their positions ready for the kick-off, leaving the bemused Chelsea team stranded, flower-laden and feeling rather foolish. They were rescued by their trainer into whose arms they piled bunch after bunch of flowers until he staggered off completely submerged in a gigantic floral display. The crowd roared with laughter and the Russians had unwittingly won a great round of gamesmanship. Unwittingly, because to them it was an accepted ritual and was not intended to cause confusion or surprise. At important matches in Russia, observers noted later, both teams would be armed with bouquets. After a brief flower-swapping ritual, the floral offerings were tossed into the crowd and no one was left stranded or embarrassed.

As soccer has become increasingly international and more and more heavily televised, local variations in pre-match rituals have become less of a problem. Everyone knows now what to expect on the great occasions. But for the players, the whole charade of pre-match formalities is a hated delay in getting down to the main function of the Tribal Gathering, soccer's Central Ritual: the game.

11 The Central Ritual

The focus of the Soccer Tribe's week, the Central Ritual around which all other tribal activities are built, is the suspense-laden, strictly controlled, ninety minutes of play. Sliced into two halves by a brief interval, begun and ended by a shrill blast on the referee's whistle, this is the time when, for the devoted tribesman, the rest of the world briefly ceases to exist. It is the time for non-stop concentration, for almost unbearable tension˙ and uncontrollable joy, for deep depression and wild elation.

The key to understanding these passions lies in the structure of the game. Every match is a contradiction, being at once both highly predictable and highly unpredictable. The simplicity of the rules and the familiarity of the tactical moves make every moment of play immediately understandable to the watching eyes. But despite this, nobody can ever be sure what will happen next. The themes may be severely limited, but the variations are infinite.

This contradictory quality means that, no matter how experienced a tribesman becomes at following the sequence of play, he is never able to relax for a second. In an instant, everything can change. What seemed to be a quiet, safe moment suddenly erupts into a lightning counter-attack, and relief turns to panic once more. It is as though, from the time when the referee signals the start of the match, the ball becomes a live grenade and no tribesman can take his eyes off it until it has either exploded in the back of the net or been inactivated by a break in play.

This idea of a 'live' and 'dead' ball is useful in understanding the basic pattern of play. Each match consists of about 2,000 *ball-contacts*, 1,000 before half-time and 1,000 after it. Most of these contacts are, of course, kicks, but they also include headings, chestings, throw-ins, accidental body-deflections and, in the case of goalkeepers, catches, throws, punches and fingertip touches. The 2,000 action-units of the game occur in a long series of irregular bursts, some brief, some extended. In a typical match there are about 100 of these periods of intense activity, during which the ball is 'alive'. At the end of each *action-sequence* the ball goes 'dead', either because there has been some infringement of the rules (giving rise to a free-kick or a penalty kick), or because the ball has gone out of play (leading to a goal-kick, a corner-kick or a throw-in), or because a goal has been scored (producing a new kick-off).

The game can therefore be seen as a string of alternating *live-ball action-sequences* and *dead-ball awards*. During the former the ball is moved swiftly about the field, available in theory to any of the 22 players at all times; during the latter it is stationary and is available, for the moment, to only one of the 22 players, who is restricted to a single ball-contact when returning it to active play.

None of the dead-ball moments lasts for many seconds (unless there has been a serious injury), so the spectator can never allow his attention to wander, even during the breaks in the action-sequences. In short, he is kept on the edge of his seat, or on his toes, throughout most of the ninety minutes, in a way that is unique to soccer.

The speed of the game is important in this respect. Ten international matches analysed action-by-action gave an average of 2,322 ball-contacts per game, the lowest figure being 1,911 and the highest 2,622. This means that, overall, there were 26 contacts per minute, or roughly one every two seconds. This must be close to the optimum required for exciting the human brain. If the input were any faster it would become too confusing – we would get mental indigestion; if it were any slower, we would have time to become distracted by other thoughts and other images. But the rate of strike of the typical soccer match is perfect for trapping our attention and then holding it.

Aiding this process is the great variability in the details of the ball-by-ball sequence. In many sports there is official 'turn-taking' which makes their pattern of events rather too predictable. Whether it is golf or snooker, tennis or cricket, we know who will act next because the rules tell us so. A follows B follows A follows B. But in soccer there is no way of telling. If a blue player has the ball, we do not know whether, at the next kick, he will still hold it at his own feet, will have passed it to a blue team-mate, lost it to a red opponent, kicked it out of play, or scored a goal. All things are possible at all times. True, we may suspect that one particular sequence is building up, but we can never be absolutely sure. It can always go wrong. Even a simple back pass can occasionally slide beyond the keeper for a tragic own-goal.

To understand this optimum-speed/optimum-unpredictability excitement of soccer more clearly, it helps to dissect the anatomy of one selected game. Obviously this should be a match that observers consider to be one of the greatest ever played. The game chosen is that between Argentina and France in the 1978 World Cup. Argentina won 2–1, but it was an evenly balanced encounter and so brilliantly contested that Bobby Charlton was moved to exclaim, 'It's one of the best international matches I've ever seen.' Since he was not alone in this view, the game was subjected to a ball-by-ball analysis to find out what a near-perfect encounter has to offer in terms of action-sequences, patterns and structures.

The first point to emerge was that it was the fastest game of a number studied. Play hardly seemed to pause, even for the 'dead balls'. The referee kept things moving at a furious pace and the players never slackened in their efforts for a moment. The total of 2,622 ball-contacts was spread over the ninety minutes as follows:

A moment of play from the Argentina–France game which is analysed in detail on the following pages.

Number of Ball-contacts					
First 15 Minutes	Second 15 Minutes	Third 15 Minutes	Fourth 15 Minutes	Fifth 15 Minutes	Sixth 15 Minutes
ARGENTINA	197	245	215 G	162	205 G	217
FRANCE	234	237	259	196 G	215	240

G = goal scored within this period

Despite the great amount of energy expended, the last quarter of an hour of play had slightly more ball-contacts than the first, both sides making a final, desperate effort to score. And there was only a very slight, general fall-off between the first half and the second:

Number of Ball-contacts			
	First Half	Second Half	Total
ARGENTINA	657	584	1,241 (= 113 per player)
FRANCE	730	651	1,381 (= 126 per player)
Total	1,387	1,235	2,622

There were no fewer than 780 successful passes made during the match. Argentinian players passed to their team-mates 368 times; the French 412 times.

The ball changed possession 464 times. During the first half each side had

Analysis of the World Cup Match between Argentina and France

FIRST HALF

INTERVAL

The 1978 World Cup encounter between Argentina and France. (Argentina played in striped shirts of white and pale silvery-blue, with dark shorts and white socks; France played in plain shirts of bright blue, with white shorts and red socks. In order to provide maximum contrast in the chart above, Argentina are shown as *blue*, and France as *red*.) Every spot in the chart represents a single ball-contact, as shown in the key.

Key

- Ball-contact
- Pass
- Dribble
- Lose to enemy

∟ Corner-kick
△ Free-kick
✳ Goal-kick
▽ Throw-in

⊡ Penalty
☆ Goal
● Goalkeeper possession

⌐O Whistle
□ Yellow card

SECOND HALF

⚥ ● ● ●▬● ●▬●▬● ●▬● △ ● ●▬●▬● ● ●▬● ● ●▬● △ ● ● ● ● L ● ●▬● ✳ ● ●▬● ● ●▬●
●▬● _●_ ● ● ● ● ●▬● ● ●▬● ● ● ● ● ● ●▬●▬● ● ●▬● ● ● ● ● ● ●▬● ● ●▬●▬●▬●
● ● ● ●▬● ● ● ● ●▬●▬● ● ● ● ● ●_●_ ● ● ● ● ● ● L ● ● ● ● ● ●▬● ● ●▬●▬●▬●
●▬● ● ● ● ● ● ● ● ● ● ●▬●▬●▬● ● ● ● ●_●_ ● ●●▬● △ ●▬● ● ● ● ●▬●▬●
●▬● ● ● ● ●▬● ●_●_ ●▬●▬●▬● ● ● ● ✳ ●_●_ ● ● ● ● ● ▽ ● ● ● △ ● ● ● ● ●
● △ ● ●▬●▬● ● ●▬●▬● ● ● ● ● ● ● ▽ ● ● ● ● ● ● ●▬●
● ● ● ● ●▬●▬● ● ●▬● ▽ ● ● ● ● ▽ ● ● ● ● ● ● ●_●_ ● ● ●▬● ● ● ● ▽ ● ● ● ●
● ● L ● ● ✳ ● ●▬● ● ● ●▬●▬● ● ● ● ●▬● ● ●▬● ●▬●▬● ● ● ● ● ☆ ⚥
● ● ● ● ● ● ● ● ● ● ▽ ● ● ● ● ● ● ● L ● _●_ ● ● ● ●▬● ● ● ▽ ● ●▬●
●▬● ● ● ● ●_●_ ●_●_ ● ● ● ✳ ●_●_ ● ● ● ● ● ●▬● ▽ ● ●▬●
●▬●▬● ● ● ●▬● △ ● ●▬●▬● ● ● ● ● △ ● ✳ ●_●_ ● ● ● ●▬●
●▬●▬● ● ● ● ● ● ● △ ● ● ● △ ● ● ● ● ● ● ●
●▬●▬● ● ● ● ● ▽ ● ● ● ●_●_ ● ●
● ●▬● ●▬●▬● ● ● ✳ ●_●_ ● ● ● ● ● ● ● ●▬● △ ● ✳ ●_●_ ●
●▬●▬● ● ● ● ● ● ● ● ● ● ● △ ● ✳ ● ▽ ● ● ● ●
●▬● ● ● ● ☆ ⚥ ● ● ● ● ● ●▬●▬● ● ✳ ●▬● ▽ ● ● ● ● ● ●▬●
● ●▬●▬● ● ● L ● ● L ● ● ●▬● ✳ ● ●▬● ● △ ●▬● ● ▽ ● ● ●▬●
●▬●▬● ▽ ● ● ● ● ●▬● ● ● ● ● ● ● ▽
● ● ● ● ● ● ● ●▬● ● ● ● ● ● ● ● △ ● ✳ ● ▽ ● ●
△ ● ● ● ● ● L ● ● ● ● ● ● ● ● ● ●▬●▬●
●▬●▬● ● ● ●▬● ● ● ● ● ● ● ● ● ●
●▬●▬● ● ● ● △ ● ● ●▬● ●▬● ●▬● ●_●_ ●▬● ●▬●
●▬● ● ●▬●▬● ● ● ● ● ● ●▬● ●▬● △ □ ● △ _●_
●▬●▬● ● ● ● ● ● ● ●▬● ● ● ▽ ●▬●▬●▬●
●▬●▬● ● ● ●▬● ● ●▬● ● ● ● ● ● ● ● ● ● ● ✳ _●_ ● ●▬●▬●
●▬●▬● ● ● ●▬● _●_ ●▬●▬● ●▬● △ ● ● ●▬● _●_ ● ● ⚥   FULL TIME

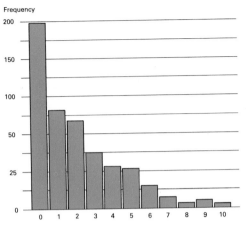

Frequency

The number of passes made between team-mates in one possession-sequence before they lose the ball to their opponents.

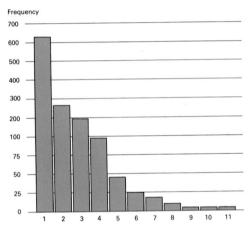

Frequency

The number of ball-contacts made by a player before he passes or loses the ball. A single touch of the ball is clearly the most common occurrence.

The Argentina–France World Cup game in 1978 (right) was judged to be one of the finest international matches ever seen. It was also one of the fastest, involving no fewer than 2,622 ball-contacts, which is 300 above the average.

possession 119 times; during the second half 113 times.

These figures mean that, since Argentinian players *passed* the ball a total of 368 times and *lost* the ball 232 times, there were 600 different occasions when an Argentinian player possessed the ball. For the French, with 412 passes and 232 losses, the total was 644. Together this gives a grand total of 1,244 changes in *man-on-the-ball* during the game.

It is this high rate of switch-over from one player to the next that gives the match one of its most important features: high-speed cooperation in the face of intense competition. The cooperation is expressed through the 780 passes and the competition through the 464 losses of the ball. Each time one of the teams passes or gains the ball, the supporters of that team feel a brief moment of pride and pleasure; each time the opposing team passes successfully, or gains the ball, these same supporters feel a moment of anxiety and tension. Given the hundreds of shifts of mood experienced at every match, it is hardly surprising that the more ardent of the Soccer Tribesmen feel satiated, even exhausted, after the final whistle has blown. The game is designed in such a way that both their positive feelings of loyalty and their negative feelings of opposition are given full rein. No other sport provides quite such a balanced feast of emotional contrasts.

There is, of course, nothing regular about the way in which possession passes from one team to another or one player to another. Each team will try to keep possession of the ball as long as possible, but eventually they must risk losing it in order to shoot at the enemy goal. Even without coming close to shooting, the longer they are in possession, the greater is the danger of being robbed of the ball. It follows that shorter possessions are more common than longer ones, but there is never any way of telling which particular possession-sequence is going to be a brief one and which will be successfully extended. Herein lies yet another source of suspense for the watching tribesmen.

Looking closely at the Argentina–France game, it is clear that the number of passes put together before losing the ball to the enemy varied between 0 and 10, with the higher numbers being rare. But there was no way of predicting on the basis of the last sequence what the next one would be. So the watching tribesman had to be alert to a possible loss or gain at any time.

From a study of even finer points of detail, it emerges that a similar pattern

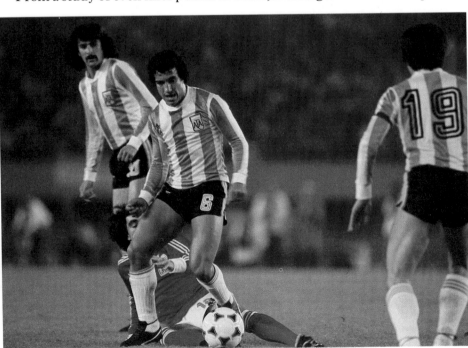

During this match the ball changed possession from one team to the other 464 times. This high figure is one of the special features of soccer that make the game uniquely exciting to watch.

is true for each man-on-the-ball unit of the match. If a player had the ball at his feet, he might give it a single kick, either passing or losing it with a single touch, or he might make several contacts before parting with it. The number of kicks (or other forms of contact) performed in one *personal* possession of the ball varied from 1 to 11, again with the higher numbers becoming increasingly rare. The fact that single contacts were most common underlines the extent to which one-touch, quick-passing play has overshadowed the old-fashioned dribbling style. On only *three* occasions in the entire Argentina–France game did the man-on-the-ball make more than eight contacts with it before passing or losing it. By contrast there were 628 cases of single contact. 'First-time football' has come to dominate the modern game.

As explained earlier, all these ball-contacts are clustered in *action-sequences* interspersed with *dead-ball moments*. In this particular game there were 121 action-sequences, varying in length from a single ball-contact to one stretching for as long as 108 contacts.

The 121 dead-ball moments alternating with these action-sequences consisted of the following:

	Corner-kick	Throw-in	Free-kick for Foul	Offside	Goal-kick	Kick-off	Penalty Kick	Total
ARGENTINA	6	14	25	2	17	2	1	67
FRANCE	5	15	17	6	8	3	0	54
Total	11	29	42	8	25	5	1	121

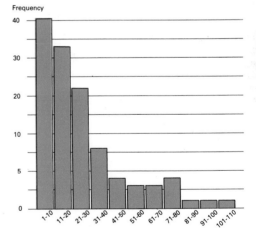

Frequency

The total number of ball-contacts made (by both sides) before an action-sequence is terminated by a dead-ball moment.

This dissection of the Argentina–France match, and other similar post-mortem studies, may help to explain the excitement of the soccer game, but they do not explain its beauty. In the end, none of these careful analyses and detailed figures can tell anything at all about the *quality* of a match, about its aesthetic properties, or what makes this move elegant and that one clumsy. All that the figures do is to provide evidence for the great potential of the soccer game as a superb vehicle for the imaginative interpretation of physical strategies and tactics.

Ultimately, however, even the most elegant patterns of passing and running become meaningless unless they build successfully to the great Ritual Climax of the Tribal Gathering: the goal.

12 The Ritual Climax

THE SCORING OF GOALS

In early folk-football the goals were distant landmarks to which the ball had to be carried. At Ashbourne in Derbyshire they were two mill-wheels, one of which still survives (bottom). The other has been replaced by a stone monolith (below).

The moment of truth in the Soccer Tribe's Central Ritual is when the ball is driven into the goalmouth. Today this action is described as 'scoring a goal' and it is a choice of words with a long history behind it.

The word *goal* has gone through a number of phases of changing meaning. Originally it was used for an obstacle or barrier of some kind; then for a limit or boundary; then, more specifically, for a boundary-marker such as a stone, a pillar, a pole or some other landmark. Narrowing its meaning still further, it became the special marker indicating the starting-point or end-point of a race. Eventually it was defined as the place which had to be reached in a competitive sport.

It was in this last sense that it became used in the earliest games of medieval folk-football, where the goal was the object to which the ball had to be carried to win the game. The nature of this object varied from place to place. At Ashbourne in Derbyshire the goals were two mill-wheels, several miles apart (one of which still survives and is used to this day in the annual Shrovetide game), and when the ball was touched on to one of these wheels it was said to be *goaled*. The victorious player did not 'score a goal', he 'goaled the ball'.

When football became more organized and the field of play more restricted, suitable pre-existing goal-objects were not always available and purpose-built goals had to be erected, in the form of wooden posts. Instead of touching the ball on to these posts, the players now had to drive it between them or carry it past them. Because it was now easier to 'goal the ball', games were no longer decided on a single 'goaling'. Instead, victory went to the side that 'goaled' most often in a fixed period of time. It became necessary to keep a record as the game proceeded and this was done by cutting notches in the wood of the goalposts.

The cutting or *scoring* of the goalposts led to the introduction of the phrase *scoring a goal*. At first this referred exclusively to the recording of the winning actions, but as time passed it came to stand for the winning actions themselves. In this new meaning, *scoring a goal* replaced the earlier phrase *goaling a ball*.

This is why, when a modern soccer player drives the ball between the goalposts, it is said that he 'scores'. And it is also why the word 'goal' now has two entirely different meanings, referring not only to a piece of equipment – the two posts, the crossbar and the net – but also to the triumphant achievement of placing the ball inside the goalmouth.

It is in this sense that 'goals' have become the climactic events in the lives of the Soccer Tribesmen. They talk lovingly of beautiful goals, dramatic goals, sensational goals – the goal of the month, the goal of the season, the goal of a lifetime, the goal of the century. Nothing creates greater ecstasy or greater dismay. They cheer them and weep over them, long for them and dread them. Theirs is a tribe dominated by the very thought of goals.

Endless records are kept and mulled over, counted and re-counted, calculated and compared: goal totals, goal averages, goal differences, equalizers, own goals, disallowed goals, penalty goals, hat tricks, top goal-scorers. Charts are drawn, tables made, statistics studied. It is the Soccer Tribesman at his devotions.

One of the qualities that make goals so important is their rarity. In modern professional soccer the most common score for a team, by the end of a ninety-minute game, is *one*. The next most common score is *nil*. To score more than a few goals in a match is so rare that it is a cause for great rejoicing. It is this immense difficulty in scoring a goal that makes the moment of triumph, when

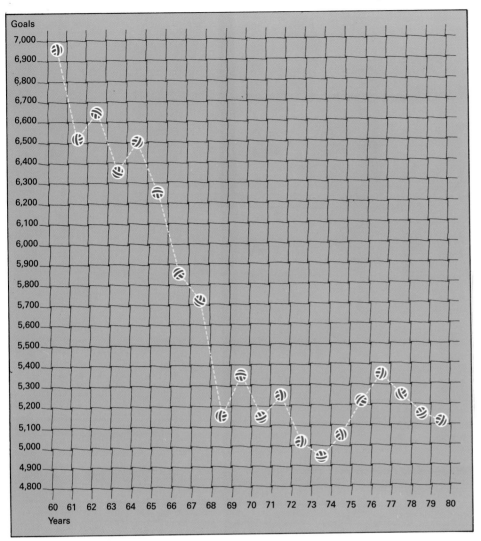

(left) The total number of goals scored per annum in English League football fell dramatically during the 1960s, from roughly 7,000 to 5,000. After that, in the 1970s, it levelled off. Clearly improvements in defence have outstripped improvements in attack.

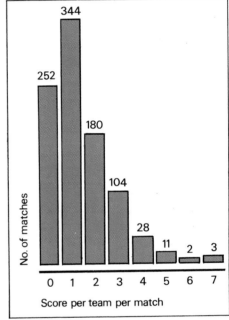

The most likely score a supporter will see his team make is *one* (above). The second most likely score is *nil*. (Based on the 462 English First Division League matches of the 1978–9 season.)

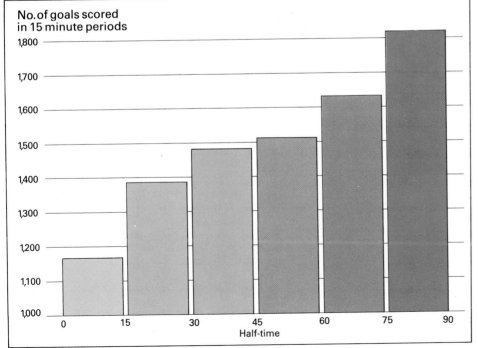

(left) The frequency of goal-scoring in each fifteen-minute segment of the ninety minutes of play. The likelihood of a goal being scored increases steadily throughout the game. This means either that the defence grows gradually weaker or that the attack gradually improves (or both) as the minutes pass.

The figures are based on the times recorded for 9,000 goals scored in English League and Cup matches from April 1978 to November 1980. (The 1,500 line shows the number of goals-per-segment expected if there was no bias.)

The climactic moment for the Soccer Tribesman is the scoring of a goal by his team and it matters little whether this is achieved by a formal penalty kick (bottom) or a more creative movement during fast play (below and right).

it finally comes, so exciting. As the last chapter revealed, each team makes contact with the ball just over a thousand times per game. This means that whenever a player strikes the ball he has a chance of scoring that is less than one in a thousand. So there is little wonder that, when it does happen, it produces such a powerful reaction. Little wonder, also, that that rare specimen, the prolific goal-scorer, is elevated in tribal folklore beyond the level of a mere hero, to become a godlike figure who is idolized and worshipped by his devoted followers.

Undoubtedly, the greatest such figure in modern times has been the Brazilian striker Edson Arantes do Nascimento, known to the world by his nickname 'Pelé'. During his career he scored 1,363 goals, a total unapproached by any other modern player. As a result of his unique abilities, the fanaticism of his followers reached such a level that extraordinary incidents occurred, the like of which have never been seen before or since in the history of the Soccer Tribe.

Once, when a referee dismissed him from the field for disputing a decision, the spectators were so incensed that they stormed the pitch. The police barely managed to save the wretched official's life and he was hustled away to safety while one of his linesmen took over the referee's whistle. The crowd would not allow the game to continue until Pelé was returned to the field and, to prevent bloodshed, the officials agreed – the only time in the history of the game that this has been permitted. The most remarkable feature of this incident is that it did not occur in Pelé's home town, or even in his own country, but in Colombia.

Stranger still was the occasion when his presence stopped a war. In Nigeria, it was agreed to call a two-day truce in the tragic conflict with Biafra, so that both sides would be able to watch him play. His fame has spread to so many countries that he has had meetings with no fewer than ten kings, five emperors, seventy presidents, two Popes and thirty-eight other heads of state. One of the Popes sought an audience with *him*. His name has been sung in over ninety different songs and he has received more awards than bear counting, including a football made of gold and a crown of gold leaves.

All these events stem directly from his amazing goal-scoring ability and, not surprisingly, it was the moment when he chalked up his thousandth goal that produced one of the most emotional scenes in his long career. He scored the goal from a penalty kick near the end of a match in the giant Maracana Stadium in Rio and there was immediate pandemonium. The players from both sides rushed to congratulate him. The photographers and reporters behind the goal broke ranks and joined them, followed by a huge crowd which surged on to the pitch. Pelé's jersey was torn from him and replaced by a silver shirt bearing the number 1,000, and he was carried shoulder high around the field, to the hysterical applause of the vast audience. Fireworks exploded and gigantic bunches of balloons rose into the sky bearing the message of the thousandth goal. In the streets of all the Brazilian cities, where millions had been waiting for the news on their transistor radios, the ecstatic populations danced all traffic to a halt. Back at the stadium a weeping Pelé fled the field and disappeared, leaving a substitute to complete the final minutes of the match. When the game was over, he reappeared to unveil a plaque in the wall of the stadium, commemorating the great event.

Although this was undoubtedly Pelé's most famous goal, his most dazzling display came at another match in the same stadium. It is generally accepted to be the most astonishing goal in the whole of modern soccer. 138,000 pairs of eyes watched unbelieving as he gathered up the ball in his own penalty area and then proceeded to dribble and weave his way past no fewer than nine opponents, right down the length of the pitch, to slam it into the back of the enemy net. A film of this feat was shown on Brazilian television every day for a whole year, without a single complaint from the viewing public.

Top goal-scorers, such as Pelé of Brazil (above), Greaves of England (top right), and Kamamoto of Japan (right), become tribal legends, worshipped as great heroes by their faithful followers.

There are many critics who feel that the increasingly defensive style of play during recent years is damaging the game because it reduces the number of shots at goal – both those that score and those that are dramatically saved. They would much prefer to see a game won 4–3 than 1–0. They point out that even a bad game can be entertaining if it is high-scoring, whereas a good game is, in the end, frustrating and disappointing if it results in a goalless draw. Several suggestions have been offered to improve the situation, including making the goalmouth wider and altering the offside law. Another idea was to change the League points system in which a win gives two points and a draw one point. If a draw, or at least a goalless draw, scored no points, it was felt that teams who could no longer 'play for a draw' to gain a single, valuable point would be obliged to adopt a more aggressive, attacking style.

All such suggestions have met with the traditional resistance which, as we have seen, serves to protect the purity of the tribal ritual. Only in the United States have alterations been instituted.* There, the offside rule has been modified by the introduction of a thirty-five-yard line, so that it is now impossible to be offside until within thirty-five yards of the enemy goal. The Americans, with some justification, feel that it is boring to halt a game for an offside decision against a player who may be only a few yards inside enemy territory. But the international Tribal Law-makers will have none of it.

The other innovation in American soccer is the dramatic 'shoot-out' at the close of a drawn match. The North American Soccer League decided that to end a match with a draw is boring and unsatisfying for the spectators. As one authority put it: 'It is as exciting as kissing your sister.' So they banned the draw from American soccer. Someone *had* to win, come what may. If normal time ends with the two sides equal, they play a fifteen-minute period of extra time (7½ minutes each way). If this fails to break the tie, they then stage the shoot-out procedure. In this, five players from each side take it in turns to dribble a ball from the thirty-five-yard line and attempt a solo goal against the opposing goalkeeper, with a time limit of five seconds. The goalkeeper is allowed to move. This is similar to the traditional 'penalties solution' to important tied matches in other countries, except that there the players take turns to shoot ordinary penalty kicks from the penalty spot. Usually, of course, a tied match (outside the United States) is replayed at a later date, but sometimes, in international competitions, it is not possible to organize such a replay, and then the penalties rule comes into operation. The Americans did try this method at first, back in 1974, but changed to the shoot-out system in 1977 because they found the penalties contest 'too stereotyped'.

In addition to these two changes in the game itself, American soccer has also radically altered the League points system. As far back as 1967, they scrapped the two points for a win, one point for a draw arrangement and replaced it with six points for a win and a bonus point for each goal scored, up to a maximum of three. If the score was, say, 3–2, then the winners would net nine points and the losers two.

These three changes, although approved by FIFA for North American soccer, were not accepted for games elsewhere, despite the fact that they were all designed to increase attacking play and raise the number of goals in each match, and despite the fact that they seem to have achieved their object and provided more entertaining soccer for American spectators. This has put the die-hard traditionalists in something of a dilemma. They complain about the excessively defensive style of the modern game and urge the need to make it more open and attacking, yet they cannot bear to accept new-fangled ideas from a comparative newcomer to the international soccer fraternity. The battle between their desires and their dignity has still to be resolved.

---

*But in 1981 the English Football League introduced a trial period of three points for a win and one point for a draw.

13 The Victory Celebrations

THE AWARDS, THE LAP OF HONOUR
AND THE HOMECOMING

When the final whistle blows, the supporters of the winning team let out a great roar of victory and clap their players from the field. The players themselves sometimes acknowledge this ovation with raised arms and a slight wave. Then, if the encounter has not been too bitter, they shake hands with their opponents and disappear into the tunnel, heading for the communal showers in the dressing rooms.

At an ordinary, routine match, there is little more to the victory celebration than that. But on important occasions, such as promotion matches, cup finals and international tournaments, the scenes are much more dramatic and the ritual procedures more elaborate.

After a great conquest, the players' emotions are in shreds and many of them collapse on to the turf, sprawled out, curled up, or bent over in a posture resembling a praying Moslem. Others cling to one another in relief and disbelief at their new status as conquerors. The Brazilian star Pelé describes the moment when his team became champions of the world, with these words: 'I had a strange feeling I was going to faint ... I felt my knees collapsing under me and reached out to prevent myself hitting the ground; and then I was being lifted, raised on the shoulders of my team-mates and being carried around the field. Everyone was crying, tears streamed from my eyes as I hung on wildly ... we marched around the field with the crowds in the stands on their feet, cheering us, with a mob of fans beside us and behind us ... The tears continued to flow, leaving trails in the sweat that still covered our faces.'

A common sight at the close of important matches is a small but attractive

In some countries such as Czechoslovakia (below) and Japan (left) the coach or captain of a victorious team is ritually tossed in the air by his players at the end of a final match. In Japan this action is called 'Do-a-Ge' – given here to the captain of the winners of the Emperor Cup.

At the close of important matches players perform the shirt-swap ritual (above) in which each man tears off his sweaty shirt and exchanges it with that of his opposite number. Many players then put on the enemy shirt in a sweat-mingling act of mutual respect.

ritual known as the 'shirt-swap', in which each player pulls off his football jersey and exchanges it with that of his opposite number. It is not clear who invented this ceremony, but it has a strange appeal both for the players and the spectators. It somehow signals that, despite all the fouls and hard tackles, all the grimaces and flaring tempers of the match itself, there remains an element of mutual respect between the opponents, a respect too strong to be expressed by a mere handshake. An exchange of gifts is required to satisfy the intensity of the emotions.

Having handed over their shirts, the players either leave the field bare-chested, carrying their informal, sweat-stained trophies, or they put them on and depart wearing the colours of their enemies. On very important occasions, where there is a cup presentation to be made before they can retreat to the dressing rooms, this can create a curious spectacle. The winners troop up to receive their trophy with some players wearing the colours of their opponents while others, who have yet to locate their opposite numbers and make the exchange, still wear their own club colours. This mixed-up display proved displeasing to certain Tribal Elders of the English FA, who took the military line that such teams were improperly dressed. After pondering the problem, they issued an order in 1980 prohibiting the exchange of shirts in public view. In future, they insisted, this action would have to be restricted to consenting players in private. In other countries no such prudery has been allowed to spoil the public's enjoyment of the only informal display of respect and friendship normally exhibited between players of opposing sides.

The collection of the trophy is itself an important victory ritual. Usually, it involves the players mounting a long, narrow step-way, then turning to walk along in front of the royal or presidential seats. The team captain leads the file, offers a sweaty palm to the king, queen, president or other VIP who is presenting the trophy, and receives the precious object into his hands. At this point it is *he* who becomes the most important person in the stadium, momentarily out-ranking even a head of state and, as if to emphasize his new status, he then commits what in any other context would be a gross breach of protocol. He turns his back on the trophy-presenter and, facing the pitch,

After the presentation of the cup, the team begins the long descent to the field, past the outstretched hands of eager well-wishers (above).

holds the huge object aloft for all to see. This is the supreme moment the supporters have been waiting for, throughout all the hard-fought struggles that have led them to this triumphant conclusion, and a roar goes up that exceeds everything that has gone before.

As his team-mates receive their individual medals, the captain starts the long descent past the outstretched hands of well-wishers and takes the trophy down on to the pitch. Joined there by the rest of his team, he begins the lap of honour, running joyfully past the stands of cheering fans, with crowds of agitated photographers in hot pursuit or running awkwardly backwards in front of the team group, desperately trying to focus their cameras.

After a short run, the photographers manage to halt the group and persuade them to cluster together for a victory team photograph, during which the trophy is passed from player to player and ceremonially kissed and embraced.

Soon they break away again and continue their circuit of honour, the trophy changing hands from time to time as they go, so that before they have finished, each player in turn will have experienced the joy of holding it aloft to show it to the admiring crowd.

Finally, they disappear into the tunnel to continue the celebrations in the dressing room, drinking champagne in the communal baths, laughing and shouting in a mixture of elation and exhaustion. Outside, their supporters take to their cars for the motor parade in which, with scarves and flags streaming from the windows, they drive home with horns blaring and arms waving.

The following day, the celebrations begin again in the home territory of the victorious tribe. The team assemble on top of an open bus and ride in

(opposite) The lap of honour around the stadium, showing off the trophy to the delighted supporters, is one of the high points in the career of a Tribal Hero.

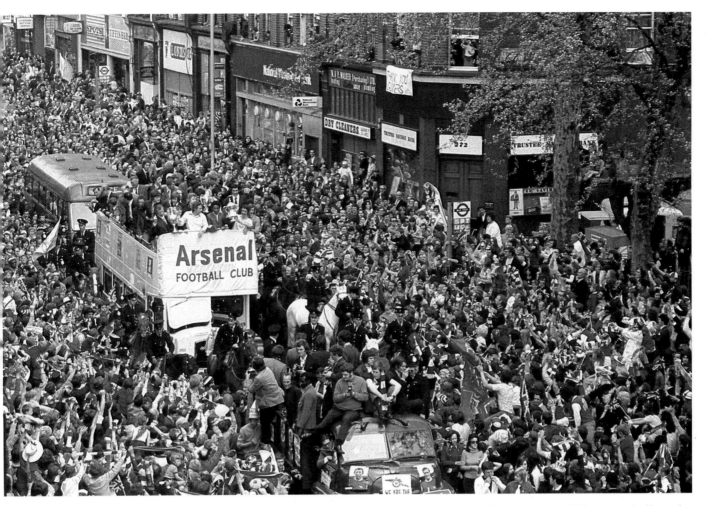

On the day following the cup final, the winning team return to their home territory (above), there to tour the joyously crowded streets in an open-topped bus, and make their way with the coveted trophy to the city centre for a heroes' feast.

(opposite) The victorious heroes celebrate noisily in the dressing rooms and relax cheerfully in the communal baths.

triumph to their local town hall for a civic reception. Thousands line the streets to cheer them home and then crowd together to await their appearance on the balcony, where once again the trophy is held aloft and displayed for all to see.

At such a moment there is an intense feeling of tribal cohesion, with the victorious team taking the role of the triumphant hunters home from the chase, holding up the kill to show to their fellow tribesmen before the feasting begins.

This homecoming celebration is as old as the game of soccer itself, and has hardly changed in any detail except the mode of transport. A newspaper report for the year 1889 describes the scene in Preston when the local team returned from winning the cup final without conceding a goal, having already won the first League championship without losing a single match: '... as soon as the mills and workshops closed the people began to flock into the streets, so that by seven o'clock there could not be less than 30,000 in the vicinity of ... the incline leading to the railway station entrance ... When the train arrived ... there was a large crowd on the platform, and a couple of bands at once formed up in front of the saloon and struck up "See the Conquering Hero Comes". Immediately behind these came the members of the team, around whom swarmed hundreds of fanatics, each of whom struggled to get a handshake with some member of the team ... Immediately the crowd set eyes on "the bit of silver plate", the wildest enthusiasm prevailed. Hats were thrown up, handkerchiefs waved, and sticks flourished. From this point the procession to the Public Hall wended its way ...'

A similar story has been told year after year, wherever the conquering heroes of the Soccer Tribe have returned triumphant to their home. Perhaps

Ecstatic fans parade the team colours through the city streets in a wild carnival of celebration.

the most frenzied scenes are those witnessed in South American cities when a national team has won the World Cup. Reports tell of carnivals lasting all night, of streets so packed that even moving trucks and buses are forced to a halt by the press of bodies, of fanatical supporters throwing themselves towards their heroes in desperate attempts to touch or kiss them, of squads of police and firemen fighting a way through for the team, so that they can escape being crushed to death by frenzied well-wishers, of traffic brought to a standstill throughout whole city centres, of balconies jammed with people throwing confetti, torn newspapers and firecrackers, setting off rockets and roman candles, and firing guns.

Reading these reports, one is left in no doubt about the intensity of feeling engendered by the activities of the Soccer Tribe. Allowing for local variations, the scenes are basically similar, always with the same overwhelming display of raw passion, as if the symbolism of the game somehow manages to tap deep sources of communal emotion in the human animal. It is the players who are the focus of this emotion and it is to them that we must now turn in more detail, in the chapters that follow.

The Tribal Heroes

14 The Background of the Heroes

THE SHAPING OF A PLAYER

Today's stars of the Soccer Tribe are true heroes of the people. They come from the same background as the majority of their devoted followers – the working classes. It was not always so. The earliest Tribal Heroes were the affluent public schoolboys of Eton and Harrow, and Oxford University. But all this changed when professionalism entered the sport and soccer was rapidly taken over by the industrial world of Victorian England. The factory workers filled the grandstands and it was their sons who performed for them on the pitch.

As soccer spread around the globe, the same pattern was repeated in many different countries. The local workers flocked to the matches and, in the back streets of the great industrial towns and the slums of the sprawling cities, young boys were to be seen kicking a ball about in the dust. On parking lots and in alleyways, on dirt tracks and near rubbish tips, anywhere they could find an open space on which to play, the offspring of the industrial revolution started their apprenticeship. Before long, the more agile of them were struggling desperately to succeed in schoolboy teams and the lucky few, who were unusually gifted, would find themselves approached by scouts, ever on the lookout for new soccer talent. They were offered a trial with a local club and, if they showed promise, a coveted place on the books as a young professional. Then, after months of training and development, came the first adult game before a paying audience.

This was the route taken by the majority of soccer players. The upper and middle classes were hardly involved. In most countries this has remained the general rule throughout the twentieth century. In some Northern European countries the game has become more classless, but in the British Isles, the Mediterranean region, South America and elsewhere it has largely retained its social roots. Most of today's great stars kicked their first football in a back alley or a side-street.

The illustrious Pelé began in this way. He recalls: 'Our field was the street where I lived . . . and our goals were the two ends of the street . . . Our sidelines were where a kerb might have been had the street been paved.' Too poor to afford a proper football, he and his friends used to borrow socks from clothes-lines, stuff them full of rags and paper until they were as round as possible and then tie them tightly with a piece of string.

The Irish star Danny Blanchflower learnt his craft in much the same way, kicking a ball about 'at every opportunity in the streets of the housing estate where he lived, in the school playground, under the railway arch and beneath the lamp-posts on dark evenings'. One of his childhood heroes was the great Stanley Matthews who, in his turn, as a boy, had 'worked hard to improve his natural skill with the aid of a cheap rubber ball and the garden wall. Kicking the ball against the wall for hours on end, and dribbling it round kitchen chairs, strategically placed to simulate opposition, were methods he employed to train the ball to obey him.'

Scenes such as these are recalled again and again in the memoirs of the Tribal Heroes. A childhood world, often impoverished in many ways, was enriched by the simple presence of a ball and a crude playing surface. Hour after hour of practice at a tender age developed intuitive skills which became so deeply ingrained that they survived for a whole lifetime. The passion grew so intense that the small boys became foot-jugglers, ball-acrobats, magicians of leg movement and body balance. The ball itself became almost part of their

All over the world, youngsters are to be found – like these boys in a back street of Rio (right) – practising their ball-skills and dreaming of cup final victories in the years ahead.

Top players, such as Stanley Matthews (opposite, left), Bobby Charlton (centre, with his mother) and George Best (right, with his father), nearly always come from soccer-obsessed families, where they have been devoted to the game since early childhood and encouraged by helpful relatives.

own beings. George Best sums up the mood well: 'In those days when I was a kid the only thing I shared my bed with was a football. I used to take a ball to bed with me. I know it sounds daft but I used to love the feel of it. I used to hold it, look at it and think, "One day you'll do everything I tell you". I only lived to play football.'

Apart from developing their skills, the future heroes also had to acquire a tough, competitive spirit. The austere environment often came to their aid. Billy Bremner remembers the rough district in which he grew up: 'You had to be hard yourself, to survive there . . . if you didn't look after yourself, then you could be sure of one thing, nobody else would.' And Pelé admits that 'I always seemed to be fighting in those days, either in school or out, either on the football field or at home, either with kids bigger than me, kids my own size, or kids smaller than me. Almost any little thing seemed to get me started.'

In addition to the physical skills and the fighting spirit, a deeper understanding of the game was also needed and in the background of many Tribal Heroes an important element was that crucial figure, the 'helpful relative'. Many future stars grew up in families containing fanatical followers of the game, who encouraged them and tutored them. Some, such as Joe Mercer, Geoff Hurst, Alan Ball and Pelé, had fathers who were themselves professional footballers. The famous brothers Jackie and Bobby Charlton had no less than five professionals in their family circle – a grandfather and four uncles – and from the day they were born they were surrounded by the

Whether poor or rich, in an alley (left) or a luxury stadium (above), children everywhere are drawn by the magic of soccer and hope that one day they may become great Tribal Heroes.

atmosphere of the game. When Jackie was a baby, his mother responded to queries about her new son with the words 'his feet are fine', such was the emphasis on soccer in the Charlton home.

The fathers of other top players may not have appeared on the pitch, but most of them were avid followers of their local teams. Their own occupations cover a wide range of working class jobs – they include dockers, miners, bricklayers, shipyard workers, joiners, fitters, porters, metalworkers, electricians and labourers – but each one helped to instil a love of soccer in his growing son.

For the vast majority of the Tribal Heroes, therefore, the world of soccer has been a deep personal involvement from early childhood and success in its ranks the eternal dream and fantasy of youth. The exceptions to this rule are so rare that they have attracted special attention. One such case is Liverpool player Steve Heighway, a man with a middle class background and a university education in economics and politics. During his early childhood he attended a small private school where there were no organized games. He never played soccer and did not watch a single match. Later, at grammar school, he played rugger, and it was not until his fourth year there that he 'decided to have a go at soccer'. In complete contrast with almost all other budding Tribal Heroes, he did not take it seriously: 'Soccer was fun, a game to be enjoyed . . .' Despite this almost sacrilegious attitude to the sport, he excelled at it. As a university student he played with such success that he was spotted and signed up for Liverpool by Bill Shankly. When he walked out on to the pitch for his first match at the famous Anfield ground, he astonished a team-mate by asking him, 'Which end is the Kop?' – a question which most of the other players could have answered on their first day at school.

Perhaps in the future the Tribal Heroes will come from a wider background. Heighway may prove to be one of the first of many scholarly heroes. Certainly on the continent of Europe there are other national and even international stars with academic qualifications and degrees. And the flowering of soccer in North America may see the addition to the ranks of the heroes of players with more educated backgrounds. But it is more likely that this will remain only a minor trend. The demands of professional soccer are such that early specialization is a great advantage. In order to succeed, most youngsters must become single-minded so early in life that there is little room for bookish pursuits. Wherever the budding hero may be, secretly in his mind he is running across the turf with a ball at his toes. For him, soccer is not seen as a 'future occupation', a mere job, it is an obsession and it drives out all other serious thoughts. As George Best recalls: 'I hated all the bloody jobs they made me do ... the work was so boring. When I was at work or supposed to be working, I'd fantasize about games I was going to play in. It was always at Wembley and there were 100,000 people in the crowd and it was a cup final ...' Such is the stuff of which future Tribal Heroes are made.

Many a father, whose own playing days are past and whose belly is no longer flat, can still enjoy the fantasy of soccer triumphs through the developing skills of a much loved son.

15 The Personality of the Heroes

COMPETITION AND COOPERATION

The role of Tribal Hero involves a basic conflict. To succeed he must be intensely competitive, but he can only achieve success by behaving cooperatively as a member of a team. On the one hand he must be aggressively self-centred and egotistical; on the other, he must be self-effacing and helpful. This fundamental contradiction goes a long way to explain the personality of the modern soccer player.

First, the competitiveness: it has often been said by those who view sports as 'character-building' that it is not the winning which is important, but the taking part. This is the Olympic ideal, but it would be naive to imagine that it has much bearing on modern professional soccer. Victory has become the most important aspect of the game. As one trainer put it: 'Winning isn't everything, it's the only thing.' The urge to dominate the opposition and to assert oneself is therefore central to the player's personality. If he is to succeed he must be able to take an almost sensual pleasure in the symbolic destruction of the enemy.

Some critics have recoiled from this idea, seeing in it a danger of glorifying human aggressiveness. George Orwell, the gloomy prophet of the nightmare world of *1984*, expressed his misgivings in extreme terms: 'Serious sport has nothing to do with fair play. It is bound up with hatred, jealousy, boastfulness, disregard of all rules and sadistic pleasure in witnessing violence. In other words it is war minus the shooting.' How seriously should one take this attitude when attempting to assess the character of the Tribal Heroes? Are they really full of hatred and jealousy?

The truth is that the aggressiveness of the soccer player is real enough, but highly formal. It is there, as an essential element in his personality, but it is contained. His battles are symbolic, not real. Far from having a 'disregard of all rules', he is completely hemmed in by them. If he breaks them, he is punished. The worst he can do is to bend them a little and hope to avoid detection. Any player who repeatedly loses control of himself will soon be discarded. Raging hostility that cannot be tamed is no use to the sportsman.

This said, it must be admitted that there is nothing in the philosophy of the Soccer Tribe that encourages an *internal* self-restraint. It is the rigid external rules that control the player. He obeys these rules more than he respects them, like the driver of a car who keeps to the speed limit, not because he feels it is morally right to do so, but because he fears being caught by the police. In the past, whenever the game has become unduly violent, it has not been a gentleman's agreement between the players that has re-established restraint, but an increased severity on the part of referees.

In essence, then, the personality of the soccer player must contain a lust for victory that is powerful but controllable. There is no question of 'art for art's sake' – playing for the fun of playing. That is the amateur approach, and the full-time player employs the word 'amateur' disparagingly. His professional world is one of ambitions and the seeking of rewards – the winning of glory, money and status.

To satisfy these aims, the player must have an inherent toughness of character and a strong romantic streak. Publicly, he must be down-to-earth, even cynical and self-mocking to protect himself from ridicule, but privately he must dream of glittering prizes and great triumphs. He must have a powerful ego, but one that is prepared to suffer to achieve its goals – in both senses of the word.

Assertiveness and determination are vital characteristics of a successful player. On the field it is easy for these qualities to become over-stimulated to the point of open aggression and anger. If this happens too often, there is a danger of being seriously penalized by the referee.

One of his biggest problems is how to handle defeat, for he knows from the very beginning that no road to soccer glory can be taken without encountering many set-backs. And he knows that these set-backs cannot be hidden. All his mistakes will be glaringly public. In this, his lifestyle differs from that of most other adults. If the scientist makes a mistake in the laboratory, he corrects it privately. He is not forced to publish his errors. If an artist paints a bad picture, he can destroy it before anyone has seen it. But every slip the player makes is visible to thousands of pairs of eyes and, for good measure, may be seen again in action replay on television by millions more. His personality must be strong enough to deal with this exposure. He must find some way of defending his ego.

The toughness of his childhood may help him here. The boy who has learnt to accept set-backs as a routine part of living is better able to keep them in perspective as an adult. As a star player, he already knows that he is capable of succeeding despite them and, if they do become serious, he will have developed special techniques for protecting his faith in himself. These include *rationalization* – blaming failure on an injury; *mysticism* – explaining away a poor game because it was against a 'bogey-team' or on a 'hoodoo ground'; *projection* – accusing the referee of being biased; *denial* – claiming that the game was not important enough to bring the best out of him; and

compensation – showing off wildly in some social context, with girls, gambling, or drinking, as a boosting device.

These tricks for handling defeats work well enough if they are short-lived and merely cover the let-down period of dejection, but they are dangerous if they become persistent. When this happens, they start to interfere with the learning process – the honest self-analysis which enables a player to learn from his mistakes. He cannot do this unless he is prepared to admit, within a day or so, that he *did* make mistakes. His personality must be such that he is then able to throw away his excuses and analyse precisely what went wrong. For a top sportsman, this means having an ego big enough to face temporary humility without damaging the self-esteem so vital to a champion. The humble champion is greater than the brash champion, not because he is pleasantly modest about his weaknesses, but because his ego is powerful enough to withstand corrective criticism. By comparison, the brash hero is an inferior personality who has extended the mechanism of compensation into a permanent crutch to support his shortcomings.

The intense competitiveness of successful players gives them a personality that is *stable* – they must keep going; *disciplined* – they must obey the rules; *tough-minded* – they must face risk of injury; *conscientious* – they cannot afford the luxury of laziness; *self-controlled* – they must harness their strongly aroused emotions; and *self-assured* – they must be seen to be assertive. Above all, they must be *egocentric*, almost narcissistic, because 'they' is all they have. A businessman can take great pride in the business he has built, an architect in his houses, a painter in his pictures, but the soccer star, like an actor, has only his own body. It is he himself who is great, not something outside him that he has made. If he says, 'I played well today,' it is like a painter saying, 'I am pleased with my new picture.' It is a detached statement and yet, at the same time, it is self-oriented because the self is all there is – the running, leaping, kicking body. This means that it is impossible to be a successful player without being 'selfish', but it is a selfishness inherent in the nature of the role. To deny it would be to disregard the very tools of one's trade.

This quality gives the solo sportsman less of a personality problem than the team player. The cooperation needed in a team sport requires additional strengths in the personality if success is to be achieved. Once he is on the pitch, the player's 'self' must become welded to ten other 'selves' to convert the team into a super-being – a twenty-two-legged monster with a single ego. Anything less would be disastrous. There might be virtuoso individual performances, but matches would be disjointed and defeat the ultimate result. So the Tribal Hero must employ special mental tricks to marry his inevitable, egocentric selfishness to a selfless team spirit.

On the field he does this by thinking of the team as part of himself – their victory becomes his victory, a companion's goal becomes his goal. Some players have described vividly the way in which personal animosities and jealousies evaporate the moment the referee blows his whistle at the kick-off. Players who were bickering the day before suddenly become as one. A strange form of almost telepathic intimacy develops. Eamon Dunphy expresses it in these words: 'If you take two players who work together in midfield, say, they will know each other through football as intimately as any two lovers . . . It's an unspoken relationship, but your movements speak, your game speaks . . . You don't necessarily become closer in a social sense, but you develop a close unspoken understanding.'

Off the field another team-reaction occurs. Players adopt an ego-mask. They hide their self-concern behind jokes and sarcasms. They use the word 'star' as an insult. If they indulge in self-praise they do so with self-mockery, deliberately inviting joking attacks. If they praise others, that, too, is expressed in some humorous way with much laughter and back-chat. The player who breaks this rule quickly becomes the butt of team teasing and, in

Between matches, teasing and friendly mockery is commonplace among team-mates as a useful levelling device in their closely knit group.

extreme cases, of ill-concealed hostility. The solo sportsman can talk earnestly about his performance without fear of ridicule, but the team sportsman seldom knows such a luxury, at least while he is in the company of his colleagues. He must wait until he is away from them and the atmosphere of bantering ego-concealment.

Beneath the good-humoured surface, however, the egos remain safely intact, ready to erupt at any moment when personal loyalty clashes with team or club loyalty. The outcome of such a conflict is never in doubt – self wins over team every time. If a player is offered a good contract with a better club, or more money by a club that is no better than his own, he will not hesitate to abandon his old team-mates. Nor would they expect him to – they would do the same if they had the chance. He would be accused of letting the side down if he played poorly during a match, but he would never be accused of doing so if he transferred to a rival club, even if it meant that he would be playing against his old team-mates in future matches. That is the professional code.

Managers are well aware of this. Southampton's Lawrie McMenemy has commented: 'It's a game that breeds selfishness. You try to encourage team-work and selflessness but in the end the professional is only in it for himself and what he can make out of it. The system, the money, the bonuses all make players think of their own interests first.' This may be true, but the clubs are as much to blame as the players. It is the directors and managers – and the fans – who demand *winning* as the top priority, rather than elegant, gentlemanly sportsmanship. It is they who reward competitiveness so massively and who discourage feelings of consideration and compassion. If they select and foster players with personalities that will be aggressive and assertive on the field, they cannot have it both ways. They cannot expect such men, chosen and trained for these properties, suddenly to turn round and display amateur sentiments when it suits them. Furthermore, every player knows full well that when he starts 'slowing up', after he has passed his thirtieth birthday, he will soon be discarded by the club and left to fend for himself. The club will show little loyalty towards him then, so his attitude is far from being one-sided, a fact which most club officials choose to ignore.

(opposite) When a violent collision occurs, tempers sometimes snap and a fight threatens to break out. As soon as this happens, restraining hands quickly appear and convert the incident into the traditional 'hold-me-back' ritual.

16 The Motivation of the Heroes

WHAT DRIVES THE PLAYERS ON

As each Tribal Hero walks out on to the pitch at the start of a game he carries with him his skill, his experience and his fitness. His skill makes him an acrobat with the ball; his experience gives him his understanding of strategy and tactics; and his fitness provides him with an athlete's body. But these are only three of the four foundation stones on which he must build his performance. The fourth, perhaps the most important of all, is his mood – his mental state.

It has been said that many a game has been won before the kick-off, because teams have come on to the field with a ruthless determination to win at all costs. In some cases their confidence or their desperate desire to triumph has overcome their mediocre skill, their inexperience and their inferior fitness. Little teams have become giant-killers when their will to win has been strong enough.

All these words – mood, determination, confidence, desire, will – can be summed up in the single term 'motivation'. What is it that motivates the players? What is it that drives them on? Why is it that, for no apparent reason, they seem stale one week and then 'play above themselves' the next? These are questions that supporters, directors, managers and even the players

Matches are won by a combination of skill, experience, fitness and motivation. In top class soccer all the players are skilful, experienced and fit, but their motivation can vary dramatically. When a game is going badly, their mood of determination can be dangerously weakened and it is then that a good captain can act as a vital motivator.

The most important task of the manager is to motivate his team, raising each player to his optimum level of arousal just before the match begins.

themselves are always asking, and yet remarkably little serious study of the problem has been undertaken inside the Soccer Tribe.

One reason for this lack of investigation is the deep tribal suspicion of psychologists and psychology. The Soccer Tribesmen are by nature conservative and view all 'new-fangled' scientific ideas with mistrust. There is also a practical difficulty. The soccer season is so crowded with fixtures that there is no time to experiment – to try out novel methods and test new theories. The scientist would be prepared to vary procedures from week to week until he found the best approach to a motivational problem, but the soccer club cannot afford to take such risks. In the close-fought League and cup competitions, they dare not throw away a single game with a rash experiment. So they rely on tried and trusted methods, using intuition instead of science.

Sometimes they persist in the old ways even in the face of obvious flaws. To give an example: training sessions are carried out at most clubs in the mornings. The players arrive early and train hard until lunchtime, after which they can relax for the rest of the day. This has the effect of establishing a dominant bio-rhythm, one which favours peak activity in the first third of the day. This routine is followed despite the glaringly obvious fact that all their matches are played in the afternoon or evening. It is almost as if they are deliberately training themselves to be off-peak at the very times when most is expected of them. Their bio-rhythms, those mysterious inner sequences of mood change that occur throughout the day, are bound to be wrong.

When this oddity is pointed out, it is met with a shrug and quickly forgotten. The tradition of morning training is so entrenched that scientific sense cannot shift it. As a routine, it seems to have become established as a 'toughness display', because early rising is thought to be manly. The idea of players rising late and spending a relaxed morning before coming in to train clashes with the pseudo-military attitude of coaches and trainers. Yet this is clearly the correct way to establish a bio-rhythm that peaks at match-time. The only redeeming feature of the old arrangement is that, since all teams use it, they are all off-peak to an equal extent. So it is at least fair.

The men directly concerned with such matters – the managers, coaches and trainers – are all ex-players who are now too old to play and must content themselves with an advisory role. Their most important task is to motivate their players, yet they lack any formal training in motivational psychology. This is rather like asking retired aircraft mechanics to fly jumbo jets. Such a remark is not intended as an insult to the managerial staff. It is merely an observation of an age-old soccer tradition. And in many respects the system works amazingly well. The good managers quickly adapt to their new role and apply every ounce of intuitive cunning at their disposal to handle their often temperamental charges. Defending themselves against scientific arguments, the managers and coaches point out that the week-by-week and moment-by-moment problems they face with their teams not only keep them too busy but are, in any case, too complex and subtle for the application of crude psychological tests. There is some truth in this, but the danger is that the attitude hardens to an extent where all new, scientific approaches are resisted automatically. The managers, feeling ignorant of the details of the psychological procedures, reject them out of a fear of appearing incompetent. Their role as group leaders demands that they shall appear all-powerful, and therefore all-knowing, to their young players. To dither about with this and that scientific novelty would undermine their authority.

Fortunately, their intuition, built up over years of playing, solves many of their problems. Bio-rhythms apart, they manage to handle the moods of their players extremely well. They know that on match-day, as the hour of kick-off approaches, they must treat their teams with special care. Each player has a personal level of arousal at which he plays his best. The old, crude idea of 'psyching up' all the players to a fever of excitement is not good enough for soccer. It is still used in some other forms of football, where violent body-charging and massive physical contact is the order of the day, and where a kind of savage animal anger is needed at the start of each contest, but soccer requires more diversified skills. As manager Lawrie McMenemy eloquently put it: 'The perfect balance for a team is seven road-sweepers and four violinists.' Some players slog away with stamina and a high work-rate, while others apply a skilfully deft touch at vital moments, and the different qualities involved require different treatment in the match build-up.

The more introverted, highly strung players, usually the strikers, often arrive at the ground with a level of mental arousal that is too high. They are already over-stressed by the situation and require relaxing. The more extroverted, happy-go-lucky players, usually the defenders, need greater arousal or they will be too relaxed. The first category must be treated gently, complimented and made to feel at ease. The second category must be encouraged and heightened to a more determined condition. The careful manager knows this and gives individual attention to the different players, bringing each of them, not to their maximum arousal, but to their *optimum*. The careless manager treats them all as one and either assails them with a pep-talk, which suits some and panics others, or presents them with a calm affability, which again suits some, but leaves others under-stimulated.

There is a myth that players of different nationalities require different forms of treatment from their managers. The Italian Vittorio Pozzo is quoted as saying, 'English players can be treated collectively. Italian players must always be treated individually. They like to know you are on their side.' He is right about the Italian players, but he does not know English teams well enough to draw such a contrast. All players, of whatever nationality, benefit from personal treatment – unless, by a rare coincidence, a team has been

Good players are highly motivated in most of their games; great players are *always* highly motivated. It is their consistency that sets them apart, in a class of their own.

formed consisting of eleven players with identical temperaments. Only then could they be dealt with 'as one man', on all occasions.

Although the individual approach to player motivation is a sound principle, there are times when it has to be overridden. If a team has been playing disastrously during the first half of a match, a half-time 'roasting' from the manager can sometimes work wonders. All the men are sunk in depression together and all can be lifted together by a verbal 'arousal onslaught'. At other times, a whole team may become over-anxious and so highly stressed that they can all benefit from a calming, confidence-boosting approach by the manager. The most imaginative example on record concerns a team that found themselves playing in an important final against illustrious opponents. The manager hired a local comedian to tell them jokes before the match, even in the dressing room as they changed, to create a relaxed mood. The device had an unexpected bonus, for the players were still laughing as they stood alongside their powerful opponents in the tunnel, waiting to make their ceremonial entrance on to the pitch. This so unnerved the superior team, who had no idea of the reason for this strange behaviour, that their own mood was destroyed and they lost the match.

Another unusual approach was adopted by a manager who would stand in the players' corridor and greet every member of the opposing team in turn. He then retired to his own dressing room and proceeded to inform his players of the terrible condition of each of their dreaded enemies: 'Brown has been out night-clubbing again. You should see the bags under his eyes. Smith is still carrying his hand-bag. Jones has obviously had a terrible row with his wife,' and so on, right through the team. Although it was treated as a great joke by his players, it nevertheless served to release the tension and boost his team's confidence.

Perhaps the most bizarre example of motivational manipulation comes from Australian soccer, where one coach went to the length of showing his team a film of Nazi atrocities before an important match because he felt that the players, as a group, were insufficiently aroused. After watching twenty minutes of concentration camp gassing and shooting, the men were told to imagine that they each had a son, wife or mother in the camp and to revenge their deaths. The team, facing opponents who had beaten them easily in the past, stormed out on to the field and symbolically 'massacred' their enemy, winning the game hands down. This particular motivational device backfired, however. When news of it became public, the over-imaginative coach was forced to resign, the President of the Australian Football Federation declaring that his action had been 'against all that soccer stands for'.

Another trick that can easily go wrong for a manager is the deliberate riling of a team or of particular players. If he feels that they are becoming stale and jaded, he can publicly pour scorn on them. In one case, with a London team made up of southerners, the manager gave an interview in which he said his men lacked toughness and, as a result, he was looking for a few northerners to strengthen the side 'because there is no doubt that they are tougher players'. When his team read this they were furious, but said nothing. Instead they set out to prove him wrong, gritting their teeth and beating their next opponents 6–1. In the following match, against a team of 'tough northerners', the angry southerners fought even harder, winning 7–1. After this, the players forgave their manager his harsh words and accepted that they had been playing poorly before he had goaded them into action. But it was a dangerous device for him to have employed. If they had not done so well it could easily have left a permanent scar on the manager-team relationship. The method is especially risky when applied to an individual player. Even if he is provoked into better play, he finds it hard to forget the public attack made on him by his own manager and before long there is news of an unexpected transfer to

An experienced manager knows exactly when to administer a rebuke, offer encouragement, provide individual sympathy, or assail his whole team with a savage verbal roasting. Each player needs personal attention to bring the best out of him, but there are other occasions where the team must be treated as one.

another club. He may recall the incident as a joke later, quoting the particular attack made on him ('He looks like Tarzan but plays like Jane' is a famous one), but such public insults tend to stick in the throats of all but the most insensitive players, and managers who use these tactics are taking a serious risk.

This is where the lack of psychological training of managers begins to show. They are often heavy-handed. Their own insecurity, coupled with a feeling that the ruggedness of the sporting context requires an authoritarian approach with a military flavour, pushes them in that direction. They, too, are under severe pressure and they sometimes overreact.

There are a number of psychological innovations available to them to broaden their range of motivational devices, if they could afford the time to study them. Maurice Yaffé, a London-based clinical psychologist and for several years an honorary consultant to the Crystal Palace Football Club, recently summarized some of the latest findings in the field of sport psychology.

One technique is known as *autogenic training*. In order to obtain a more positive frame of mind before a match, a player is asked to perform a series of alternating tensing and relaxing exercises. He must lie down in a comfortable position, close his eyes and go through a period of deep breathing. Then he has to tense all his muscles as hard as he can, concentrating on each part of his body in turn. After holding this wire-tight condition for a few moments he must relax his muscles completely and go limp. These two contrasting states are then alternated – tense/limp, tense/limp. When he is in the tensed-up condition he is asked to imagine the enemy he is about to face. After a session of this kind, the player's performance on the pitch will be sharper and more effective.

Another method is *assertion training*. A player who is losing his confidence and cannot muster sufficiently aggressive feelings on the pitch can be helped by focusing his mind on a 'hate image'. He is asked to hit a punch-bag repeatedly while concentrating on some private, personal object of hatred. Each time he punches the bag he must hold the image in his mind and must always picture the same scene, so that it becomes fixed. This enables him to relate an uninhibited act of aggression to the particular image. Instead of bottling up his aggression, as he would have to do during ordinary social life, he lets it go, in a violent physical movement. This helps him to become familiar with a high state of aggressive arousal. When he is out on the pitch and he feels his assertiveness ebbing, all he then has to do is to call up the private 'hate image' and concentrate on it for a few moments. This will recharge him and give him back his lost drive.

A similar device is the development of *coping images*. These are used to reduce feelings of panic or depression when the game is going badly. The player is asked to select a pleasant memory, such as the moment when he scored a brilliant goal in an earlier match, and to concentrate on this repeatedly before a difficult game. He does this until it is firmly fixed in his mind, rather like a phrase from a popular song that one 'can't get out of one's head'. Then, during the match, when the play is going against him, he can switch on his special memory as an internal booster.

An alternative is *mental rehearsal*, in which the player imagines the worst possible disasters that can befall him during the game. But he does this before the match, during a period of calm and relaxation. Then, when he encounters them in reality on the pitch, he will respond with a lower level of panic.

Some players face a different kind of problem. They are not panicky or unassertive, they are *too* aggressive. As a result they repeatedly commit fouls and find themselves penalized. Studies in Germany involving the analysis of more than 1,800 soccer matches revealed several characteristic features of fouls: losing sides commit more fouls than winning sides; visiting teams commit more fouls than home sides; low-scoring games produce more fouls than high-scoring games; lower-placed teams commit more fouls than high-ranking teams. Similar results were obtained by Belgian investigators, and it seems likely that they apply generally to all countries.

Clearly the chances of fouling are increased by a sense of frustration. A team that is losing a match, is failing to score many goals, or is low down in the League ratings, feels intensely thwarted and this triggers off more illegal actions. The away team fouls more than the home team because it cannot help reacting to the hostility of the home supporters.

Individual players who are prone to react with unusual violence to frustrations of this kind, and who are repeatedly booked by the referee for their lack of control, can be helped by a process of *desensitization*. This involves showing them video-taped recordings of themselves at their most 'foul' during previous matches, while they are practising special relaxation exercises. If they watch themselves performing violently on tape while their bodies are deeply relaxed, this helps to reduce the chance of future 'explosions' on the pitch.

Perhaps the strangest discovery made by the scientific analysis of match play concerns the *friendship factor*. Every manager assumes automatically that each player in his team will pass the ball to the team-mate who is in the most useful position to receive it. This is such an obvious requirement of the game that it goes without question. At least, it did go without question until Hungarian investigators studied it more closely. They discovered that the basic rule is often broken. Players pass the ball more often to team-mates who are close friends than to those for whom they have weak or negative feelings. They do not do this all the time, of course. They frequently pass balls to the most useful recipient, but the frequency is lower than was imagined. When the game is going well, the friendship factor interferes little with play, but when the side is losing badly, or when momentary panic sets in, it becomes more dominant. In need of security, a player may then pass the ball to a close friend he trusts, rather than to someone else, even if his friend is in a poor position to receive it. Needless to say, this makes matters worse, the panic grows, and the process becomes intensified.

Some managers have intuitively sensed the need to combat this problem, without even identifying it accurately. Vittorio Pozzo, the Italian manager, when travelling to away matches with his team, made special sleeping arrangements for the players at their hotel. If two of them had fallen out and were always quarrelling, he would insist that they shared a bedroom. There were always strong protests at this, because it is a tradition that each player shares a room with his closest friend. But by ignoring these objections, Pozzo was able to wear down mutual antagonisms and improve the overall team relationships.

A more systematic approach is to carry out friendship tests on the members of a team and produce an *affiliation chart*. This shows the strengths of the bonds that exist between each player and the rest of the team. In successful teams, positive relationships exist between most of the players, but in unsuccessful teams there is a greater number of 'solitary players', with no bonds of attachment. When sequences of ball-passing are analysed from video-tapes of matches, it soon becomes clear that the solitary players are being starved of the ball. Managers can use this information in one of two ways. They can either set about strengthening the friendship bonds of the 'isolated players', or they can present the whole problem to the players themselves, so that they can see the folly of their actions and correct them. In this way, team cohesiveness can be improved.

One important side-light of this study concerns team changes. German research has revealed that teams which remain constant in personnel are more successful than those where the make-up of the squad is repeatedly

Two affiliation charts showing the strengths of the friendship bonds (indicated by the number of lines joining the players) between team-mates. The red players are from a Hungarian club at the top of the first division. The blue players are from a club at the bottom of the division. Each man was asked five questions about his friendships within his squad and when the results were mapped it emerged that there were more solitary players in the team that was doing badly.

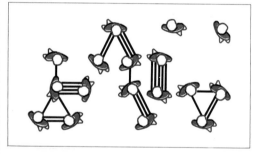

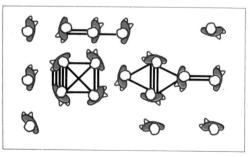

changed. The reason is obvious enough, when one considers the operation of the friendship factor. By removing an old established player from a team and replacing him with a new member, friendship ties are lost. Sometimes when a player moves to a new club, and the home supporters have been led to expect great things of him, they are quickly disappointed because he seems to contribute so little to his first games. Some club members misguidedly believe that he is not trying, or that he has not settled in, but if they analysed video-tapes of the matches they would find that, despite valiant efforts to impress his new club, the unhappy player was simply not receiving the ball enough in passes from his team-mates. It is not he who is failing to settle in, but the established players who are failing to accept him and trust him in moments of high tension. The more the problem of the friendship factor is brought out into the open and discussed by players, the greater the chance that they will be able to defeat its damaging effects on team success.

These, then, are some of the ways in which motivational problems can be explored and resolved, but it would be naive to imagine that the Soccer Tribe will accept them with any degree of eagerness. Some reasons for this have already been given. Many managers feel that it is unprofessional to devote too much energy to such issues. Some feel they should be ignored altogether. One wrote in his club programme: 'People should realize that motivation should be part of a player's make-up without any help from outside agencies . . . when the whistle goes I expect a fair day's work for a fair day's pay. It has nothing to do with motivation. A player who is being well paid to do a job should not have to be continually inspired by his manager. If that is necessary then he, and the game in general, is in a sorry state . . .' This hardline attitude, which relies on buying ultra-stable players and selling moody, emotional players (even if they are potentially brilliant), is best summed up in the acid words of an American coach who once exclaimed: 'If you aren't fired with enthusiasm, you'll be fired with enthusiasm!' It may work well enough in some instances, but the indications are that a few managers, at least, are now paying more attention to motivational aspects of the game. This trend is likely to increase in the future, as playing standards continue to rise and the soccer contest becomes more of a battle of nerves between equally skilful sides, where mood and determination are the ultimate weapons of victory.

The intelligent manager treats his players both as a team and as individuals. Different players require different degrees of arousal before a match – some need calming and some need stimulating. The best managers achieve the perfect balance for every man.

17 Away-itis

THE CHALLENGE OF PLAYING ON A RIVAL TERRITORY

If proof is needed that psychological factors play a vital role in winning soccer matches, the phenomenon of Away-itis can provide it. Away-itis is a complaint suffered by all visiting teams playing on enemy territory. Its main cause is the hostility felt at the alien ground and its symptoms are a dramatically reduced ability to win away-matches and score away-goals. Every Soccer Tribesman is aware of the problem, but few have measured it accurately or taken positive steps to combat it. It is simply accepted as an inevitable tribal disease.

Away-itis is as old as soccer itself. The English Football League played for twelve seasons in the nineteenth century and match results are available for every game. If the number of *home-wins* in all twelve seasons is added up and the total is divided by the number of *away-wins*, it is possible to express Away-itis in terms of a simple ratio. The result, for all First Division matches, is 2·6 to 1. This means that when one of these early teams played at home, it had a two-and-a-half times better chance of winning than when it played away.

If a similar exercise is carried out with all English First Division matches for the modern period following the Second World War, from the 1940s to the 1980s, the ratio of home-wins to away-wins emerges as 2·1 to 1. There has been a slight decline in the 'fear of foreign grounds', but home-wins are still twice as likely as away-wins.

If one examines the ratios year by year they show few if any erratic changes. The lowest nineteenth-century ratio was 1·7 to 1 (in the 1896–7 season) and the highest 3·4 to 1 (in 1895–6) but the majority are very close to the average figure.

The lowest modern ratio is also 1·7 to 1 (found in the seasons 1946–7, 1950–1 and 1954–5) and the highest is 2·8 to 1 (in 1976–7), but again most of the years show a figure close to the average.

This demonstrates that, in the years most plagued by Away-itis, it was roughly three times as hard to win away as at home, while in the best years it was still nearly twice as hard. This reveals the enormous influence of the territorial factor in soccer. It is so great that any team which could overcome the problem would soon rise to become champions.

This thought prompts a comparison between the degree of Away-itis displayed by top teams with that found in bottom teams. If the English First Division games for the whole of the 1970s are analysed, comparing the top-of-the-division teams with those at the bottom each year, it is possible to see whether they both suffer from the same degree of Away-itis, or whether the top teams are free of it. The average, overall ratio for the period in question was 2·2 to 1. The average for the top teams proved to be 1·7 to 1 and that for the bottom teams 2·9 to 1. In other words both the highest and the lowest teams suffered from the dreaded disease, but the bottom teams were almost twice as badly afflicted. So top teams fear away-grounds less, but they are still unable to shake off the curse completely.

Another comparison can be made, this time between the whole of the English First Division and, for contrast, the whole of the Fourth Division. The Fourth Division was first introduced in the 1958–9 season and if one adds up all the match results from that time until the end of the 1970s, the following ratios emerge: First Division home-wins to away-wins: 2·1 to 1. Fourth Division home-wins to away-wins: 2·5 to 1. Again, the more lowly teams suffer slightly more than the higher teams.

Nor is Away-itis a purely English disease; similar calculations were made

Home–Away Result Differences for English First Division Clubs 1946–79

Season	Home Wins	Away Wins	Ratio
1946–7	232	140	1·7
1947–8	236	122	1·9
1948–9	232	97	2·4
1949–50	219	111	2·0
1950–1	218	130	1·7
1951–2	227	122	1·9
1952–3	240	106	2·3
1953–4	254	109	2·3
1954–5	223	128	1·7
1955–6	248	119	2·0
1956–7	246	107	2·3
1957–8	246	122	2·0
1958–9	239	132	1·8
1959–60	232	131	1·8
1960–1	245	120	2·0
1961–2	246	110	2·2
1962–3	223	126	1·8
1963–4	228	126	1·8
1964–5	251	105	2·4
1965–6	245	114	2·1
1966–7	232	120	1·9
1967–8	244	107	2·3
1968–9	233	89	2·6
1969–70	205	114	1·8
1970–1	215	112	1·9
1971–2	227	106	2·1
1972–3	236	96	2·5
1973–4	218	95	2·3
1974–5	235	103	2·3
1975–6	229	106	2·2
1976–7	240	85	2·8
1977–8	223	107	2·1
1978–9	209	109	1·9

Average ratio 2·1

for Italian soccer, covering the period from the end of the Second World War to the late 1970s. There was slightly more variation, the lowest ratio being 1·9 to 1 and the highest as large as 4·3 to 1, but the average came out at 2·5 to 1, remarkably close to the English figure. So the phenomenon appears to go beyond national boundaries. Indeed, it is highly likely that it is worldwide.

One interesting similarity between the Italian and the English figures is that the post-war year in which they both show their lowest ratio was the very first season that soccer was resumed in each country after the end of the Second World War. It seems as if people in those austere, lean years were so grateful to see a soccer match again that they welcomed even the visiting players. Without local antagonism, the away team would have found themselves slightly less prone to Away-itis than usual.

Another device for measuring the strength of Away-itis is to look at the number of goals scored, instead of the number of matches won. The ratio of home-goals to away-goals should give a similar picture. Here are the figures:

Ratio of home-goals to away-goals for nineteenth-century English First Division games (1888–1900): 1·8 to 1.

Ratio of home-goals to away-goals for modern English First Division games (1946–79): 1·5 to 1.

Ratio of home-goals to away-goals for modern English Fourth Division games (1958–79): 1·7 to 1.

Several points emerge from this. Again there has been a slight decline in Away-itis, measured in this way, from the early days of soccer to more modern times. And again there is stronger Away-itis in the lowly clubs of the Fourth Division than in the giants of the First. Also, the ratios show that although Away-itis influences goal-scoring strongly, the effect is slightly less marked than with game-winning. To put it into very crude terms: if it is twice as difficult to win away, it is only one-and-a-half times as difficult to score.

Given all these facts, how can Away-itis be cured? The answer, in a word, is that it can't. It is concerned with a territorial reaction that is too basic to permit any clever manipulation. Consider the elements of the 'away-day' as they make their impact on the visiting players. First, they must rise at a different hour, ready to catch the train or coach that will carry them to the enemy ground. If they avoid this match-day trip by staying at an overnight hotel near the place of battle, they must instead deal with the problems of sleeping in an unfamiliar room and a strange bed.

Second, they will not be able to eat in the friendly surroundings of their own house and with their own family. When they are playing away there is a tense meal to be taken in some unknown restaurant. Third, if they are travelling on match-day, there is the long and tiring journey with which to contend.

Fourth, as they approach the enemy ground, they will see the alien colours of the home team's supporters, moving menacingly through the streets and heading towards the stadium. If the visiting players are spotted they may be jeered and heckled. This mood of hostility increases as they near the ground and dismount from the coach. Once inside the visitors' dressing room they will again be assailed by unfamiliar details. They will have to find their way around, strangers in a foreign land. Outside, the noise of the supporters will remind them of the hostile chanting that will soon be hurled against them. When they inspect the pitch, that too will be slightly strange. Every ground has its own peculiarities – a different slope, different drainage, a wider perimeter track, and so on. All these details will combine to make the visitors feel ill at ease.

When they finally run out on to the pitch at the start of the game, the silence or actual booing that greets them will contrast all too vividly with the

Home–Away Result Differences for Italian Clubs 1946–76

Year	Home Wins	Away Wins	Ratio
1946	197	86	2·3
1947	260	60	4·3
1948	211	70	3·0
1949	221	75	3·0
1950	232	64	3·6
1951	205	76	2·7
1952	157	61	2·6
1953	151	58	2·6
1954	143	63	2·3
1955	148	64	2·3
1956	157	56	2·8
1957	159	53	3·0
1958	152	61	2·5
1959	157	50	3·1
1960	166	57	2·9
1961	146	75	2·0
1962	153	61	2·5
1963	135	68	2·0
1964	153	55	2·8
1965	147	58	2·5
1966	133	56	2·4
1967	119	50	2·4
1968	112	43	2·6
1969	109	53	2·1
1970	95	39	2·4
1971	112	43	2·6
1972	107	48	2·2
1973	109	39	2·8
1974	107	39	2·8
1975	111	46	2·4
1976	109	48	2·3

Average ratio 2·5

great roar of appreciation that goes up as the home team take the field. By now, the accumulated impressions of the day have so loaded the visiting team with bad feelings about their role as detested invaders that, when the starting whistle finally blows, they will enter the match at a grave psychological disadvantage. It is this that causes the Away-itis and the poor results.

There is no way in which all of the away-day factors can be eliminated. Helicopters to fly in the visitors would certainly reduce the journey dramatically and remove many of the minor disturbances of the ordinary travelling arrangements. But helicopters are too expensive for most clubs and some players might find such a journey even more stressful. As an alternative, the interiors of the coaches could be converted from ordinary seating to flat sleeping bunks where the players could rest in the dark, with tranquillizing music played over headphones. This would replace the agitation of long hours of gambling and card-playing. But for many players, the card-playing acts as a valuable time-filler, distracting them from thoughts of the dangers ahead. Left to themselves, they might find their minds full of anxious fantasies, and arrive at the ground in an even worse psychological condition.

If there is little that can be done about the journey itself, there are steps that could be taken to improve the arrival at the foreign ground. Special arrangements could be made with the team's fan club to rendezvous at the entrance of the enemy stadium, so that as the players arrive they see, not the alien colours, but a mass of their own supporters, cheering them into their dressing room. The dressing room itself could be decorated with team colours which are deliberately kept on show in the team's own, home dressing room at other times. This would help to label the strange room as 'theirs' and make them feel more at ease. But beyond that, and hoping that as many of their fans as possible have come to cheer them along, there is little that the visiting team can do to combat the nerves of 'invading an enemy territory'. Away-itis will continue to haunt the Soccer Tribe for many a year to come, and only the most astute manager will be able to calm the nerves of his tense, anxiety-ridden players.

Every team feels tense during the long journey to an away match (left). Some distraction is needed to fill the hours of travelling and this nearly always takes the form of simple card games.

When the visiting players run out on to the enemy field (above) the tension on their faces shows clearly the apprehension they feel as they face the alien environment.

18 Gamesmanship

STRATAGEMS AND LOW CUNNING

The Tribal Hero of today must keep his wits about him. It is not enough to run fast and aim accurately, he must also be able to think quickly and react deviously. As every novice professional soon discovers, he is entering a world full of subterfuge and trickery, where gamesmanship is almost as important as the game itself. Unlike his amateur ancestors he has two challenges to face – the official one of soccer and the unofficial one of chicanery.

Rival gamesmanship is a special 'contest' that all clubs indulge in and which is appreciated inside the tribe as a kind of second language of soccer – an additional line of communication that opens up as soon as two teams embark on an important encounter. Here is a brief guide to the most popular stratagems and dirty tricks employed in modern times:

1 Smoke-screen

This is a device of wily managers to confuse their opponents. In a pre-match press statement they bravely insist that their team will refuse to adopt cowardly, defensive tactics. Instead, they will be playing attacking football of the kind that pleases the crowd. If they are fooled by this, their opponents decide on a suitable formation and devise strategies to deal with the expected all-out attack, only to discover that they are facing a totally different kind of enemy who is putting up a massive defensive wall and playing 'on the break'. Or the manager announces that he will be happy to play for a draw, and then throws his men forward in an immediate assault on the rival goal. Another trick is to exaggerate an injury to a star player, casting doubt on whether he will be able to play. The opponents then change their marking tactics. Just before the match, when the team lists are issued, they discover their mistake. Not only is the star playing but, as they soon find when the game begins, he is in peak condition.

2 Super-host

At international matches, the host organizers sometimes go to great lengths to entertain their visitors. Their hospitality is often difficult to refuse and if it is suitably excessive it can act as a valuable weapon. One foreign team visiting Vienna for an important match was offered a sight-seeing tour of the city, which they accepted out of politeness. It was arranged for the morning of the game, when the players were collected from their hotel and taken off *on foot* to inspect all the points of local interest. After walking for miles they were beginning to feel exhausted, but their guide insisted that they must see the birthplace of Johann Strauss. He claimed it was only just around the corner, but when the corner turned out to be two miles long, the weary visitors went on strike and, courtesy or no courtesy, refused to budge.

Local banquets provide another source of gamesmanship. The visitors are expected to eat strange and spicy foods – familiar to the stomachs of their hosts, but quite alien to their own normal diets. A European team in Central America, facing a difficult match on the following day, was offered the following delicacies: a first course of large lumps of fat fried to a crisp; a second course of dried rice covered in brown sauce; a third course of sheep's intestines 'wobbly as an ice-cold jelly' and prepared by 'covering them in cactus leaves and burying the whole lot in the ground for several hours'; and 'a kind of wine with a grub floating around in it'. European soccer players are notoriously conservative about their diets and this banquet, most of which they refused, left them ravenous. Those who were brave enough to swallow the exotic foods were laid low by 'Montezuma's Revenge'.

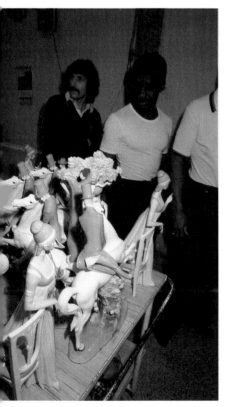

Many soccer hosts arrange special tours and sight-seeing visits for their guests at international fixtures. Most of these gestures are genuine and well-intentioned, like this visit to a factory making china ornaments, but occasionally the devious trick of Super-host is played. This type of gamesmanship involves exhausting the visitors before the match, or feeding them unsuitable foods. Today managers and coaches take special precautions to avoid these pitfalls.

It has been estimated that approximately one-third of all European players visiting hot-climate countries for foreign matches used to suffer from some form of gastroenteritis before they returned home. Some authorities have now become so concerned about this problem that they insist on taking their own cooks and their own foodstuffs with them to all international contests, and visiting managers are much more strict about their players' pre-match festivities.

3 Insomnia

A favourite device of the 'dirty tricks department' is to rob visiting players of their much-needed sleep before a big match. Arranging for them to stay at a hotel near a noisy night-club or discotheque is the simplest stratagem. Alternatively there is the 'happy revellers' parade in which excited supporters of the local team pass the pre-match night away by moving up and down in front of the visitors' hotel, singing, banging drums, tooting their car-horns and exploding fireworks, with only the mildest of restraint applied by the local police.

The noise of drumming in the streets is cheerfully accepted by everyone when it follows a great victory, but at other times it may produce a different response. Carried out as Insomnia gamesmanship, late at night outside the hotel of a visiting team, it can easily lead to angry incidents.

In deeply religious countries, the church can also play its part. On one of their foreign tours, the Liverpool team discovered to their dismay that the bells in the church next door to their hotel had to be rung every hour on the hour. This was hard enough to bear, but as they settled down in their beds, the interval was mysteriously changed to every half-hour. Manager Bill Shankly stormed over to the church to demand peace and quiet, but was told that the bell-ringing rule could not be broken. He offered to send his trainer over to muffle the bells by tying bandages around them, but this too was politely refused, and he was forced to spend the rest of the night arguing with the local authorities until finally he managed to silence the noise and gain his players the remnant of a night's sleep.

Perhaps the most devious stratagem of all was the housing of a visiting team in a hotel next to a brothel. English manager Fred Ford had taken his team abroad to play a local continental side and had deliberately arranged for his young players to be put up at a hotel in the countryside, some miles from the city where they were to play. But on the day before the match, his hosts persuaded him to move them into the city itself in order 'to avoid a long and tiring journey the next day'. He agreed and was delighted with the new accommodation until he went on his rounds to make sure that all his men were safely bedded down for the night. To his surprise he found a number of them missing and, once he realized what had happened, spent the rest of a sleepless night chasing one after another of them out of the adjacent house of pleasure.

4 Scandal

An extreme device in the pre-match war-of-nerves is the involving of one of the star players of the visiting team in a scandal of some kind. Although the 'set-up' is easily uncovered as a fraud, it none the less has an unnerving effect because of the vast amount of publicity and media-intrusion that it causes. The most notorious incident of this kind took place during the run-up to the 1970 World Cup, when England captain Bobby Moore was falsely accused of stealing a £600 emerald bracelet from a shop in Bogota, Colombia. Despite the fact that the evidence against Moore was inconsistent and contradictory, he was forced to submit to four days of detention and questioning before finally being released and allowed to join the rest of his team. Further attempts were made to discredit other members of the team. Striker Jeff Astle, who suffered from a fear of flying, was feeling ill when he arrived at Mexico City airport after a bad flight, and photographs were published of him in this condition, along with the claim that he was drunk.

The climax came when the local paper *El Heraldo* dubbed the English squad 'a team of drunks and thieves'. Outrageous though this comment was, it nevertheless succeeded in fanning the flames of pre-match hostility to the point where the English flag was massively jeered in the opening ceremony. It required a deep understanding of soccer gamesmanship on the part of Bobby Moore and his team to reduce the harmful impact of such a situation.

5 Hold-up

Irritating delays that are apparently unavoidable are always useful ways of demoralizing a visiting team. They take a variety of forms. One method is for the bus carrying the home team to be so heavily mobbed by delighted supporters that it fails to reach the stadium on time. The visitors meanwhile have changed and 'warmed up' and are then left in a frustrated condition, becoming more and more tense, while local officials repeatedly apologize for the hold-up. As gamesmanship of this kind has intensified over the years, managers have become increasingly wary about agreeing to their players being sent out on to the pitch. When he was England manager, Sir Alf Ramsey developed the habit of checking that his opponents were ready before accepting the invitation of a local official for the English squad to go out for the pre-match kick-about. Nor would he hand over his final team-sheet until the host's sheet was also made available.

Another device is refusing to allow the visitors' bus to drive up to the dressing room door. Billy Bremner has described how this was done to his Leeds team when they were playing abroad, despite the fact that the same coach had been permitted to enter the ground when delivering the players earlier in the day, for a morning kick-about. No reason was given, but the players were forced to dismount outside the stadium gates and then fight their way through a dense crowd of hostile local supporters. By the time they reached the sanctuary of the dressing room they were angry and shaken. Gamesmanship had triumphed again.

He also recalls an occasion in an Eastern European country where the entire team was jammed in a lift for most of the half-time interval. The lift had delivered them smoothly enough for the kick-off at the start of the match, but when they crowded into it to go up for the vital team-talk at half-time, it stopped on the way up and refused to budge. They were freed just in time to reassure their frantic manager that they were still alive and well, before cramming in again to descend to the pitch for the second half. Their descent was perfect and they were convinced that they had been deliberately sabotaged.

6 Safety-first

An unnerving routine is to insist that local feelings are running so high that the visitors must be heavily protected by gun-toting guards or police. Manchester United have met this device when playing on foreign soil and have sometimes been refused permission to leave their hotel without a heavily armed escort. The psychological impact of such measures, if they are carried out in a sufficiently melodramatic manner, is to raise the level of tension in an already stressed group of players, much to the advantage of the home side.

The England team met with similar treatment on one occasion, when they were refused permission to inspect the pitch before a foreign match. This was a vital procedure in order to determine the correct type of studs to be worn on their boots. The excuse given was that all the entrances to the pitch were locked to prevent the visitors being 'disturbed by outsiders' and it was only after a point blank refusal to continue with the contest that officials reluctantly gave way and the inspection went ahead.

When playing Monster, players with fang-like teeth make sure the enemy see the evidence of hard tackles in previous matches by offering menacing grins and grimaces.

7 Hot-house

Additional gamesmanship may occur inside the visitors' dressing room, where northern teams visiting hot-climate countries have been known to find their windows jammed tight. In one case the internal temperature was high enough to create a debilitating furnace atmosphere, in which they were forced to struggle into their playing gear and then wait for many minutes, sweating and cursing, before their escape to the fresh air of the pitch.

8 Colour-clash

Turning the tables on the home team, some visitors have 'innocently' arrived from abroad with playing gear in an identical colour to the hosts' traditional costume. It is always a great psychological advantage to play in one's own colours in any match, and it is extremely rare for a team not to wear its traditional 'strip' when playing on home territory. Whenever a colour clash occurs in an ordinary League match, it is always the visiting team who must change into their second colour. But on certain international occasions, the foreign visitors have simply refused to do this. In one instance a traditionally red-and-white team from the East came to play a match in Western Europe, where the local team's strip was all-white. To the hosts' astonishment, the visitors emerged into the tunnel also wearing all-white. No amount of argument could persuade them to alter their costumes and in the end the home team had to change, rather than risk a riot among their massed supporters.

Those are eight of the most striking pre-match 'dirty tricks', but that is far from the end of the gamesmanship. Once the starting whistle has been blown there are many more devices available to the wilier players. They include:

9 Monster

There are several ways of playing Monster, in which the aim is to make oneself appear as menacing as possible to the opposition. One is to go unshaven for several days, so as to look tough and uncaring. Another is to grow a jutting beard to hide a weak face. Another is to snarl and grimace ferociously when coming near any opponent, and to refuse to exchange any pleasant words during lulls in the play. Alternatively, a player who has had his teeth knocked out in earlier games can offer a fang-like grin to remind the enemy that he is used to rough-stuff. And spitting skilfully on the ground near an opponent's feet may be added to give further proof of 'hardness'.

10 Agony

Once a player has been felled, he can exaggerate the foul by spinning on the ground like a rolling log, ending in a writhing heap. With contorted face and arching body, he then allows himself to be treated by his trainer. After hobbling about for a few moments he bravely resumes play, but appears to be badly slowed down. The device has three advantages. In the first place, he gains much sympathy from his supporters, who start a storm of booing against the fouler and may continue to harass the man for the rest of the game, jeering him whenever he gains possession of the ball and thereby putting him off his stroke. Secondly, the Agony player may manage to convince the referee that the foul was bad enough to warrant a booking. Thirdly, by appearing to remain wounded after the incident, the Agony player will seem to be less of a threat to the opposition. In an unguarded moment they may give him a slight advantage, whereupon he miraculously recovers and speeds away with the ball, to score a shock goal.

The most extreme form of Agony is the one played in the midst of a sudden scuffle, when so much is happening so quickly that the referee cannot see the trick being carried out. It requires a thick skull and a brutal mentality. By aiming a deliberate head-butt at an opponent, the trickster hopes to do as much damage as possible. He then immediately falls flat on his back to give the impression that the blow was delivered at *him*. This has been seen even in international matches involving top players. On one such occasion the crowd started whistling to draw the referee's attention to the fact that a player was wandering about in a daze, with blood streaming down his face. Near him, lying prostrate on the ground, was an opponent. Team-mates clustered around their half-stunned friend who was able to mumble: 'He butted me in the face and then he just lay down!' The referee came rushing over and promptly booked the blood-spattered victim for a foul, assuming that the man flattened on the ground must have been the innocent party. As soon as the trainers had left the pitch, the trickster rose to his feet, laughed in his victim's face and sauntered away upfield. Still groggy from the blow and now thoroughly disgruntled by his unfair treatment, the victimized player predictably lost his concentration, and the 'dirty tricks department' had triumphed yet again.

As a cunning stratagem, Agony has the longest pedigree of all forms of football gamesmanship. It is far older even than soccer, going right back to the earliest games of folk football. Indeed, as long ago as the fifteenth century, it was recorded in England as a genuine 'miracle'. To be precise, it was Miracle no. 91 in a collection of posthumous miracles of Henry VI. The chronicler of this remarkable event comments as follows: '. . . our hero had

How badly is this man hurt? It is almost impossible to tell. One of the hardest tasks for a referee is to decide when a player is performing an Agony display and when he is truly in great pain.

thrown himself into the midst of the fray, when one of his fellows, whose name I do not know, came up against him from in front and kicked him by misadventure, missing his aim at the ball.' The victim of the kick, one William Bartram, 'suffered long and scarce endurable pain', but was suddenly restored to health when he saw a vision of 'the glorious King Henry'. Modern soccer players will understand the nature of this miracle well enough.

The problem faced by a referee confronted with a player writhing on the ground, while the opposing supporters chant 'Give him an Oscar!' or 'Bring on the Bostik' to indicate their scepticism, is to decide whether the man really is hurt or not. Referees are as cynical about such incidents as anyone else, but they are in a difficult position. Players do receive serious, genuine injuries while playing and as officials they cannot afford to make a mistake and ignore a man who may be in urgent need of medical attention. So the artificial agony ploy works far better than many other forms of gamesmanship.

11 High-dive

A popular variant of Agony is 'taking a dive'. This is usually confined to the opponents' penalty area. A player is mildly tackled by a defender as he speeds towards the enemy goal and instead of trying to regain his balance, deliberately lets himself fall. The movement is performed with a spectacular plunge, in the hope of being awarded a penalty, but referees have become more and more wary of such incidents. When the dives do work successfully, however, they are capable of winning matches and as a consequence have become increasingly common. So frequent are they today that officials have even developed a special gesture – the mimed action of a high-diver's arm-movements as he takes off from a diving board – to indicate that they are not being fooled.

12 Helping-hand

Less common is the 'hurtful helper'. Having felled an opponent, this trickster then leans over him and helpfully tries to pull him back on to his feet. But he does so in a way that causes even more pain. If he is lucky, his victim then loses his temper and becomes so violent that, in the end, it is he who is punished for retaliation. On one occasion two players were seen gently lifting an injured opponent between them and carrying him carefully to the side of the pitch where he could receive attention. Once there, however, they 'accidentally' dropped him and walked innocently away.

The most devious form of Helping-hand is the type recorded by Martin Peters, encountered in an international match: 'If you were knocked to the ground they would endear themselves to the crowd by stooping to pick you up and shake hands with you. But while the right hand was shaking, the left would sneak up your forearm and pinch you. And the crowd would say, "Look at that ungrateful swine, the man's shaken his hand and he's trying to clout him."'

13 Blindside

The referee has only one pair of eyes and, even with the help of his linesmen, he cannot always see what is happening. Bodies obscure his line of vision. Hidden fouls deliberately inflicted on his blind-side are a common form of gamesmanship. Blindside Elbow is a favourite of the striker who is being too closely shadowed by a burly defender. When the shadow moves up close behind him and both men are turned to look down the pitch, where the action is attracting attention in the other half of the field, he suddenly jabs his elbow backwards into his enemy's chest and then moves away to a safe distance. There is little the defender can do about such a trick, except wince and bear it – and perhaps keep a more respectful distance in future. Blindside Shirt-

(far left) In this sequence the referee signals for a penalty and the angry defender rushes towards the fallen figure, convinced that his opponent has 'taken a dive'. The tripped player, delighted by the penalty decision, laughs in his face and gets a kick on the rump in reply – an action that could easily have led to a booking had the referee not been preoccupied with the preparations for the penalty kick.

High-dive has become so popular, especially in the penalty box, that referees have developed their own mime to indicate their scepticism (left).

Blindside shirt-holding during a tackle (right), executed with sufficient cunning to escape the referee's attention.

When a defensive wall forms up, the referee cannot see what happens behind it. This is therefore an ideal moment for Blindside gamesmanship. The most obvious trick is to pull aside one of the defending players at the very instant the free-kick is taken, leaving a gap in the wall through which a team-mate can score. In the lower of the two examples shown here, the device worked and a vital goal was scored.

A rare form of soccer gamesmanship is Jester (below), in which a player deliberately acts the fool as a way of riling his opponents. In this case, a foul is followed by an exaggerated, abject apology on one knee, which has the effect of making the opponent even more angry than he was before.

holding is another variant, used to impede an enemy without detection. And there is the 'phantom push-in-the-back'. Deftly performed, this can easily gain a free-kick. Two players go up to head a goal-kick. They are close together, one behind the other, and facing in the same direction. As the ball descends towards them, the one in front, nearer the referee, snaps his body forward in a sharp jerk, as if he has been hit in the back or pushed hard from behind. Since this is a foul when it occurs in reality, the referee is very likely to blow his whistle and the Blindsider has won an important advantage for his side.

14 Retaliation

This has already been mentioned in relation to the Helping-hand device, but it also occurs in a verbal context. One player approaches another and insults him under his breath, preying on some special, known weakness of the man. It may be a racial comment, where a black player is concerned, or perhaps some reference to the sex life of the player's wife. The essential feature of the insult is that it must be sufficiently vile to enrage the enemy to a point where he loses control and lashes out with his fist. The tormentor then does a spectacular wrestler's fall, or holds his face pathetically like a beaten child. The referee rushes over, shows a yellow card to the victim and the Retaliation game has chalked up another success. It is a dangerous game to play, however, especially if the victim is well muscled.

15 False-call

A sneakier trickster is the False-caller. His device is to shout out to an opponent, calling for the ball to be passed to him, or left for him, as if he is a member of the enemy team. Team-mates often shout to one another in this way and, in the heat of battle, it is easy enough to mimic an enemy voice and gain possession of the ball without having to make a tackle. Referee Arthur Ellis recalls a particular match in which this happened. As a ball came across from the wing, a forward shouted 'Right!' and caused an enemy defender to let it pass: 'The forward got possession as a result and scored. I disallowed the "goal" because I considered it was ungentlemanly conduct and I was booed by the crowd for a considerable time.' Many a referee fails to act with such firmness, however, and the False-caller is then unfairly rewarded for his simple deceit.

16 Jester

Every so often, soccer throws up a court jester, a clown who becomes known for making mock of the solemn ritual of the game. His aim is merely to disrupt the concentration of the opposing team, but the device is rare because it can backfire on to his own team-mates and destroy their mood as well. One man who risked this was England player Len Shackleton. Once, when taking a free-kick, he gathered up some loose earth and piled it into a golfer's tee. Placing the ball carefully on top of the cone of earth, he was about to kick the ball when the referee stopped him. Characteristically, he informed the official that there was nothing in the rules of soccer to prevent what he was doing. By the time the argument had been concluded, his opponents had become irritated and impatient, and their concentration was spoiled. Yet the Jester had in no way broken any law, which was the strength of his stratagem.

On another occasion Shackleton performed an astonishing action that was also, strictly speaking, within the law. The ball was passed to him, he halted it deftly with one foot, then promptly sat down on it. As he squatted there with a completely deadpan expression, the other players looked at one another dumbfounded, until the referee roared 'Play on!', whereupon the Jester leapt up and swept away with the ball. Again, the exasperated referee was incapable of calling to mind any rule that had been broken and was powerless to penalize the bizarre behaviour that had thrown the enemy into confusion.

17 Innocent-arm

Every time a player kicks a ball out of play he automatically appeals to the referee, claiming that the throw-in should be his. He knows perfectly well that it should go to the opposing team, but the simple act of raising his arm costs him nothing, so he tries it on. In marginal cases, where two players are close to the ball as it is driven over the touch-line, there is always a chance that the official cannot see which foot is the last one to touch it, and if both players raise their arms, the guilty man may occasionally win. Innocent-arm has irritated some sportswriters, who view it as childish, but it will never disappear as long as there is the slenderest hope of gaining an advantage by it, especially as it is too mild a misdeed ever to be penalized by the referee.

18 Creeper

Another mild form of gamesmanship is Creeping. The man throwing in the ball creeps along the touchline as he does so, gaining a few feet in the direction of the enemy goal. It happens almost every time and the advantage is so marginal that most referees ignore it. Only when it becomes a blatant advance of several yards do they interfere, but it repeatedly irritates and even angers the watching crowd. As an act of gamesmanship it is one of the most common and one of the most pointless devices.

A much more useful trick is Creeping up on a free-kick. The rule states that opposing players must stand at least ten yards away from the free-kicker, but this is rarely observed, despite repeated attempts on the part of the referee to persuade the defenders to withdraw further. The double advantage of this device is that it delays the free-kick and unsettles the kicker, while at the same time boxing him in and making the kick more difficult to take. Often one defender will encroach more outrageously than the rest of his team-mates, as part of the stratagem to destroy the kicker's concentration. By so doing, he risks becoming a villain in the eyes of the referee and if he repeats the process too often is likely to be booked. To prevent this some teams work a rota system in which a different player acts as encroacher in each free-kick, so that no one man becomes the referee's special target.

A most extraordinary case of the Creeper device nearly going wrong occurred once when the referee took his ten-yard position and held out his arm to indicate the correct line to the row of Creepers edging towards the free-kicker. Although his signal was for them to move back, and they knew this perfectly well, they held their ground to delay matters. But the kicker accepted the arm signal as the sign for taking the free-kick, tapped the ball sideways, and a team-mate immediately scored. The referee caused a near-riot by disallowing the goal and insisting on having the free-kick retaken. This outraged the goal-scorers who pointed out that they had been robbed of a goal by the illegal action of their Creeping opponents. The incident created bad feeling for some time afterwards and illustrates clearly the immense difficulties that gamesmanship causes for harassed referees.

Here a foul is clearly committed just outside the penalty area, but the tripped player sprawls inside the box and optimistically appeals for a penalty kick. The referee, who has doubtless met this trick many times before, is not fooled by it and laughs in the protester's face.

19 Penalty-ploy

When a penalty kick has been awarded, the soccer player is given his only official invitation to indulge in gamesmanship. The whole object of the penalty is to fool the goalkeeper and make him go the wrong way. The penalty taker must use every trick of body language to avoid signalling his true intention. He can do this by glancing almost imperceptibly in the direction in which he will *not* strike the ball, as if judging the angle, or he can swerve slightly during his run-up, to confuse the keeper about the aim he is taking.

One man employed a much more extreme measure. He ran up to the ball on the penalty spot, but instead of kicking it he put his foot over it without making contact. Then, as the keeper flew through the air sideways in an attempt to save it, he calmly tapped it into the centre of the net. When attacked for this device he claimed that it was his way of punishing goalkeepers for moving before the ball has been struck. His action created yet another problem for referees, who could not provide chapter and verse regarding any law he had broken. Since his time, other players have tried using short pauses in the run-up to taking a penalty, but referees have nearly always classed such behaviour as ungentlemanly conduct and have insisted on the penalty being taken a second time. So this particular type of trick has become extremely rare.

20 Time-filler

When a team is winning and there is little time left to play, they indulge in a variety of Time-filling actions. Some of these are difficult for the referee to penalize, but if they become too obvious he will add on extra playing time and thereby defeat the stratagem completely. As a successful device, Time-filler must therefore be operated with cunning. Short-ball is a useful way of doing this. The keeper kicks a ball out to a defender, as a short goal-kick. His team-mate then returns it to him, but takes care to do so just before it has left the penalty area. As this is not permitted, the referee is forced to demand that the goal-kick be retaken, and precious moments have been filled. A cruder dodge is 'accidentally' to loft the ball, kicking it so high that it sails right over the top of the grandstand. This necessitates bringing a spare ball into play, which has to be inspected by the referee before it can be used, in case it has the wrong pressure. Again, valuable moments have passed.

These, then, are the top twenty forms of gamesmanship, operated both before the match and during it. Together they make a minefield for the unwary player and demand quick thinking and considerable mental agility. The public's popular cartoon image of the Soccer Tribe's hero as a slow-witted, inarticulate dunce clearly has to be false. And yet James Thurber's famous remark about a footballer, that 'While he was not dumber than an ox, he was not any smarter,' has many echoes. These can be detected even inside the Soccer Tribe itself. Manager Tommy Docherty was once heard to exclaim: 'Brains? There's a lot of players who think that Manual Labour is the Spanish President.' This sounds rather like Hitchcock being provocatively rude about film actors, but at least one manager has come to the players' defence. Brian Clough has been quoted as saying: 'Show me a talented player who is thick and I will show you a player who has problems.'

The truth is that a highly successful soccer player must *also* be highly intelligent. The mistake people make is to assume that all forms of intelligence can be measured in the same way. Most authorities who discuss intelligence are themselves clever in a scholarly, bookish way and automatically assume this to be the norm. But many a great painter has been inarticulate, even crudely so, when it comes to juggling with words. His world is one of shapes and colours, patterns and images, and his particular form of brilliance is entirely visual. The soccer player's brilliance is muscular. His intelligence is finely tuned, not to words and phrases or numbers and figures, but to running and leaping, turning and kicking. Like the great artist, he finds it hard to translate the subtleties of his feelings into verbal statements. But to say that his brain is therefore unsubtle is greatly to underestimate him. And his devious expertise at the complex business of soccer gamesmanship, described here, serves to underline this.

19 The Skills of the Heroes

FITNESS AND ACROBATICS, TRAINING AND COACHING

The individual skills of the Tribal Heroes depend on two things – an acrobatic ability when controlling the ball and an athletic fitness to provide the stamina needed for a full ninety minutes of play.

It is important to realize that these are two totally different qualities. A player who is a great acrobat, one who can trap the ball perfectly and juggle it this way and that with great accuracy, may be a weak athlete who quickly tires during a fast-moving game. Another player, who is a super-fit athlete and who could continue running at top speed long after the final whistle, may have only mediocre ball control. It is essential for all top players to excel in both departments.

The easier area for coaches to work on is simple fitness. At the start of each season, several weeks before the first competitive game is played, the players reassemble after their annual break and give themselves up to the tender mercies of their trainers. The routines are demanding – a cross between a commando course and ballet practice. Many hours are spent each week on long runs and PT exercises until, with the arrival of the first fixture, the players are in peak physical condition.

The majority of players hate this fitness training but accept it as a necessary part of their professional lives. Rodney Marsh comments: 'Pre-season

Most players would prefer the tortures of weight-training to the embarrassment of ballet training (above) but some coaches now recognize the value of dance exercises as a way of loosening up the body. When the postures of dance routines (opposite, above) are compared with those of match-play (opposite, below) the similarities are striking and the relevance of the new-style training methods becomes obvious.

A top player must not only possess acrobatic skills with a football, he must also have the stamina of a long-distance athlete, and must subject himself to many hours of training each season (left).

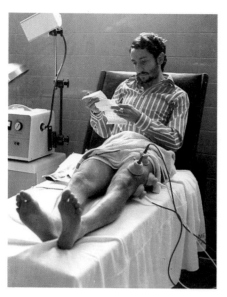

No matter how match-fit players become (below), there are so many knocks on the field each week that few escape the need for regular visits to the club's treatment room.

training is the foundation of the whole season ... The body cries out with pain. Your pulse throbs. You wonder why you are in the game, and convince yourself there must be easier ways of earning a living. But you know you must do it because there is no easier way to peak condition.' A sharp distinction is made between being 'fit' and 'match-fit', the latter being the all-important target. And because it is so easy to fall just below peak condition during the long, arduous nine months of the soccer season, the training routines continue week in and week out, even after competitive playing has begun. The normal pattern is for the pre-match training to comprise day-long sessions of a really punishing kind, and then for these to be reduced to half-day sessions of morning training only, when serious play has started.

Having created a group of 'match-fit' players, the trainers face the more difficult task of improving acrobatic skills. The problem here is that good ball control and playing rhythm are hard to teach, being to some extent a natural ability, and for many players this aspect can only be improved by actual game-play. Practice matches therefore figure largely in training sessions. But coaches also like to introduce special novelties which they claim will strengthen certain elements of their players' agility, and this is where controversy occurs.

It is not the simpler procedures – shooting, passing, dribbling, heading – that players object to. They have even been prepared, on occasion, to undergo ballet training with professional instructors, or to use dance routines

Good diet is crucial for high performance that lasts to the final whistle. Special tests at Oxford United in 1972–3 proved the value of a high glucose diet. For a Saturday afternoon match, players were trained to exhaustion on Thursday, but given no further training during the 36 hours before the game. On Friday they were fed the high glucose diet and on Saturday morning care was taken to keep them relaxed and avoid prolonged adrenalin flow. The result was a startling improvement in the team's performance during the final stages of each match. Over 20 games (see graphs) they scored more goals in the final stages and far fewer goals were scored against them during this phase. Because of their increased stamina they also suffered far fewer injuries than previously.

Glucose solution

Without glucose solution

Goals For

0 mins   30   60   90

Goals Against

0 mins   30   60   90

to develop their sense of balance. But when coaches become over-elaborate, introducing strangely distorted game-patterns, many of their victims begin to feel that they are having their natural talents suppressed. 'Coaching', says Eamon Dunphy, 'should be about showing people how to express themselves … Not subjection, but liberation. A lot of coaches see coaching as a way of subjecting people to their particular theories.' He describes the way in which this can go astray. A particular coach decides that one week his players must have practice games in which they are only allowed to score by heading the ball, or in which one-touch play is the rule and no one is allowed to strike the ball a second time until somebody else has hit it. The players do their best, spurred on by the reassurance that this kind of training will strengthen that particular element of their game. But the effect, all too often, is to make them stale at it. Such a regime can even lead to over-compensation, so that when match-day arrives they will do anything *but* head the ball or make one-touch moves. The manager then becomes exasperated and accuses them of being perverse, when all that has happened is that they have exhausted their intuitive reactions to these overworked elements of play.

Other training devices, such as 'conditioned games' in which the men are instructed to use two footballs on the field at once, or to score in any of four goals set up in the corners of the field, are so artificial that they can easily destroy the pattern and flow of the team's ordinary match-play. Eamon Dunphy complains that coaches study too many clever books. Of one man, he comments: 'He's going on about this really fantastic book he is reading, and then coming out with these incredible routines; they have no relation to football at all. They are just pure exercises in teaching … It's funny the way coaches have this thing about conditioned games, and all these weird theories they get out of the FA Coaching Manual … You go out on a Saturday when you've been playing these games, and it destroys you. Drives you mad. Because rhythm is a very important part of your game, but these things screw up your rhythm.'

The majority of players would agree with this assessment and secretly believe that coaches and trainers are more concerned with appearing to be knowing and clever than with giving their men a chance to improve their natural talents. The best routine would seem to be one that concentrates on tough fitness training, good diet, the tuning up of simple acrobatic skills, the playing of plenty of practice matches, and then, in addition, the teaching of new team tactics and strategies. Most players would clearly welcome it if all the more complex coaching systems and artificial game-patterns were omitted from this general plan. Indeed, there are those who claim that too much training of *any* kind is bad for players, suggesting that only match-play itself is of any real use. Repeated experience on the real field of battle is, in their opinion, the only proper training. They also consider that real games of soccer are the only measure needed to maintain match-fitness and that all the new-fangled concentration on intensive training is merely a by-product of the kind of modern professionalism that has made soccer players into full-time employees, who must be seen to be earning their large salaries. Most authorities would claim that this approach is a gross exaggeration, although it has to be admitted that some of the sport's top players have been notoriously bad about religiously following a full training schedule.

Unfortunately for this renegade view, the speed of soccer has greatly increased in recent years. The great stars of earlier decades, who underwent far less training, would, if transported on to a modern pitch, look pathetically inferior, despite the romantic legends one reads about them in the soccer history books. Today's soccer player has little choice but to accept that, if he is to compete successfully, he must undergo the annual tortures of heavy physical training.

20 The Superstitions of the Heroes

MAGICAL PRECAUTIONS AND LUCKY CHARMS

Because they are involved in a high-risk occupation, many of the Tribal Heroes are highly superstitious. Every time they set foot on the field of play there is a danger of injury and a possibility of disgrace if they are heavily beaten by their opponents. And there is a strong element of luck on the grass pitch. A ball can bounce badly for them. They can be robbed of a goal by slipping on wet grass, or give one away because the ball hits a small bump and accidentally finds the toe of an enemy striker.

Injury, disgrace, a sudden slip, an unlucky ball – all these thoughts flit through the minds of the players as they prepare for each match. They know that no amount of coaching, training, skill or fitness will protect them completely from these hazards. They also know that when ill-fortune catches up with them, it will do so in full view of thousands of critical eyes. Theirs is a public ordeal. There is no escape, no way of hiding a mistake.

Faced with this threat, they seek additional aid of a kind their trainers and managers cannot give them – the supernatural aid of superstitious practices. They have no idea how such actions can help, but they perform them all the same, 'just in case'. They frequently call them ridiculous and stupid, but they dare not omit them. And some of the most rational of players treat them so seriously that they will go to extraordinary lengths to ensure that their own personal rituals are not interfered with or disrupted in any way.

The most intense period of superstitious activity is the time just before a match begins. Of one hundred soccer superstitions, collected at random, no fewer than 40 per cent were concentrated in the pre-match dressing room, where tension is at its highest. Many other 'good luck' actions were performed on the way to the match, in the tunnel leading to the pitch, and on the pitch itself.

But the magical process begins even earlier, on the days before the match, when the build-up to the great ordeal is starting to make its impact. One player is growing a lucky moustache, another a lucky beard. The team that

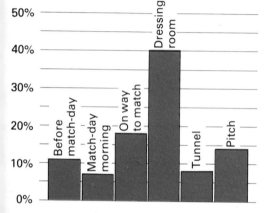

Of 100 soccer superstitions, collected at random, 40 per cent involved some ritual action performed by a player during the tense waiting period in the dressing room before the match.

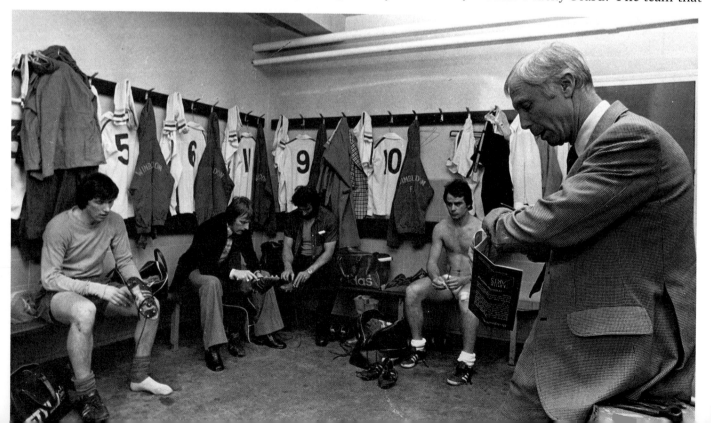

must travel insist on staying at their lucky hotel, or *not* staying at one which proved unlucky on a previous occasion. One member of the team has packed a piece of lucky silver in his bag, another has to carry someone else's bag rather than his own. Several more are carefully packing and unpacking their belongings in a rigidly set sequence that must not be broken. One whole team must play a round of golf on a particular course, or suffer dire consequences. A particular player insists that his wife must accompany him – not for sexual reasons, but because he always has bad luck when she is away from him. He is outraged when, on a long foreign trip, this request is refused, and his game suffers for it.

A London team, experiencing a bad run of defeats, become convinced that they have a bogeyman in their midst. Whenever they arrive at a hotel before an away match, a local newspaper reporter is always staying there and greets them cheerfully. He is friendly and sympathetic, but gradually they come to associate him with their disasters and finally convince themselves that he is to blame for them. His presence becomes an ill omen and they go to lengths to avoid him.

Sometimes the 'bogey' becomes, not a man, but a particular ground. Derby's stadium, the Baseball Ground, was once thought to be suffering from a gypsy curse. The ground acquired its name because it was the site of an unsuccessful attempt to establish the sport of baseball in the British Isles. Before that, it had been the location of a gypsy encampment, and when it was taken over as a soccer stadium in 1895, there were those who felt that the displaced gypsies had put a curse on the place. In the years that followed, the Derby team suffered four cup semi-final and three cup final defeats. In 1946 they again reached the FA Cup Final. Taking no chances this time, they sent their captain to a gypsy to have the curse lifted, and promptly won the final by four goals to one.

When the players awake on the morning of the match, a new set of irrational rules comes into operation. One man decides to remove an unlucky moustache, another goes out for a ritual haircut and a stroll over a specific route. Other people become involved. A player's wife has to clean the windows at home, because she was doing just that when he last had a great victory. The children of another must wear special colours all day for a similar reason. Even the manager may have to appear before his team wearing lucky garments because he knows that to omit them might cause anxiety. In one case, it was a pair of blue socks, and each player would be careful to inspect him to make sure that he had not forgotten.

As the team sit down to the pre-match lunch, more beliefs are acted out. Sometimes the order in which the men take their seats is strictly regulated by their irrational fears of breaking a lucky routine. The food eaten and the manner of its eating may also come under superstitious control.

When the coach leaves for a particular ground it must take the same route as before – assuming, of course, that last time the team triumphed. Once, long ago, when a famous English amateur team, the Wanderers, was visiting Leiden in Holland, they were driven to the ground in a coach pulled by four black horses, decked out in black, funeral plumes. The coach took a route which went through the local cemetery, next to the ground, and the Wanderers lost their long undefeated record. After the match they refused point blank to return by the same sinister road, for fear that it might affect further games.

The players themselves are often laden with lucky charms as they head towards their match-day encounter. For one it is a pair of special cuff-links, for a second a gold charm given to him by an elderly supporter one day after a winning game, for a third a pair of sun-glasses, even in the rain, or a medallion around the neck, or a toy rabbit, or a rabbit's-foot tucked in a pocket, or some lucky article of clothing.

The gestures of these players clearly reveal the tensions of waiting for the start of the second half of a cup final. As they take to the field they will move out in a fixed order, each man holding a special, lucky position in the advancing column.

Dutch star Rudi Krol wearing a lucky necklace to protect him against ill-fortune during the match.

Once in the dressing room, yet another set of rituals begins. Again there are special things to be worn – lucky stockings, lucky laces, lucky boots; a lucky wedding ring to be kissed ceremonially. There are special actions to be carried out – a towel to be hung on a peg instead of placed in its usual position on the bench, two sticks of chewing-gum to be chewed while changing, a ritual swig of whisky, not for alcohol but for luck; for one player, the anointing of the tips of his boots with a splash of whisky, for another a splash of water. Some players have to enter the dressing room in a particular way. One has to be the last in, to avoid bad luck; another always has to come in through the boot-room entrance instead of the main door; another must be there, fully changed, exactly forty minutes before kick-off; another must always sit in the same corner. Yet another must carefully shake hands with every one of his team-mates before leaving the dressing room, or his game will suffer.

The most rigidly observed procedures are those connected with changing clothes. Some are simple enough – putting on the left sock before the right, or the right boot before the left – but others are more complicated. One player must remove his trousers and put on his jock-strap before removing his jacket. Another must dress completely in his playing gear, then take it all off again, and put it on once more. Another must go through the actions of lacing and unlacing his boots three times.

Perhaps the most extraordinary example of 'ritual dressing' took place during Portsmouth's successful cup run in 1939. Sportswriter John Cottrell records the scene before the cup final climax: 'In accordance with strictly observed pre-Cup-tie tradition, Portsmouth's veteran outside-right Freddie Worrall bent down and ceremoniously buckled a pair of clean white spats on to the feet of club manager Jack Tinn. These were magic spats normally stored in the Portsmouth FC safe. The left one had to be buckled first. Then they brought you luck. So far they had taken Pompey safely through cup-ties ... with only a single goal being scored in reply. This time, however, Portsmouth were not relying exclusively on the lucky spats. Just to make sure that they were favoured by the gods, Worrall carried a miniature horseshoe in his shirt pocket, a sprig of heather in each sock, a lucky sixpenny-bit in a boot, and a china white elephant tied to one of his garters.' The magic seemed to work. They beat their opponents, the clear favourites, by four goals to one.

Timing is crucial in some rituals. One player would wait fully changed except for his shorts, which he held ready in his hand, until the referee's buzzer sounded. Only then could he put them on and make his way quickly to the door. England captain Bobby Moore had a very similar ritual. For him it was important to be the last person in the dressing room to put his shorts on before the game. Moore's team-mate Martin Peters was fascinated by the way he stood around holding the shorts, waiting for everyone else to finish dressing. Peters later admitted, 'He never realized, but I used to take the mickey. When he had put on his shorts I would take mine off. He would immediately do the same and not put them back on until I had done so. I used to do this frequently, but he never caught on.'

Bobby Moore was not the only player to be treated in this way. Rodney Marsh recalls that, 'Jimmy Langley always refused to touch the ball in the changing-room before a match. He would be wild if he did, and Alan Mullery used to play on this in their Fulham days. Alan is a great niggler, and he would get hold of a ball and start kicking or throwing it at Jim. Jim used to leap all over the place, trying to avoid it.'

It is surprising that one player would try to upset another's rituals in this manner and thereby risk unsettling him for the match to come, and such disregard for the superstitions of others is comparatively rare. In most cases team-mates respect one another's beliefs and avoid tempting fate. If something goes wrong with a superstition, friends often try to help. The great Pelé once gave away one of his playing shirts, only to find that his game suffered afterwards. He asked a friend to try to trace the fan to whom he had given it, and recover it. After a week, the friend returned wth the missing shirt and explained that he had gone to much trouble finding it. Pelé was immensely grateful, donned the shirt, and his champion's touch returned. His friend was careful not to tell him that his search had been futile and that he had simply handed back to the great man the shirt in which he had lost so miserably the previous week. The power of superstitions is all in the mind.

When the players leave the dressing room and file out into the tunnel, the rituals are not over. There is a special order to be followed. One player must always be third in line, another second from the last, another must always walk behind the no. 10. The favoured position, however, is last out, and this creates problems when a team has two 'last-outers' in its squad. Alert soccer-watchers will have seen the result of this dilemma at certain cup finals, where the two players at the end of the line, as it marches on to the pitch, are carefully positioned side by side. Other tunnel-rituals include turning round in a complete circle after leaving the dressing room, never carrying a ball, always carrying a ball, or bouncing a ball twice on the ceiling.

Once out on the pitch, certain players ritually touch the grass with one hand as they enter the playing area. Many Catholic players cross themselves and kiss their thumbs. One player, rather less decorously, takes his chewing-gum out of his mouth, rolls it into a little ball and kicks it with his foot. If he misses this ritual gum-kick, he will play badly. Another player has to be the first one to aim a kick at goal during the warm-up period and his keeper dare not save it, even though it is only a practice shot, because if he does so the kicker will have a poor game. Another player is taking his boots off and putting them on again, another is kissing the goalposts. A keeper is carefully placing his small bag of paraphernalia in the right-hand side of the goal. If he accidentally put it on the other side, or if anyone moved it, he would be unable to make his 'magic saves'.

All of these many different superstitions have been solemnly performed by particular players and particular teams. Each and every one of them is recorded in the memoirs of players and the writings of soccer historians.

As the players wait in the tunnel to go out on to the Wembley pitch, their captain obeys his private superstition of bouncing the ball against one of the walls to bring good luck.

Reports indicate that similar irrational actions take place all around the globe, wherever important matches are played and the Tribal Heroes suffer from pangs of anxiety and apprehension. Some players, it is true, make a point of stressing that *they*, unlike their team-mates, have no superstitions whatever and consider the whole business to be a silly waste of time and effort. They are in a minority, however, and the clue to what lies behind their statement is perhaps given by the player who announced, 'My superstition is not telling other people what my superstitions are.'

For some players the magic rituals assume astonishing intensity. World Cup centre-half Jackie Charlton even went to the length of refusing the captaincy of his club team rather than break his pre-match ritual. It was vital for him to be the last player on to the pitch and, as captain, he would have been forced to lead out his team. Rather than risk this, he let the captain's honour go to Billy Bremner.

But perhaps the most complicated magic routine of all belonged to a goalkeeper, Alan Rough, who publicly admitted that he went 'in fear of missing out some part of my match-day ritual'. The pattern was as follows:

1 He must not shave on match-day mornings.

2 He must carry a key-ring with a thistle motif.

3 He must also take with him to the ground an old tennis ball.

4 He must put in his pocket a miniature football boot he found in his goal-net one afternoon.

5 He must wear a small, star-shaped medal.

6 He must always use peg no. 13 in the dressing-room.

7 He must put on his original no. 11 jersey, from the days of his first soccer club, underneath his keeper's sweater.

8 As he goes through the tunnel, he must bounce the ball off the wall three times.

9 When he approaches the goalmouth, he must kick the ball into the empty net.

10 Throughout the match he must blow his nose as many times as possible, using handkerchiefs tucked inside his keeper's cap specially for the purpose.

He concludes this formidable list by saying that, 'I don't think I could play without going through these preparations. And nothing discourages me, not even a seven-goal hammering.'

It is easy to laugh at these incredibly elaborate precautions, and to scoff at their validity, as Michael Parkinson does in his 'Soccer Star's Superstition Interview' parody: 'When I go out into the white-hot cauldron which will be Wembley tomorrow, I shall not have picked my nose for ten days, I shall be wearing two left boots, I shall be carrying my wife's lucky handbag, I shall be wearing my grandfather's vest. It is my lucky charm. It might seem silly but it is going to put Liverpool/Newcastle out of the cup.' But the fact remains that irrational actions not much less extreme than these *are* carried out everywhere, every week of every season, by large numbers of otherwise sensible and down-to-earth players. It has to be accepted that they are of great value. This does not mean that there is any supernatural or mystical connection between the performance of the rituals and the outcome of the play on the field. This is not necessary, providing the players concerned strongly *believe* in such a connection. If they can convince themselves that their strange actions will make them play better, then it will be so, simply because the rituals will help to reduce their anxieties and give them added self-confidence. Greater faith in their own abilities is often the only thing that separates the winners from the losers in an otherwise well-balanced contest.

For this reason, superstition will always be commonplace in the high-risk occupation of sport, as it was in primitive human tribes where the whole way of life was fraught with risks and dangers and where magical thinking was born.

Jackie Charlton refused to accept the captaincy of his club because it meant that he would be forced to lead his squad out on to the field at the start of a match. One of his superstitions demanded that he should be the last out on the pitch and rather than abandon this, he let the captain's role go to Billy Bremner, seen here leading out the team.

At the Barcelona stadium there is a special chapel where the players can pray for success in the contest to come and deposit their club pennant as an offering – the soccer equivalent of lighting a holy candle.

21 The Bravery of the Heroes

COURAGE AND CLOGGING, PAIN AND INJURIES

There is so much violence on the modern soccer field that it has become an act of bravery merely for the players to run out on to the pitch at the start of a contest. It is an extremely rare event for the full ninety minutes to pass without at least one player receiving treatment for an injury. And there is hardly a player alive who has survived a whole season of soccer without suffering considerable pain.

The fact that this threat of damage does not deter the Tribal Heroes is due to the traditional acceptance of violence as an inherent part of the sport. The young men who aspire to become professional players arrive pre-programmed to expect the knocks along with the glory. Later, they carry the scars almost as a badge of courage, rather like primitive tribesmen who have undergone ritual scarification. One advantage for the Soccer Tribesman is that the pain is not inflicted in cold blood. It occurs in the heat of battle, when the mental and physiological state of arousal makes it easier to bear. Nevertheless, many players have shown remarkable bravery and determination in the face of excessive physical battering.

There are a number of cases on record of players continuing to the end of a match despite suffering from broken bones. When he was only sixteen, goalkeeper Gordon Banks was severely hurt when he threw himself at the feet of an attacking forward. Without realizing it, he played out the rest of the game with a broken arm, and still carries a screw in his elbow as a souvenir of this act of tenacity. Another goalkeeper, Bert Trautman, played through an FA Cup Final with a broken neck. Striker Jimmy Greaves played a game with a broken wrist, and the legendary Ted Drake, renowned for having scored seven goals in a First Division match, once broke *both* wrists during a game, but stubbornly carried on until the final whistle. The extraordinary feature of Drake's attitude was that he always played more ferociously and vigorously after he had been injured, and the worse the injury, the more determined he became. This led to the famous remark, 'God help his opponents if Drake ever breaks a leg.'

The greatest battle on the soccer field is always between the fleet-footed forwards and the desperate defenders. By the nature of their encounter, it is the forwards who suffer most. It is they who are trying to run past or around their opponents, and it is the defenders who are so often forced to hack them down, or lose their reputations. A brilliant defender can dispossess a forward legally and painlessly, but as strikers have grown ever faster and more skilful, many defenders have been driven to become cloggers who deliberately hack their enemy down with a 'professional foul'. Instead of 'play the game', their motto is now 'play the man'.

It is these professional fouls that cause most of the serious damage, and a modern striker who happens to be unusually gifted will have multi-coloured legs before the soccer season is very old. When George Best was suffering particularly badly in this way, his coach held a special press conference to exhibit his star's damaged shins. One reporter commented: 'They looked as if he had walked through barbed wire.' Dutch star Johan Cruyff regarded five new wounds after a normal Dutch league match as 'routine'. The Brazilian genius Pelé was equally philosophical, saying, 'I have come to accept that the life of a front-runner is a hard one, that he will suffer more injuries than most men and that many of these injuries will not be accidental.' He even expressed a cynical admiration for a defender who carried out his hatchet-man duties with artistry. Speaking of the Italian player Betini, he has written: 'Betini was an artist at fouling a man without getting caught. Whenever he

Sometimes a player who has been taken off for treatment insists on returning to the field of play and completing the match, heading the ball fearlessly even with a bandaged head.

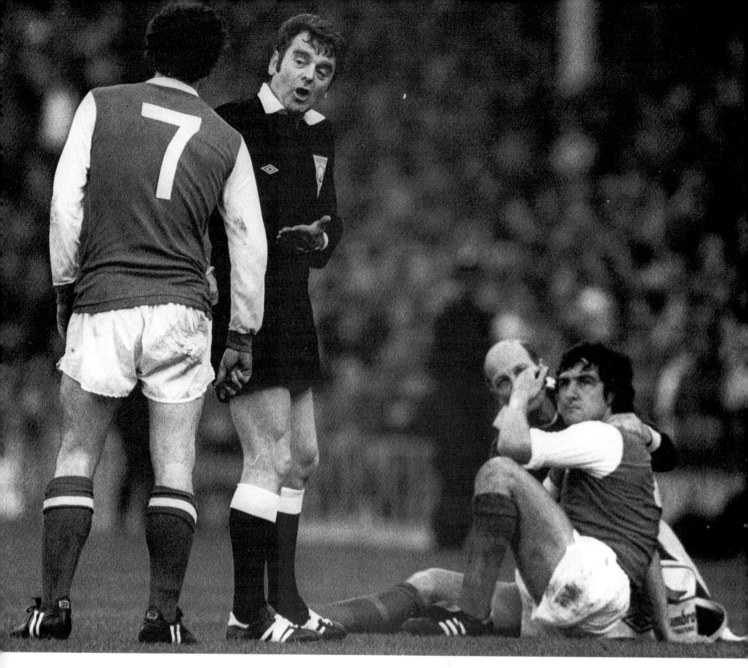

When a player is injured his anger may give added fire to his game, his change of mood more than compensating for his physical damage.

came close he managed to dig me in the ribs, or put his fist in my stomach, or to kick me in the shins during a tackle . . . Betini was an artist, I must admit.'

In 1976 one soccer manager likened the clashes between massive, brutal defenders and valiant, acrobatic forwards to the encounter normally seen inside a bull-ring: 'The hacking must stop. If it doesn't then the only people who will bother to come to football will be those interested in bloodsports – a form of bullfighting.' For a manager or coach with a seriously injured star striker, such sentiments are understandable. Even the strikers themselves, despite their bravery, occasionally find the struggle becoming too savage and are driven to voicing their disgust. In 1971, George Best exploded: 'A lot of rubbish is talked about destroyers and tough defenders. I call them dirty bastards.'

Unfortunately, against this reaction has to be set the fact that if a defender failed to make an assault on a striker who had somehow slithered past him and was now heading straight for the goalmouth, he would be booed off the park by his supporters and would soon lose his place in the team. If, on the other hand, he cut down his tormentor like an angry bull, goring him from behind with a savage professional foul, his supporters would cheer him to the rafters. So it is hard to blame soccer's beleaguered rear-guard for their brutal methods. The remedy, some feel, must come from the game's law-makers. They have two alternatives available to them to reduce the violence, but for traditional reasons they are loth to act. The first solution is to give the referee the power to impose a penalty kick as a punishment for a seriously violent foul *anywhere* on the pitch, instead of confining it to the penalty area alone. Since penalties can win and lose games, brutal attacks would be far more risky than they are at present. With the existing system of punishments, the referee is forced to use either a booking or a sending-off, along with a free-kick, when a vicious foul has been committed outside the 'box'. Because the drastic action of sending the offender off unbalances the game for the rest of the match, referees are extremely reluctant to employ it. Hatchet-men are aware of this and can therefore hope to get away with a booking and a free-kick. In many cases they decide that the benefit gained by the act of violence outweighs this punishment. It not only eliminates the opponent's immediate advantage as he runs towards the goalmouth, but it has the added appeal that it may effectively slow him down for the rest of the game. Fear of giving away a penalty would make many a clogger think twice before felling a rival.

The alternative way of dealing with really brutal fouls is to treat them as 'assault' in the legal sense of the word. Edward Grayson, a London barrister, has advocated a Safety of Sports Persons Act with the following wording: 'Any person deliberately or recklessly causing any harm or injury . . . to any person concerned with, before, during or after any sporting activity shall be guilty of an offence.' Professor Colin Tatz agrees with him, stating that, in his opinion, 'A violent assault which is outside the rules of the game is also outside the rules of the law, and therefore amenable to its jurisdiction and punishment.'

Courage is needed to face a free-kick as a member of a defensive wall, but care is taken to protect the most vulnerable parts of the body.

Sometimes, in the rush of play, it is impossible to avoid a flying boot and many players are missing their front teeth.

In cases of extreme severity such measures may be called for, but sports officials are quick to point out that they could easily destroy sport by weakening its essentially rugged character. Professor Tatz was brusquely answered by the secretary of the English Football Association, who replied, 'Legal intervention in sport ... has become the hobby-horse of many publicity-seekers. Justice on the field is undeniably rough justice, but it is accepted in sport and is something on which sport relies totally.' Some players, tired of outside meddling in their game, have gone much further. Two typically cynical remarks are: 'Violence in football today is becoming a problem – there isn't enough of it,' and, 'We're going to have to do something about all this violence or people are going to keep on buying tickets.' Most fans feel the same way and frankly admit to enjoying a hard-tackling game. Bravery is one of the qualities they expect to see displayed by their heroes, in addition to brilliant skills and athletic performance. And bravery will vanish if the threat of violent contact is greatly reduced.

It would seem, therefore, that the balance can best be kept by a measure such as the suggested penalty kick 'extension', which would empower the referee to punish severely the most extreme acts of violence without softening the game to a point where it ceases to be exciting. In this way injuries should be kept in check, although there will, of course, always be genuine accidents.

Such accidents have a long history. And some have proved fatal. The earliest known death caused by playing football occurred in 1321. The man responsible was a canon called William de Spalding: 'During the game at ball as he kicked the ball, a lay friend of his, also called William, ran against him and wounded himself on a sheathed knife carried by the canon, so severely that he died within six days. Dispensation is granted, as no blame is attached to William de Spalding, who, feeling deeply the death of his friend, and fearing what might be said by his enemies, has applied to the pope.'

Many other deaths occurred in the centuries which followed, while football remained a rough-and-tumble folk sport. Their number decreased rapidly once a set of rules was applied and soccer became an organized activity, but from time to time the game claimed a victim. At Leicester Assizes in 1878, for example, a player was charged with killing a rival by striking him with his 'protruding knee'. And during the First World War, the wooden cross above the grave of one unfortunate soldier bore an inscription which read *He died of Footballitis*. This unusual memorial was to a man who, having escaped death in the trenches and on the battlefield on a hundred occasions, was finally laid low by a kick on the temple during a friendly match with his fellow-soldiers.

A particularly poignant death befell an Arsenal defender, Bob Benson, who during the same war worked in the Arsenal munition sheds at Woolwich, making shells. His health suffered badly, and he was soon a shadow of his pre-war self. One day, sitting as a spectator at a war-time Arsenal match, he was offered a challenge he could not refuse. One of the team had failed to arrive at the stadium and Benson immediately volunteered to take his place. The crowd, remembering his days of glory, gave him a standing ovation, with the result that he literally played his heart out. Making a brave clearance just before half-time, he collapsed from a heart attack and was led from the field by a team-mate, to whom he whispered his dying wish that the game should be continued to the end.

But perhaps the most extraordinary soccer deaths occurred actually in the field of battle. When the East Surrey Regiment were attacking German positions in 1916, the Captain of one company ordered his men to dribble footballs before them as they crossed no-man's-land. A war correspondent recorded the bizarre event in the following words: 'The Captain had provided four footballs, one for each platoon, urging them to keep up a

A single, serious injury can easily end a promising career, as it did in this stretcher case (above). When a player is obviously badly hurt, the usual animosity between the opposing teams is momentarily suspended (above left) and players from both sides come to his aid.

Blood rarely flows on the soccer field, the majority of the injuries being internal, but occasionally a player damages his head (left) and leaves the field looking more like a prize-fighter than a footballer.

dribbling competition all the way over the mile and a quarter of ground they had to traverse. As the company formed on emerging from the trench, the platoon commanders kicked off and the match against Death commenced. The gallant Captain himself fell early in the charge, and men began to drop rapidly under the hail of machine-gun bullets. But still the footballs were booted onwards, with hoarse cries of encouragement or defiance, until they disappeared in the dense smother behind which the Germans were shooting. Then when the bombs and bayonets had done their work, and the enemy had cleared out, the Surrey men looked for their footballs, and recovered two of them in the captured traverses. These will be sent to the Regimental Depot at Kingston as trophies worth preserving.'

In the inter-war period there was a dramatic death at Ibrox Park during a Rangers–Celtic confrontation. John Thompson, Celtic's young goalkeeper, saved his last goal by diving courageously at the feet of the Rangers centre-forward. He managed to deflect the ball but took the attacker's kick full in the face. Sensing a victory now that the enemy goalkeeper was injured, some of the Rangers fans began to cheer, but their team's captain, realizing the severity of the injury, ran to the noisy crowd and with outstretched arms made a dramatic appeal for silence. The young keeper was near to death, but as he was being stretchered from the ground, he made one last movement, struggling to raise his body up and gaze back down the field to where his goalmouth now stood empty. It was as if, even while dying, he could not rid himself of the deeply ingrained anxiety of leaving his goal unprotected.

These fortunately are the dramatic rarities; ordinary injuries, as already mentioned, are far from rare. The head of a sports clinic recently calculated that during the 1970s there was one injury (serious enough to require at least three days' rest and treatment) for every thirteen games played by a professional. This is the average – some players seem to be unusually lucky while others are disastrously accident-prone. And he believes that this 13 to 1

The soldiers of the East Surrey Regiment playing soccer as they advance across no-man's-land through a hail of enemy fire. A patriotic poet commemorated the event: 'Where blood is poured like water, they drive the trickling ball . . . True to the land that bore them, The Surreys play the game!'

The agony of high-speed soccer (opposite). It is rare for a match to reach its final whistle without at least a few incidents of this kind.

ratio is rising, as games become increasingly competitive.

Most injuries occur in the head region and on the legs. A clash of heads, when two rival players try to head the ball at the same moment, often causes concussion. Teeth and noses are broken by flying boots or jabbing elbows. The Tottenham goalkeeper recently had so many teeth knocked down his throat by a striker's elbow that he nearly choked to death. But it was a French centre-half who suffered the most bizarre head injury. Turning a complete somersault, he kicked himself unconscious by striking his head with his own boot.

Leg wounds include cuts, bruises, torn ligaments, damaged cartilages, severed tendons and bone fractures. The list of famous players who have suffered recurrent knee trouble is endless. It is the cartilages, those pieces of gristle that ensure smooth movement of the knee joints, that succumb most often. Although we tend to think of the knee purely as a bending device, a hinge, it also rotates. It is most easily injured when it is flexed and rotating, as it frequently is during a hard game of soccer. A vicious twist, and the cartilage can be badly damaged. Around the knee there are fan-shaped ligaments, tough fibrous strands whose task is to offer the greatest resistance to stress. These can be injured either by rotation strain or by pure natural strain through impact, whether the player is standing with the legs straight or running with the knees bent.

A trainer from each club is always standing by to provide immediate first aid, if the referee permits him to run on to the field. When this happens, the traditional 'magic sponge' is usually on hand to bring about a miraculous cure.

All players know how vulnerable their knees are and how many famous names have been forced to limp out of soccer prematurely because of violent fouls. So it is understandable that tempers sometimes run high among team-mates when they see a friend callously hacked down and watch him writhing on the ground clutching one of his knees. Such incidents are particularly explosive and on a number of occasions have led to fist-fights between those players who are still upright. Referees have to be very quick off the mark to quell these outbursts, because there is always a chance that they may spread until two whole teams are locked in battle, not symbolically via a football, but directly via clenched knuckles. If no more than two or three players are involved, it is still possible for the referee to send them off and restart the match, but once a whole group have started fighting, the official has little choice but to abandon the game. This in its turn is dangerous because it can lead to rioting among the frustrated fans. The most famous occasion when this happened was during a Brazilian match, when not only all the players were brawling, but also the substitutes, coaches and trainers. There were so many fights taking place across the pitch that hordes of photographers invaded the turf to take close-ups of the action and soon the whole field was a mass of running, kicking, punching figures. Within minutes the fans on the terraces followed suit and a major riot had begun. Somewhere in the midst of all this was a distraught referee whose whistle had suddenly lost its meaning.

On one occasion player-violence of this sort erupted even after the final whistle. At the 'Battle of Berne', as it was dubbed, the Brazilians were playing their great enemies the Hungarians and the match had been particularly bad-tempered. As the teams were leaving the pitch at the end of the contest and were filing off to their dressing rooms, one of the Brazilian players claimed to have been struck in the face by a bottle. Some observers believed it had been wielded by an angry rival supporter, but the Brazilian insisted it had been one of the Hungarian team. Don Ateyo describes what happened next: 'The Brazilians immediately stormed the Hungarian dressing room, where there ensued the extraordinary spectacle of two dozen international players battering each other with boots and liniment bottles amid jock-straps and dirty sweaters. The worst casualty was a Hungarian who had his cheek laid open.'

Fortunately most player-clashes are restrained by pacifying hands long before the disputes reach such dramatic proportions. On the pitch, the usual pattern is for the outraged player, who goes to strike an opponent, to be held back by his companions. If the restraining arms are those of his own team-mates, who at the same time offer sufficiently calming advice, worse trouble can often be averted. This 'hold-me-back' scene, so common in pub brawls, is a great boon to harassed referees, who can then rush in between the two snarling rivals and apply further dampening influences.

If officials bewail the lack of self-control among modern soccer players, they must remember three things. First, the game is always played in an atmosphere of great tension and physiological arousal. Adrenalin is racing through the system. This is necessary for exciting play, but it also means that the players are primed for *any* kind of violent action. Second, the demands from the crowd to win at all costs add strong psychological pressures that keep pulsing out towards the players from the noisy, packed terraces. And third, the players have been both selected and trained for bravery in the face of aggressive opposition. This bravery is intended to win matches, but when violence erupts, it makes no distinction. In the heat of the moment, it is hard to expect courage to evaporate simply because the rules have momentarily collapsed. This is the inherent weakness of all kinds of formalized contest. It is so easy for them to burst into *real* contests and for the licensed bravery that won cheers, to become in an instant the unmasked face of naked aggression.

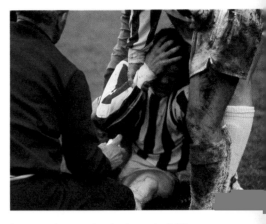

A recent innovation is the pain-killing aerosol spray – a mixed blessing that enables a player to continue the match without feeling undue discomfort, but in so doing increases the risk of the injured part suffering further serious damage.

22 The Triumph Displays

LEAPS AND JUMPS, EMBRACES AND HUGS

Immediately following the scoring of a goal the Soccer Tribe explodes into one of its major expressions of joy – the Triumph Display. With their supporters roaring, dancing and clapping on the terraces, the Tribal Heroes celebrate their 'kill' in a frenzied outburst of abandoned leaping and embracing. It is a peak moment of tribal life and it is enjoyed to the full, with all physical barriers down and all the usual inhibitions swept away.

It has not always been like this. In the earlier days of soccer, the moment of triumph was usually celebrated with little more than a handshake and a smile. As one elderly ex-player put it: 'There was none of this nonsense in the old days. When we scored everyone behaved as if nothing extraordinary had happened. The most I would do as captain would be to give the scorer a pat on the back and say, "Well done, old boy."' Critics of the new trend towards a more extravagant display include the august members of the English Football Association's ruling body. These Tribal Elders have been quoted as saying that they are ashamed of the uncontrolled emotions of their professional players. The general attitude of such critics can be summed up in the plea: 'It is to be hoped that such histrionics are nothing more than a passing phase.'

There are two possible reasons for these attacks on a tribal display which seems to give nothing but joy to all concerned and which certainly appears to do no harm. The first has to do with pure traditionalism. It is the task of the Tribal Elders to keep the tribal rituals pure and constant and to resist all change on principle. Irritating as this may be to some, it is an important role and not to be scoffed at. Without their stubborn resistance to modern trends, the distinctive quality of the Soccer Tribe might eventually be lost and its dignity degraded. On this basis, it is easy to understand their mistrust of actions as flamboyant as hugging and kissing and waving, which to them must smack more of the theatre than the sports field. In these, they no doubt see the first signs of a downward slide from a serious contest into the razzmatazz of show business.

The second possible reason for their attacks has to do with the time-honoured tradition of the British stiff-upper-lip. Cultures vary enormously in their attitudes towards the outward display of inner emotions. In some, such as the peoples who live around the Mediterranean Sea, there is an extrovert tradition which permits grown men to kiss and embrace, with few social restraints. As far as they are concerned, only a snob or an emotional cripple would fail to express his feelings with bodily actions. In other regions, such as the Far East and Northern Europe, lack of control is viewed as primitive or infantile. As one critic put it: 'When you score . . . you don't do some sort of Red Indian war dance and you do not behave like a lot of children.'

What the critics are saying, therefore, is that the Triumph Displays of modern soccer players are both untraditional and unBritish and that since soccer is traditionally a British sport there is a double reason for frowning upon this new trend. To any impartial observer, however, it is clear that they are losing the battle and it is interesting to ask why this should be, when they have been so successful in preserving many of the other ancient tribal customs and attitudes.

To start with, the trend is not particularly recent. It began shortly after the Second World War, when soccer was undergoing a massive expansion to become an international obsession, aided by the growth of television. With soccer teams able to move about more easily and speedily from country to

At the moment of triumph, the goal-scorer usually jumps for joy and is then mobbed by congratulating team-mates. This behaviour, which gives pleasure to players and supporters alike, has been frowned upon by elderly officials in some countries who see it as unsportsmanlike gloating over the vanquished opponents.

country, thanks to faster jet travel, there was a mixing of soccer nationalities on a scale that the game had never known before. Players from the Latin countries of the Mediterranean and South America became more familiar figures in Northern Europe and their physical outbursts of joy when they scored important goals came as something of a shock to the quieter, more subdued heroes of British and other northern teams. Initially the Latins were laughed at for their short shorts and their wild embraces, but after a while they began to make the stoical British look positively churlish. The old tradition of a handshake and a pat on the back began to give the false impression that the British did not care so much about scoring goals and the inhibited northerners were forced to cast off their restraint and to indulge in a few mild embraces.

Before long all the emotion-shy teams had caught up with the emotion-free Latins and had become indistinguishable in their ecstatic displays of goal-scoring triumph. To their surprise, it now seemed the natural thing to do, and the truth was out at last. It *was* the natural thing to do at a moment of such intense emotional experience. It was not the Latins who had been 'odd' in their behaviour, but the northerners themselves. It was the Latin embracing that was appropriate in the special context of the peak moment of goal-scoring, not the culturally suppressed formalities of the British.

To the Tribal Elders in the English Football Association and elsewhere, the new 'antics' of the players seemed as shocking as the waltz (their bodies are *touching*!) had done to their grandfathers before them. Worse still, these body intimacies were not only public, but male-to-male. Yet despite the scorn and despite the accusations of effeminacy, the embraces continued and even grew in intensity. And they have lasted now, as a regular tribal display, for several decades, to become firmly entrenched, not as a 'passing fad', but a new tradition in the Soccer Tribe's behaviour repertoire. What is the secret of their success in the face of so much initial hostility?

To understand this it is necessary to look back at the origins of the gestures. The first time we experience hugs and pats, kisses and embraces, is in the arms of our mother when we are tiny babies. These body contacts soon come to stand for loving and being loved. When we grow older we begin to reciprocate. As young children, we run to hug our mother just as she used to hug us, and the result is a mutual embrace of love. The important point here is that this is not sexual love, it is pre-sexual love. When sex arrives during the teenage years, the intimacies between parent and offspring decline and there is even some embarrassment. Before long the young adults have shifted their physical attentions from parent to sexual partner and the intimate body contacts begin to flower again. The hugs and embraces of juvenile love have now become the caresses of sexual love. It is this new sexual emphasis that, in some cultures, leads to a suppression of body intimacies outside the sexual pair. If friendly embraces do occur between close friends they are muted and formal, for fear that they may carry some sexual meaning.

In other cultures this limitation does not take place. There, the juvenile embrace that means non-sexual loving survives among close friends as an expression of warmth and strong feelings for one another. It continues into adulthood in its original non-sexual form without any of the 'northern' inhibitions.

Seen in this way, it is clear that the embracing of soccer players is in no way 'borrowed' from the sexual sphere, but rather that it is the sexual sphere that has borrowed these actions from the pre-sexual phase of childhood. They are so basic to *generalized* loving that, when a particularly intense emotional moment arrives, it is the most natural thing in the world for a human being to throw his arms around a close friend and embrace him warmly. So it is the slurs on the manliness of the hugging footballers that are 'odd', not the actions of the players. This is why, despite the criticisms, the players felt

somehow that what they were doing was 'right' in the special context of the frenzy of joy at scoring an important goal. The fact that some of their actions looked superficially very sexual was a cultural accident rather than a biological truth. And this is why it was the Latin exuberance that infected the northern players, rather than the northern suppression of emotional displays that spread to the Latin teams.

This said, it remains to examine exactly what does happen after a goal is scored. There are two phases: the display of the scorer and the response of his team-mates. The actions can be separated into a number of distinct units:

1 The Scoring Sprint

Immediately after a goal, the man who has scored often takes off on a wild sprint back down the field, usually with his mouth wide open. As one famous player put it: 'My particular way of expressing excitement and elation is to run and leap, waving my arms wildly in the air like a berserk kangaroo.' There are two reasons for this display. One is the great upsurge in disinhibited energy felt by the scorer, following the pent-up tensions of the match. The sprint helps to release these tensions. Another reason is that the rapid movement removes any suggestion that the scorer is waiting for congratulations. One player explains: 'I don't . . . stand conceitedly waiting for the acclaim of my colleagues; in fact, some of them complain at times that, when they have tried to congratulate me, I have showed more speed than I do during the rest of the game.'

When a player has scored a vital goal he often races off down the pitch in a *Scoring Sprint* (above). The elation of the moment fires him with a sudden burst of energy that demands expression and his team-mates are forced to rush after him to offer their congratulations.

Many goal-scorers feel the need to hail their supporters with a *Raised Arm* salute (opposite, above left) and some go further, exaggerating the gesture into a *Leaping Air-punch* (opposite, above centre) in which the raised arm beats the air in a symbolic blow, as if hitting the vanquished enemy over the head. A variant of the jumping action is the *Leaping Fists-aloft* (opposite, above right).

Sometimes a team-mate responds to a goal by leaping on to the scorer's back (right), while he is performing an *Arms Aloft* display. Clasping his body with both hands and legs, he looks like a cross between a mating frog and a small child clinging to his father.

2 The Raised Arm

A less dramatic response to scoring a goal is for the scorer to turn away from the goalmouth and raise one arm vertically above his head. This is performed not so much to his team-mates as in salute of the roaring crowd. The action has been attacked by critics as being 'like some Caesar back from the wars taking his plaudits from the populace', and scolded with the words, 'Players must mind their manners.' Yet the description of a hero accepting the acclaim of the spectators is a perfectly valid one and warrants no scorn. On the contrary, it is a courtesy to the crowd. The alternative of jogging back quietly to the centre spot while ignoring their cheers would, by contrast, be ill-mannered.

There are three forms of the Raised Arm display: the flat-handed version, rather like a Roman Hail; the tight-fist version, rather like a Communist or Black Panther Salute; and the forefinger version, in which the single digit points to the heavens, as if signalling the number one – one more goal.

3 The Leaping Air-punch

As the scorer runs back along the pitch he suddenly leaps in the air with a raised fist and then brings it down in a powerful over-arm blow. The blow strikes the air, but symbolically it is crashing down on the defeated heads of the enemy. This over-arm downward-striking punch is the basic attack movement of the human species. It is seen in very tiny children when they first start to fight in nursery schools, and in the panic moments of adult riots. The frontal punch of the boxer has to be learnt, but the over-arm down-punch seems to be inborn, and it is this one that we revert to when wishing to make a symbolic demonstration of our triumphant power.

4 The Arms Aloft

Perhaps the most common of all Triumph Displays is the full raising of both arms. This has the effect of making the scorer seem larger and taller. In describing his feelings he is likely to use such phrases as 'I felt ten feet tall' and his arm-raising is a physical expression of that sensation. In animal terms, by scoring the goal he has instantly raised his status in his group. Throughout the animal world, high status is displayed in ways that heighten or enlarge the individual, so in this respect the scorer is performing a very basic piece of animal behaviour.

5 The Leaping Fists-aloft

In this action the scorer increases his height twice over. His raised arms add about two feet to his height and his upward jump provides another two feet, to give him a fleeting moment of 'being ten feet tall'. This combination is about as far as the display of size-magnifying can go.

6 The War-dance

This is a rare variant but has become more frequent recently. It is not a caricature of a native war-dance, mimed as a joke, but a curious little movement similar to running on the spot, or running very fast with the legs while the body moves only very slowly forward. It seems to be a 'condensed' version of the Scoring Sprint, representing an outpouring of emotion expressed in token form.

7 The Back-tilt

In this the goal-scorer leans sharply back, from the knees, and slightly raises his clenched fists. This is another way of signalling with his body language that he is 'the opposite of defeated'. Just as the Arms Aloft posture is the antithesis of the Downward Slump posture of the goal-losers, so the Back-tilt

The triumphant goal-scorer sometimes performs a *Back-tilt* at the moment the ball enters the net. In doing so, he is adopting the posture opposite to that of a beaten player, who droops his head forward.

The celebrating players often run across the field with their arms outspread in an *Embrace Invitation* display.

contrasts strongly with the forward lowering of the defeated head and shoulders. It is usually seen only at the very moment when the ball enters the goalmouth, after which it gives way to other displays.

8 The Embrace Invitation

In this the players run towards one another with their arms stretched out sideways as far as they will go, signalling, 'I am about to embrace you.' This is done during the Scoring Sprint and sometimes there is an obvious conflict between inviting an embrace and raising the arms aloft, with the result that they point diagonally upward.

9 The Embrace

As the players meet, they fling their arms around one another and hug tightly in a full frontal embrace. While they do this other players start racing towards them.

10 The Multi-embrace

As more and more players cluster together, they do their best to add their embraces to the original one, throwing their arms around one another's shoulders and forming a dense clump.

11 The Frontal Leap-cling

A curious extension of the ordinary embrace occurs when the first player to reach the scorer leaps up at him and succeeds in embracing him, not only

with his arms, but also with his legs, clasping him like a small child leaping into its father's arms. Often this leads to the collapse of the scorer, who topples over on to the grass with his congratulator still clinging to him.

12 The Rear Leap-cling

Occasionally, the leap-cling is performed from behind, in which case the couple are likely to topple over backwards and come to rest on the ground in a confused heap.

13 The Horizontal Embrace

If the scorer has collapsed on the ground after striking home the goal, or if he has been flattened by his embracing team-mates, the hugging may continue on the grass and it is at this point that it does look remarkably like a sexual encounter. The embracers, however, remain quite oblivious of such accidental similarities. For a while their minds are almost blank and they feel no embarrassment. As one player recalls: 'I remember diving on our nearest man . . . and we rolled over on the ground together like madmen.' They may have *looked* like sexy lovers to the scornful, but to themselves they felt like madmen, released from all the cares and pressures of reality for a few brief moments.

14 The Gang-lift

The collapsed player may sometimes be lifted by his team-mates and then embraced as his body is dragged upwards. Again, this looks superficially erotic, almost as if a gang-bang is in progress, but once more the mood of the players is on a different plane altogether.

A goal-scorer and his nearest team-mate sometimes perform a *Leap-cling* celebration together (above). When this is frontal, the weight of the 'child' on the 'parent's' body is so great that the two players often topple over and continue their abandoned embrace on the grass of the pitch (right).

Many scorers quickly find themselves swamped by a growing cluster of embracing team-mates (opposite), all eager to share in the moment of glory. Despite the fact that this is a natural response to a moment of great emotional intensity, it has been criticized in some quarters as 'unmanly' behaviour.

15 The Kiss

To the amazed eyes of some elderly spectators, players sometimes crown their embraces with a kiss. This is not common, and when it does occur, the movement usually stops short of actual lip contact and becomes diverted into a pressing together of faces. Many players who approve of the expressive Triumph Display feel that perhaps kissing *is* going too far: 'I am not against the occasional cuddle, for it can be manly,' says one, 'but I must say that I am against kissing, which I feel is better left to the end of the game, and then preferably with the opposite sex.' Here the old intimacy taboo is breaking through again, with the kiss heavily loaded as a sexual action. However, the kiss, like the embrace, has a non-sexual origin. It stems from an ancient mother-offspring contact, when regurgitated food was passed mouth to mouth as a weaning device (in the centuries before the advent of commercial baby food). In this way the kiss acquired a loving quality that was pre-sexual. Male-to-male kissing as a non-sexual act of warm friendship still takes place in many cultures, but in the West the kiss has become so strongly loaded with erotic significance when performed between adults, that it remains a rarity even in the most abandoned clusters of displaying goal-scorers.

16 The Hair-ruffle

During the clusters it is extremely common to observe hair-ruffling of the kind normally seen between fathers and their sons. In less intense situations, where perhaps the scoring of a goal is of comparatively little importance (as when a losing team rises from 5–1 down to 5–2 down with no hope of winning the match), the hair-ruffle action may occur as the only sign of congratulation as the scorer walks back past his colleagues.

A collapsed goal-scorer may be raised up by his companions in a concerted *Gang-lift* operation, in order to facilitate embracing him (opposite, above). Other intimate actions of celebrating players include the *Hair-ruffle* (opposite, below) and the *Kiss* (above).

17 The Back Pat

Patting on the back is a similar, low-intensity action that may be seen as the only form of display, but it can also serve to augment the cluster embrace. Head-patting, another mock-fatherly action, is often added.

18 The Handshake

Even in these uninhibited times, the polite Victorian handshake has not been totally submerged and still appears occasionally as triumphant players pass one another during the reassembly for the restarting of the game. Its most common use today, however, is as a formality between a player who is going off the field during the match and a substitute who is replacing him.

These, then, are the Triumph Displays of the Soccer Tribe. In their more extreme forms they have gone through three historical phases. First they were performed only by Latin players. Then they were taken up by others and became particularly intense. As a 'new fashion' they were overworked, with every goal being greeted with prolonged displays of body contact. During the 1970s, their intensity subsided slightly, so that they were reserved more and more for the goals that really mattered. Now one can see them at full strength in a vital match, or at a much lower intensity in a routine encounter. This third phase is the most genuine one, with the actions forming a true reflection of the mood of the players, rather than a blanket response to a new fad. Having passed through these initial stages and having overcome all the attacks and snide remarks, the Triumph Display is now almost certainly here to stay.

23 The Heroes in Defeat

POSTURES AND EXPRESSIONS, FRUSTRATION AND DESPAIR

There are three moments which all Tribal Heroes dread; the moment when the referee inflicts a severe punishment, such as a penalty kick or a sending-off; the moment when the opponents score a goal; and the moment when the final whistle blows to signal victory to the enemy. These are the times when defeat is either anticipated or has arrived. They are occasions when a great wave of dejection passes through the punished or losing team. As with the triumphant players, this special mood carries with it a set of specific postures and actions.

In many respects these actions are the opposite of those of the happy opponents, especially in the seconds following the scoring of a vital goal. The scorers are moving fast – the defeated are stationary or slow-moving; the scorers are leaping and jumping – the defeated are slumped; the scorers are noisy and their faces full of expression – the defeated are silent and deadpan. The contrast is striking and highly predictable.

Closely related to the postures of dejection are those of exasperation. When a striker narrowly misses an all-important goal, he feels it like a miniature defeat. Although in reality it is a 'failed success', which is different from a direct defeat, he reacts to it with similar emotions of frustration and despair. The result is that the actions he performs in his moment of torment are akin to those seen when he suffers the agony of enemy conquest.

Here is a brief classification of the twelve most commonly observed reactions to defeat:

1 The Outrage Display

When there is an element of doubt about the validity of the referee's decision to award a penalty or a goal, the suffering side may risk his wrath by disputing it. With faces full of outrage, anger or dismay, they confront him and argue their case. All this is to no avail, with one possible exception. The referee

The *Outrage Display* is performed when players cannot accept the referee's decision (below, left); the *Frustration Face* is seen when a seemingly certain goal is miraculously saved by the enemy keeper (above). The *Head Clamp* or 'blinkers posture' (below) that often follows the Frustration Face is a way of shutting out the horror of the outside world.

himself cannot change his mind, if only because he must be seen to be unwavering in his decisions, but if they can persuade him to consult one of his linesmen, there is still a ray of hope. If the linesman has spotted an offside or some other infringement hidden from the referee, there is a slender chance that perhaps he will make a correction and, in effect, overrule himself. So the outrage display is not entirely a waste of time. But it has to be performed with some degree of restraint, or the referee himself will react angrily and book the protesting players for dissent.

Once it is clear that he is unmoved, the Outrage Display disintegrates rapidly into gestures of disbelief and implications of insanity. Anger gives way to exaggerated shrugs, the melodramatic wringing of hands, and much head-wagging and temple-tapping, indicating that the unhappy players are convinced either that the gods have deserted them, or that the world has gone mad.

2 The Frustration Face
The striker who is forced to watch as his brilliant shot at goal is miraculously saved by the keeper, or who makes a tantalizing near-miss with the ball skimming just outside the woodwork, adopts a special posture of frustration. With his arms outstretched or his fists clenched, he throws back his head as if appealing to the heavens. His face is contorted with a silent scream, his mouth wide open and his eyes closed, as he expresses to the crowd that his own disappointment is as acute as theirs.

3 The Forehead Clasp
The frustrated striker, with his head still tilted to the heavens, may then add another element to his display – the clasping of his forehead with both palms. This is one of several common hand-to-head actions used by distraught players and has a double function. It acts both as 'cut-off' and self-comfort. The position of the hands blocks off the man's vision and shields his eyes from the horror before him. Cut-off of this type is widely employed in many forms of unpleasant encounter and helps to damp down the visual input,

making the situation slightly easier to bear. The self-comforting element comes from the contact of the hands with the head. This is a form of auto-contact, a widespread device used when the individual feels in need of a reassuring embrace, but has no one immediately available to offer one.

4 The Hair Clasp
This is similar to the Forehead Clasp, but without the cut-off element. The hands come up to the back of the head, where they press tightly against the hair, while the eyes continue to study the scene in front. Again, this acts as a self-comforting contact.

5 The Neck Clasp
Another variant, in which the palms of the hands hold the sides of the neck. For the performer it gives the ghost-impression that someone else has rushed up and embraced him in a comforting way.

6 The Head Clamp
This is a 'blinkers posture' in which the forearms are almost wrapped around the face to cut off the scene of disaster, while the hands are clasped around the back of the head. It makes the player look like a horse wearing an outsize pair of blinkers.

7 The Face Cover
This is the ultimate in cut-off and self-comfort. The player stands with both palms pressed tightly to the face, the fingers pointing upwards. It not only switches off the visual input and provides a comforting auto-contact, but it also obliterates all facial expressions.

8 The Head Down
The simple lowering of the head, with a downward-directed gaze, is part of the general slumping of the body that accompanies defeat. While the triumphant team cavort head-high, the defeated players display the opposite posture. This Head Down makes them look smaller, which mirrors the way they would express their mood verbally, if asked about their feelings at the time.

9 The Arms Akimbo

One of the most common postures of defeat, the Arms Akimbo, is essentially an anti-social gesture. The hands are placed on the hips and the elbows jut out sideways, like pointed barriers fending off anyone who might come too close. The elbows are, in effect, saying 'keep away'. As the goal-scorers embrace one another, the goal-losers use the Arms Akimbo display as a kind of 'anti-embrace', again transmitting body signals that are the opposite of their successful colleagues'. Once this particular action has been identified as a posture of defeat, it is amazing how many times it can be observed. It is so widespread and automatic that almost every goal produces a sudden rash of Akimbos in the defeated side, with at least half of the team standing in this characteristic posture while their opponents' wild celebrations burn themselves out.

10 The Body Collapse

After the final victory has been awarded to the other side, the energy of the losers instantly evaporates and many of them collapse on to the turf. They remain there, slumped, crouched or prostrate, for some moments before disconsolately dragging themselves up and away. This extreme form of reaction, however, only occurs at the end of a vitally important match – a promotion or relegation struggle, or a major final, when the players have given their all, after a particularly tense build-up that has left them utterly exhausted. The pressure is often so great on such occasions that even the victors sometimes find themselves incapable of jumping for joy in the usual manner. They, too, may collapse briefly on to the grass in postures almost identical with those of the losers, but there are usually slight differences in body language that distinguish the two groups. The collapsed winners are often in positions more reminiscent of attitudes of prayer and thanksgiving than of total disintegration.

11 The Brave Face

In contests such as cup finals, where the members of the defeated team are expected to parade past their fans, to offer them a wave of thanks for their support, many contradictory body signals can be seen. The players attempt to put a Brave Face on their defeat, trying to convert it psychologically into a near-triumph. They offer a valiant hail of the arm or a defiant thumbs-up gesture as they walk past, but these actions are contradicted by the desperate disappointment in their eyes and the weakness of their forced smiles.

12 The Weeping Face

The final display of utter despondency is open weeping. Although this may erupt before the players reach the privacy of the tunnel and the dressing room, it is more commonly hidden from the gaze of the crowd because it is considered unmanly. Despite this, it is surprising how often the Tribal Heroes do give way to crying when a great victory has been snatched from their grasp. This reflects no softness, merely the incredible intensity with which they face their greatest encounters.

Steve Heighway describes his feelings at one of Liverpool's rare cup defeats: 'Of course, we went up for our losers' medals, and we tried to put on a show of bravado for the benefit of the Liverpool supporters. But ... back in the dressing room, I was choked, because I was one of the losers. I shed tears, bucketsful of them – but I kept a towel over my head and face, so that no one would see. I found out later that I wasn't the only one to cry.' This is the typical picture when weeping can no longer be controlled; by contrast, Pelé describes a much more public incident of a most unusual kind: 'We were playing in Dakar, in Senegal ... That particular day I was in rare form ... Twice in the first ten minutes ... I fooled the goalkeeper into getting out of position and dribbled the ball around him, rolling it into the net. Suddenly, after the second goal, I saw him raise his hand for the referee and I saw he was crying as if his heart would break ... the next thing I knew the goalkeeper had walked dispiritedly from the field, still crying uncontrollably, and a replacement had to be found before the game could continue.' During his long career, Pelé must have made many goalkeepers want to weep, but this was probably the only time that he, or any other striker, succeeded quite so dramatically.

When overcome by dejection, players adopt a *Heads Down* posture (above). This is so common that, in soccer slang, the phrase 'They've got their heads down' is always used to indicate that a team has lost its fighting spirit. (Soccerese for the opposite condition – high spirits – is 'They've got their tails up.')

At the end of a major contest such as a cup final, the defeated players often collapse on the turf (below left), their energy suddenly drained away. After a while, they may be able to force themselves to perform a lap of the field to applaud their loyal followers. When they do this, they try to put on a *Brave Face* (below), but even as they give a friendly thumbs-up gesture, the sadness of their crumpled expressions is impossible to conceal.

24 The Social Life of the Heroes

PASTIMES AND FAMILIES, GAMBLING AND SEX

If art, science and politics vanished from society tomorrow, the heroes of the Soccer Tribe would have little comment to make for the simple reason that they would hardly notice. Footwork is their art, strategy their science, and promotion their politics. They have few needs for any other form of expression. Almost to a man, they live totally inside the sphere of sport and view the outside world as if it were an alien domain. As manager Tommy Docherty put it: 'I talk a lot. On any subject. Which is always football.'

A great deal has been written about the shallowness of the soccer player's social life. A newspaper editorial recently commented that, 'Footballers off the field tend to have an existence more tedious than a 0–0 draw in Division Four.' The player's response would be that if their critics were engaged in an occupation as filled with tension, excitement and physical danger as professional soccer, they too would welcome a little 'tedium' in their personal lives. He might add that most men's *work* is so tedious that it is only natural for them to seek more active, stimulating pursuits in their spare time.

The main point about the player's profession is that it gives his ego a chance to enjoy itself in a virile, manly, risk-laden way every week. He proves himself publicly on the pitch and it takes so much out of him that he has little need to prove himself at other times. Like a tribal hunter or an ancient warrior, he can spend his off-duty hours in quiet relaxation and mild social amusements without feeling any lack of fulfilment. All his imagination and energy are reserved for the crucial contests on the field of play.

This said, how does he occupy himself? What are his likes and dislikes, his hobbies and entertainments? With a few notable exceptions, there is a remarkable uniformity in social lifestyle. A survey of a random group of top players reveals that, for almost all of them, the main interest outside soccer is watching or participating in other sports. The great favourite is golf. It is not too vigorous, lacks any danger of injury, and provides useful practice in

The professional footballer's main pastime is some other form of sport, always of a relaxing and non-violent kind, such as golf, tennis or snooker.

If players take a special interest in animals there is usually a competitive element involved. A few of the top players own racehorses; others keep racing pigeons.

'aiming skills'. Tennis is the next most popular, with squash a close third. Indoors, table-tennis, darts, snooker and pool are all widely enjoyed, but there is apparently an almost total lack of interest in the more physically violent sports, such as wrestling, boxing and the other forms of football, such as rugger. These seem to be too stimulating and, in some cases, much too close to home, to provide the necessary relaxation.

A second major preoccupation is gambling. When they are in the company of their team-mates, endless leisure hours are spent playing simple card games, such as brag. These games are always played for money, but the stakes are usually low. The fun is in the winning, not the taking of a friend's cash, which could quickly damage team relationships. The games are played in an atmosphere of great humour and back-slanging, noisily laced with roars of anger and peals of laughter. They help to pass the long hours of travelling endured by every professional team, on buses and coaches, in trains and hotel rooms.

Rather more serious is the business of betting on horses and dogs, and a

The main hate of professional players, who are forced to travel a great deal, is the boredom of long journeys. For many, the boredom is banished by endless games of cards and light-hearted gambling for small stakes.

few of the most successful players even own and race their own animals. In some cases the betting becomes obsessional and managers grow concerned when matters start to get out of hand, in case it interferes with the playing mood on match-days. One manager, however, used his team's betting activities to advantage, in a most unusual way. There happened to be a greyhound stadium right next to the soccer ground and on one Saturday afternoon all the home team players had placed a bet on one particular dog. The race was due to be run while the League match was in progress, and the manager arranged to have the result signalled to him from the greyhound stadium. The dog won at three to one, which was more than could be said for the home team, who were trailing by one to nil. On hearing the good news the manager sent a tic-tac signal out on to the pitch, telling his team of their luck, and within minutes they had turned their goal deficit into a two-one lead.

When they are not playing games or gambling, the Tribal Heroes spend a good deal of time at the cinema or watching television. Their general preference is for thrillers and action films. On television their main hates are soap-operas, political programmes and religious programmes, in that order. Their choice of favourite film actors and actresses is revealing. The male fantasy image is predictably the strong, silent, violent man of action. Interestingly, the favourite actresses are quiet blondes rather than the more fiery sex-symbols. Clearly there is a preference for a fantasy female who is more like the girl-next-door and less of a threat than the great sex-goddesses. The soccer star wants his ideal woman to be feminine, beautiful and fun-loving, but not too much of a challenge. He has enough challenges to face on the pitch and wants a more peaceful relationship in his sex life.

Tastes in music are limited largely to the pop and rock world. Reading is mainly restricted to sports biographies, soccer magazines, tabloid newspapers, detective fiction and thrillers. Only one of the top players admitted to reading comics. Interest in current affairs is zero. One man went so far as to say: 'The world could be coming to an end and I wouldn't know unless it was on the sports pages.'

Politically, one might expect the players' background to make them slightly left-wing, but this does not seem to be the case. In the early 1970s Hunter Davies quizzed the whole of the Tottenham Hotspur squad on their party affiliations and the results were: right-wing (Tory) – 9; left-wing (Labour) – 3; no interest in politics of any sort – 6. Even those who gave a positive answer often added, 'But I am not really interested.'

The favourite reading of the soccer player includes sports magazines, the sports pages of newspapers, sporting biographies and thrillers.

Many players' wives (below) conform to a particular type – blonde, attractive and very feminine. They create homes for their warrior-mates that are peaceful retreats from the violence and stress of the field of play.

Surprisingly, quite a number of players smoke, despite the fact that the modern game demands high athletic skills and endurance. Managers do not encourage smoking, but rarely try to stamp it out, recognizing its great therapeutic value as a means of reducing stress at moments of high tension.

Footballers make better than average family men and excellent parents, partly because, like soldiers at war, they value the quiet moments at home more than other men, and partly because, having fought hard on the field, they feel less need to throw their weight about when they return to their families at the end of the day.

The players' attitude to food is also rather conservative. Many of them enjoy eating out, but they prefer simple, ungarnished dishes, with steak and chicken as the top choices. Light beers are favourite drinks, but few players imbibe to excess. Surprisingly, quite a number of them are smokers, including some of the greatest names in soccer, a fact which might seem strange to athletes in other branches of sport. Managers are none too happy about this, but seldom apply strict rules, because they recognize the soothing value of a cigarette at moments of great tension and consider that this outweighs the health hazards in men who are so highly trained and in such a peak of condition.

Among the soccer stars' pet dislikes are the boring and frustrating aspects of travel, which they must face all too often. Also high on the list are household chores such as gardening and car-washing. The attitude to housework generally is massively chauvinistic and would horrify the feminist movement if they ever encountered it (which is unlikely, since an active feminist would be anathema to any soccer player). Goalkeeper Pat Jennings stated bluntly: 'I never help in the house. I couldn't change a nappy, I've never washed a dish. In Ireland, men don't do any housework. I just sit back in the house and I'm the boss, at least I like to think I am.' Other players admit to 'helping a bit' but claim they are no good at it. Whether this is the truth, or merely a public display of expected manliness, it is hard to say.

Certainly, the type of girl selected as a mate by the Tribal Hero fits the pattern one would predict. Typically, she is gentle but lively, pretty and often beautiful, feminine, domesticated and genuinely admires her man as much as she loves him. She is the warrior's girl, the hunter's wife, and together they make good, lasting marriages, rear their children with warmth

and pride, and enjoy a home life rather more satisfying than the average family of today. Again, the reason seems to be the enormous intensity of the drama of soccer that makes the contrasting relaxation and security of the home so highly valued. Just as soldiers away at war thought more longingly and lovingly about their families back home and of their greatly missed fireside peace, so the soccer sportsman feels warmly about his nest as he faces the weekly battle on the pitch.

But soccer sometimes takes its toll. The hours are unusual. The players are often at home at strange times and away playing or travelling when other men are at leisure. Christmas and Easter are often ruined by a heavy fixture list. And unless the wife is sympathetic to the world of soccer, she is liable to find the permanent obsession with it suffocating. This problem is best summed up by a heartfelt advertisement which appeared in an Argentinian newspaper: 'Husband wanted who understands nothing about football, has never heard of football and will swear, when married, never to utter a single word about football. I am the divorced wife of a footballer who is fed up to the teeth with football.'

One of the greatest disadvantages for a soccer wife is that she cannot share her husband's travel to exotic and faraway places. When he goes abroad to play, it is always with the strictly all-male group of the squad and managerial staff. So she misses the delights of wandering around foreign cities. Ironically, the players do too. But in their case it is through choice. The opportunities are there but the men seem strangely uninterested. Cocooned in their inner world of team life, they prefer to remain in their hotels playing cards, rather than set off exploring.

This lack of curiosity about local sight-seeing has provided some memorable comments. When an English team travelled to China for a soccer tour in the 1970s, they were offered an enviable chance to visit the Great Wall, undeniably one of the wonders of the world. Few bothered to accept. One who refused remarked: 'When you've seen one wall, you've seen them all;' another, who went, said: 'I've bent balls round better walls than that.' Fortunately for international peace and goodwill these comments were not translated.

England captain Bobby Moore recalls one of his squad 'being offered a free ticket to the top of the Empire State Building in New York. Later, when asked had he been and enjoyed it, he replied: "Oh yes. I stood at the bottom and looked up."' England international Nobby Stiles feels that the lack of sight-seeing curiosity is due to the fact that players prefer being with people to enjoying inanimate objects: 'I won't give the Mona Lisa a second glance if there is a gurgling baby in a pram I can look at instead.' He goes on to describe the way in which his team was taken on a special diversion when in Italy, so that they could see the famous Leaning Tower of Pisa: 'When we finally arrived there we were playing cards on the coach. Somebody said: "Oh look, the Tower." A perfunctory glance over our shoulder, and we were back to the nine-card brag without ever getting out of our seats.'

This attitude came as a great shock to Liverpool's Steve Heighway, one of the few top professionals with a university education. When he first joined the Liverpool squad he found his social encounters with his team-mates almost as daunting as his on-field clashes with his opponents. 'Socially he was a misfit,' reports a sports commentator. 'On trips abroad, when the cards came out, Heighway would disappear on sight-seeing missions, a sure sign to his colleagues that he was a stuck-up intellectual. On his return, they'd give him a withering look and ask if he wanted to be dealt in.'

Heighway was unhappy about being the odd man out and did his best to adapt. This is the 'gang' feature of team life that creates such uniformity of interests. If one player had an unusual private interest, he would feel uneasy about being 'different' from the gang, and being teased for it. So each

All-male team travel occasionally puts a strain on soccer marriages. When players tour abroad, their wives are left behind and are unable to share the excitement of visits to exotic and faraway places.

Liverpool player Steve Heighway, whose educational background set him apart from other players on social occasions until he learnt to adapt.

'Training Session' by Mike Francis, Nicholas Treadwell Gallery, London

Like most young warriors, players enjoy a fantasy idea of a curvaceous female partner and their lusting is captured in Mike Francis's somewhat surrealist 1975 painting called 'Training Session' – a scene not depicted in the FA coaching manual.

The professional footballer's body is so physically fit that his sexual performance is far above average, and unmarried players attract many beautiful girls. George Best claims to have bedded more than a thousand girls in his earlier years as a star player.

member of a squad tends to move slightly more towards its centre, as an adjustment to the group lifestyle. The motto might be: 'Something simple shared is better than something special solo.' With younger, unmarried players this may even extend to girls.

The Tribal Hero's attitude to sex involves the classic double standard. When he marries he is typically a loving husband who cares deeply about his wife. But before this, when he is single, he tends to treat girls like crude sex objects, to be bedded as quickly and as often as possible. Being young and in the peak of condition, he has strong physical appeal for the many groupies to be found on the fringes of the tribe. Drawn by the glamour of his public image, they offer the possibility of repeated sexual conquests and his obsession with 'scoring' soon takes on an additional meaning.

There seems to be remarkably little jealousy in these high-scoring sexual games. Groupies are often passed on from one player to the next without any squabbling, and after a while some girls have been known to take 'team photographs' of their assembled bed-mates. Such is the intimacy of team-members that they are even prepared to make love to their groupies while watched by their friends. Sometimes the girl in question has no objections and the onlookers are unconcealed, but George Best tells of occasions when they were carefully hidden from view. When his team was away on tour he and his friends used to 'try to organize a situation whereby I got a bird in bed and the rest watched from wardrobes or behind curtains or whatever'. On one occasion the manager suspected something was going on and the performance had to be cancelled: 'We'd charged 50p each for that and we had to refund the money. There was nothing dirty in it. It was just a big laugh for the lads. The girls never knew and I'd have screwed them in any case, so what's the difference?'

In Michael Parkinson's revealing biography of George Best, the player attacks the notion that sex-before-matches 'weakens you'. He claims to have played some of his best matches shortly after rising from a much-rumpled bed and would certainly not have approved of the strict routine of some continental clubs, where players are closeted in monastic seclusion for several days before an important game. His only complaint about the easy availability of sex was that, in the end, it became too much even for him: 'It got on my nerves. I'd open my bedroom curtains in the morning and there would be a line of young birds looking through the window . . . It was incredible. I never had to take them out to dinner or any of that crap. They'd ring me up or hang about in the boutique and straight upstairs . . . They used to fall over themselves to get into bed with me . . . I know that a lot of them just did it to say they had slept with George Best . . . just as they were going to climb into bed with me they'd say, "I hope you don't think I'm doing this just because you are George Best" . . . I didn't mind so long as I enjoyed myself.'

He claims to have enjoyed himself with more than a thousand of these willing girls and set the target for the aspiring young soccer star's lifestyle in the 1960s. Tragically the strain eventually proved too much for him – not the sexual strain, but the public exposure – and his career began to suffer. Critics said that his playboy existence was to blame, but he refutes this: 'Birds kept me sane . . . Whenever things got too tough . . . and I couldn't take all the limelight and wanted to get away I used to find myself a bird.'

Best is undoubtedly exceptional, both as a player and in his social life, but it remains true that all pleasure-seeking, off-duty soccer stars regard their spare hours mainly as time to be filled between fixtures and use it to prepare themselves both physically and mentally for the tensions and dangers that they must face on the vital match-days. By restricting themselves to the simpler pleasures of the flesh and the mind, the majority of them succeed in this remarkably well, even if, in the process, their private lives seem to some critics to be lacking in imagination and a sense of social involvement.

The Tribal
Trappings

25 The Ball

FROM BLOWN BLADDERS
TO BROWN LEATHER TO MULTI-COLOURS

The central focus of all the Soccer Tribe's activities is the ball. As a physical object, its main property is that it has *unbiased mobility*. Being an inflated sphere, it moves in any direction with equal responsiveness, its speed and flight-path determined solely by the way it is struck. This may sound obvious, and yet it is the very essence of the game of soccer. The ovoid ball used in rugger and American Football, and the flattened puck employed in ice hockey, for example, lack this quality. Their degree of mobility is biased by their non-spherical shape. In the case of rugger, this makes rapid kicking of the ball unpredictable; with ice hockey it reduces the range of play largely to one plane – the surface of the ice. The use of a spherical ball, by contrast, permits the development of a very high level of 'kicking skill'. The unbiased response of the sphere allows the kicker, rather like a juggler or acrobat, to refine his footwork to the point where he can control the flight and direction of the ball with immense precision. It is the degree of sensitivity attainable in the performance of these kicking actions that raises modern soccer from a crude knockabout game to the level of an art form.

The precision of the modern sport is, of course, dependent on the manufacture of high-quality footballs, standardized throughout the world. The player who has spent years practising his ball skills must be sure that, when he walks out on to a foreign playing field, perhaps thousands of miles from his home country, the ball he is about to kick is of exactly the same size, weight, texture, hardness and elasticity as those with which he has trained himself. This has not always been the case. In the earlier days of international soccer, different countries favoured different types of ball and many disputes arose, sometimes with dramatic results. On one occasion, back in the 1920s, when a European team was playing in South America, the visitors protested that the ball produced by the local authorities was too small and too heavy. They insisted that the game should be played with one of their own larger, lighter balls, two of which they had taken with them for practice purposes. Furious argument ensued and the start of the game was delayed for over half an hour. Eventually the South American hosts gave in and agreed to play with the European ball, much to the annoyance of the local spectators. An eye-witness reports what then occurred: 'The game had not been in progress many minutes before the ball was kicked among the spectators, who immediately whipped out their knives and stabbed the ball several times with a viciousness that seemed unnatural towards such an innocent thing as an English football. Another ball was produced, but one of the spectators walked off with it as soon as it went out of play. Eventually, in sheer desperation, the visitors agreed to play with the small ball of the local team.'

Even within Europe itself, arguments of this kind were still going on as late as the 1940s. In one international match, the larger ball was again insisted upon by the visiting team, but when they scored a goal with it, the home team's goalkeeper, according to one reporter, 'must have then employed some superb sleight of hand as he picked the ball out, for shortly afterwards the visiting players noticed that they were playing with the smaller ball, after all'.

Happily such disputes no longer occur, because of the strict standardization of all aspects of the game that has been enforced by the International Board set up by FIFA. The regulation-size ball is now always employed, according to the standards laid down in the official Laws of the Game. Law 2 is worded as follows: 'The ball shall be spherical; the outer casing shall be of

Referee Jack Taylor inspecting the balls to be used in the 1974 World Cup finals, ensuring that they weigh between 14 and 16 ounces (396–453 g.), as required by the Tribal Laws.

leather or other approved materials. No material shall be used in its construction which might prove dangerous to the players. The circumference of the ball at the start of the game shall not be more than 28 inches and not less than 27 inches. The weight of the ball at the start of the game shall not be more than 16 oz. nor less than 14 oz. The pressure shall be equal to 0·6–0·7 atmosphere, which equals 9·0–10·5 lb/sq. in. (600–700 gr/cm²) at sea level. The ball shall not be changed during the game unless authorized by the Referee.'

The International Board have added to this law a comment that 14–16 ounces is to be taken as 396–453 grammes, for international purposes.

These precise requirements for a professional football are made possible by the efficiency of modern manufacturing techniques, but such refinements have not always been available. The origins and subsequent evolution of the modern ball is an intriguing story.

The idea of a spherical ball that rolls easily when touched must have been available to prehistoric man, through the natural presence of certain spherical fruits and nuts, and smooth pebbles. It is inconceivable that prehistoric children failed to discover the play-potential of such objects for simple rolling and throwing games, but we have no evidence from early rock carvings or paintings that, during the prehistoric period, ball-games had any serious, adult role. We do know that Stone Age people manufactured well-shaped stone balls, and it has been suggested that a group of such balls found in an ancient temple in Malta were used in some sort of bowling game, but this is unlikely. It is more probable that they were employed for a mechanical purpose, as a primitive version of modern ball-bearings. Other stone spheres were used in ancient times as weapons or implements, and that was undoubtedly their dominant function, as far as our early ancestors were concerned.

The oldest playing balls in the world that have survived to the present day come from the civilization of ancient Egypt. Three of them are owned by the British Museum. They are red, green and yellow in colour and are made from linen stuffed with cut reed or straw. Clearly too delicate for rough play, they must have been used for simple rolling or catching games, probably played indoors as a casual pastime, rather than an organized, competitive sport.

Other civilizations developed similar kinds of balls for use in games, sometimes with a linen covering, sometimes with curved skins stitched

The oldest known balls in the world. Relics of ancient Egypt, these three stuffed linen balls now belong to the British Museum. Little is known of how they were used, but like most ancient balls they could not have withstood much rough treatment and were probably reserved for indoor games.

These two balls hanging in the bar of a Derbyshire hotel are made of painted leather stuffed with cork shavings. One is for use in the local Shrovetide Game on Shrove Tuesday and the other on the following day – Ash Wednesday.

together, and filled with a variety of substances, such as earth, grain, plant fibres, corn husks, hair or feathers. Objects of this type were suitable for throwing and catching games, but of little use for the more violent running and kicking sports. Inflated animal bladders provided a more mobile, bouncy ball, but again it was technically inefficient because it burst too easily when kicked hard. For this reason, competitive kicking games did not take on a significant role in ancient Greece or Rome, or in the earlier periods of European history. Even when the stage had been reached at which the outer casing could be efficiently stitched together from strong leather strips, the reliance on easily burst, inflated animal bladders for the inside of the ball made its bounciness too vulnerable to puncture. Medieval ball-games were therefore played with solid balls, usually a leather covering filled with cork shavings, or some such light material. This made them suitable for catch-and-throw-and-run games, such as the traditional Shrovetide Football, and it was out of this type of sport that modern rugger and its related forms evolved, with only a minor emphasis on accurate kicking.

It was not until the introduction of rubber to Europe that this technical problem was to be solved. The special qualities of rubber were first observed by Europeans during Columbus's second voyage to the Americas, when the local inhabitants were seen playing a game with balls 'made of the gum of a tree'. It was noted with interest that these balls were lighter and bounced better than those used in Europe at the time.

This game played with rubber balls was not a local fad or a child's pastime. It was a sport as important to the social life of the ancient American civilizations as soccer is today. Because of the local availability of rubber, to provide efficient, high-bouncing balls, a serious, competitive sport known as Tlachtli, or Pok-a-tok, had developed in Central America as long ago as 500 BC. What the European explorers witnessed was a ball-game with a 2,000-year history behind it, and a long tradition of savagely contested encounters. Almost every city in the world of the Aztecs and the Mayas had at least one sacred ball-court, where a violent game was played between two seven-man teams using a solid rubber ball about the size of a modern bowling ball. There were special terraces for the supporters of the two teams and huge sums of money were gambled on the outcome. There were hooligans and riots even in those days, and Montezuma, the last of the great Aztec emperors, once had to go out on to the field of play himself to break up a heated argument. On one occasion he even took part in a game as a player, against the chief of Texcoco, to resolve an argument. (For those interested in statistics, the final score was Montezuma 2, Texcoco 3.) It has often been claimed that the members of the losing team were slaughtered, as an early method of 'motivating the players', but this is an exaggeration. The assertion is based on one set of relief carvings showing the seven players of each team, with the captain of the winning team holding in his hand the decapitated head of the losing captain. But this was undoubtedly a representation of one particularly important match of special magical significance, and not a picture of the outcome of a typical, routine encounter.

This development of a major social sport in ancient America, with its huge stadia, terraces full of passionate supporters, elaborate organization, riots and gambling, and intense ritual significance, clearly took place as the direct result of the discovery by the local inhabitants of the magical, bouncing quality of the rubber-tree gum. The presence of this substance, and the efficient ball it could make available, led to the growth and prolonged success of a ball-game that is the closest parallel in history for the modern soccer phenomenon. It might be imagined that, as soon as rubber was discovered by the European explorers, the use of the bouncing ball would have spread rapidly, causing an immediate explosion of serious ball-games across the world. But that was not to be. It was several hundred years before rubber goods became commonly manufactured in Europe and the substance acquired an important status as a new technical commodity. Not until the nineteenth century did a Mr Macintosh discover a suitable solvent for the raw rubber, enabling him to make his famous waterproof 'macintoshes' and other products employing thin rubber sheets. This soon led to the development of inflatable rubber bladders of great strength. Because these could withstand heavy pressure, they were obviously ideal 'inner tubes' for leather footballs, and the very first ball that was *both kickable and bounceable* could be created. So it seems certain that, without the growth of rubber technology, the modern international sport of soccer would not have emerged in the way it did. And it is surely no accident that both this technology and the game of soccer sprang up together in the nineteenth century.

The heavy, brown-leather, rubber-inflated balls of early soccer were to remain largely unchanged for many decades. They were usually made from eighteen sections of tanned leather, arranged in six panels of three strips each. The sections, held inside out, were stitched together by hand with five-ply

Occasionally a particular ball becomes so famous that it is preserved in a sports museum, like this cup final ball of 1903. As with all earlier soccer balls it is made of heavy brown leather.

hemp, leaving a small lace-up slit on one side. Next, the whole sphere was reversed, to turn the outside out, and a collapsed rubber bladder inserted through the slit. The bladder was then inflated to the approved pressure and the slit in the leather laced up tight. One craftsman was able to turn out about forty balls a week using this method and, since they enjoyed a long life even with the heavy battering on the field, the world was soon being flooded with these new, standardized objects of play.

The main objection to this type of football was that, when players were heading back a powerfully driven ball, the action could be extremely painful if they happened to make contact with the ball's lacing. Also, on wet days, the ball grew unpleasantly heavy as the leather soaked up the water and became caked with mud. As time passed, research into improved balls provided answers to both these problems. A new type of inflation valve was invented that permitted a completely laceless ball, and the leather surface was protected by water-proofing substances so that it did not become unduly sodden in the rain.

In 1951 a white ball was permitted for the first time. Up to that point all footballs had been of traditional, dark brown leather. It was felt that a white ball would be easier for spectators to follow, and white has been the predominant colour ever since. An exception to this is the use of a red or orange ball during conditions of heavy snowfall.

In recent years there have been a number of fancy developments in ball decoration, not all of which have met with universal approval. The traditionalists feel that a simple, plain ball is preferable because any pattern that breaks up its shape reduces its visibility during high speed moments of the game. If there has to be a pattern, they say, then let it at least be symmetrical. This condition applies to the three most popular of the new-style balls: the Black Pentagonal/White Hexagonal Ball, the Multi-circle Ball, and the American Red-starred Ball. All three of these are based on a new type of panelling. The old-style design with its eighteen strip-panels is replaced by thirty-two smaller panels, alternately pentagonal and hexagonal in shape. The five-sided units are slightly smaller than the six-sided ones and, in the first of the three new-style balls, are painted black, contrasting with the pure white of the hexagons. The Multi-circle Ball, favoured in recent international matches, is also black and white, but in this case the pentagonal panels are made the centre of large white circles. In the American Red-starred Ball, used in NASL games, the hexagonal panels are white, while each pentagon is filled with a red, five-pointed star on a blue background.

Only one of the modern balls has adopted an asymmetrical pattern and that is the new English Football League Official Ball. Again, it is a thirty-two-panel ball, but in this instance a whole band of panels running right around the ball is bright red, while the rest of the surface is a contrasting pure white. When this type of ball is kicked into the air and spins round, the rapidly rotating red panel is dazzling to the eyes and it is this ball that players have objected to so strongly, much to the League's disappointment. When it was first introduced, the League officials requested that it should always be used when a League game was being televised, but many clubs have ignored this request and still prefer to play with a plain white ball. Manager Allan Clarke has put on record the general reaction: 'I don't like it. The red and white panels distract the players. They spin round like children's tops. We'll burn them or flog them or give them away.'

Nobody is complaining, however, about the quality of the craftsmanship and materials used in the latest balls. They are of a remarkably high standard and their surfaces are protected better than ever before by special polyurethane preparations which have eliminated water absorption by the leather, maintaining a perfect ball weight even in heavy rain. Some balls are

In snowy conditions today the white ball is replaced with a more conspicuous red or orange ball.

The six types of football in use today: the 18-strip-panel White Ball (above left); and, with 32 panels, the Pentagonal/Hexagonal White Ball (above right); the Black Pentagonal/White Hexagonal Ball (centre left); the Tango Multi-circle Ball (centre right); the North American Soccer League Red-starred Ball (below left); and the red-banded English Football League Official Ball (below right).

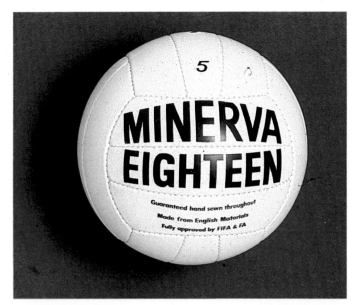

In ancient folk-football the ball was the prize to be carried home to one's *own* goal, not driven to the enemy goal. The 'goaler' was rewarded by being allowed to keep the ball – like these two successful contestants in the annual Shrovetide Game at Ashbourne in Derbyshire.

now made completely of synthetic, polyurethane materials which are highly resistant to cuts and scratches. They are footballs which the ancient Aztecs would be proud to think of as the modern descendants of their early rubber spheres.

Leaving the technicalities of the ball and turning to its symbolic role, different people have seen it in very different ways. The Aztecs apparently saw it as a symbol of the sun. This has been given as the explanation of why they were forbidden to touch it with their hands during their long and violent contests. The object of their game was to drive the ball through stone rings set high up on the side walls of the playing field, and the flight of the ball is claimed to represent the cycle of the sun through the heavens, the rings representing sunset and sunrise. After the match was over, the ball was ceremonially burnt. This interpretation sounds rather fanciful, but it has to be admitted that the ball-courts of ancient America were always built in the direction of the sun's movements through the sky – from east to west.

Another imaginative explanation of the origin of football, in other parts of the world, sees the ball as representing the severed head of a sacrificed animal. The two teams who fought for its possession were trying to carry it off to bury it on their land as a magical way of ensuring the fertility of their crops. Yet another story sees it as a symbolic version of an ancient game in which the decapitated head of a slain human enemy was kicked about by a savage crowd intent on inflicting a final humiliation on the fallen foe. This version comes from the town of Kingston-on-Thames in England, where Shrovetide Football was played annually to commemorate an ancient victory. A record dating from 1790 states: 'The captain of the Danish forces having been slain, and his head kicked about in derision, the custom of kicking a Foot Ball on the anniversary of that day has been observed ever since.'

In the Shrovetide Football still played annually at Ashbourne in Derbyshire, the object of the game is to carry the ball to *one's own goal* (an old mill-wheel) and touch it on to the goal three times. That act not only ends the game, but also makes the goal-scorer the proud owner of that year's special ball. The symbolism of the ball in these earlier games is clearly quite different from the modern sport of soccer. In the medieval game, the ball was the prize to be fought for and carried off. In the modern soccer game, it is a missile to be aimed at the enemy goal. In the first, it is the symbolic prey to be carried home in triumph by the pseudo-hunter. In the second, it is his killing weapon.

This change in the role of the ball has made modern soccer into an essentially attacking game, in which the goalmouth is repeatedly assaulted by the enemy, rather than one in which the ball is a protected thing, to be defended against the enemy who are seeking to steal it for themselves.

For some, these symbolic interpretations are of minor significance. They see the modern game as an abstract contest of human physical skills, rather like a vast chess game, with the addition of the ball as a 'wild piece'. The French writer Jean Giraudoux sums up this view in the following words: 'Football is the king of games . . . All the great games of man are games with a ball . . . In our life, the ball is that thing which most easily escapes from the laws of life. This is its most useful quality. It has, on earth, the extra-terrestrial quality of some force which has not been fully tamed. It is in no way related to the concept of the animal being, which is that of constriction . . . Football owes its universality to the fact that it can give the ball its maximum effect . . . Beyond its own principle, that of resilience, of independence, the team imparts to the ball the motor of eleven shrewd minds and eleven imaginations. If the hands have been barred from the game, it is because their intrusion would make the ball no longer a ball, the player no longer a player. The hands are cheats . . . The ball will not permit any cheating, but only effects which are sublime.'

26 The Costumes

SHIRTS, SHORTS, SHOES, STUDS AND SHINPADS

The costumes in which players do battle have changed a great deal since the early days of the game. Their development is a story of conflict between protection against climate and skin damage, on the one hand, and freedom of limb movement, on the other. It has been a one-sided contest, with athletic freedom of movement becoming more and more dominant.

Looking back at the earliest pictures of nineteenth-century players, the degree of 'cover-up' is striking. The finalists in the first-ever cup final in 1872 took to the field wearing heavy boots, thick woollen stockings, three-quarter-length trousers that reached down over the stockings or were tucked into them, heavy woollen long-sleeved jerseys, and clinging, fisherman-style hats, or short-peaked caps. Protected in this way, they played out a game in which not even the smallest patch of bare leg was exposed to the elements, or to scratches and cuts inflicted by their opponents.

In these early matches, heavy cricket-style pads were often worn, strapped to the whole of the front of the lower leg. Such protective clothing clearly had the effect of slowing down the players, but soccer in the nineteenth century was a much slower, more ponderous game than it is today. As it began to speed up, items of clothing that hampered free movement of the body had to go. Except for goalkeepers, the hats and caps had to be discarded. They remain today in only two contexts – for the keepers when there is bright sunlight shining in their eyes, and as a relic form of clothing traditionally awarded to players who achieve the status of National Team members. To play for your country is to be 'capped' and to receive a peaked cap as a memento – one which will never be worn, but which is carefully stored away as part of a star performer's treasured souvenirs. In this award, we are seeing the fossilized remains of the most ancient form of soccer apparel.

As play grew more agile, the costumes became gradually lighter in weight and started, as it were, to shrink. The sleeves of the jerseys became shorter and the trouser hems rose from the calf to just above the knee. Bare knees were now exposed to cold and damage, but were able to enjoy much easier movement during the fast moments of play. The cumbersome leg-pads, originally strapped on top of the stockings, were also reduced in size and tucked down inside. But the boots, if anything, became stouter and heavier.

Although shorter, the trousers were still cut rather tight on to the leg and this was the next tradition to be broken. Despite the fact that it increased the draughtiness, they were restyled to make them looser and baggier. The thigh

What the well-dressed footballer was wearing in 1901 – from beltless knickers and flannelette shirt to Shurekik boots and shin-guards.

England Captain Bobby Moore celebrates the award of his 100th cap. His first 99 caps – one for each of his previous international appearances – are displayed on the heads of young fans from a school in West Ham.

The evolution of soccer shorts is a story of progressive reduction in length. (left to right) The full-length trousers of the earliest days (re-created here in 1972); the long shorts of the turn of the century, exposing the knees; the baggy shorts of the mid-twentieth century; the short shorts of the late twentieth century; and the latest trend – hem-nicked shorts, a style borrowed from the athletic field.

muscles may have been colder, but they now, like the knees, had greater ease of movement. These shorts were still very long by modern standards, however, coming down almost to the knees. This was the typical form of costume for the soccer player during the first half of the twentieth century. The hem of the shorts may have crept an inch or two higher as the years passed, but basically the 'baggy shorts and heavy boots' style remained the dominant costume theme, right up until the Second World War.

It was in the post-war period that the next major change was to occur, largely due to the dramatic increase in international fixtures made possible by greatly improved air travel. Players from the traditional home of soccer, in the cold countries of Northern Europe, began to encounter a new and exciting breed of player from the warmer climes of the Mediterranean and South America. These men experienced a climatic problem that was the exact opposite of the northerners'. During fast play they suffered from overheating and rarely had to endure the biting cold that had kept the northern players so heavily swathed in the earlier days of the sport. Their solution had been to encourage an even greater shrinkage of the soccer costumes. They favoured exaggeratedly short shorts, very light-weight materials, short sleeves and light, flexible boots that were little more than studded track-shoes. In other words, they dressed for soccer as the athletes they were. When these scantily clad figures first appeared on northern pitches, they produced mild astonishment. The rugged northerners viewed their prancing, skin-exposed bodies as soft and 'pansy'. But the quality of their play soon changed this attitude. Their skill and speed were undeniable and before long the tables were turned. Now it was the northerners whose costumes looked silly, with their baggy, billowing shorts suddenly clumsy and old-fashioned. In no time at all, they were being shortened, and shortened, until finally they too became the mini-shorts that the whole of soccer now takes for granted as standard apparel. And the heavy, old boots all vanished as well, confined for ever to the glass cases of museums.

Shirt designs still vary, some clubs preferring simple round-neck designs, while others insist on V-necks with or without collars and token buttons. The sleeves may be long or short.

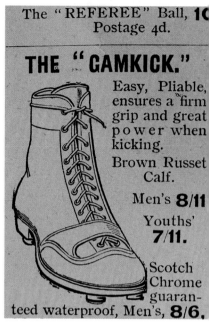

Certain teams from hot countries – like this one from Africa's Gold Coast – prefer to play soccer barefoot (opposite, above left). By contrast, the earliest English footballers wore tall, ankle-hugging boots (opposite, above right). These decreased in size as the years passed. Stanley Matthews's much smaller boots (above) were typical of mid-twentieth-century soccer. Modern designs and materials have since been introduced (above right) converting the earlier boot into little more than a modified track-shoe.

On freezing days (left), players sometimes resort to 'ballet tights' and gloves to protect the circulation.

Shin-pads also grew smaller and many players discarded them altogether, preferring to play the later stages of games with their socks rolled down, defying shin damage in order to gain extra freedom.

In the coldest months of winter, in the north of Europe, this new athletic style of soccer clothing does sometimes cause problems that the old-style kit avoided. Leg muscles can become severely chilled during the less active periods of play and a few individuals have made a quiet, almost secretive return to the full-leg coverings of yesterday. This has been achieved by the wearing of an almost invisible form of tights, similar to those worn by ballet dancers. Their use is still rare, however, because of their susceptibility to ridicule from the crowd and from other players, but for lonely forwards who must often stand around on icy pitches while the play is concentrated near their own goalmouth, they make a great deal of sense.

For goalkeepers the problem is even more acute. If their team happens to be dominating play for much of the match, they are required to stand frozen between their goalposts for long periods of time. If the opposing team suddenly breaks away and comes tearing down-field to strike at goal, the shivering keeper must somehow activate his icy limbs to make an accurate save. In dead of winter, many goalkeepers give up the struggle and return to the ancient costume of full-length leg-covering, putting on a thick jersey and track-suit bottoms. Some also wear heavy gloves with surfaces that give improved grip and which, at the same time, help to increase the circulation in their fingers.

Since the demise of the baggy shorts in the mid-twentieth century, and the global adoption of light-weight playing kit with abbreviated shorts, there has been little change apart from the introduction of new and shinier fabrics that display the team colours more intensely to the dedicated supporters. Only details have been altered. Experiments have been made with various necklines, some round, some V-shaped, some with collars and some without. Different teams prefer different shirt styles and there seems to be no clear answer as to which is the most efficient garment for the increasingly athletic mode of play. The argument for short sleeves versus long sleeves also seems to be unsettled and sometimes both alternatives are seen within one team.

The latest detail to have undergone a change is the shape of the hemline of the shorts. This is another trend borrowed from the world of athletics, where in recent years a cutaway hem has been introduced. The new fashion is intended to improve ease of leg movement during fast running and many soccer teams can now be seen wearing athletic shorts of this type, with an upward nick in the hemline in the region of the outer thigh. This is about as far as the long process of soccer costume-shrinkage can go. The players are now as lightly clad as is possible for their role as football gymnasts and, short of a dramatic alteration in the style of play, it is unlikely that we will see any further changes for many years to come.

When representing their teams, modern footballers tend to wear immaculate non-playing clothes, usually plain suits or blazers. This is done largely to satisfy the pseudo-military demands of their managers, and if the smartness rule is ignored even famous players are liable to be fined for being 'scruffily dressed'.

27 The Colours

THE DISTRIBUTION OF TRIBAL COLOURS

At first glance, the bright colours worn by the Tribal Heroes appear to be decorative, but this is misleading. They make an attractive picture, swirling about in a changing pattern above the green of the turf, but visual appeal is not their primary function.

In reality, they are vital tribal signals. Like the display colours of many animals and flowers, they carry important messages about their 'owners'. This function restricts their variety. There are no teams, for example, playing in shirts covered in large pink spots over a background of purple spirals. Nor are there clubs that send their heroes out on to the field wearing grey and brown stripes. What at first appears to be a wild cacophony of dazzling colours and patterns, proves on closer examination to be a strictly limited range of styles.

A survey of the top teams of England, Scotland, France and Italy reveals

The frequency of the different shirt colours in the top clubs of England, Scotland, France and Italy. Red, blue and white are the most popular. (A red-and-white or red-and-black shirt is classed as red here, blue-and-white as blue, etc. This is because in such cases the bright colour would be the one the officials would consider when deciding whether there was a colour clash requiring a change strip. Only where there are two equally powerful colours present, such as red-and-green, are the shirts classified here as fully 'bi-coloured'.)

DOMINANT SHIRT COLOUR	ENGLAND %	SCOTLAND %	FRANCE %	ITALY %
Red	26	11	30	42
Blue	29	29	15	17
White	22	13	20	8
Yellow	5	5	10	3
Orange	2	5	5	3
Amber	4	8	0	3
Sky (pale) Blue	2	3	5	6
Claret	3	0	0	0
Pale Violet	0	0	0	3
Maroon	0	8	0	0
Green	1	5	5	3
Black/White	3	11	5	6
Red/Blue	0	0	5	3
Red/Green	0	0	0	3
Red/Yellow	0	3	0	0
Blue/Yellow	1	0	0	0

The 92 English League clubs
arranged according to their colours

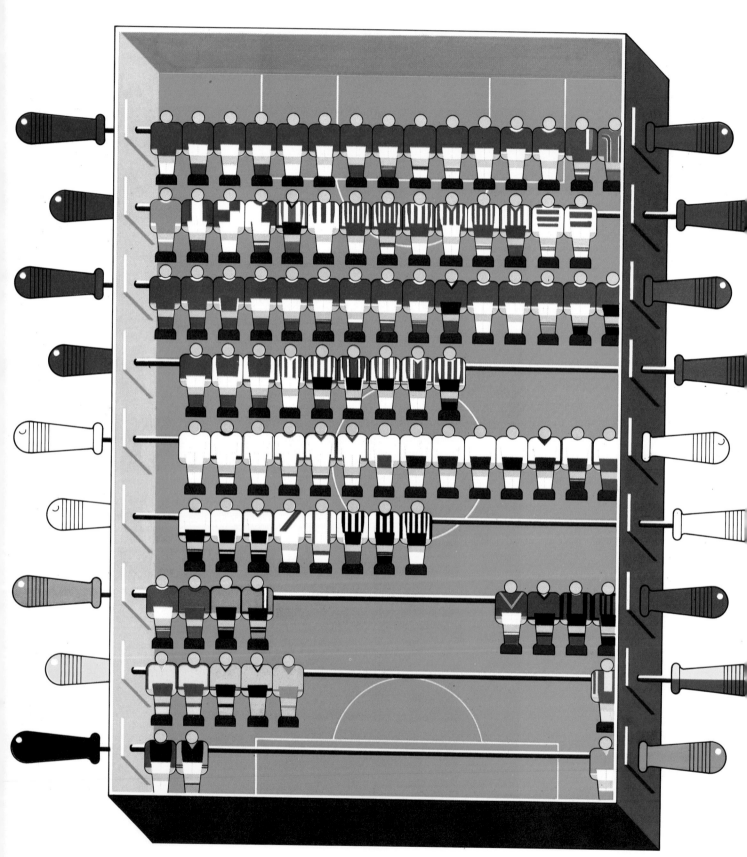

that, in all four cases, the most popular shirt pattern is one in which a single colour predominates. (The shorts and stockings usually echo this colour, or contrast with it in plain black or white.) The most popular colour in England and Scotland is *blue*. In France and Italy it is *red*. The second favourite in England is *red*; in Italy *blue*; and in Scotland and France *white*.

After red, blue and white, the next most favoured colours are the yellows and oranges, although these are nowhere particularly common. Rarely used colours include green, claret, pale sky blue, maroon and violet. Pinks, greys, browns and blacks are virtually non-existent.

The most popular shirt pattern, apart from a single dominant colour, is bold, vertical striping. Horizontal bands of colour, referred to as hoops, are also moderately popular in some regions, although they seem to be completely absent in certain continental countries. Other patterns seen include a broad diagonal sash, or a vertical sash down the left-hand side of the body. 'Quartered' and 'halved' shirt patterns are among the rare forms.

Why do these colours and patterns predominate? Why are there no flowered patterns, spots, blobs, curves or spirals of colour on the heroes' shirts? Why are there no multi-coloured shirts in bold, abstract patterns? To answer these questions it is necessary to analyse the basic functions of the Tribal Colours. They operate as visual signals in the following way:

1 They must make the wearers look *conspicuous*.
This eliminates all the dull browns and greys and the pale, delicate or washed-out pastel shades. It also rules out any broken or patchy colour arrangements, as these would tend to camouflage the players. Even certain bright colours or bold patterns are unsuitable in the context of the soccer match, because of special features of the game. The presence of a large round ball means that strong circular motifs are taboo. There are no large spots or circles to be seen on any soccer shirts (although they are common enough on the tunics of jockeys, in the horse-racing world). The fact that soccer is always viewed against the green background of the turf means that even the

Colour rarities of the soccer world: the purple of Anderlecht's fans, and the dark brown of Coventry's change strip.

Although most clubs wear plain colours, some prefer a patterned costume. The designs are nearly always simple, the most common being a set of vertical stripes. The chart shows a variety of patterns in use today.

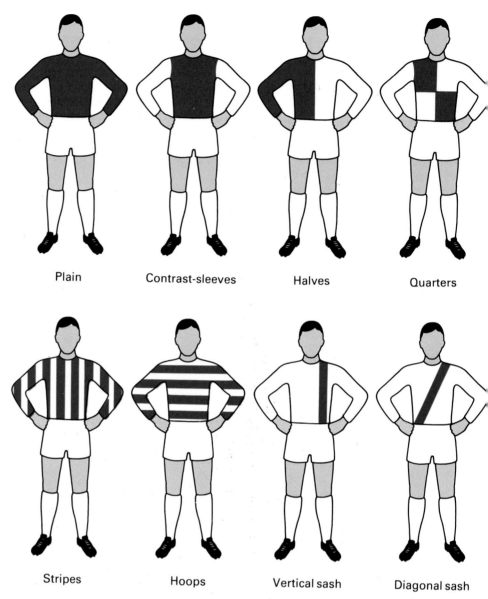

Plain   Contrast-sleeves   Halves   Quarters

Stripes   Hoops   Vertical sash   Diagonal sash

The dominant shirt patterns of the top clubs in England, Scotland, France and Italy

Dominant shirt pattern	Eng. %	Sc. %	Fr. %	It. %
Plain	64	55	70	61
Stripes	24	11	15	22
Hoops	2	16	0	0
Vertical sash (on left side)	2	8	5	8
Vertical sash (on right side)	0	3	0	0
Diagonal sash	1	0	5	3
Large V	2	3	5	0
Paired lines (vertical)	2	5	0	0
Quarters	1	0	0	6
Halves	1	0	0	0

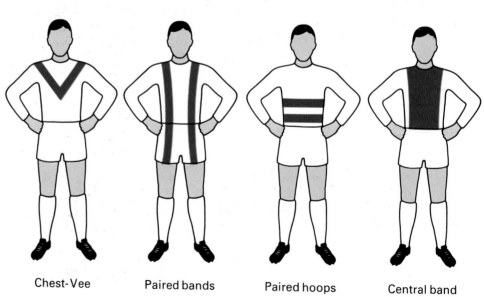

Chest-Vee   Paired bands   Paired hoops   Central band

The rare blue-and-red pattern seen above, with its single chest-bar, is probably uncommon because the horizontal band of colour is too reminiscent of the top of a bikini, when viewed at a distance.

brightest green costumes are in danger of becoming inconspicuous as the players race about across the field. As a result, green is the rarest of the 'bold' colours.

The most important requirement here is that the colours, especially the shirt colours, should make the players as conspicuous as possible *at a distance*. At close quarters there is no problem. Even a mud-caked costume is visible enough when only a few feet away. But when a player is making a long-distance pass to a team-mate, he needs to be able to catch sight of him, often out of the corner of his eye, in a split second, and it is then that a bright, bold, simple splash of colour will be the best guide. For this purpose, a pure red is the most valuable of all colours.

2 They must make their wearers look *different from their opponents*.
Both for the players and the spectators, it is vital that there should be maximum contrast between the colours of the two teams. There are two ways of achieving this. In the world of horse-racing, every owner has a unique set of colours for his jockeys. This demands rather elaborate combinations of hues and designs, to avoid confusion. But there is no alternative because every jockey is competing with every other jockey. There are no teams. In soccer, it is only necessary to contrast with one rival colour-pattern at a time. This means that if each team always wears its own colours on its home ground, but has a second colour (called a 'change strip') available to be worn at away matches, there is no problem. Many away matches will not, in any case, necessitate a change from the home colours, but where there is a clash, the change strip can come to the rescue.

For psychological reasons, players prefer to appear in their home colours and are usually unhappy when they have to switch to their second colours at away matches. Their travelling fans – often sporting the home colours in the shape of flags and scarves – also prefer to see their heroes in their more familiar costumes. So there is some pressure to avoid making too many changes. This has the effect of keeping the design of the costumes as simple as possible. If, for instance, a particular club had a bold red, yellow and blue shirt, it would mean that officials would demand a switch to a change strip at all away matches where the home teams were predominantly red, yellow *or* blue. This would cover the majority of rival teams and would require the club to play in its change strip at almost every away game. If, by contrast, the home costume had only a single, dominant colour, say, red, then there would only be a need for change when visiting 'red clubs'. This is why simple, predominantly one-colour costumes are the most popular, and is another reason why complex and elaborate colour schemes are so extremely rare. The advantages of having a unique, globally identifiable costume are outweighed by the desire to keep the home colours flying at as many away matches as possible.

3 They must make their wearers look *different from their near neighbours*.
Wherever a big city has two major soccer clubs, there has to be a major colour contrast, for territorial reasons. The followers of the two clubs wish to be able to distinguish themselves from one another and it is particularly important that, at the annual 'local derby', when the rival local sides meet, each should be wearing their home colours. So it is that Manchester United are red and Manchester City are blue; Liverpool are red and Everton are blue; Nottingham Forest are red and Notts County are black and white; Bristol City are red and Bristol Rovers are blue and white; Dundee are blue and Dundee United are orange. With the largest of cities this becomes something of a problem. In London, there are no fewer than twelve professional League clubs, and this stretches local colour-contrasts to the maximum. The London solution is as follows:

Dominant Colour	London Club	Shirts	Shorts	Socks
RED	1 Arsenal	red with white sleeves	white	red
	2 Charlton	all-red	white	red
	3 Brentford	red and white stripes	black	black
BLUE	4 Chelsea	all-blue	blue	white
	5 QPR	blue and white hoops	white	white
	6 Millwall	all-blue	white	blue
WHITE	7 Spurs	all-white	blue	white
	8 Fulham	all-white	black	white
	9 Orient	white with two red lines	white with two red lines	white
	10 Palace	white with blue/red sash	white	white
CLARET	11 West Ham	claret with blue sleeves	white	white
YELLOW	12 Watford	yellow with black/red sleeve-stripe	black	black

Looking at this list it is clear that, apart from West Ham and Watford, there has been no rush to strange colours to avoid clashes in the densely populated London region. Instead, the three top favourites – red, blue and white – have remained popular. The confusion this could cause has been lessened by two factors. First, there has been a great deal of minor variation added to the basic shirt colour – different coloured shorts or socks, or the use of shirt patterns with stripes, hoops and sashes. Second, there has been a 'class distinction', with top clubs more or less ignoring the colours of lowly clubs which they are seldom likely to meet. For instance, the four London clubs most often found in the First Division (sometimes with a brief slide down into the Second Division) are Arsenal, Spurs, Chelsea and West Ham. Between these four there is no colour clash, since they are respectively red, white, blue and claret. The four clubs most often found in the lower divisions are Brentford, Orient, Millwall and Watford. Again, there is no colour clash between these four because they are respectively red, white, blue and yellow. So even in club-crowded London a colour contrast system is operating, although at first sight it appears to be absent.

4 They must give their wearers a *psychological advantage*.
Highly conspicuous colours are not merely easy to see when passing a ball to a team-mate, they are also intimidating to the enemy. At the unconscious level they send messages saying, 'I am fearless – I am not frightened to show myself.' The brighter the colour, the fiercer seems its wearer. In this respect footballers are rather like dangerous animals. Any species of animal that possesses a special defensive weapon, such as the snake with its venom, the wasp with its sting or the skunk with its sickening smell, needs to advertise the fact to its potential enemies. It does this by wearing a 'warning coloration' of some kind, one to which the enemies will react quickly, as soon as they see it. Poisonous snakes often have bright bands of orange and black; wasps are sharply marked in yellow and black; skunks are striped in black and white. Nearly all the poisonous or dangerous animals announce their presence with warning colours and it is surprising how often these make them look as

The bold, simple, conspicuous colour-patterns of footballers are very similar to the warning display colours of certain poisonous animals. This has the effect of making the men seem threatening and 'dangerous'.

though they are wearing a football jersey. The parallels are striking, especially with the striped and banded patterns. The advantage of wearing contrasting patches of colour is that the contrast-lines remain, no matter how the background changes. And this applies to animals and footballers alike.

It may well be that 'venomous' colour patterns of this type give the wearers' enemies an unconscious sensation that they may be 'stung' or 'poisoned' by too-close contact. Even if this psychological advantage operates at a very low level, it is still not to be ignored. The players themselves may laugh at such a suggestion, but it is hard to be certain of the impact of different colours when worn by a body that is hurtling towards you. There is a strong chance that, if the body is clad in vividly bold and contrasting colours, like a giant stinging insect, it will be more threatening than if it is adorned in baby blue or some soft pastel shade.

Given this thought, it might seem logical to expect a predominance of reds, yellows and oranges among the Tribal Colours, instead of the reds, blues and whites. Blue, even dark blue, seems to be lacking in fierceness for such a popular colour. And white seems too washed out and colourless. The yellows and oranges, on the other hand, are so popular among dangerous animals that it is puzzling not to find them in greater numbers. What is the explanation for these differences?

It seems as if there are other, special psychological associations at work, which come into conflict with the simple display value of the colours. Yellow, although it is the cheerful, radiant, optimistic colour of sun and sand, is also a colour associated with cowardice – the yellow streak. The phrase 'he's yellow' is so well known and widely used as an insult that this association has probably been one of the main factors working against the popularity of this colour. The colour orange might seem to escape this damaging label, but it suffers from another drawback. It is an intermediate colour – halfway between yellow and red. All intermediate colours fare badly in the Soccer Tribe, as do all pale versions of strong colours (such as pale blue, soft pink, etc.). It seems that an intermediate colour has the psychological disadvantage of 'indecision'. It cannot make up its mind, as it were, where it stands. Is orange a yellowish red, or a reddish yellow? This destroys the sharpness of its image and, as a result, reduces it to a comparatively rare Tribal Colour.

Looking at the popular colours, red is easy to understand. It is the most conspicuous of all colours, especially at a distance, and it has a powerful symbolic impact as the colour of blood, energy, life, force, power and intensity. It is the perfect colour for any sporting team and it is difficult to understand why, in some countries, it is not even more popular than it already is.

The great popularity of blue is harder to explain. In many ways it is the opposite of red, being the colour of peace, calm, harmony and loyalty. Perhaps its secret lies in the direction of its message. Perhaps its greatest attraction is the comforting signals it sends out from one team-mate to another, rather than the message of violence transmitted by bright red costumes towards the enemy. If this is so, it would make up for its lack of fierceness in attack by having a calming, confidence-building effect within the ranks of the team wearing it.

White is another colour (or rather, to be technically accurate, a *lack* of colour) the popularity of which is hard to understand. Symbolically, white is the colour of death and fear, ice and snow and cold, purity and innocence – hardly the associations most needed on the sports field. In addition, it quickly soils and looks grubby during a match. And yet white is one of the three most favoured colours. The only explanation for its popularity (apart from its general conspicuousness) is that it does have one other symbolic 'label', namely that of the hero. At the time when many clubs were becoming established, at the end of the nineteenth century or the beginning of the twentieth, there were two phrases in common use: 'that's white of you' and 'the black side of him'. In these contexts, white meant honourable or fair-dealing, while black meant villainous or sinister. This distinction was based originally on an early racist view of white supremacy over black savages and has survived in colour symbolism even where the racism has vanished. We still talk of 'black days' meaning bad days, or of 'black-hearted villains'. White, by contrast, becomes the colour of valour and honour and heroism. It is in this way, presumably, that it has survived as one of the top three Tribal Colours.

Those, then, are the four main functions of the Tribal Colours. If we look back at their long history, we find that they have changed little over the decades. Plain colours, stripes, hoops and quarters were all there in the nineteenth century. Hoops, in particular, seem to have been popular in those early days, but have lost ground in many places. They are favoured today in Scotland, which seems to have kept more closely to the original patterns, but on the continent of Europe, they are almost completely absent. Why this should be is not clear.

In recent years a number of fancy patterns have been added to the simple shirts and shorts, as clothing designers have taken an interest in the world of sporting costumes. In the United States, in particular, some rather dramatic innovations have surfaced involving such decorative items as stars and zigzags, but these have yet to appear elsewhere. A much more widespread and curiously unattractive trend has been the adding of advertisements to the players' shirts. Major companies are prepared to pay large sums to sponsor clubs and to have their names written across the heaving chests of the local heroes. While this may be a sound commercial proposition, it nevertheless attacks the heroic mould in which the players are cast, reducing them to scampering sandwich-board men and robbing them of much of their tribal dignity. Sadly it is a trend that seems to be growing as many clubs struggle with the increasing financial problems of today.

The changing face of soccer costumes. (above) Traditional horizontal hoops have been worn for over a century. This example dates from 1865.

(below) Elaborate designs such as this combination of stripes, zigzags and stars represent a new trend and are still extremely rare. This particular example comes from North America where it is worn by the Portland Timbers team.

Some clubs are now wearing advertisement names across the fronts of their shirts, a commercially attractive idea which nevertheless robs the costumes of some of their tribal dignity (below right).

28 The Emblems

THE CLUB BADGES AND INSIGNIA

Like native tribes, each soccer club has its own Sacred Sign. Known as the 'official club emblem', the design is usually protected by copyright, so that nobody may copy it or use it without the permission of the Tribal Elders. In this way, it becomes uniquely associated with the club and takes on the role of a Totemic Device, to be respected, protected and rallied around, like a regimental flag or a royal standard.

The main function of the emblem is to become an intensifier of tribal emotions. As a unique visual motif, its conspicuous presence serves to strengthen feelings of club loyalty. Merely to catch sight of it, fluttering on a club banner or scrawled on a brick wall, should quicken the pulse of any devoted tribesman. In addition, the emblem acts as a label of identity, appearing on club badges, ties, notepaper, programmes, pennants, souvenirs, flags, stadium buildings and offices. As an ever-present symbol, it helps to keep alive the sense of club attachment and, at the same time, acts as a threat and intimidation to rival tribesmen.

At many clubs, the emblem is incorporated into the playing costume of the Tribal Heroes, where it is positioned on the left side of the chest. Placing it over the player's heart in this way is an important symbolic act. It transmits the message to the Tribal Followers that the man's heart 'belongs to the club'. In reality this may be true or false – he may be devoted to the club for which he is playing, or he may be desperately seeking a transfer to another club – but this matters little during the emotional atmosphere of a hard-fought game. While the battle rages on the field, his clearly labelled heart beats only for the watching eyes of his supporters.

Historically, club emblems have gone through two main stages. In the early years, most clubs took as their insignia the coat-of-arms of their local communities. City crests were the most common form of soccer emblem in those days, but many have since vanished. Some of them disappeared because they were too widely used by other local organizations and the soccer clubs wanted a unique label of their own. A few soccer crests do still survive, but most have been replaced by more modern designs.

In almost all cases the new emblems are much simpler than the old crests. Another weakness of the earlier emblems was that they were too fussy and complicated. Being heraldic devices, they involved too much finicky detail to be easily remembered and copied. They lacked any sharply defined, dominant element that could be used as the club totem. The new designs, usually based on a single image, such as an animal, are easier to commit to memory and to identify at a distance.

In selecting the images for these new emblems, the clubs have frequently chosen either a bird or some kind of wild beast. In adopting these totemic animals, they have provided not only a striking visual symbol for their followers, but also, in many cases, a useful club nickname.

Two influences seem to be operating in the choice of animals in these modern emblems. The first is the idea that a fierce animal is needed to reflect the power and savage determination of the players. Predictably, large carnivores such as lions, tigers and wolves are popular. Birds of prey, such as eagles, hawks and owls, are also favoured, symbolizing swift and remorseless attacks that give their victims little chance of escape. Among the non-carnivores, creatures of great power or belligerence are singled out – the mighty elephant crushing all before it, the great charging bull, the valiant stag with its huge antlers, the duelling ram with its massive horns, the courageous, rearing stallion, or the bloodthirsty fighting-cock. All these

Each club has an official emblem which acts as a label of identity and as a magic talisman (above). Many of the older clubs incorporated heraldic devices in their emblematic designs. Chelsea (below) display a blue lion standing on its hind legs and looking backward (in heraldic terms, a lion *rampant regardant*).

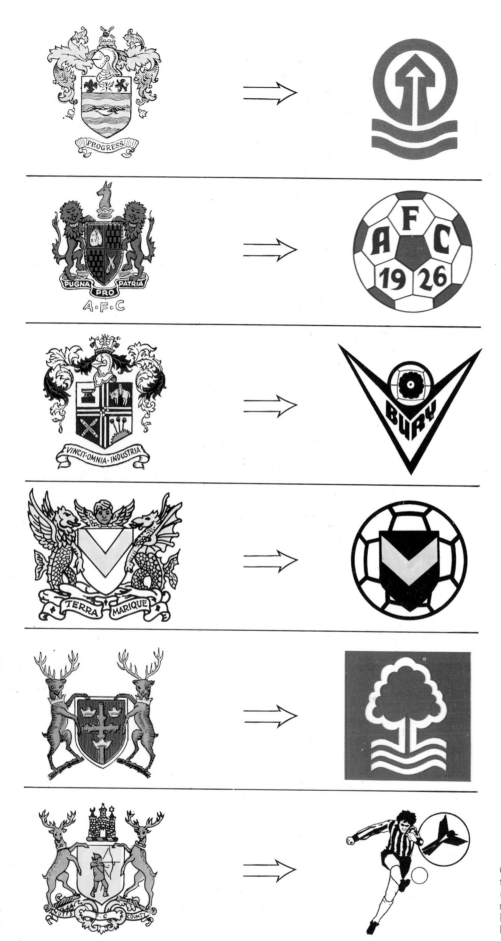

Clubs which started out with elaborate crests based on the coats of arms of their home cities, have often modernized and simplified these emblems to produce designs that are easier to recognize at a glance.

Club emblems (opposite) frequently take as a central image an Agile Bird (top row), a Weapon of War (second row), a Hunting Killer (third row), a Powerful Beast (fourth row), or a Bird of Prey (bottom row).

creatures provide ideal symbols of the aggressiveness and force of the club's team on the field of battle.

A second type of highly favoured totemic animal is, at first sight, harder to understand. Many clubs have chosen to put their faith in small and often rather inoffensive birds of one kind or another. There are totemic robins, bluebirds, magpies, canaries and seagulls, none of which seems to be particularly suitable as a symbol of a rugged contest. It is not their source that is difficult to explain – they usually reflect the team's colours (robins for a red team, magpies a black-and-white team, canaries a yellow team, and so on) or the club's geographical position (seagulls for a seaside town) – but their physical weakness as 'savage beasts' might be thought to make them an odd choice. Their secret, however, lies in another quality they possess, namely swift flight through the air. Flying at high speed, darting this way and that, they symbolize both the athletic skills of the players and the rapid movement of the football as it flies down the field.

Although the most popular choice, animals are not the only form of totemic image. Weapons, too, are favoured, especially swords and lances. There are cannons, axes and hammers, and knights, swordsmen and warriors; also fortified buildings such as castles and towers. The aggressive, warlike nature of such symbols is obvious enough and underlines the role of the soccer match as a pseudo-battle.

In the United States a different form of power-symbol has, for some reason, come to dominate the emblematic scene. The untamed forces of nature have provided a new source of motifs and nicknames. There we find the hurricane and the tornado, the blizzard and the crashing surf, the earthquake and the searing flames. And when the ball flies through the air it is not seen as a fast-winging bird, but as a comet speeding into the cosmos.

Another difference between American and European clubs lies in their official attitude to the nicknames that derive from the tribal emblems. In Europe these nicknames, no matter how well known or commonly used, are never included in the club names or titles. In America they have become formalized and always appear as part of the official club name. If, for example, the English club at Norwich followed the American pattern, it would be known as *Norwich Canaries*, rather than by its typically ponderous title of *Norwich City Football Club*. In the same way, *Derby County Football Club* would carry the title of *Derby Rams*. The traditionalism of European clubs, naming their clubs exclusively after their tribal homes, does not appeal to modern American tastes. They prefer more colourful titles which 'sell' their nicknames to their followers by institutionalizing them, rather than leaving matters to chance and the slower, natural growth of totemic symbols. If, to European eyes, this seems like a case of American 'hustling', and the imposing of ready-made folklore on the American Soccer Tribesmen, it must be remembered that in North America soccer is still a sporting underdog, struggling to loosen the powerful grip of those long-entrenched rivals, American Football and Baseball. In its fight to gain greater public support it cannot afford the dignified luxury of the more antiquated and traditional titles so beloved by European soccer clubs.

The most popular source of emblems for North American soccer clubs is a natural force of some kind, such as high winds, earthquakes or pounding waves.

29 The Trophies

CUPS AND CAPS, SHIELDS AND STATUETTES

The symbolic prize awarded to the victorious members of the Soccer Tribe is referred to as the Trophy, and this name has a special significance. In ancient times, triumphant warriors would hang up certain spoils of war as a memorial of a battle won. The Romans usually took such trophies home to Rome, where they were put on display to mark yet another great victory over their foreign enemies. In more recent times, big-game hunters used the word 'trophy' to refer to the stuffed animal heads they displayed on their walls after returning from a successful hunt. In both cases, the great significance attached to the bringing home of such objects harked back to mankind's primeval hunting life, when the most important act of the males of the tribe was to return home carrying the carcass of the quarry killed in the hunt, for a tribal feast.

In modern, symbolic terms this is also the supreme task of the heroes of each Soccer Tribe. At the end of a long 'hunting' season, the champions return home with their coveted trophy, to display it to their faithful followers. They parade with it through the streets and then appear triumphantly on a balcony, holding it up for all to see. After this, they disappear inside for a great feast of celebration, with the trophy standing in a place of honour, like the severed horns of some great beast whose carcass they are devouring.

The typical soccer trophy is not, however, a pair of horns, but a giant silver cup, and it is worth asking why this particular type of symbolic object should

Trophies of this sort are the Soccer Tribe's most coveted prizes. They are almost sacred objects, to be held high as proud possessions.

have been chosen as the supreme tribal prize. To find the answer, it is necessary to go back to classical times. Ernest Crawley, writing about early drinking habits, records that: 'Health-drinking, the *propinatio* of the Latins, has some variations. One form is the sharing of a drink; the person doing the honour drinks first, and hands the cup (in Greek life this became the property of the person honoured) to the other.' This gives the vital clue. To honour someone you hand them a drink, taking a mouthful yourself first to demonstrate that it is not poisoned. This act is commemorated by the honoured person retaining the cup as a memento of the occasion. The cup thereby becomes the symbol of the act of 'being honoured'.

This can explain the giving of a small cup, but the vessels given to victorious soccer heroes are huge. To understand the reason for this, we have to look at the way the classical ritual developed in later years in England. For centuries, there was a custom at great banquets of passing round a large 'loving cup'. This was an outsized vessel containing wine, or some other form of celebratory drink, which was passed from man to man around the dining tables. Each individual had to drink and then pass it on to his neighbour. In this way each man was seen to be honouring his friend. Each one treated his companion symbolically as his 'honoured superior', in a general display of group loyalty. The giant 'loving cups' used on these occasions were the prototypes of modern sporting cups. This shift in function probably began at banquets where a famous sportsman was being honoured and, in the old Greek tradition, was allowed to keep the 'loving cup' after it had been passed around. It is easy to see how this gradually became a fixed ceremony, with cups being specially made for presentation alone and the drinking of one another's health being performed from ordinary glasses. When soccer developed in the nineteenth century it merely took over this already established sporting practice.

The first important soccer trophy was the Football Association Challenge Cup, usually referred to simply as the FA Cup. The idea of holding a knock-out competition for a prize was born in the offices of a London newspaper, the *Sportsman*, on July 20th 1871. Seven men gathered there, including the secretary of the FA, Charles Alcock, and it was his suggestion that a cup competition should be introduced to add excitement to the newly developing sport. When he had attended the elite English public school of Harrow, he had been impressed by the emotions aroused by the knock-out inter-house competitions held there, and felt that a similarly intense reaction could be

(opposite) Six of the many cups awarded as soccer trophies today:

(above left) The Football Association Challenge Cup, usually known simply as the FA Cup, has the longest history. The original one was first awarded in 1872, but was stolen from a shop window in 1895 and never recovered. A second was made and used until 1910, when it was presented to Lord Kinnaird for his services to the sport. The one shown here is the third, introduced in 1911 and still in use today.

(above centre) The Football League Championship trophy is awarded to the top club in the annual League points competition.

(above right) The lower echelons of the soccer world also have their awards, such as this, the Football League Division III Championship Cup.

(below left) The French-inspired European Champion Clubs Cup, usually called simply the European Cup, was introduced in the 1955–6 season.

(below centre) The European Cup-winners Cup, which first appeared in the 1960–1 season, is fought for by the winners of each of the national cups.

(below right) The Football League Cup, another newcomer, was also introduced in the 1960–1 season. (In the background is the FA Charity Shield, awarded since 1908, usually to the winners of a special match played between the FA Cup holders and the League Champions.)

At the moment of victory, the honour of holding or touching the trophy is shared between the team members, as if it were a loving cup to be passed from man to man.

produced at national level by using the same form of contest for the member teams of the Football Association. His idea was accepted on October 16th of that year and £20 was raised to purchase a modest silver cup, slightly less than 18 inches high, standing on an ebony plinth. It was shaped like a goblet, with a pair of curving handles and a figure of a player standing on top of the large lid. It had a capacity of about one quart.

Fifteen teams entered for that very first cup competition (compared with over 600 in recent years) and the final was played on March 16th 1872 at the Oval in London before a crowd of 2,000, each of whom paid one shilling for the privilege of seeing soccer history in the making. As has so often happened

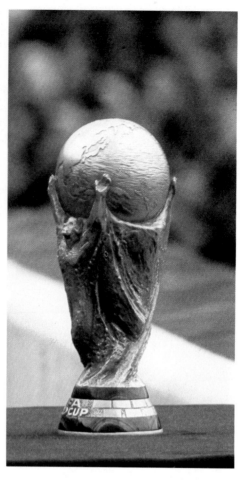

The World Cup competition is the sport's supreme contest. The first of the two World Cups, the Jules Rimet Trophy (far left) was made of solid gold and stood 32 cm high. First awarded (to Uruguay) in 1930, it was stolen from an exhibition in Central Hall, Westminster, in 1966. Unlike the original FA Cup it was eventually rediscovered, wrapped in newspaper, beneath a bush in a South-east London garden. In 1970, when it was won by Brazil for the third time, it was awarded to them as a permanent honour and replaced by the present trophy (left) – a 'Cup' that is no longer a cup.

since, the underdogs (the Wanderers) beat the favourites (the Royal Engineers).

This event was to change the whole face of competitive soccer. As football historian Geoffrey Green has put it: 'The influence of the cup ... is incalculable. It was the spark that set the whole bonfire of football alight, for very soon this "little tin idol", as the trophy was called, spread its magic wings across all the fields of England, drawing more and more clubs under its spell. It altered the whole pattern and the whole purpose of the game.'

It is hard for us today to imagine soccer without such competitions, but clearly their importance in boosting the growth of the sport was enormous and they soon spread outwards from England across the whole face of the globe, culminating in the creation of the greatest of all soccer contests, the World Cup, in 1930. Today there are cup competitions at national, continental, and international level all over the world, and the size and value of the trophies awarded have increased dramatically since that first humble FA Cup of 1872. Some are now so vast that it becomes something of a feat for the exhausted victors to hold them aloft at the end of the final match. Some are no longer cups at all, but instead are made in the form of statuettes or shields. The first World Cup was a mixture, half figurine, half cup, the stem of the traditional goblet having grown into the shape of a winged Victory. Her arms were raised above her head to hold what was now a rather small vessel, hardly suitable as a 'loving cup'. When this trophy had been won three times by Brazil, the Brazilian soccer authorities were allowed to keep it permanently and a new one had to be designed. In this, the vessel has disappeared altogether, to be replaced by a solid globe. The concept of the 'cup' is, however, so ingrained in football thinking that the new statuette is still referred to by all Soccer Tribesmen as 'the World Cup'.

There are two additional World Cup awards – the Golden Boot (above) for the leading goal-scorer, and the Golden Ball for the best player. Like the main trophy, these are awarded once every four years, after the contest's final game.

The Tribal Elders

30 The Tribal Council

THE CHAIRMEN AND DIRECTORS

At the head of each Soccer Tribe sits the Tribal Council. In England this is known as the Board of Directors, so-called because in the distant past their names were inscribed on a wooden board hung on the wall of the tribe's inner sanctum. This room, the tribal 'Holy of Holies', is still known today as the Board-room and usually contains a modern echo of the ancient inscription panel in the form of a tableau of coloured photographs of the faces of the present directors, with their names printed below them.

At the centre of this tribal nerve-centre stands the Board-room Table, around which the directors gather for their regular Board Meetings. The seating is formal and rigidly fixed, with the Chairman sitting at the head of the table, flanked by his Vice-Chairman and Secretary, and with the other directors spread out from him in order of decreasing seniority. The business of these meetings also follows a formal and highly predictable sequence. As with all committees, there is a curious, unwritten rule that 'the more trivial an item, the longer it is discussed'. This is partly because the really important issues, like the sale of a player, are settled privately beforehand and are merely rubber-stamped at the meeting, leaving plenty of time for debates on the number of pages in next season's programmes, and similar matters. These are discussed passionately and often late into the night.

All this changes when the curtain goes up on that long-running drama, the Board-room Split. For restraint and rational thinking, this has all the qualities of the ousting of the leader of a pack of baboons, with the grunting and posturing often spilling out of the Board-room and into the columns of the local newspapers. For a while the air is thick with threatened resignations

The Holy of Holies of each club is the Board-room, but few can boast such a magnificent display as Real Madrid's trophy-laden inner sanctum.

and recriminations, until the dust settles and a new chairman is enthroned as the tribal ruler, or the old one finally triumphs, bruised but unbowed. Typically, there is an aftermath of simmering grudges that continue to bubble through the tribal corridors for some time to come, ready to boil over whenever the tribal fortunes are damaged by particularly inglorious defeats on the field. But outwardly peace soon reigns again and the Board returns to its routine preoccupations with lottery tickets, admission prices, servicing of floodlights, repairs to the main gates, and other equally trend-setting innovations.

Since the activities and appearance of English football clubs have changed little during the past hundred years, it is clear that the behaviour of the directors is as much a ritual as the game itself, their main role being to maintain the ancient traditions of the tribes, rather than to foster progress and expansion, as would be the case in other businesses. The only change they strive for is one of increased goal-scoring.

Their moment of truth comes on the vital match-days, when they engage in their other main duty, that of playing Hosts and Guests. The rites begin with the assembly in the Board-room of the Home Team Directors, to greet the Directors of the Visiting Team. Each home director is careful to shake hands with each visiting director as he arrives, and there follows the serving of drinks and a period of friendly small-talk during which the genuine mutual hostility is submerged in equally genuine sympathy. Each director recognizes in his counterpart a fellow sufferer and responds accordingly. The fact that they are silently longing for one another's impending defeat is hardly allowed to surface, except in an occasional joking exchange, during this Greeting Ceremony.

This friendly match-day contact is unique to the directors. Other sectors of the rival tribes enjoy no such encounters. The opposing players try to ignore one another at this point and quickly retreat to the isolation of their separate dressing rooms. The opposing fans stream into their designated areas of the terraces and, even before the match has begun, start to hurl chanted abuse at one another. Only the directors in their figurehead roles are expected to indulge in smiling chit-chat and formal compliments.

This phase is ended abruptly by the ringing of a bell or buzzer, announcing the fact that the players are about to run out on to the pitch. Donning their overcoats, the directors then troop up from the board-room to the Directors' Box, a specially sealed-off section of seating, where they formally split into two groups, home directors on one side and away directors on the other. This physical separation of the hosts and the visitors during the actual playing time contrasts strikingly with their friendly mingling down below in the board-room, and is a device which enables them to express aloud, and sometimes noisily, their disgust at the foul tactics of the players of the opposing team, without the embarrassment of having to do so down the necks of their hosts or guests.

This break in friendly contact ceases as soon as the half-time whistle is blown, when the home directors usher their guests back down to the board-room for the Tea Ceremony. Conversation is a little more stilted now, as the cups of tea are dispensed. Friendly anecdotes are replaced by comments on the run of play and the probable insanity of the referee. A television set giving half-time results of other matches provides a welcome distraction until the buzzer sounds again to herald the start of the second half.

As soon as the final whistle has blown there is the 'Well done!' Ritual, in which the losing directors, with great effort, force a smile on to their faces and proffer a hand to be shaken by each of the winning directors. The words 'Well done!' or 'Congratulations!' are repeated with each handshake, and each winning director replies 'Thank you,' as if he himself has personally achieved the victory.

The tension of the match is clearly reflected in the tight-lipped expressions on the faces in the Directors' Box (left). According to popular mythology, this tension is forever exploding into violent behind-the-scenes rows between managers and chairmen (as depicted in an illustration from a 'Roy of the Rovers' story, above) but in reality such incidents are extremely rare.

Back in the board-room for the third and last time, there is an enlarged tea ceremony, including a miniature feast, little of which is eaten, but which has to be provided as part of the Hosting Display. While the sipping and nibbling goes on, there is an exchange of post-mortem remarks, all of which are clichés and highly predictable. Tension is relieved by the watching on television of all the final results of the other matches that have been played that day. After this, tea gives way to alcohol from the bar and a final return to a few friendly anecdotes before the visitors take their leave and are wished a safe journey home. As soon as they have departed, the home directors either indulge in a mild celebration or a grim-faced analysis of 'what went wrong'. This usually involves the manager, who either extols the virtues of his players and the brilliant way in which they have followed his directions, or, if they have lost, explains how stupid they are in failing to follow his directions. Shortly afterwards the match-day rites come to an end and the directors drift home to await the reports in the following day's newspapers, to relive once more their ecstasy or their agony.

Outlined in this way the role of a director does not seem too arduous. Indeed he is often viewed as something of a joke. A famous international player, when writing his autobiography, included a chapter with the title 'The average director's knowledge of football'. Beneath this title was a blank page. This sums up the attitude of many managers as well as players. One manager reached such a peak of success with his team that he felt secure enough to risk referring to his board of directors, in public, as a bunch of 'noodles' (using the word in its dialect meaning of 'simpletons'). This same manager is on record as saying, 'The only important decision any director has got to take is the appointment of the right man to conduct the affairs of the club.' Another manager was even more scathing, describing the ideal board of directors as consisting of three men, 'two dead and the other dying'.

These feelings about directors have a long history. Originally, before the advent of managers, directors were local business leaders who knew little about soccer but nevertheless insisted on dealing with such matters as team selection, often with disastrous results. Managing the players on a more trivial day-to-day basis was left to the team captain. But as professionalism grew and the game developed, it became necessary to appoint a retired player as a go-between, and the modern manager was born. At first, his life was made a misery by constant interference from the directors, each of whom felt that he knew more about the technicalities of the game than the manager, despite the latter's playing record. When managers complained about this, the usual retort was, 'I have been watching football for thirty years and I know what I am talking about.' Finally, one manager retorted, 'And my wife has been watching me drive for many years, too, but I'm damned if I will let her take over the driving seat.'

Matters came to a head and managers eventually insisted that all decisions concerning the players and the team strategy, tactics, training and selection should be the exclusive concern of the managerial staff and that directors should restrict themselves purely to the business side of the clubs. Most boards now accept this position, but the triumph of the manager has proved to be something of a double-edged sword. Having gained control of the players, he has now become the main focus of attack when the team does badly, and the directors are all too ready to sack him on the spot, offering him up as a kind of tribal sacrifice.

Given the restricted role of the members of the Tribal Council, in which they are forbidden to direct the thing they are supposed to direct, it is hard for some people to understand why anyone should wish to join the board of a football club. One suggestion, sometimes heard, is that 'they are in it for the money'. But nothing could be further from the truth, at least in British clubs. It is strictly against the rules for directors to be paid for their services. This is the last surviving relic of the early days of amateurism. While the salaries of players and managers have soared, and all the ordinary office staff of the clubs are paid professional wages, the directors remain the last outpost of what might be called the amateur enthusiasm of the Victorian era. And so we have the strange contradiction of a vast, modern sporting industry run by unpaid part-timers as a kind of hobby. Why do they do it?

One answer was offered by club chairman Arthur Wait, who exclaimed: 'They go in because they are football crazy – or football mad. You have to be bloody crackers to be a director of a football club anyway. Who'd pour money into football when you can earn ten per cent with it – twenty per cent with it?' Many directors would agree with this comment, especially after travelling two hundred miles to an away game to see their team hopelessly defeated on a freezing winter afternoon.

Cynics would reply that the truth lies in the sense of authority and self-importance that their figurehead role gives them. With little to do except watch over their tribe, they can bask in the pride of their dominant position. This was the view expressed repeatedly on the pages of *Foul* magazine, which described itself as 'The Alternative Football Paper'. One commentator wrote: 'Essentially the director of a football club is there because he wants control over employees and supporters. Power to him is material and he wants it to a large extent for its own sake.' Other writers in *Foul* are at pains to blame the directors for all that is wrong with the modern game: 'The directors of professional football clubs have changed little in attitude to their players and clubs since the early days ... To them must fall the burden of responsibility for the archaic industrial relations, autocratic control, unbending administration and generally narrow vision which characterizes the game today ... Directors ... form a self-perpetuating oligarchy whose influence is excessive ... Their role was created and defined a century ago – but that role is badly in need of revision to make them more responsive to the needs of the game in general and their fans and players in particular.'

If these seem strong words, they pale into insignificance alongside the attacks made by skinhead football writer Chris Lightbown in his *Football Handbook to end all Football Handbooks*. In his 'A to Z of Football', he includes the following definition: '*Directors*. Every Football Club has a

The satirical image of the senior director, as conceived by Paul Rigby in Chris Lightbown's *Football Handbook to end all Football Handbooks*.

Board of Directors ... they are ignorant, idle slobs who are just in it for the prestige. They can be distinguished by the lengthy cigar, Rolls-Royce, blonde personal assistant sitting on the lap during the game and general all-round repulsiveness.' He explains how they are selected to sit on the board: 'Candidates are put through a Sociability Test – this involves their being shut in the same room as a *footballer*. If, after 70 minutes, nothing has been said, the candidate is adjudged to be of director material.'

It is doubtful whether many of today's directors would recognize this image of themselves. Most of them would laugh at the idea that they were power-mad, prestige-hungry autocrats. They would describe the typical director as a successful businessman with a deep and life-long devotion to the game, who is prepared to give up a considerable amount of time and energy to help his local club and see it through its moments of crisis and financial difficulty. If such a man seems to the outside world to be antiquated in his approach, it must be remembered that he is, in a very real sense, the chief guardian of the Tribal Traditions. If he resists progress it is because he intuitively feels the need to retain the age-old mood of rigid ritual that gives the soccer game so much of its intensity. The problem with such an attitude is that, if it is successful, it provides little for the more controversial soccer scribes to write about. This, in part, explains their hostility. To thrive, they need change and turmoil, progress and revolution, but this is clearly alien to the Soccer Tribe's fixed traditionalism.

Much of the serious work done by club directors is unseen and unsung. Many hours are devoted to advising on and organizing the business aspects of the tribal activities, but these hold little interest for the supporters on the terraces. A great deal of money is involved in club transactions and this needs careful handling if the tribe is to prosper. The board of directors, at a well-run club, acts as a group of consultants for the permanent secretary, who is in charge of day-to-day administration, the commercial manager, who is concerned with promotional activities, fund-raising and lotteries, and the team manager, who is responsible for all playing staff. A survey of the boards of English League clubs reveals that, as might be expected, the vast majority of all directors are businessmen. In addition, there are 23 solicitors and 18 from various branches of medicine, both categories with obvious contributions to make. Beyond these there are no distinct categories. The list of directors includes men with such diverse occupations as: architect,

The latest addition to the ranks of the Tribal Council is the 'celebrity director'. Comedian Eric Morecambe (above) served on the board of Luton Town and pop star Elton John (top and left) has risen to become Chairman of Watford. Such men make a striking contrast with the more traditional directors, like those of Tottenham Hotspur (right).

university professor, film producer, comedian, broadcaster, politician, musician, psychologist, sports commentator, zoologist, clergyman, head-master, entertainer, chemist, and bank manager.

One unusual new category is the 'celebrity director', brought in to add a little colour to the board. The most striking example of this trend is to be found at Watford Football Club, where pop star Elton John is not merely a director but has become chairman of the board. His passion for soccer is no passing fancy or publicity stunt, but has assumed the proportion of a major obsession. Helicopters are used to rush him to Watford matches that happen to clash with his concert engagements, and he is deeply involved in the day-to-day running of the club. In 1979 he went on record as saying: 'The club is the most important single thing in my life right now . . . music will always be important to me. But it's something that will have to run alongside my responsibilities to Watford.' His only complaint is that being chairman has almost spoiled his enjoyment of the game: 'It's torture sitting there, watching us play. When I was just an ordinary director, I used to leap about and have a lot of fun. Now I just sit there and suffer. And I find it terribly embarrassing when we lose.'

Other chairmen will recognize these symptoms all too well, and it is the intensity of Elton John's involvement that has finally gained him the respect of the Tribal Elders, despite his exotic clothing and far-from-conservative lifestyle. Above all, the other directors recognize the huge financial sacrifice that he has made in order to hold his position as Watford chairman. Most millionaire pop stars live abroad as tax exiles, but he has chosen to stay put and take the brunt of the British taxation system, rather than desert his club.

Elton John's devotion to Watford sums up clearly the overwhelming passion that overtakes many of the men involved in running the Soccer Tribes. It is the final answer to all the snide remarks about the 'idle directors' and 'pompous chairmen'. And it is typical of nearly all the Tribal Elders. Some may indeed be self-important and pretentious, but whether haughty or humble, magisterial or modest, they share an almost pathological love of the sport. To overlook this, as their critics prefer to do, is a grave injustice. Whether a young pop star or an elderly business tycoon, they would all agree with Bill Shankly's now famous remark: 'Some people think football is a matter of life and death. I don't like that attitude. I can assure them it is much more serious than that.'

31 The Tribal Judges

LEAGUES AND ASSOCIATIONS, REFEREES AND LINESMEN

High above the individual Soccer Tribes sit the remote and lordly Tribal Judges. Feared and respected by most of the local Tribal Councils, these senior officials and their organizations, the National Associations and Leagues and the International Federations, hand down their judgments and punishments, settle disputes and enforce the rules of inter-tribal battles.

To the average tribesman, the supporter on the terraces, they are of little interest and are given scarcely a passing thought. They merely exist as the organizers of the season's fixtures, deciding who will play whom and when and where. The soccer fan knows that someone must settle such matters, but sees the Tribal Judges as little more than office-boys compiling charts and arranging the venues of great championships. They are grey, shadowy figures of little popular significance when placed alongside the true Tribal Heroes, the players on the field.

To the players themselves, the Tribal Judges are the elderly overlords who scold them at Disciplinary Tribunals when they have misbehaved, or shake hands with them at the start of an important cup final or international match.

Their most important task, in general terms, is undoubtedly that of maintaining an atmosphere of tribal dignity and fairness. In the intensely competitive atmosphere of modern soccer, it is their role to ensure that no hint of double-dealing or sharp practice can ever be levelled at the sacred sport. The soccer ritual must be incorruptible and the running of the clubs and their contests must be scrupulously fair, or all is lost. Anything which, in their own words, 'brings the game into disrepute' is pounced on and dealt with in the severest possible way by the Tribal Judges.

The fact that all the major soccer organizations are, in effect, total monopolies gives them almost feudal powers which they wield with the sternness of a military court. They have often been criticized for this hardline

Players rarely encounter the high officials of the Soccer Tribe except at cup final ceremonies (above) and disciplinary hearings (below left, as depicted by cartoonist Bill Tidy).

When FIFA authorities meet (above) they look more like great statesmen or political leaders at a summit conference than the organizers of a simple ball-game.

approach, which to some seems out of place in these modern, democratic days. But in their defence it must be said that they are dealing with a set of tribal communities with such passionate rivalries that only the strictest judgments can hope to keep control of a potentially explosive situation. If at times they seem harsh and unbending, it must be remembered that, up to the present, they have successfully organized inter-tribal affairs and contained them so efficiently that the game of soccer has remained comparatively free of many of the ailments that beset other spheres of sport. Political interference, drug abuse, gambling rackets and financial fraud have all been kept to a minimum, which has not always been the case elsewhere. On the rare occasions when these problems *have* arisen inside the Soccer Tribe, they have been swiftly and deftly eliminated. The average fan may not be interested in such organizational triumphs, but he would soon become sadly aware of the damaging effects of corruption and unpleasant outside influences if the 'grey men' were less successful than they are. It is their own efficiency that keeps the Tribal Judges in the shadows.

If the high court judges of the sport remain out of sight and out of mind of the fans, their low court counterparts are, by contrast, very much in evidence. For at every match the Tribal Judges are represented by three intrepid emissaries – the referee and his two linesmen. It is these travelling judges who must bear the brunt of the angry fans' abuse, must stand exposed in the centre of the arena, and must make instantaneous, unalterable judgments on every second of game-play. They may only be junior officials in the cumbersome hierarchy of the Tribal Elders, but once the starting whistle has blown and a match is in progress, they are the temporary masters of all they survey and no one, not even the highest official in the land, may interfere with a single decision they make.

The Average Soccer Tribesman's Guide to Referees

1 The Blind Ref Sees himself as the friend of the fast-flowing game. Appears to have lost his whistle and lets anything pass. Beloved by the hard men of the game.

2 The Whistling Ref The chronic whistleblower wears his Acme Thunderer as if it were a permanent brace on his teeth. Much hated by supporters, he blows up for every minor misdeed, fragmenting the game with a thousand irritating stoppages. Beloved by the soft men of the game.

3 The Homer Ref Believes that every savage foul by the home team is nothing more than an enthusiastic tackle. Knows that the visiting team are a bunch of animals and acts accordingly. Is usually nervous, timid, inconsistent and agitated. Suffers from the worst disease that can afflict a referee: the desire to be loved. For some mysterious reason, usually has lily-white legs.

4 The Headmaster Ref Treats all players as naughty little schoolboys. Gives them patronizingly sarcastic glances at every opportunity. When warning them, insists that they 'Come here!', beckoning derisively. Given to much finger-wagging and stern lecturing. Particularly hated by all players.

5 The Flashy Ref Immaculate costume. Always knows where the TV cameras are positioned. Uses flamboyant gestures and often acts out fouls in mime. Appears to have had ballet training and is said to wear hairspray.

6 The Smiley Ref Has seen it all before and believes that humour is the best way to defuse potentially explosive situations. Is usually one of the older men and is given to much athletic sprinting to prove that he is not. Nearly always smiles when he gives a severe warning – even when swearing at hotheads in their own language. The players' favourite.

7 The Perfect Ref Firm but fair. Restrained but decisive. Unmoved by emotional outbursts and the baying of the crowd. Unimpressed by special pleading, and can tell a trip from a dive at fifty yards. A rare species, but not yet extinct.

Some of these categories are illustrated on the page opposite, but which is which is left to the reader's imagination.

The worst problem for the referee during the course of a match is that he knows, without a shred of a doubt, that every decision he takes will be intensely unpopular with at least eleven players and all their loyal supporters. Nothing he can do will please everyone, and it is a hard fact to live with. Being human, he is bound to be swayed to some extent by the atmosphere at the club where he is officiating. There will always be far more home supporters than away supporters and he will be acutely aware that decisions in favour of the home team will make him far less unpopular than decisions against them. The result is that, to a lesser or greater degree, he is often persuaded to favour the home team – to become, in the language of soccer, a 'homer'.

Experienced referees are so sensitive to this danger that they consciously try to combat the urge to please the home crowd. The best succeed extremely well, but the worst fail miserably. If their failure becomes too obvious, they set up a mood of resentment in the visiting players, who then begin to grow more violent and ruthless in their play. If the home team retaliate, the game is rapidly on its way to disaster, with a weak referee gradually losing control. When this happens, his decisions become increasingly inconsistent and the

In earlier days referees were occasionally attacked by outraged fans (right, at a Spanish match), but greater precautions are now taken to protect officials, including the provision of underground tunnels to give safe entry to and exit from the field (opposite).

crowd becomes increasingly enraged. The final outcome may be violence on the terraces and outside the ground. In some cases, it can lead to a full-scale riot.

Although today the referee's role is generally respected and serious incidents are rare, in the early days of South American soccer there was crisis after crisis. If the home team failed to win a match the referee's life was literally in danger. Frequently the wretched man had to be smuggled out of the ground in heavy disguises, sometimes dressed as a policeman, or even as a woman, to avoid the angry crowds waiting to lynch him. Some frightened referees went on to the field of play armed with a hidden weapon. One, after being punched on the nose for allowing a goal which was thought to be unfair, was quickly surrounded by a whole team of players threatening to extend the damage unless he changed his mind. His answer was to produce with a flourish a cut-throat razor which he had concealed in his clothing.

Another unfortunate referee, who refused to award a penalty in favour of the home club at a South American match, was shot for his decision. The president of the club whipped out a revolver, took careful aim and fired, the bullet striking the man in the head. Yet another was forced to flee the field after flattening a local policeman who had approached him menacingly. The swiftly delivered upper-cut laid out the lawman long enough to enable the now panic-stricken referee to sprint across the pitch towards the players' tunnel, from the safety of which he started blowing his whistle, frantically trying to end the game.

In Central America the picture was much the same. As one goalless draw was nearing its close, the referee awarded a penalty to the visiting team. He was promptly stoned to death by the home team. Such incidents are not unknown in other continents. In West Africa, a home team of Mali players went berserk at one of the referee's decisions, beat him to the ground, smashed his watch and then forced the offending visiting player to kneel at their feet and beg forgiveness. And in Copenhagen, a referee was clubbed unconscious by a visiting Turkish team which, according to his ruling, had been defeated in the closing minutes.

Anyone who has witnessed a violent attack of this type is left in no doubt about the hazardous nature of the referee's task, and it is little wonder that recruitment of good young referees has become increasingly difficult. Fortunately, the worst offences have declined in recent times, as heavier

The referee's instrument of authority: the famous Acme Thunderer whistle.

barriers have been erected around the perimeter of important soccer pitches. The standard of refereeing has also improved, thanks to careful training sessions, and the punishments meted out to riotous clubs have also become harsher. But if physical damage to referees has been nearly eliminated, other forms of abuse still survive, and every referee who runs out on to a field of play at the start of a match needs a strong stomach and a cool head. As one put it, the perfect referee must have 'a skin like a rhinoceros and be as deaf as a doornail'.

Why anyone should wish to be a referee under these circumstances is a puzzling question for an outsider. The answer lies in the intense desire of certain men to be intimately involved in the game of soccer. If they are inadequate as players and know in their hearts that they will never rise to an important level as actual team-members, then the next best thing is to be out there alongside the teams, as a referee or a linesman. They may be insulted and cursed and snarled at, game after game, but they still manage to feel the excitement of the sport at close quarters. This is something that, despite the onslaught of obscenities and despite the poor pay, they are not prepared to forgo. And the rest of the Soccer Tribe must be grateful for this, because without them there would be chaos and the whole world of soccer would disintegrate.

32 The Tribal Witch-doctors

MANAGERS AND COACHES, PHYSIOS AND TRAINERS

Every tribe needs its witch-doctor, to cast spells and work magic. In the Soccer Tribe he is known as the manager or coach. It is his job, through sheer strength of personality, and a few ritual incantations, to convert a team of cynical, hard-bitten professional sportsmen into a group of possessed fanatics, ready to give their lives – or at least their limbs – for the tribal cause. He must be able to transform what might be seen as 'just another day's work' into a dedicated crusade. To do this, he must – like all good witch-doctors – be part hypnotist, part psychiatrist and part sorcerer. For he can never set foot himself on the field of play and can never influence the game directly. Everything he does must be carried out through indirect influence of a kind that can be wantonly ignored if his players have not been brought under his spell.

If the difference between a good manager and a bad one has to do primarily with the ability to impose one's will on others, then it follows that the greatest managers should be rather strong personalities, and this is indeed the case. The most successful among them are remarkable for their magnetism and their ability – in the dressing room or on television – to keep an audience hanging on their every word. How they do it is a mystery, for they have no formal training. As Lawrie McMenemy has admitted: 'Football managers aren't educated people. We aren't trained for management, for making speeches, for being businessmen. We pick it up. We are hoisted into a situation where we have to compete with people who gained their education at the right end of their lives.' Yet somehow, through a mixture of intuition and native cunning, they are able to survive as intensely public figures, interviewed as frequently as politicians and quoted as often as authors.

Part of their success depends on their skill at turning ball-play into word-play. Back in the days when they were team-members themselves, they had to outwit their opponents with feints and tricks of movement. Somehow, it seems, this develops a particular kind of mental process which stands them in good stead in later years. It builds into their brains a quick-wittedness which, if converted from a muscular device into a verbal one, can give them an enormous advantage. It provides them with the instant conversational comeback and makes them good at lateral thinking. They can parry a difficult question, twist a probing remark to their advantage, deflect an insult. They employ the skills they perfected on the pitch, but now in the form of speech rather than footwork.

Of the ninety-two League managers in the 1980 season in England, eighty-eight were ex-professional players. The remaining four were ex-amateurs. Because some of the most famous managers have been ex-defenders, it has sometimes been argued that defenders make the best managerial material. On closer examination this does not seem to be the case. Of the eighty-eight ex-professionals, twenty-seven had been forwards, thirty-two midfielders, twenty-eight defenders and one a goalkeeper. Apart from the scarcity of ex-keepers, there appears to be nothing remarkable about this list. Each main zone of the field supplies its fair share of successful managers, and any bias that may appear to have existed is probably no more than coincidence. Each zone has its special qualities as a training-ground for future managers: the forwards are agile and quick-thinking; the midfielders versatile and hard-working; the defenders resolute and tough. Any man who can transform these attributes from the physical to the administrative, has the makings of a good manager when the time comes to hang up his boots.

Most managers start out by being thrown in at the deep end. One day they

Thoughtful, forceful, cajoling, tense, demanding, pleading, angry, depressed and disappointed – the varied expressions of the managers and coaches, as they watch their teams in action, tell their own story.

are 'ageing' players, in their thirties, struggling to make their legs keep up with their experienced brains, and the next they are 'the boss', talking to a group of young players in the way they themselves have been talked to for the past fifteen or more years. There is seldom any complaint about the suddenness of this transition. It is not easy for a retired player to find exciting work. The job of team manager is the one that most of them pray for, and they are not about to question their luck. So eager are they that they thrust to one side the thought that they are accepting the most insecure post the Soccer Tribe has to offer.

The average life-span of a professional manager at any one club is slightly less than three years. The lucky ones depart to become managers of more important clubs in higher divisions, but the majority leave because they are sacked by their board of directors for failing to produce a winning team. The press statements often announce that a particular manager has resigned and is leaving by mutual agreement with his club, but, as one of them plaintively remarked: 'Believe what you like – no manager ever resigns.' This is the nightmare with which all such men find themselves living, season by season.

The reason why the manager becomes the tribal scapegoat is clear enough. A club cannot afford to sack its entire team if they are performing poorly or if they are relegated to a lower division. Nobody would buy such a team and the club that has suffered from poor results is in no position to give all its players away and start with a completely fresh batch. So the team is comparatively safe. The same is true of the board of directors. They usually hold enough shares between them to survive the onslaught of the shareholders at the Annual General Meeting. The club secretary has not been involved in decisions concerning the playing staff, so he too is secure. That leaves the solitary figure of the manager and it is he who is finally sacrificed on the tribal altar. Like the primitive witch-doctor whose people are suffering from a great drought, despite his repeated rain-making magic, he becomes a despised figure and is shown no mercy.

This attitude is understandable, but it is sometimes grossly unfair. His board of directors may have interfered with his policies, urging him to take steps of which he does not approve. They will no longer make specific demands as they did in the old days, but they may have dropped subtle hints, of a kind he finds it hard to ignore. To pacify them and to keep good relations, he may have given in on a number of issues. Certain directors may have had

In addition to casting a spell over his team, travelling long distances to watch others play, and wheeling and dealing in the purchase and transfer of players, the successful manager must also become an efficient diplomat and PR man, capable of handling difficult press conferences (opposite, above).

At major international matches the modern manager travels with a large entourage. The dug-out is crowded with assistant managers, coaches and trainers. In this case (opposite, below) they are all anxiously awaiting the final whistle signalling victory, to release them from the almost unbearable tension.

After it is all over (right) there is sometimes a traditional dousing in the team showers for the happy coach, following a great conquest.

team 'favourites', particular players of whom they have become personally fond, and they will have used constant pressure to bias the manager even when he knows, from his professional experience, that the men in question have serious flaws that can lose matches. If eventually he is proved correct, the damage will already have been done, and the directors will conveniently forget the role they have played in the team's downfall. They may also forget that, because of financial difficulties, they refused to allow him to buy a vital player he desperately wanted earlier in the season.

In addition to trouble from above, the manager may also be assailed from below. He may find that some of his best players are uncooperative or even rebellious. Being indispensable, they feel free to challenge his authority and in this way they undermine his control of the other team-members. One coach cynically summed this up by remarking that, 'Success for a new manager means keeping the five players who hate you away from the six who have not yet made up their minds.'

Alternatively, a club may be beset with injuries that eliminate key players for long periods, unbalancing the team and again leading to a string of defeats.

If a manager threatened with dismissal points to these and other extenuating circumstances, it will seldom save him. By the time the club is sinking into the relegation zone, the displeasure of the directors will already have spread to the terraces. The fans will be greeting the manager with slogans and chants demanding 'Smith OUT! Smith OUT!' at the end of each disappointing match, as defeat follows defeat. They too will select him as their scapegoat and will be baying for his blood to purge the tribe of its sour memories. And fanning the flames will be the local journalists and commentators, always ready, in their weekly search for controversy, to dissect and enlarge his every error.

When the dam finally bursts and he is forced to leave, under a dark cloud, his future is bleak. There are always plenty of assistant managers and other retired players anxious to take his place. Despite the risks, it is never difficult to fill a managerial vacancy.

So the beleaguered manager is threatened on all sides – from the directors above him, the players below him, and the supporters and media all around him. Little wonder that, even during periods of temporary success, he (and his long-suffering family) feel a nagging sense of insecurity. It is this permanent anxiety as much as anything that has driven him, over the years, to favour a more and more cautious, defensive form of football. He is more scared of losing than eager for winning. The inevitable result is less daring, less entertaining soccer.

It is hard to see a solution to this problem. If a strong managers' union were formed to protect its members from unfair dismissal and to ensure for them a much greater security of employment, the boards of directors would have to toe the line. But the supporters would never tolerate this. The terraces would explode and the manager's life at a club would quickly become unbearable. The tribal role of witch-doctor is simply not amenable to the usual union controls. He will probably always remain the tribal scapegoat – working his magic one moment and then being banished the next. But the times when the magic does work offer a great deal of compensation. All those long, frustrating hours spent huddled in the dug-out, wincing and yelling, coaxing and snarling at the players on the field, always desperately longing to leap out there himself and show them how it used to be done, can, with luck and judgment, bring moments of overwhelming joy and pride. When his team responds to his magic spells like a thing possessed and soars to the greatest heights of triumph, his sense of victory is as great and as rewarding as their own. In those moments, the months of agony and nail-biting insecurity suddenly all seem worth while, and the true lure of the soccer manager's role is there for everyone to see, clearly reflected in the uncontrollable, climactic expression of fulfilment on his delighted face.

The moment of cup final victory, when all the hours of agony and effort and insecurity are suddenly worth while.

The Tribal Followers

33 The Ranks of the Followers

SUPPORTERS AND REPORTERS

To watch the approach roads to a great stadium on the day of a championship match is like seeing a medieval army assembling for battle. Dense columns of moving figures, brightly clad and carrying flags and banners, converge on the towering arena, singing and chanting, calling the names of their tribes and their heroes, beating drums, hooting horns and clapping their hands in ritual rhythms. These are the Tribal Followers and they have become as important to the excitement of the game as the players themselves. Without the atmosphere they create, without their fierce loyalties and their intense longings, the whole sport would collapse, not merely for financial reasons, but because it would lose its spirit – its tribal agony and its tribal joy.

Who are these devout followers and where do they come from, the millions who flock to the soccer matches every week throughout the long season? The vast majority are city-dwellers, the offspring of the industrial revolution. Their typical week is spent in the factories and offices, the shops and streets of the busy urban world of the twentieth century. Their work lacks any sharp climax and is often monotonously repetitive, so that when match-day arrives they eagerly anticipate the peaks of high tension and emotional drama that the game will bring, breaking their steady routine with surging moments of almost unbearable excitement.

Each follower is interested enough in the technicalities of the sport to watch any soccer game on television, and will support his national team on special occasions, but his heart is always with one particular team and his tribal allegiance to his home club transcends all other considerations. Even when his team is playing poorly and suffering a run of defeats, the loyalty of the true follower remains unshaken. He may moan and grumble, but he does not desert them. He has learnt that no team, however brilliant, can win all its games, and he waits for the good times that must surely come.

The most fanatical of the followers have an almost encyclopaedic knowledge of their club statistics and seem to possess a photographic

On great occasions, the Tribal Followers set out for an important encounter looking like a medieval army. Converging on the stadium with their colours flying, they dramatically heighten the tension of the event and convert it into a spectacular pageant.

memory of hundreds of tribal incidents. Names of players are recited like a litany. Match results and goal-scores are recalled in staggering detail. Their heads are full of team compositions, the outcome of disputed offsides, the clashes of star players, the shifts in League positions, the goal-ratios, the transfer dates of their heroes, and a thousand other match facts and figures. If there were university courses in such things, they would all be brilliant scholars. If it was church they were attending, they would all be able to recite the gospels word for word.

As they enter the stadium on match-day they divide up roughly into two groups – the Old Supporters and the Young Supporters. The old ones go to the seated areas, while the young ones stand on the terraces. There are exceptions, but this is the general rule. At first glance they look like an amorphous mass, a great sea of heads craning to watch the action, following it second by second, almost as if they have become united cells in a single giant organism. But on closer scrutiny it is possible to isolate a number of distinct categories – special types of follower who crop up again and again at each Tribal Gathering. Here is a brief guide to some of the more interesting of these:

The Old Supporters

1 *The Loyalists*
These are the followers who have devoted their lives to their club. For them, their team can do no wrong. Their motto is, 'Our team never loses but occasionally it runs out of time.' A poor result is always due to unfair refereeing, the brutal behaviour of the opposing team, or a spell of bad luck. They become angry with anyone who suggests that their team did not play well and they never shout abuse at them, even under the most extreme provocation. Their bias is total and all-consuming.

2 *The Experts*
These are the individuals who know more about the team than the manager, and would explain everything to him if only he would listen. They analyse every move and are always highly critical of team selection, the buying and

At first sight, the sea of faces at a routine, local match (above) looks like an amorphous mass, but on closer inspection a number of distinctive types can be isolated – the ever-optimistic Loyalist, the long-suffering Martyr, the know-all Expert, the angry Barracker, the eternal Joker, and the rest. Each one brings his own moods and prejudices to the game, exerting powerful pressures on the players by his noisy support or his critical hostility.

selling of players and the choice of formation. From their seat in the grandstand, they keep their long-suffering neighbours fully informed of the complexity of every incident and sometimes become so engrossed in their shouted comments that they miss a vital goal. They are skilled at making excuses about their wrong predictions and always very wise after the event.

3 *The Jokers*
These are followers who have developed a repertoire of caustically amusing comments which they shout out loudly whenever there is a pause in the game. Their remarks are nearly always exaggerated insults. If the referee misses a foul, the Joker shouts, 'They wouldn't let him bring his guide-dog on the pitch.' If an opposing player is down with an injured leg, he cries, 'They shoot horses, but you're all right, they don't shoot donkeys.' If the referee gives the opponents a penalty, he yells, 'When they circumcised you they threw away the wrong part.' If a player is not trying hard enough, he bellows, 'You are as much use as a chocolate teapot.'

4 *The Barrackers*
Like the Jokers, these are loud shouters, but their remarks are based on anger rather than humour. They usually confine themselves to simple insults such as 'You're a load of rubbish,' or 'You're a bunch of pansies.' Such remarks are directed at their own team when the game is going badly, much to the distress of the Loyalists, who sometimes round on them and tell them to shut up. When things are going well, they fall silent and rarely if ever raise a cheer at moments of triumph. They seem to attend matches primarily as a way of venting their spleen. When this is directed at the opponents it is usually in the form of 'You're animals, go back to the zoo.' For the Barracker, the match is a special kind of therapy, rather like visiting a public 'rage room'.

5 *The Martyrs*
The Martyr never shouts out. He moans quietly to himself and shakes his head sadly. He knew things would be bad even before the match had begun and suffers throughout it. He enjoys his martyrdom so much that if things are going well he is driven to grumbling about the one player who is not pulling his weight, or to gloomy predictions that 'it won't last'. He dreads the team losing and dreads even more the threat of relegation. He says he cannot imagine why he goes to matches when they cause him so much pain, but he always comes back for more.

6 *The Eccentrics*
Every club has its odd characters who regularly turn up wearing some outlandish costume, or carry special food with them, or make a conspicuous exit before the game has ended, muttering to themselves. They live in a world of their own, but seem to need the company of a crowd in order to emphasize to themselves their difference from the common herd. No one discovers their true feelings about the game and they remain a law unto themselves.

7 *The Outsiders*
Almost everyone in the grandstand is a regular and knows the ropes, but occasionally a few Outsiders find their way in and immediately stand out by their lack of understanding of the tribal rituals. They may be foreigners or visitors to the city and they are conspicuous by their clothes and their reactions to the events on the pitch. If they become excited enough to shout out, their comments immediately lack the tribal ring, and the regulars exchange knowing glances.

The Young Supporters

1 *The Tiddlers*
The hard core of the young supporters are the Fans, the brightly clad,

Two of the many categories that make up the Ranks of the Followers: the Eccentric (above), clad in outrageous costume and covered in club emblems; and the Loyalist (below), with bright rosette, cheerful expression and optimistic gesture.

The youngest fans tend to cluster around the edges of the pitch (above). This does not always give them the best view of the game (above right) but it brings them closer to their idols.

chanting, clapping army of fanatics who mass together on the terraces, but around them are other young supporters who are not fully absorbed into their ranks. The youngest of these are the Tiddlers, very young boys who are just old enough to attend matches on their own. They inhabit the fringes of the massed fans, often squeezed into corners, leaning over low walls, or with their faces thrust between the railings of the barriers. They hover around the players' tunnel, trying to get a close glimpse of their idols, or with luck to touch them with outstretched hands. They are the most mobile of the young supporters, often scampering about from one vantage point to another and waiting eagerly outside the players' entrance with autograph books at the ready in the hope of obtaining a star signature to carry home in triumph and show to their friends. They are the serious fans of tomorrow.

2 The Novices
One step up in the hierarchy of young supporters come the Novices. Slightly older than the Tiddlers, they cluster on the immediate fringes of the main body of fans, but are still too young to thrust themselves into the tight ranks of the fanatics. They stay close, however, and no longer scamper about playfully, but watch the actions of the older fans attentively and learn their tribal chants and clapping rhythms. In each ground they tend to concentrate in one special section of the terraces – perhaps just in front of the main fan army, or to one side.

3 The Fans
The true Fans can be identified in a number of ways. Their clothing is adorned in some manner with their team colours. They assemble outside the ground long before the match is due to start, then move in and take up their special position, clustered together in one particular section of the terraces. This is their sacred territory and woe betide any stranger who enters it. In most clubs it is the stand behind one of the goals which, through hallowed tradition, has become known as the 'home end'. The police are careful to keep visiting fans away from this section, for if alien colours were spotted there, fighting would soon break out and the invaders would be driven forcibly away to some other part of the stadium. The home end often has a special nickname – the Liverpool Kop is one of the most famous of these. To be a member of the fan-cluster that gathers in such places is a tribal privilege and

'Compartments II' by Graham Dean, Treadwell Gallery, London

The Toughs – aggressive followers who are ready and eager to put the boot in, in support of their club. Stripped for action, they have abandoned the colourful accessories of the slightly younger fans.

it requires the observance of certain customs and rules. The Fans must all join in the ritual chantings, hurling abuse at their opponents and offering praise to their Tribal Heroes. During a season, more than two hundred different chants may be sung and the words must be ready on the tip of every tongue. Clapping rhythms and other actions are also a vital part of the true Fan's performance. Like the players on the field, he is an integral part of the main ritual of his tribe. As we saw earlier, it is much easier for a team to score home goals than away goals, and the passionate atmosphere of fanatical support created by the main fan-cluster is the largest factor influencing this difference. With a huge army of fans roaring and clapping their support and displaying the team colours, the players are given a greater urgency and confidence in themselves. They feel they 'can't let the fans down'. Knowing this, the most ardent fans organize special buses to carry them to away matches, or make long train journeys, to try to create a more supportive atmosphere for their players who are doing battle a long way from their home territory. It is rare for this travelling band to outnumber the home fans, but some teams enjoy such fervent support that their followers are almost capable of making them feel 'at home' wherever they may happen to be. These invading fans often have to be protected by the police and marshalled from bus park or railway station in large groups to prevent fighting outside the ground. Once inside, they have to be herded into a visitors' section at the far end of the pitch from the home fans, so that the two rival groups are kept as far apart as possible. The fans who travel regularly to away matches are the most respected members of their ranks.

4 *The Leaders*
Inside the general fan-cluster there are several specialized categories. Although no external organization is imposed on the fan army of any particular club, there is some degree of internal organization. There are certain individuals who assume the role of natural Leaders. Some are Aggro Leaders, who take command when violence breaks out. Others are Chant Leaders, who invent new songs and phrases and then lead the chanting, setting up a new rhythm, or initiating the clapping sequences. Others are Travel Organizers, who make the arrangements for buses, meeting places and the other transportation details.

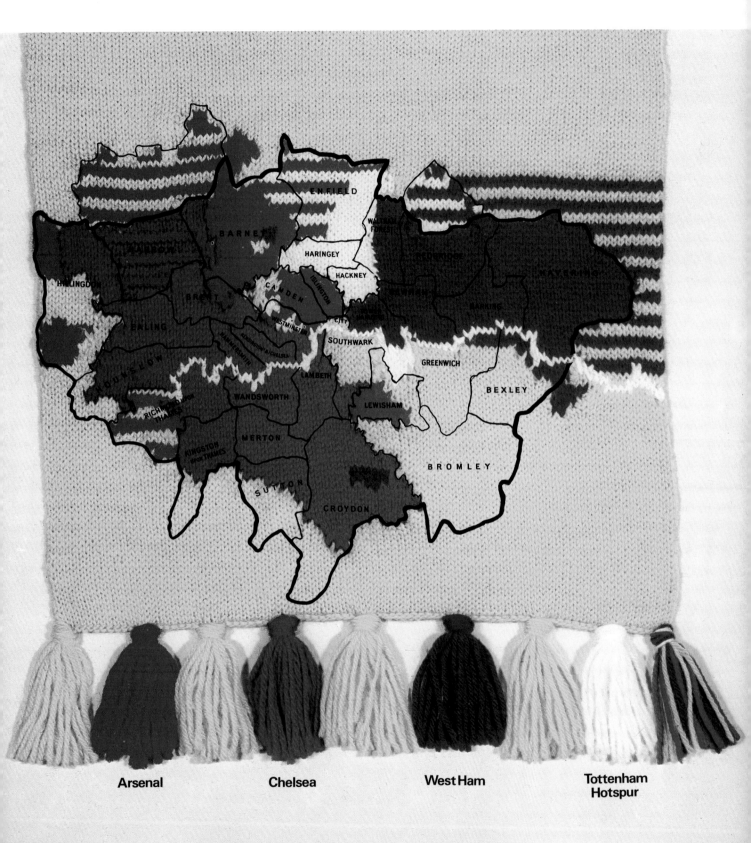

Soccer gangland in London. Each major club draws its support
from specific areas of the capital. Like territorial animals, the
soccer gangs defend their regions against intruders – especially
when these are wearing the display colours of their rival clubs.
(Adapted from a map compiled by Chris Lightbown.)

5 The Hooligans

Among the body of fans there are many who are always ready to defend their club's honour against rivals. For most, this amounts to ritual threats and stops short of actual fighting. They may hurl abuse and make surging runs to 'see off' rivals on or near their sacred territory but they rarely come to blows. Being particularly 'showy' in their aggressive displays, they appear more dangerous than they in fact are.

6 The Toughs

There is a special category of slightly older fans who can be distinguished from the others by the complete absence of club colours. They wear plain denims and T-shirts because they feel they have graduated beyond such displays and are now known to the rest by their personal reputations. They tend to group together and are the ones most likely to take their aggressive rituals over into real fighting when trouble breaks out. They are the hard men of the terraces and the most feared by the opposing fans. But they plan their strategies carefully and are by no means out of control. The ordinary fans look up to them as dominant members of the main group.

7 The Nutters

Every club has its few wild men. They go by a variety of names, such as Headbashers or Nutters. They are not liked by the other fans, because when there is trouble they do lose control and commit serious acts of bodily violence. They sometimes carry concealed weapons and may provoke police body-searches at particularly sensitive encounters, where traditional rivals are meeting. They also precipitate severe police action which annoys the general body of fans because they become tarred with the same brush. In the public mind the worst actions of the Nutters are synonymous with the behaviour of all soccer fans and they are all wrongly labelled as 'savage thugs' because of this small minority.

8 The Drinkers

One category of slightly older fans uses heavy drinking before the match as a form of status display. They gather in pubs and bars before the kick-off and arrive on the terraces in a more or less drunken state. This too irritates some of the fans because their disorganized behaviour tends to disrupt the synchronized rituals of chanting and clapping, but others look upon them as an entertaining side-show.

9 The Creeps

Around the fringes of the main body of fans there are varying numbers of pseudo-fans who pretend to belong to the fan-cluster and try to join in their actions, but who are too stupid or cowardly to be classed as true members of the group. Ineffectual hangers-on, they are often used as scapegoats by the others.

10 The Straights

Finally, there are many young supporters who position themselves away from the mass of fanatical fans and who attend the matches only to watch the game. They may cheer and shout and applaud, but they do not join in the special chants and displays of the true fans. They may be intensely loyal supporters of their team, but they prefer to remain as individuals rather than become members of a fan army.

These, then, are the Ranks of the Supporters. Far from being the amorphous mass that it at first appears, the soccer crowd is a complex social unit, full of subtle distinctions and categories, each of which recognizes the other types and sees itself occupying a particular role in the Tribal Gatherings. The description given here is based on the pattern seen at typical English clubs. In

Among the clusters of fans, certain individuals stand out from the crowd. They may be Chant Leaders or Aggro Leaders, Travel Organizers or simply drinking champions, but they are all capable, through the force of their personalities, of becoming respected members of the complex sub-culture of the soccer terraces.

(opposite) All over the globe, in all conditions, from freezing rain to blinding sun, the followers of the Soccer Tribe gather to pay homage to their heroes. They may come from dramatically different backgrounds but from the moment their eyes focus on the centre spot at the start of a match, they share the same obsessive preoccupation.

other countries there are variations, but many of the categories are found at almost all clubs around the globe.

Where differences do occur in the pattern, there are usually special national peculiarities to explain them. For instance, in countries where the clubs are widely separated geographically, there is far less chance of groups of fans travelling to away matches. This immediately removes the confrontation factor, and alters many of the displays of the fans. In the United States, where the principal ball-game is American Football, the constitution of the soccer crowds is of a special type. It is made up essentially of an 'ethnic element' and a middle class element. The so-called ethnic element comes from recent immigrants whose families grew up in the soccer-dominated societies of South and Central America and elsewhere. For them the old soccer traditions can now find a new outlet in the rapidly expanding activities of the North American Soccer League. Middle class America, on the other hand, is coming to view soccer as a sophisticated novelty, rather like an imported luxury item, and is flocking to it as a family entertainment. This creates a totally different crowd structure and match atmosphere.

Finally, there is one specialized group of followers who assemble at each Tribal Gathering – the *Recorders*. They are the Scribes and Soothsayers of the Tribe – the sports journalists and the match reporters, the radio and television commentators, and the photographers and cameramen. They record every tiny detail of the play and make rash predictions about the future fortunes of the various clubs.

Apart from the photographers, who set up what appears to be a large market for camera equipment behind the goal-line (and which sometimes acts as an uncomfortable crash barrier for the flying bodies of players), and the television cameramen who perch high up around the stadium like snipers, the bulk of the Recorders are confined to the isolation of a special glass booth called the Press Box. This sets them apart from the general crowd of followers to such an extent that their presence is hardly noted or commented upon. To the supporters they seem as remote as a projectionist does to cinema-goers, and it is only on the following day that they are remembered and their words avidly scanned for confirmation of events that are already well known and have been endlessly discussed after the final whistle. But they are an essential part of the tribal structure, the time and space they devote to the sport giving documentary proof of its ritual importance.

The recorders of the tribal history – the long-suffering commentators and the photographers with their probing telephoto lenses. Filling countless hours on radio and television and acres of space in the papers, they help to keep alive the sense of importance attached to tribal events.

34 The Adornments of the Followers

TOP HATS AND TATTOOS, WAR-PAINT AND ROSETTES

Attending a cup final today is like going to a fancy dress ball. Nowhere in modern society is there such a riot of colour and design. It has not always been so. In the early days of soccer the great crowds, although just as passionate in their loyalties, were uniformly drab.

In the years before the First World War, the soccer follower took off his working clothes and donned his best suit to attend the match. Running a magnifying glass over the surviving photographs of the crowds of that period, it is possible to analyse their soccer-going costumes. Of a hundred spectators, taken from a picture chosen at random, ninety men are wearing flat cloth caps and eight are sporting bowler hats. The other two are women in large bonnets. Of the men, almost all are dressed in jackets and shirts with collars and ties. Four have light-coloured scarves wrapped tightly around their necks and tucked inside their jackets. That was the typical pattern of dress in football crowds in the early part of the century, and other photographs confirm this, although the proportion of bowler hats was sometimes slightly higher.

In the inter-war period, the bowler hats began to decline in number, to be replaced by trilbies, but the flat cap still predominated. Additional adornments now, for the more venturesome, were rosettes and rattles, with bright scarves marked in the team's colours. Suits and ties remained the typical form of clothing.

After the Second World War there was a period of austerity during which little advance was made in costume display, the only changes being the demise of the bowler hat and the appearance of a much greater proportion of bare heads. But as the years passed there began a great flowering of soccer adornments, with the arrival of team-coloured hats, flags, badges and

The top hat is a remarkable survival from the earliest days of soccer, when it was worn as the formal headgear of top officials. By the middle of the twentieth century it had become fancy dress wear for the more flamboyant of the fans (above) and, in recent years, has grown in height to become a 'super-topper' so huge that it obscures the view of those behind (opposite).

In earlier days the Tribal Followers put on their best suits and hats to cheer their teams. In this 1923 crowd (left) there is hardly a bare head visible, but the flat caps that dominated the scene before the First World War are now rivalled by the trilbies.

emblems in addition to the traditional rosettes and scarves. This trend has continued right up to the present day, although it is confined largely to the younger fans. It reaches its peak at major cup matches, where the emotional mood often persuades even the more elderly followers to abandon their drab plumage and join in the carnival atmosphere.

These peacock displays are not merely for fun. They are deadly serious and, despite the fact that there is a great deal of carnival drunkenness and laughter, the colours and costumes are signals of an intense tribal loyalty. Anyone misguided enough to treat them as a joke would suffer grievous bodily harm. It is this passionate loyalty that lends even the most seemingly ridiculous costume a certain dignity.

There are no guidelines for a fan's costume beyond his team colours and club emblem. Any pattern, any design, any badge, any article of clothing, any accessory he likes to devise, is acceptable. Some uniformity does occur, of course, because in many cases he will buy items to wear from his club shop, and these will inevitably be mass-produced. But for important occasions he will also spend a great deal of time making his own special, personal adornments which will add variety to the spectacle.

We can make a tour of the fan's body, starting at the top. Hats now come in all shapes and sizes. There are bright caps in contrasting segments of the team colours. There are knitted berets surmounted by pom-poms, and even the occasional coloured fez. But the most dramatic form of ceremonial headgear is, of all things, the top hat. This appears over and over again at cup matches and is a remarkable survival from the very earliest days of soccer, back in the nineteenth century. In that formal era, top hats were the normal wear for the 'toffs' who frequented the first amateur matches and 'toppers' were still worn by high officials in the early part of the twentieth century. They reappeared as part of the fans' cup final garb in the 1920s, gaily painted in vertical bands of the team's colours. It was as if the fans were saying, 'Now *we* are the top officials.'

The rapid turnover of space-age fashions has not eclipsed the top hat. The stubborn traditionalism of the Tribal Elders is echoed throughout the Soccer Tribe and, on the heads of the most devoted followers, the top hat still thrives. In some cases it has grown enormously in height, extreme examples being two and even three feet tall, so that they are difficult to keep in place. The bands of colour are still there and are sometimes long enough to carry names and slogans. The brims, too, are brightly patterned and there may even be an insignia of some kind on the very top, soaring into the sky. In reaching these proportions the 'super-toppers' clearly put display before consideration for the view of the people standing immediately behind the wearer, which is in striking contrast to the old-fashioned flat cap – a form of headgear ideally suited to group viewing on the densely packed terraces. But at the start of really important cup matches it is display that comes first and many of the huge banners and flags must also obscure the view of large sections of the terrace crowds. Once the game begins, however, these are usually dropped out of sight, as watching replaces displaying, and are raised again only in moments of triumph and victory. The same is probably true of the largest of the top hats.

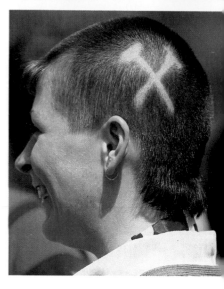

Moving down from hats to hair, there are two extreme forms of display. One is the dyeing of the hair in the colour of the team. To make this colour sufficiently vivid the hair is first bleached and then dyed. Bright crimson and bright purple hair have been seen at recent matches and, where there are two club colours, two-tone hair-dyeing has appeared on occasion, but all these examples are rare. The reason, of course, is that this kind of tribal display cannot be removed easily after the match is over. It shows a devotion to the tribal cause that goes beyond mere costume and is reminiscent of the permanent skin-scarring that is carried out in certain native tribes. Perhaps

When young fans daub themselves with bands of tribal colour (above) they are (consciously or unconsciously) coming very close to the primitive skin-displays of many native tribesmen.

(opposite) Dyeing the hair in team colours (in the blue, green and yellow of Cosmos, and the red of Manchester United) or clipping it in the shape of the club emblem (here with the crossed hammers of West Ham) are more drastic, longer-lasting forms of display.

the most extraordinary example of soccer hair display observed recently was on the head of a young fan who had shaved bare scalp patches in the design of the tribal emblem (a pair of crossed hammers), a gesture of allegiance that would take some months to disappear.

Coming to the face, there are two forms of display employed. One is face-painting, again using the club colours. Sometimes the face is divided into two halves with one colour on each cheek. Sometimes a more elaborate pattern of colours is marked all over the face, giving the look of a painted savage.

An alternative style of facial display is the use of masks of some kind. These may be pseudo-terrorist, with a complete head mask covering everything except eyes and mouth, or they may be more theatrical – skull masks, or horror faces bought from joke shops. Such devices not only have a powerful shock value but also successfully hide the identity of the wearer.

A more extensive display involves a whole-body theatrical costume, frequently in the form of a club's animal mascot, so that the wearer becomes, in effect, a walking emblem or totem.

Returning to our anatomical tour of the different parts of the body and descending from the face to the neck, we come to that perennial soccer garment, the coloured scarf. Its popularity has continued to soar and thousands are sold each year, many clubs offering several different designs based on the same colours. Scarves owe their origins to the need to keep warm on the freezing terraces of the damp and draughty British stadia in the dead of winter, and are far more popular among British soccer supporters than in other countries. But they have become much more than mere neck-warmers. Not only are they still worn in the comparative warmth of the spring cup finals and in August at the start of the new season, but there is also an increasing tendency to wear them tied to the wrist rather than around the neck. This wrist fashion has spread rapidly because it makes waving displays

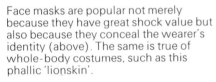

Face masks are popular not merely because they have great shock value but also because they conceal the wearer's identity (above). The same is true of whole-body costumes, such as this phallic 'lionskin'.

easier and, in particular, because it demonstrates that the wearer is too manly to need the comfort of warm clothing.

Moving further down, the shoulders are often draped in a club flag, worn almost like a magic cloak, and the back and chest are frequently used to display insignia, badges, stickers or rosettes. Emblems are also sometimes tattooed permanently on the arms. Descending to the trousers, stickers are again in evidence, especially on the ubiquitous jeans and, in rare cases, coloured bows of silk may be stitched right down the length of the trouser-legs – a device used by both males and females.

These attractive trouser-bows reveal the latent urge for costume display that is present in ordinary people. When given a good reason for embellishing their everyday clothes, they cast off their usual inhibitions and exhibit a daring they would find embarrassing in a less intense social context. As with Hell's Angels and disco dancers, soccer fans are prepared to go to unusual extremes to demonstrate the strength of their involvement. The important point is that the trouser-bows are not merely decorative. They have the specific function of repeating over and over again the tribal club colours. It is this that converts them from a rather precious, peacock display into a fiercely loyal costume advertisement, and enables them to be worn as proud, knightly favours rather than as pretty conceits.

Even the most extreme and zany costumes can overcome ridicule in this way. Whether they be the head-to-toe Union Jacks of tail-coated England supporters at World Cup international matches, or totally bizarre conglomerations of assorted garments flung together in praise of the club colours, they all manage to retain a curious kind of tribal dignity.

This dignity is aided by the fact that so many of the costumes are obviously home-made. They have not been quickly bought off-the-peg for mere money, but reflect the club loyalty involved in the time and effort spent on their production. As with the ceremonial gatherings of native tribes, they make it clear that many days of planning and preparation have gone into the build-up to the great event.

Given their richness and inventiveness, it is surprising that no serious

Trouser-bows (above), which have a long and ancient costume history, are a British speciality rarely seen elsewhere. The coloured scarf has become almost symbolic of the British soccer fan but continental supporters wear it far less. They do, however, share a weakness for hand-decorated denims (below).

study has been made of the costume displays of the Soccer Tribe. It is living folklore right in our midst and yet it has been largely ignored. The irony is that, were it a *dead* folklore relating to customs of past centuries that survive only as tourist attractions or artificially revived historical pageants, it would excite great attention from folklorists and heritage conservationists. And were it a ceremonial display by some *remote* native tribe, it would attract lengthy investigations by studious anthropologists. Such is the blinkered world in which many academics live today.

One important exception is the work of Peter Marsh, a social psychologist who spent three years living among the young tribesmen of the Oxford United Football Club in England, recording the subtle differences in their costume displays and other tribal customs. He discovered that the attitudes of young fans to one another were strongly influenced by small details in their habitual choice of clothing and he devised a test to analyse this. First he made a number of films and video tapes of the fans in their tribal costumes. From a study of these he was able to isolate the important display elements. He then commissioned a series of watercolour paintings depicting a typical fan dressed in the most popular combinations of these elements. These pictures were taken back and shown to a number of the fans themselves and they were asked to describe the kind of club supporter who would normally dress in this way. They were intrigued enough to take the test seriously and examined each of the pictures in turn, commenting in their own tribal terminology on the personality of each individual. Since the face and build of the fan depicted was the same in every case, their answers were, of course, entirely influenced by the minor differences in dress.

The results of this test were fed through a computer and some interesting trends emerged. The investigator sums them up in the following way: 'Denim jackets made the models look "harder" than those without denim jackets. Club scarves, naturally, were a sign of "loyalty". Scarves on the wrist rather than round the neck indicated exceptional loyalty *and* hardness. Fans wearing such combinations as scarf, flag, T-shirt, and white baggy pants struck many boys as "right hooligans", but they did not seem as hard as most of the other models. Jeans, boots and denim jacket *without* a scarf pointed to hardness without loyalty, while models without scarves and who were otherwise dressed rather conventionally in casual jacket, trousers and shoes seemed both hard and loyal.' This last interpretation seems strange and requires explanation.

What is happening here is that the fans are using combinations of costume elements to identify two separate qualities: *hardness* and *loyalty*. A 'hard' fan is one who is prepared to stand in the pouring rain or freezing cold to watch a match and who will join in the ritual battles with rival fans, skirmishes with the police and various minor acts of hooliganism. A 'soft' fan is one who is more likely to use his scarf, for example, to keep him warm and who is likely to hang back as an observer when trouble starts with rivals or the police. The clothing worn by fans apparently gives a fairly precise indication of where each one stands on this scale of *hard to soft*. Independent from this is another scale for *loyal to disloyal*. Here, a 'loyal' fan is one who never misses a match and who will spend a great deal of time and money travelling hundreds of miles to attend away fixtures. A 'disloyal' fan is one who only bothers to turn up for the more important home matches and perhaps an occasional, easy-to-reach away fixture. Again, certain clothing details and combinations of elements provide an accurate clue to a fan's degree of loyalty to his tribe.

This means that there are four extreme types of fan. The first is very hard and fiercely loyal. He is always ready to threaten the enemy and he religiously attends all the matches in which his team appears, even when they are doing badly. Second is the fan who is very hard but rather disloyal. He is always prepared for trouble, but only attends a few of the better matches and will drift away altogether if his team are on a losing streak. He is really more interested in the hostilities than the sport. Third is the fan who is soft but intensely loyal. He will travel the length and breadth of the country to follow his team, but he always tries to avoid involvement when trouble starts. Finally, there is the fan who is both soft and disloyal. His interest in the tribe is minimal. He only bothers to attend matches when they have aroused some special excitement, such as an unusually good 'cup run', and he has no interest whatever in the tribal hostilities with rival fans or the police.

These four types, with all their intermediates, are recognized by the combinations of clothing items which they wear. The loyalty factor is obvious enough: the more tribal colours you put on, the more loyal you are. In this connection, the scarf is the most important element, with flags, badges and stickers available as boosters.

The hardness factor is represented by thin T-shirts and the wearing of scarves around the wrist rather than the neck, as signs of disregard for the cold; tough clothing such as denim jackets and jeans suitable for rough wear and fighting; and big heavy boots for kicking rivals.

Most of the fans demonstrate moderate hardness and moderate loyalty, and their clothing-displays are clear enough, but those who go to extremes create some contradictions. The fan who dons the hardest of clothes, such as denims and T-shirt, and then drapes himself in an abundance of club colours, in the form of scarves, flags, stickers and badges, is going so far that he is slightly suspect. His loyalty may not be questioned, but he is perhaps too weighed down with accessories to be taken seriously as a 'hard man' who will be ready for instant action when there is trouble. He is in danger of becoming something of a court jester. This does not mean that he is looked down upon as a clown, but rather that he is seen as jokingly aggressive instead of sternly so.

The individual who, by contrast, understates his dress display and wears rather ordinary casual clothes belongs in one of two distinct categories. He is either a Straight or a Tough, and it is easy for an outsider to confuse the two. Straights are not fans in the strict sense of the word. They take no part in the social life of the tribe, but attend matches from time to time simply to watch the game. Toughs, on the other hand, are fans who have graduated from the colourful-display stage to an older grouping where, on their past record, they are *known* to be important and carry their hardness and loyalty with them as a personal reputation rather than as a form of dress. It is as if, with their plain clothing, they are saying that they do not *need* special costumes to be recognized as impressive trouble-makers and loyal supporters, and the young, more brightly clad fans must show due deference to them as dominant members of the tribe. On the terraces the Toughs stand among the fans. The Straights are scattered elsewhere, keeping away from the main zone of passionate fan activity. So when the test paintings were being considered in the clothing experiment, it was natural for the plainly dressed figures to be seen as part of the general fan-cluster and therefore labelled as Toughs, rather than Straights.

This investigation of the clothing signals of fans was carried out in the mid-1970s at only one tribal centre and there are undoubtedly many differences at other places and at other times. But what it shows clearly is that there is a remarkable degree of order in the apparent chaos of the terrace crowds. This is not a disorganized mob, but a structured group with sets of dress conventions as rigid as those found among city gents or in any other stratum of society. It only *appears* chaotic to inexperienced eyes. The same is true, of course, of any tribal decorations, as anthropologists have repeatedly discovered. And this is one of the many reasons why it is possible to use the term Soccer *Tribe*, not as a superficial joke-label, but as a reflection of a deep similarity between the soccer community and other tribal societies.

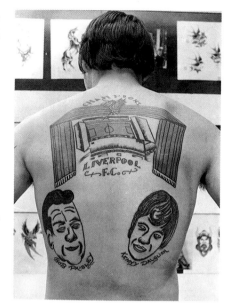

Perhaps the most extreme form of devotion is the giant tattoo (above), a permanent homage to the fan's team, in this case complete with portraits of the club's manager and the star player.

(opposite) The costume language of the soccer fan. These paintings were used by psychologist Peter Marsh in tests which demonstrated that subtle differences in clothing altered the 'personality' of the wearer – making him appear harder or softer and more loyal or less loyal.

35 The Displays of the Followers

FANFARES AND FLAGS, CLAPPING AND CALLING

It is not enough for the ardent soccer fan merely to dress the part and then stand dumbly on the crowded terraces. Nor is it enough simply to clap and cheer, or boo and hiss and whistle with commonplace signals of approval and disgust. Instead, the more fanatical ranks of the Tribal Followers have gradually built up their own special repertoire of mass-displays. Some are noisy and some are a feast for the eyes, but most are both at once and can lift the soccer gathering from a simple ball-game to the level of a dramatic tribal ceremonial.

As with many of the costumes, these ritual displays are impressive because they have grown naturally from within the ranks of the fans themselves. They have not been imposed from outside by official display-masters. There are no professional cheer-leaders as in American Football, to guide the fans like orchestra conductors. The fans are their own composers and their own conductors. If there *are* leaders they are ordinary fans embedded deep in the crush of bodies surrounding the sacred turf of the pitch, and all they do is to start off a particular display at a particular moment, which then explodes, almost instantly, like a massed offering.

1 Tribal Fanfares

One of the earliest displays recorded is the whirring of hundreds of wooden rattles. A handle bearing a ring of wooden teeth is held up and rotated so that a flat piece of wood slaps against each of the teeth in turn as the arm of the rattle swings round and round. The effect is to fill the air with the noise of an army of clattering machines, revving faster and faster. This was the popular sound display of the inter-war period but for some reason it has now gone into a sharp decline. In its place has arrived an even more ear-piercing device, the hooter or honker. This started life as a portable ship's fog-siren and consists of a canister of gas with a horn mounted on the top of it. When a plunger is pressed, the gas escapes under great pressure and sounds a violent blast on the horn. By pushing the plunger down rhythmically it is possible to emit a deafening pattern of noise that often acts as the trigger for a similar clapping-rhythm to be taken up by thousands of pairs of hands.

On the continent of Europe the Soccer Tribes also employ more traditional fanfares. Many of the followers take with them bugles and trumpets and other musical instruments, not so much to play tunes as to emit bursts of sound in urgent rhythms throughout the match, whenever they feel the mood is slightly less than hysterical. They are often accompanied by drummers, sometimes whole rows of them beating away like natives working up a war-dance with tom-toms.

To British ears, these continental hooting and drumming routines are too random. They seem to go on and on, without sufficient relationship to what is happening on the pitch. The British Soccer Tribes prefer their noise displays to come and go with the dramas of the game.

There is one instrumentalist who arouses particular anger. The Phantom Whistler takes a referee's whistle with him to the match and every so often blows it in a special rhythm. At the first peep of an outburst of phantom whistling it sounds as though the referee is stopping the game for some reason and even the players are sometimes fooled by this. But after a few moments, when the rhythm has been identified, it is obvious enough that the whistle is not coming from the referee on the pitch and it creates no problem. On

occasion the referee will report the matter to club officials and a plea is put out on the loudspeakers in an attempt to silence the Phantom Whistler. The success of this request usually depends on the size and muscular power of the man standing next to the offender.

2 Paper Storms

A South American speciality that has now spread to Europe is the spectacular Paper Storm, which greets the home team as it walks out on to the pitch. This is a ritual enjoyed by everyone except the sweepers who have to clean up the ground after the match is over. At World Cup matches the storm of tiny fragments of paper, carried into the stadium in sackloads and thrown joyfully up into the air, is so vast that it can completely obscure the huge crowd. If a sharp wind is blowing, the storm continues for some minutes as the white clouds swirl around the terraces. Often the pitch itself looks as though it is covered in giant snowflakes.

The display has an ancient origin. It is derived from the throwing of confetti at marriages, religious festivals and carnivals. This, in turn, was a modified form of the very ancient practice of throwing handfuls of grain, usually wheat or rice, over the heads of people at special celebrations. As a primitive custom the hurling of grains of food is often described as a fertility rite, especially at weddings, where the food is thought to represent fruitfulness and plenty. This interpretation would make it a strange ceremony for the entrance of a soccer team, unless of course one imagines that it is the goals that must multiply and be fruitful. A more convincing explanation is that the custom has its roots in the art of driving away evil spirits. Viewed in this way, the throwing of the grains of food was meant to appease the evil spirits who were always conjured up by a great event and who would then try to ruin it. By throwing them good food it was thought they would take a lenient view and presumably, in the case of soccer matches, this would mean that no goals would be scored against the home team and no injuries would befall them.

Another ancient way of dealing with evil spirits at important gatherings was to set off firecrackers, burn fires, or make smoke, and these are all actions

In many countries the simple wooden rattles of earlier days have been augmented or replaced by drums and other musical instruments. These (seen here at matches in Spain, above, and Nigeria, above left) beat out deafening rhythms on the terraces, creating a pulsating atmosphere reminiscent of a native war-dance ceremony.

(following pages) In some countries, especially in South America, the arrival of the players is greeted by a dramatic Paper Storm accompanied by the flinging of long paper streamers, adding a carnival element to the already intensely aroused mood of the spectators. A variant of this display, confetti-throwing, is sometimes seen in Italy (below left) where, from a distance, the fans soon look as though they have been caught in a snow blizzard. At many British matches a crude equivalent of the throwing of carnival streamers is the traditional Toilet Roll Display. The size of these improvised streamers is such that they often interfere with play and have to be cleared away before the game can proceed.

seen today at certain soccer matches. The throwing of smoke-bombs (often producing smoke in the appropriate team colours) has become something of a menace, frequently obscuring play and causing the stoppage of the game while panicked officials stamp bravely on the burning smoke canisters. But like the Paper Storm, even these actions have an ancient precedent among superstitious peoples – and nobody is more superstitious than the Soccer Tribesmen.

At great soccer events, the throwing of long paper streamers usually accompanies the Paper Storm, adding dramatic streaks of white to the general cloud of floating fragments. An improvised version is seen at almost every British soccer match in the form of the Toilet Roll Display, where a large streamer of uncurling lavatory paper arcs out over the pitch, usually in the goal area, where it is hoped to cause a distraction for the enemy goalkeeper.

3 The Flag Forest

The most widespread soccer display is the waving of a forest of coloured flags. Although it is reserved for only the most important matches, it can be seen in almost any part of the world. On a great occasion a horde of flag-carriers converges on the stadium in ragged columns, their colours above them as they advance, like the standard-bearers of a medieval army. Once there, they parade around the outside of the ground and then, having taken up their places inside, hoist the flags high and wave them slowly from side to side. The spectacle reaches its peak at the moment when the teams walk out on to the pitch. It resurges again at each goal and at the final whistle. There can be few more massively colourful displays in any sphere of modern society.

When more routine matches are being played the great forest of flags is absent but there are often a few token standard-bearers in the crowd and isolated flags can still be seen to wave, or to be draped over walls or barriers. Those fans who regularly wear a large flag around their shoulders, like a special cloak, when travelling to away matches, can stretch this out with the help of several friends, should the home team perform with particular brilliance.

On the continent of Europe there has been a recent trend to construct bigger and bigger flags, some of which reach such gigantic proportions that the view of a whole section of the crowd must be obscured by them. Complaints, however, are rare, because the vast size of the 'standard' acts as a form of status-display – the bigger the flag, the higher the status of the tribe – and who dare argue with that?

4 Scarf Displays

The British habit of wearing coloured soccer scarves has led to two special displays: the Stretched Scarf and the Twirled Scarf. The most common and dramatic is the Stretched Scarf, when a whole mass of supporters hold their arms high above their heads with their scarves stretched out horizontally. This gives a maximum frontal exposure of the tribal colours and when it is performed simultaneously by hundreds or even thousands of supporters, it presents a boldly magnified display of these colours, aimed straight at the rival supporters at the other end of the ground.

The Stretched Scarf display is usually confined to those moments when the team has done well and is winning the match, but it can also erupt whenever the mood takes the massed fans on the terraces to demonstrate their shared loyalty. Significantly, it is usually accompanied by the singing of the tune 'You'll never walk alone', which helps to reaffirm the sense of tribal belonging.

The Twirled Scarf display is not so frequent. It arose from the habit of

The colourful Flag Forest, one of the most spectacular displays of the massed followers, is seen today at all important finals and international matches, creating a vast, undulating sea of the team's colours and providing an important ego-boost for the players. It also helps to intimidate their rivals.

tying the scarf around one wrist, instead of draping it around the neck. Fans can then raise one arm high in the air and rotate the fist, almost as if they are holding an invisible wooden rattle of the old type. This twirls the scarf rapidly round in the air, creating a sea of coloured movement.

5 Jumping for Joy

The most natural response to a goal is to leap wildly up and down on the terraces, waving the arms in the air. As such, it is not a formalized display, but rather an emotional outburst. It has, however, developed into something approaching a ritual at other times. On these occasions, a mass of bodies suddenly starts leaping vertically, until a whole section of the crowd appears to be heaving and swelling like a rough sea. This 'Pogo-jumping' is comparatively recent and may well have been influenced by the dances performed at punk rock concerts.

One important traditional element of the Jump for Joy that has almost faded away is the antique 'throwing-of-hats-in-the-air'. Throwing something in the air at a moment of victory had become a popular ritual in earlier years but it has been seen little since the 1950s. Joe Mercer, writing in 1964 about a 1950 match, confirms this: 'I stood there . . . and saw a sight I have not seen since, not even at Wembley . . . Programmes were going up in the air, coming down and being thrown up again. Men and women and boys were dancing in circles, shaking hands and slapping one another on the back and throwing hats (which did not belong to them) in the air. I bet there were thousands of hats lost that day and I bet no one cared.' Since that date men have become increasingly hatless and programmes have become increasingly valuable as collectors' items, which may in part explain the demise of the Throw-in-air Display. The only time when things are thrown with any regularity now, it seems, is when the victorious team at a major match are making their lap of honour to show the cup to their fans. Then, many of the fans will hurl their hats, scarves and mascots over the fence in the hope that one of the Tribal Heroes will honour them by picking their favour up and wearing it or carrying it around the arena. Usually several of the team-members oblige and, in so doing, make the sacrifice of the garment worthwhile.

6 Synchro-clapping

This is an English invention originating, it is claimed, in the Liverpool Kop. It must have grown out of the clapping of ordinary applause, but it is now distinct in every way. Not only does it sound completely different, but it occurs at times when ordinary clapping is not taking place. It has three special qualities: it has a rhythmic pattern; it is highly synchronized throughout the displaying fans; and it is performed with the hands held high over the head instead of in the usual position in front of the chest. This gives it a characteristic staccato sound and also renders it highly visible.

The degree to which the different fans are 'in synch' with one another is astonishing. Slow motion films taken of a group of Synchro-clappers revealed that the degree of synchrony is greater than 1/64th of a second. The slow motion film runs through the camera at a rate of 64 frames per second and by examining the changing positions of the clapping hands frame by frame it can be seen that they are all in phase on each single frame. Psychologist Peter Marsh, who made this analysis, was amazed that such a degree of synchrony could be achieved by any group: '. . . Staccato hand-clapping takes on a precision which is probably higher than that achieved by well-drilled military bands . . . The degree of error is only a few inches at the most. How this remarkable precision is achieved, within what most people would see as a disorderly rabble, is a mystery . . . it is orderly to an almost absurd extent.'

The Horizontal Scarf Display is most likely to erupt when the team is playing or scoring particularly well. It is the display of proud supporters who feel an urge to pay homage to their heroes with a huge blanket of tribal colours.

The most popular rhythm for Synchro-clapping is CLAP/CLAP/CLAP-CLAP-CLAP/CLAP-CLAP-CLAP-CLAP/CLAP-CLAP. (The hyphens indicate a shortening of the pause between certain claps.) As the sequence ends it is usually climaxed by a loud shout giving the name of the team. Then the clapping sequence is repeated, and so on, for some time, until either it peters out or some drama on the pitch interrupts it.

A less common rhythm goes *CLAP*-CLAP-CLAP-CLAP/*CLAP*-CLAP-CLAP-CLAP/*CLAP*. (The claps in italics are louder than the others.) As before, the sequence is repeated several times before it fades out.

Other rhythms are closely linked to particular chants. The words of these chants are discussed in Chapter 43, as part of the Tribal Tongue, but the clapping elements are as follows:

When the name of the club is chanted repeatedly it is interspersed with a rapid triple-clap. For instance: United!/CLAP-CLAP-CLAP/United!/CLAP-CLAP-CLAP/United!/CLAP-CLAP-CLAP . . .

When the famous rendering of 'You'll never walk alone' rings out from the terraces, it often ends with a fast double-clap being interspersed between the words: YOU'LL NEV/CLAP-CLAP/ER WALK/CLAP-CLAP/ALONE. This breaks the words up into double sounds that balance the double claps that come between them.

The popular old song 'She'll be coming round the mountain when she comes, when she comes . . .' has been modified as a rallying call asking the fans to attend the next away match. If that is at, say, Blackpool, then they sing, 'If you're all going to Blackpool clap your hands' but in place of the repeat-phrase ('when she comes') of the original song, they perform a Synchro-clap that imitates the song phrase rhythm: CLAP/CLAP-CLAP.

At the start of the match, when the fans are waiting for their team to appear on the pitch, they usually chant BRING ON THE CHAMPIONS. The phrasing is: BRING-ON THE-CHAM *PIONS*, and this is then copied with a similar clapping rhythm: CLAP-CLAP/CLAP-CLAP/CLAP. The whole offering is then repeated several times until it dies away, or until the champions actually appear, when it explodes into a great roar of welcome.

Three other clapping devices are the 'beating-time', the 'speeding-up train' and the slow handclap of derision. The beating-time is used as a support to songs such as 'When the saints go marching in', when it is performed as a synchronized on-beat stroke. The train clap imitates the sound of carriages rattling over the tracks, getting faster and faster. It seems to be a plaintive way of asking the team to speed up their play. The slow

The most contrived form of ritual is the Death Display, in which a carefully decorated coffin is paraded around the ground or left on the touch-line as a forlorn reminder of defeat for the enemy (below and opposite, above). If the opposing team happen to win the contest, the equipment needed for this type of display can become something of an embarrassment.

handclap, again in a synchronized rhythm, occurs when the playing of both teams is so boring that the crowd becomes restless. There is an unfortunate East–West difference here, because in Russia, for example, the slow handclap is the height of *praise* for performers, the exact opposite of its meaning in the West. Russian teams visiting England, or vice versa, might find this rather confusing, as do some theatrical performers when they first encounter it.

7 The Multi-gestures

Hand signals are common at soccer matches. The Victory V-sign, the thumbs-up, the OK ring-sign, and wildly waving hands are all used when things are going well. When the mood of the crowd shifts to anger or derision, the signs change to shaken fists, wagged forefingers, insult-V-signs (in England), horned hands (the *cornuta* of Italy), the finger (USA), and many other local specialities. Most of these, however, are not displayed en masse as a group ritual, but merely explode individually as certain spectators find it impossible to control their feelings. There are only two examples of commonly used Multi-gestures, in which a whole forest of hands comes up together to perform the identical gesture. These are the Wanking-taunts and the Score-taunts.

The first is a comparatively new arrival. The home fans use it when a rival player has been ineffectual in some way on the pitch, or when the away fans have chanted something that annoys them. Hundreds of hands shoot up into the air and, with curled fingers, mimic the act of male masturbation. The implication is that the rival fans are so unmanly that they cannot attract girls and must resort to masturbation to satisfy their sexual needs.

The Score-taunt is used only by fans whose team are winning the match. Each fan raises his arm in the air with his team's score shown by the number of extended fingers. He then moves his hand forward as if 'throwing' the score at his distant enemies. This is done quite slowly to an accompanying chant of 'two-one, two-one', or whatever the score happens to be.

8 The Jungle Calls

Massed calling includes the obvious booing (at bad decisions or foul tackles by the enemy), cheering (when their own team scores a goal), roaring (in anticipation of success), jeering (as a complaint at a bad failure), groaning (with relief after an escape from disaster), and moaning (to express disappointment following a brave failure). Whistling is sometimes used as a substitute for booing, especially in Italy, but in England it is more often reserved for a plea to the referee to blow the final whistle and end the game. This is done, of course, when the team is barely clinging on to a narrow lead.

These are primitive non-verbal calls that owe nothing specifically to soccer, although they tend to be used more at football matches than at other public events. But there are at least three Jungle Calls that seem to be unique to the Soccer Tribe. They are the Massed-snarl, the Goalie-scream and the Monkey Call. The Massed-snarl is a strange kind of animal ARRRRGH sound that begins with a small group of fans and then spreads across the terraces, stretching out and growing in strength to create a sinister atmosphere of frustrated aggression. The Goalie-scream is given when the enemy goalkeeper is about to take a goal-kick at the end of the ground where the home fans stand. It is a massed shout, starting low as an ERRR sound and gradually rising through an OUUU sound to end in a high-pitched AAAH. The effect is of a groan mounting to a roar and then soaring to a high-pitched scream. It is augmented by a simultaneous rising whistle. The sound is designed to reach its peak at the very moment the goalie kicks the ball, in the hope that it will put him off his stroke. Finally, the Monkey Call is reserved exclusively for black players of the opposing team. It is an ape-like OUUGH-OUUGH-OUUGH sound and is chanted by fans whenever the player in question is running with the ball, in an attempt to destroy his concentration.

To an outsider the Monkey Call seems unpleasantly racist, but this is perhaps a rash judgment. Any obvious characteristic of an enemy player, whether he has black skin, red hair, short legs, or a big nose, is liable to be used against him, and the Monkey Call is not so much anti-racial as anti-rival. Black players are fully aware of this and treat it as just one of the hazards of the game. They know full well that if they score a goal their *own* fans will cheer them to the rafters. In the Soccer Tribe, allegiance to your own team and hatred for rival teams dominates all other considerations.

9 Death Displays

On rare occasions, death ceremonies are performed. These elaborate and contrived rituals are the work of a few special fanatics, rather than the massed crowds on the terraces. They take several forms. One is the burning in effigy of the manager after the loss of an important contest. A dummy of the man is made and this is then ceremonially burnt at the edge of the pitch after the game has ended. A similar event is the hanging of the manager's effigy from a mock-gallows, as happened to the Brazilian coach during the 1978 World Cup.

A third ceremony is the carrying of an imitation (but full-scale) coffin around the stadium after a powerful enemy team has been defeated. This is done by a group of supporters of the winning team as a final insult to the vanquished favourites. The coffin is usually marked with letters inviting the losers' club to 'Rest In Peace'. Another device is the issuing of death warrants for the rival club. These are printed as cards and distributed or scattered about outside the stadium before the match begins, in an attempt to intimidate the rival fans.

Finally, there is the more alarming mock-killing that used to take place at South American games. As long ago as 1920, an English observer reported that the local supporters stamped, whistled, cheered and waved white handkerchiefs when their team did well, and added: 'Those are the more sober-minded spectators, the other variety wave revolvers.' Blanks were fired into the air with these guns in an attempt to terrorize the visiting players, who were left in no doubt as to what the locals would like to do to them.

10 The Car Parade

Once the match is over, those fans who drove to the stadium in their own cars cover them with club colours and emblems and ride home hooting their horns and waving flags from the windows in a closing parade of victory. This usually only applies to the major cup games, but can also be observed in local derby matches where there are long-standing rivalries. These fans' cars will have made the journey to the match trailing scarves from the windows and with club stickers and mascots on view, but the 'winning cars' intensify their display on the way home, with added noise and sometimes with whole families protruding from the windows or perched precariously on the roof. In some Mediterranean towns and villages the decorated cars parade up and down the main street in a dense procession, bringing the life of the community to a halt while they spread the glad tidings, but in the bigger, more sophisticated cities this is difficult and the Car Parade becomes a more individual and uncoordinated affair.

After the victory, the fans take off on their ecstatic Car Parade, travelling home with their colours flying and their arms waving, to spread the glad tidings.

These, then, are the main displays of the Tribal Followers and, like their elaborate costumes, they underline the complex social nature of each soccer event. As J. B. Priestley put it so well: 'To think of football as merely 22 hirelings kicking a ball is merely to say that a violin is wood and cat-gut, Hamlet so much ink and paper. It is conflict and art.'

36 The Violence of the Followers

OUTBREAKS OF AGGRO, THE POLICE AND THE FANS

According to a recent Public Opinion Poll, many people stay away from soccer matches because of the threat of crowd violence. Roughly 10 per cent of the subjects questioned gave this reason, saying they feared personal injury from hostile fans if they attended a local game. To what extent is their anxiety justified? Do the terraces run with blood on match-days, or is widespread violence merely a popular fantasy fostered by sensational press reporting?

During the 1970s careful studies were made by psychologist Peter Marsh to get at the truth of this matter. At Leeds United, a large club with a reputation for violence, where the police were extremely active and had installed an expensive remote-controlled video-camera system for crowd surveillance, it emerged that the total number of arrests made during one full season was 273. This amounts to an average of no more than nine individuals per match from the huge crowds present. At a smaller club, Oxford United, during the same (1974) season, the total number of arrests was 83, an average of under four per match. But closer examination of the Oxford incidents revealed that of the 83, only five arrests were for offences involving violence.

This figure of five arrests for violence covering a whole soccer year, with thousands crowding into the terraces week after week, seemed remarkably low. Critics felt that perhaps the police arrests were not as frequent as they should have been and represented only the tip of the iceberg. To answer this comment, the records of the First Aid Station at Oxford United were examined. It was found that during a period of two full seasons 311 people received some kind of treatment, but more than half of these cases were simple accidents. This meant that an average of only about three people per match were hurt as a direct result of crowd violence. The majority of these injuries were trivial, consisting of little more than small cuts and bruises. But the most important discovery was summed up in the following statement: 'Out of those involving deliberate violence it was impossible to find any cases of "innocent bystanders" being hurt.' In other words, the victims were always young rowdies – the fanatical fans who are at the forefront of the clashes between rival supporters.

If these findings are representative of the general picture, and there are indications that this is indeed the case, then the people questioned in the Opinion Poll had little cause to fear the risk of injury if they attended the local matches, unless of course they specifically went looking for trouble. And there is an additional protection available to them. Every stadium has a number of separate entrances and exits. Some of these lead to the standing terraces and others to the numbered seating in the grandstands. There are plenty of safe standing areas, away from the main fan army, but for total immunity from danger the nervous spectator has only to buy a seat ticket and enter through a gate far removed from the 'trouble-spots'. He could follow this routine every week for a lifetime and never encounter so much as a threatening word, let alone a fist in his face.

All the older supporters are well aware of this and are mildly scathing about the nervy 'stay-aways'. From their grandstand seats they have a distant view of the occasional crowd upheavals on the terraces and adopt one of three attitudes towards these incidents. The first is flippant: 'There's no extra charge for the riot,' or 'The terraces are more entertaining than the play today.' The second is chauvinistic: 'Why aren't our lads holding their

When trouble is expected, police often frisk fans as they enter the ground, searching for offensive weapons.

Heavy metal fencing has become commonplace on soccer terraces, and police sometimes take the precaution of creating a no-man's-land between two groups of fans.

ground? Go on, drive the devils back.' The third is moralistic: 'Look at the fighting. They are animals, animals. It's disgusting. They should all be horse-whipped.' But that is about the limit of their involvement.

To sum up, then, there is more threat of violence than actual violence itself and what there is is confined to the rival fans. So why has there been such a fuss in recent years? Part of the answer lies in the conspicuous and predictable nature of the outbursts that do occasionally erupt. Most forms of ordinary street violence occur erratically and without warning, often late at night in dark alleyways. By contrast, trouble on the terraces takes place at set times with a huge crowd watching and under the eyes of both press and police. Also, it has been claimed that the press wildly exaggerate incidents in order to fabricate the sort of lurid stories that sell newspapers. Nobody would deny that in rare cases there are savagely violent moments, but the way these are sometimes reported makes it sound as though they are a common occurrence. Because there are a few unstable, genuinely brutal individuals at a soccer match and because it is they who reach the headlines with their anti-social behaviour, the ordinary, boisterously loyal young supporter becomes labelled as a vicious thug. With the help of the media he becomes the 'folk devil' of modern society. If, as a result, he is unfairly treated, his resentment can only make matters worse. Pushed far enough, he may even begin to adopt the role with which society has unjustly saddled him. The only way to avoid this is to isolate the true trouble-makers and take steps to prevent them from attending future matches.

Many writers have claimed that 'Soccer hooliganism is worse now than it has ever been' and ask, 'Where will it all end?' This alarmist statement is rarely if ever queried, yet there is little evidence to support it. Bearing in mind the vast numbers of people attending matches all around the globe today, the numbers of serious incidents are ridiculously small. If we examine the records of the early days of folk football, it is clear that there was much more violence then than there is now. If we go right back to the earliest days of spectator sports, the picture becomes even more turbulent. Ancient Rome suffered from chariot hooligans. There were two main factions, the Greens and the Blues, and the rivalry between their supporters was intense. The hatred between them was heightened by the fact that they adhered to different religious beliefs, rather like the soccer clubs of (Catholic) Celtic and (Protestant) Rangers in Glasgow today. The worst riot in the history of sport occurred in January of the year 512, when fighting broke out between the supporters of the Blues and Greens. It lasted several days and developed into a massacre in which at least 30,000 people lost their lives.

During medieval times, folk football was repeatedly outlawed by royal proclamation, in reign after reign, because it was so brutal and unruly. By comparison with these early events, the crowd trouble at modern soccer matches begins to appear very tame indeed. But it is worth taking a closer look at precisely what does occur.

The earliest sign of aggression on a match-day is the *Assembly Taunting*. As groups of fans begin to gather before entering the stadium, they may spot rival supporters arriving. This can lead to taunts and jeers and threats of terrible vengeance later in the day. There may be a few running scuffles, but little real fighting ever takes place at this stage.

Once the fans have massed on the terraces and their numbers have reached a 'critical density', they begin the next phase of their hostilities – the *Terrace Taunting*. This is ritualized aggression and is entirely gestural and verbal. They hurl insults at one another, not missiles. If, however, during this stage, or while the match is in progress, a few intrepid (or stupid) rival fans find themselves in the wrong part of the terraces and surrounded by a large number of their enemies, there may be *Terrace Jostling*. The interlopers may be pushed and shoved, jostled and tripped and even, occasionally, punched

and kicked, until they have been driven out of the defended territory and sent packing to their own strongholds. The physical outcome of such encounters is little more than minor bruising.

More serious trouble arises when two fan-clusters confront one another at close quarters on the terraces. This can lead to *Terrace Charges* in which one side works itself up to a point where it risks pushing forward in a great, dense rush, to try to drive back the opposing faction. At the place where these two forces meet, there is usually a certain amount of punching and kicking, until some kind of equilibrium has been re-established. The only real danger here is that some fans may find themselves badly squashed in the crush of bodies.

Occasionally, when something unfair has happened on the field of play, there is a *Pitch Invasion*. This is usually initiated by the fans of the losing team, or the team that appears to have been unjustly treated in some way – by a callous foul or a bad decision from the referee. Hordes of supporters come flooding over the barriers and on to the turf. Accepting the challenge, their rivals rush on from the other end. The game is halted while the police hurry to fill the gap between the two advancing sides. Forming a line between them, they start to herd the fans back to their places on the terraces, arresting a few of the leading trouble-makers and frog-marching these off to the 'charge room'. Once in a while, the police are caught by surprise and the two advancing fan armies come face to face. When this happens, the inexperienced observer may be forgiven for imagining that he is about to witness a pitched battle, but he is wrong. The leading fans on the two sides halt and face up to one another, mouthing insults, but the anticipated hand-to-hand fighting does not materialize. One or two hot-heads may lash out with hefty kicks and small, isolated scuffles may erupt, but little more. It is as if both sides are waiting for the overdue police intervention that will keep

When fighting does break out (above), it is usually confined to kicking and punching and, despite lurid press reports of 'savage riots', the injuries are commonly little more than minor cuts and bruises.

Police have become expert at containing crowd movements (opposite, below), but occasionally they are taken by surprise when a sudden surge of spectators explodes on to the field (opposite, above). Pitch invasions nearly always look worse than they are. In reality there is little true violence and the scampering fans are soon brought under control

them safely apart. When it does arrive, they seem almost relieved to be hustled back away from one another.

A variation of the Pitch Invasion is the *Player Assault*, in which a hated opponent exasperates rival supporters beyond endurance. One or more of them burst from the pitch perimeter and speed out on to the field to attack him with a punch or a kick. On one memorable occasion an elderly supporter was so outraged by his team's inability to score, that he rushed out from his position behind the goal-line and attacked the enemy goalkeeper. With his false teeth in one hand and his walking stick in the other, the old man ran up behind the keeper, who was conveniently bending over to place the ball for a goal-kick, and caned him across the buttocks. He was marched off by the police to a rousing chorus of 'Grandad, we love you' from the massed fans on the terraces above.

Many star players have stories to tell of attacks from enraged fans, although the high fences and deep ditches of modern stadia have largely eliminated this kind of match disruption. Hated players are still vulnerable, however, as they leave the ground after the match. England player Nobby Stiles records how he was treated as he boarded the team bus after a particularly bad-tempered international game in Southern Europe, during which he had been hit by a ripe tomato and a shoe: 'As I walked round the front of the coach a rival supporter clobbered me with his fist. I pushed him off and as I turned to get in the coach my glasses fell off. I stooped to pick them up and suddenly somebody put the lights out. A bottle had been smashed into the back of my head. I was lifted on to the coach and for a few seconds was unconscious. Then I came to, struggling and shouting: "Let me get at him." Several of the lads held me back and with blood streaming down my face I remembered Alf Ramsey's words: "It is enough to beat them." ... If we had lost they would have thrown flowers at me. The bottle, the shoe and the tomato showed we had won.'

Variations of Player Assault are *Referee Assault* and *Linesman Assault*, with the unfortunate officials being butted, punched, kicked or grappled to the ground by furious supporters who have managed to reach them before being

cut off by police. But these are extremely rare incidents. Slightly more common are *Missile Attacks*. Throwing something has a double advantage over bodily assault. It can overcome barriers and it is more anonymous. Goalkeepers are particularly vulnerable, especially in English stadia, where the spectators behind the goal are often very close to the edge of the pitch. Some clubs have recently taken to using a much finer-meshed goal-net, following incidents in which keepers have been hit by coins or other sharp objects from behind. Even if they are not hurt, their concentration is often destroyed by this form of attack. One keeper was horrified to look down and see a hand-grenade lying on the turf near him. Even though it proved to be inactive and was easily removed, its psychological impact must have given a strong advantage to the opposing team.

When missiles are aimed at outfield players they can sometimes cause serious injury, and the game is quickly disrupted. Garrincha, the famous Brazilian player, was once struck on the head by a bottle during a South American match and required stitches in his wound, an incident which clearly had a major influence on the outcome of the contest. Even less dangerous missiles can cause chaos on the pitch. On one occasion an English team on a visit to South America was pelted with oranges by an angry crowd. One player attempted to defuse the tension by calmly picking up one of the oranges, peeling it and eating it, which amused the crowd enough to gain him a few cheers, but his team-mates were less philosophical about the incident and the quality of their game was inevitably reduced.

If a local crowd becomes particularly incensed about the behaviour of a visiting team, another form of aggressive display occasionally erupts – the *Supporter Siege*. After the match a menacing mob gathers around the outside of the club building and besieges the visitors' dressing room. They may simply block the team's exit and chant abuse at them through the windows, or they may go further and hurl objects at the building in an attempt to terrorize the men inside. Later, when the team bus finally leaves the ground, it may be stoned and its windows shattered, while the players inside cover their heads to protect their faces from splinters of flying glass. Coaches carrying young visiting fans also sometimes have their windows smashed in the same way by an outraged mob of rival supporters.

Once in a while this anger is turned on the supporters' own team or manager. If the club has suffered a string of defeats and its fans are demanding the sacking of the manager, they may lay siege to the stadium offices and hurl abuse or even missiles at it to let their feelings be known to the local officials.

Under extreme circumstances, attempts may be made to demolish club buildings. *Property Destruction* of this kind has been witnessed in several countries, where it has sometimes escalated into serious cases of arson. Disgruntled visiting fans making their way home may indulge in running *Street Battles* with rival supporters, or set off on an orgy of shop-window smashing and graffiti-scrawling. Trains carrying dissatisfied fans back to their home town at the end of the day have sometimes been savagely ripped to pieces in a similar outburst.

This catalogue of mayhem sounds terrifying when listed in this way, but it cannot be stressed too strongly that these incidents are extremely rare and have, in recent years, shown a considerable decline. Clubs where outbreaks of violence have erupted have been heavily penalized by the soccer authorities and have received massive fines and even temporary closures as a result of failing to restrain their unruly supporters. Greater police control has been demanded and stronger supervision of the hordes of fans, and these have been forthcoming in most places. Two countries (Malta and India) have even banned *all* soccer for a number of weeks, following particularly damaging incidents.

If an angry fan runs on to the field and assaults a player (left), the club where the offence takes place is liable to a heavy fine from the football authorities. Because of this, more and more perimeter fences and ditches have been built.

Even assaults have their comic moments, as when this elderly 'hooligan' (right) became so enraged that he rushed on to the field and caned the buttocks of an unsuspecting goalkeeper.

Today, the worst that is likely to happen at the end of an unusually tense match is the *Seeing Off* display, in which the home fans rush wildly around trying to frighten the visiting fans as they are ushered to their waiting buses or to the railway station. But like most of the more common examples of 'aggro', this is more of a threat display than an actual attack, and little real injury occurs.

Even these milder forms of hostility have caused damaging publicity for the Soccer Tribe and the tribal authorities have devoted much time and thought to ways of preventing them. Many suggestions have been put forward, some hysterical, others carefully considered. Surprisingly it is certain managers who have responded with the most demented suggestions, demanding drowning, shooting and whipping, in moments of extreme anguish. One was quoted as saying: 'I think capital punishment is a great deterrent,' and another exclaimed, 'Get flame-throwers and burn the bastards. These people aren't human.' Ignoring these outbursts, it is worth looking at some of the more serious proposals that have been put forward in recent years. They include the following:

1 Club membership, with the issuing of identity cards to all fans.
2 All-ticket matches, advance booking only, with the sale of tickets carefully controlled by the clubs concerned.
3 The total banning of all away fans to prevent confrontation between rival groups.
4 Heavier police penalties, with large fines and periods of imprisonment for violent offenders, or the imposition of social work on match-days.
5 The formation of special 'travel clubs' for fans visiting away matches, with police escorts for the fans' buses.
6 TV surveillance of the terrace trouble-spots to identify offenders during scuffles.

7 Heavier fences and ditches to isolate the pitch from the terraces and to separate one section of the terraces from another.

8 All-seater stadia to eliminate the crowd surges that occur on the packed standing terraces.

9 Careful body-searches by police as fans enter the ground to combat the carrying of potentially offensive weapons.

10 The closing of clubs with a long record of serious violence.

11 The use of large numbers of armed riot-police, police with dogs, mounted police, and tear gas.

12 Appeals by star players over loudspeakers to ask the fans to restrain themselves.

13 Voluntary restrictions on press and television coverage of acts of soccer violence to rob the offenders of glamorous publicity.

14 Major attempts to understand and change the social conditions that lie at the root of the violent outbursts.

This last suggestion is clearly the most valuable, but also the most difficult to undertake. It amounts to a massive project of social reform that goes far beyond the boundaries of the Soccer Tribe and its ailments. Sociologists studying the background of the offenders have found that, time and again, it is the young men from the more deprived areas of the city or town, living out their daily lives in crowded slums or boring, soulless housing estates, who are the typical offenders. Their outbursts of violence have little to do with the Soccer Tribe itself, which merely acts as a dramatic stage on which they can perform. Since society has given them little chance to express their manhood in a positive or creative manner, they take the only course left to them apart from dumb subservience, and strike out in a negative and destructive way. They know that at least they will not then be ignored and that they will be able to make their mark on society, even if it is only a scar on someone else's body.

Short of major social reforms, the only efficient way to curb the excesses of the most violent of the present-day soccer followers is to identify and deal with the tiny minority of 'wild men' who cause the serious incidents. Most of the other measures proposed have some merit, but they fail to get at the root of the problem. Usually, they penalize *all* young fans – the innocent majority being punished along with the guilty minority. This causes resentment and can easily spread trouble wider, rather than contain and reduce it.

Examination of a typical incident shows what happens. There is an upheaval on the terraces and the uniformed policemen move in to quell it. The trouble has been initiated by a small group of 'hard men', eager for aggro. The mood quickly infects those around them and fighting breaks out. By the time the police have arrived at the scene there is general confusion. They grab young fans who seem to be involved and frog-march them away. But the chances are that they do not catch the real offenders, who are too cunning for them and quickly melt into the crowd. Time and again, the police-net only manages to trap the small fry, while the big fish escape to cause trouble another day.

The small fry who are punished on such occasions may have been guilty of allowing themselves to be carried away by the mood of the terraces and may have stupidly followed the lead of the hard men at the heart of the trouble, or they may have been innocent watchers of the incident, which merely spilled over in their direction, falsely creating the impression that they were actively involved. Either way, if they are the ones who finally receive the blame for what happened, their reaction is easy to predict. They will either abandon the terraces in disgust, or will turn into hard men themselves, on the principle that if they are going to be treated that way, they have nothing to lose.

The police sometimes find it difficult to keep a straight face when making an arrest (below), but other occasions (opposite) are less amusing. In certain instances the police manage to isolate and remove the real trouble-makers, but often these are too cunning to be caught and the strong arm of the law ends up netting comparative small fry who have merely been swept along by the mood of the crowd.

(opposite) When serious trouble threatens to flare up, the terraces sometimes seem to contain more riot police than spectators (below). Police dogs (above left) and armoured cars equipped with water cannon (above right) are used by some police forces, giving the stadium the air of a besieged fortress.

Faced with these comments, the police argue that they do the best they can under extremely difficult and explosive circumstances. For the uniformed men on the 'soccer beat' this is true, and they deserve sympathy for their hazardous task. But there is an obvious strategy that would help them and which, at higher levels, seems to have been ignored. This is the use of undercover agents, posing as terrace supporters, to infiltrate the ranks of the hard men and identify the real trouble-makers, the 'wild ones' who initiate the serious violence. Once they have been labelled, it should not be so difficult to weed them out and remove the savage minority that give all soccer fans such a bad name with the general public.

It is not as if these key figures in the world of soccer violence are shadowy unknowns. The fans themselves know who they are and fear and respect them. There is a small gang of them at almost every club and they are even given special names. At one club they are called the F-troop, at another the Townies, at another the Shelf Gang. Don Ateyo, in his study of sports violence, *Blood and Guts*, has described the activities of F-troop in the following words: 'It is F-troop which infiltrates the enemy end, either by guile – wearing enemy colours, cheering the enemy team, even talking in the enemy's accent – or by force. When they have gained a foothold on the rival terracing, they lash out, clearing a wide circle around them and sending visible ripples of panic through the tightly packed supporters. They are fearless – revered as "nutters" and "headbangers" by the other fans – and the sight of a dozen F-troopers tackling a thousand enemy supporters is not uncommon.' In an interview, one member of this gang stated bluntly: 'I go to a match for one reason only: the aggro. It's an obsession, I can't give it up. I get so much pleasure when I'm having aggro that I nearly wet my pants – it's true. I go all over the country looking for it.'

It seems extraordinary that if investigators studying soccer violence can identify these key trouble-makers with ease, and can even obtain interviews from them, the police cannot employ undercover strategies to track them down and ultimately bring them to justice. All this requires is a master-plan organized by the police in cooperation with the soccer authorities, and in a comparatively brief period it should be possible to rid the sport of its savage minority, without alienating the mass of ordinary, if boisterous, young fans who have no intention of cracking skulls or drawing blood, and who are quite prepared to restrict themselves to symbolic forms of aggression – ritual displays of threat and counter-threat, insult and gesture. These rituals may intimidate the tender-hearted (as they are intended to do) but they cause no physical injury. In this they are similar to the hostile displays of most other animal species.

Many would like to see even these verbal and visual displays eliminated totally from the world of the Soccer Tribe, and the match-day events become more of a happy family outing, with gentle applause and the singing of cheerful club songs, like some school outing or boy-scout jamboree. They want to domesticate the wild soccer events and convert them into a quiet, civilized pastime. But such ideas disturb even those supporters who are the most vociferous opponents of soccer fan aggro. They suddenly realize how much excitement the pent-up tension of the typically belligerent soccer crowd gives to the sport. Take away that tension and the powerful symbolic significance of the tribal rituals would be lost, their deeper meaning crushed.

The trick for the future, clearly, is to retain this tension, this intensity of involvement of the tribesmen, but at the same time to dispense with its most extreme and destructive forms of expression. The trouble is that any fire which warms you can also occasionally burn your fingers, and the Soccer Tribe has yet to invent the perfect fireguard. Hopefully it will do so before the rest of society loses its patience and douses it with water.

In the past, when railways have run 'soccer specials' to important matches, there have been serious cases of vandalism (below), but this wave of destruction appears to have subsided, as a result of more intensive police action.

37 Tribal Disasters

CRUSHES AND CRASHES, DEATHS AND RIOTS

Every tribe has its major catastrophes, the dramatic details of which are told and retold until they become legendary, and the Soccer Tribe is no exception. In the very early days, crowds were too small to generate serious disasters, but as soon as the sport began to attract large audiences, tragedy was not far away. It first struck on April 5th 1902, at Ibrox Park, the home ground of the Scottish team Glasgow Rangers.

On that particular day their stadium was being used for a popular annual event, the international match between Scotland and England, and a crowd of 68,114 had gathered to watch it. The terraces had recently been enlarged and modernized but sadly these alterations were to prove inadequate for the immense crush of spectators assembled on them.

Even before the kick-off whistle had blown, the West Stand, a huge, tiered construction over fifty feet tall, consisting of an iron framework covered in wooden planks, was creaking and swaying under the weight of thousands of densely packed Scottish supporters. Once the game had begun, the pressure of the crowd became even greater, as the sea of eyes tried to follow the action on the field. Within a few minutes the upper part of the planking gave way, showering a mass of helpless bodies to their death below. Hundreds fell to the ground through what had suddenly become a vast trap-door, the lucky ones being the last to topple down, their descent softened by the heap of dying bodies beneath them.

Because the casualties had disappeared out of sight as they fell, the spectators in the other stands were unaware that anything serious had occurred. When a wave of panic passed through the lower sections of the West Stand and some of the people there were pushed forward on to the pitch, the game was halted for a while but was then resumed. Indeed, it was played right through to end in a 1–1 draw. The contrast between the entertainment out on the pitch and the hidden agony behind the West Stand was acute. As the next issue of the *Scotsman* commented: 'The fact that the game was proceeded with was doubtless gratifying to a great number who had assembled, many of them from long distances. But to those engaged

The Soccer Tribe's first major disaster occurred at Ibrox Park, Glasgow, in 1902, when a section of the grandstand collapsed (below left) hurling 25 spectators to their deaths and injuring hundreds more. While the bodies were being removed (below), the game continued, to end in a 1-1 draw.

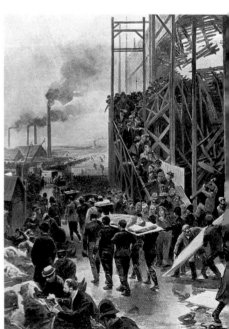

The chaotic scene at Wembley Stadium in 1923. Thousands smashed their way into the already packed ground, until they covered almost the entire field of play. The pitch was eventually cleared by a policeman on a white stallion (just visible in the centre of the picture) and the event became known in soccer legend as the White Horse Cup Final.

amongst the dead and dying, the applause which from time to time punctuated the play seemed incongruous, coming as it did as an accompaniment to the groans and moans of the injured and dying.'

Altogether there were 518 casualties, made up as follows: dead, 25; dangerously injured, 168; seriously injured, 153; slightly injured, 172. The scene resembled a battlefield awash with blood, and yet an eye-witness involved in the rescue operation records that: 'Half an hour afterwards, when all the injured had been taken out, and play was again in progress, I was surprised to see the terrace occupied again.' It takes more than death and disaster to put the Soccer Tribesman off his game.

The same was true of the next major catastrophe, which took place at Sheffield Wednesday's ground at Hillsborough on February 4th 1914. Then, during an FA cup-tie replay, a massive retaining wall collapsed injuring 75 people, but as before play was soon restarted. The record books state drily: 'The game was resumed but there was no addition to the score of 1–0 in favour of the Wednesday.' It seemed as though only a world war could halt play, and tragically this was soon proved to be the case.

Within a few years of the return of peace, the Soccer Tribe was to witness one of the most extraordinary events in its long history. Recorded in soccer legend as the White Horse Cup Final, the match played at the newly completed Wembley Stadium in London on April 28th 1923 was a scene of almost total chaos. Nearly half a million people converged on the ground that day to see Bolton fight out the final with West Ham. Those in charge of the new stadium were proud of the fact that it could hold 127,000 and imagined that this would more than suffice, since the previous year's cup final had attracted a crowd of no more than 53,000. But they had reckoned without the

lure of their brand new National Stadium. They had taken every other precaution, even going to the lengths of importing a battalion of infantry to thunder around on the terraces in heavy army boots, testing the strength of the structure to ensure that there was no repeat of the Ibrox disaster of 1902. But as the horde of eager fans grew and grew on that Saturday morning, they realized that, even if their terraces would stand firm, all their carefully laid plans were soon to collapse about their ears.

The gates were closed on the capacity crowd at 1.45 pm. There was no more room without serious overcrowding. The organizers were shocked to discover that, outside the towering walls, there was a vast crush of a quarter of a million more would-be spectators determined to get inside. Events moved swiftly. The locked-out crowd launched a mass attack on the stadium, battered down the gates, scaled the fences and hurled themselves onward into the sacred arena. The human tide swept forward until there were an estimated 100,000 extra bodies crammed into the ground. They flooded the entire pitch until hardly a blade of grass was visible. In the seething mass of humanity, several hundred people fainted and by the end of the day no fewer than one thousand casualties had been treated for shock, collapse or minor injury. But only 24 needed hospital treatment and by some miracle not one single death was recorded.

At 2.45 pm the king arrived and the National Anthem was sung, but to what purpose was not clear, since there was no space left in which a game could be played. Officials were distraught and helpless. The police and stewards seemed powerless. And then, as in all good legends, the hero of the day arrived on a white horse, to save the situation. The saviour in question was not a knight in armour, but a police constable named George Scorey, mounted on his thirteen-year-old police stallion called Billy. He picked his way carefully to the very centre of the Wembley turf and started to circle

In 1946 two disasters struck within days of one another, both caused by stadium collapses. On March 9th, 33 people were crushed to death and 500 injured at a match in Bolton, in the north of England. Only a few days earlier, on February 20th, at Lille in northern France (above), hundreds more had been trapped when a grandstand roof, weakened by latecomers climbing on top of it, fell on the packed crowd below. Seconds after the photograph was taken, the entire roof caved in.

slowly around, edging the crowd back inch by inch until a small patch of green grass began to show near the centre spot. Little by little, gently but firmly he enlarged his territory, the massive horse nudging people back further and further, while his rider persuaded the front ranks to link hands and push outwards. It took him forty minutes to remove them as far as the touch-line, at which point it became clear that driving them further was a physical impossibility.

Wisely, the referee decided to start the match despite the extraordinary circumstances, and nearly an hour late the game kicked off. From time to time players, unable to halt themselves, crashed into the crowd and disappeared, struggling desperately back on to the field as the game continued. At half-time both teams had to stay on the pitch, since there was no way they could force a passage through to the dressing rooms. Several times in the second half, play had to be stopped as spectators spilled forward on to the field, but the game was finally completed and Bolton triumphantly carried off the FA Cup.

A minor version of this chaotic incident occurred immediately after the Second World War, when, on November 13th 1945, the mysterious team of Moscow Dynamos visited England to play at Chelsea's Stamford Bridge ground. Again, thousands of fans were locked out of an already bulging stadium. Many of them were men fresh from storming buildings in war-torn Europe and their army training was once again to be put to good effect. They tore doors from their hinges and used them as battering rams on the main gates; they took ladders and used them to scale the barricades; they hurtled over walls as if on an assault course; they burst through glass skylights and clambered through every hole they could smash in the beleaguered stadium. More than 10,000 determined fans managed to gatecrash the match, but when it began there were still many thousands struggling outside. There were so many clinging to the grandstand roof and crawling about on it to gain a better view, that it creaked and groaned and threatened to collapse on the tightly packed throng beneath. Happily it held and, at the end of the day, the officials were able to breathe a sigh of relief that, as at the White Horse Cup Final, nobody had died in the mêlée. Although, as before, hundreds had fainted in the crush, fewer than twenty had need of hospital treatment, the worst case being a broken leg.

The following year, however, saw a soccer disaster with a much more tragic outcome. The date was March 9th 1946 and the match was an FA cup-tie between Bolton and Stoke, at Bolton's Burnden Park Stadium. Again, overcrowding was to blame. The pressure of the crowd broke down a brick wall and sent a wave of bodies surging forward against crush barriers which collapsed under the strain. In the human avalanche that followed, 33 people were crushed to death and more than 500 injured, at that time the greatest casualty list in the history of the game. Only twelve minutes of the game had been played. The referee, at the request of the police, removed the players to their dressing rooms while aid was given to the injured. Then, after a halt of twenty-six minutes, the game continued and was played through to its end, in traditional fashion. The full extent of the tragedy was kept from the players and, as Stanley Matthews said afterwards, 'I may be accused of hardness when I say our minds were soon on the game again, but it is the truth ... within a few minutes of returning to the field after the hold-up we had forgotten that men, who a little earlier had been cheering us, were now lying dead.' Such is the intensity of the great tribal ritual.

Following this disaster, a special enquiry was set up and made firm recommendations that, in future, improved safety regulations must be enforced and that all grounds must be restricted to a specific crowd maximum. But nothing was done. The authorities were indolent and for years it seemed as though they were going to get away with it. Then, in 1971,

The second Glasgow disaster, 69 years after the first, was even more deadly, killing 66 spectators in a crush of bodies so terrible that it twisted and buckled the heavy metal piping of the handrails as though it were made of cardboard (left).

an even bigger disaster struck. On January 2nd, at Glasgow's Ibrox Park – the scene of the first great soccer catastrophe – the horrific total of 66 people were crushed to death and more than 200 injured. It was, in a sense, a freak accident. The home team, Rangers, were losing to their hated rivals, Celtic, and with only a minute or so to the final whistle, large groups of disconsolate home supporters started to troop away to the exits. Then, with only seconds of play left, Rangers scored the equalizer. The great roar brought the early leavers rushing back, just as the main army of fans was about to depart. The two human tides met in head-on collision on a steep section of terracing, the descending wave engulfing the climbing one. Heavy metal piping was twisted out of shape in the wild crush that followed, as bodies piled on bodies until the stadium began to look like a charnel house.

This time the authorities were forced to act, but it was not until 1975 that the Safety of Sports Grounds Act was finally passed and strict conditions were applied to all stadia, with greatly reduced 'official ground capacity' figures.

If the worst hazard for a supporter was being crushed to death, the greatest risk for a player was not on the ground, in either sense of the word, but in the air. Top players since the Second World War have been required to travel a great deal by air, in order to fulfil their engagements, and on two occasions this has led to a major disaster. The first occurred on May 14th 1949 when the Italian League Champions, Torino, were returning to Turin from a match in Lisbon. Their plane crashed into the Basilica of Superga on the outskirts of Turin, killing the whole of the first team squad, including eight Italian internationals. Also on board were all the reserves, the manager, the trainer and the coach. Every one of them died. In a second, one of Europe's great soccer clubs was totally wiped out.

Nine years later, on February 6th 1958, a fate almost as bad was to befall

The Munich air disaster in 1958 (below) wiped out eight of Manchester United's star players, along with their trainer, coach and club secretary. The death of their team captain, Duncan Edwards, was commemorated with a stained glass window.

Manchester United as their aircraft failed to take off from Munich airport. They had been to Belgrade for a European Cup match, but few of them were to return. Eight of the star players died as a result of the crash, along with their trainer, their coach, the club secretary, and eight sports journalists who had been covering the trip. Since then, despite increased travelling for top teams, there have been no further air disasters for the soccer world.

There is, however, one final type of calamity to be mentioned. The first two categories – *crushes* and *crashes* – are bad enough, but at least they are predominantly accidental. The third is worse, because it involves deliberate acts of savagery. It is the mercifully rare category of *riots*.

One often hears stories of a soccer 'riot', but usually the word is not justified. A few hundred Scottish fans rushing around on the pitch at Wembley after a victory over England, smashing the goalposts and tearing up handfuls of turf, may seem like a riot to the stadium officials, but few people are hurt and it is child's play compared with the worst that the Tribal Archives have to offer.

Soccer's darkest day is undoubtedly May 25th 1964, when at least 301 people were killed and over 500 injured at the National Stadium in Lima, Peru, following a match between Peru and Argentina. The atmosphere was already tense and, when the Uruguayan referee disallowed a Peruvian goal with only two minutes to go to the final whistle, the crowd exploded in uncontrollable anger. The riot that ensued was so fierce that police were driven to using tear gas. This only increased the sense of panic and chaos, as the crowd hurled bottles, set fire to the stand and tore down iron railings. The police then started shooting into the crowd and killed four of the fans. The panic rose to new peaks of hysteria as terror mixed with anger to create a frenzy of stampeding figures. They hurled themselves against the exit gates, which were still locked, until the corpses were piled high, as if the stadium was a nightmare concentration camp rather than a simple sports arena. The

official figure of 301 dead is said by some to be too low. Others put it at 318, or as high as 350. But even in the midst of this carnage, the old soccer traditions still survived. That night a huge mob marched on the Presidential Palace in Lima demanding justice. But what precisely was their demand? An investigation to track down the thugs in the crowd who had first started rioting and who had initiated the whole incident? Some kind of compensation for the bereaved relatives of the dead? No. Their main concern was that the result of the match should be declared a draw. There can be no clearer example than this of the way in which the fanaticism of the Soccer Tribesmen for their game transcends all other considerations.

A few years later, South America was to witness another violent outburst at a match played in Buenos Aires on June 23rd 1968. During a game between River Plate and Boca Juniors, young thugs started throwing burning paper into the crowd to terrorize them. They succeeded beyond their wildest dreams as the stampedes they caused killed 73 spectators and injured 200 more.

But perhaps the most spectacular of all the great Tribal Disasters was the one that occurred in Central America in 1969. There, in a World Cup qualifying round, a match between Honduras and El Salvador led to such savage rioting that the two countries broke off diplomatic relations with one another and in no time at all were at war. This 'Soccer War', as it has been called, is the classic example of the great symbolic ritual of the game becoming de-ritualized and returning to its primitive roots. True, in this case the relations between the two countries were already poor, but the fact that a simple ball-game can carry such significance that it is capable of acting as the trigger for a full-scale war, underlines yet again the power of the sport and the way in which it dominates the minds of those who follow it so avidly, sometimes to their deaths.

Major riots are rare, but when they do occur they transform the soccer ground from a symbolic battlefield into a real one. Here, riot police are standing by with shields (opposite, above left) and guns (opposite, above right). When trouble breaks out (opposite, below – in Holland), they fan out over the field to restore order and are sometimes called upon to use their shields to rescue attacked players and see them to safety through a hail of missiles (above – in Rome).

38 Hero Worship

AUTOGRAPHS AND IDOLS, FANMAIL AND STARS

The Tribal Followers worship their heroes, but their adoration is not as straightforward as it may appear at first glance. Compared with other forms of hero worship it has some unusual features. To understand this, it helps to contrast the attitudes of the devoted fans of the soccer stars with those of the followers of film stars or pop idols.

There is a saying in Hollywood that 'you are as good as your last film', but this is not strictly the case. Film fans have a long memory and their idols can retain their mystique for many years on the basis of a few brilliant, early movies. The same is true in the world of music, but it is much more difficult for the magic of a soccer star to survive after his peak years are past. The explanation of this difference has to do with the nature of the 'product'. The actor makes a film, the composer writes a piece of music, the singer records a song. They are concerned with producing tangible things. Their films can be shown again and again, the music played over and over, year after year. Their original triumphs are always there to keep the fans' memories alive.

In theory, the same could be true of the great soccer stars. Films and tapes of their most exciting performances could be kept and shown time after time in just the same way. Yet this is rarely done. Humphrey Bogart and Elvis Presley are enduring figures in the world of popular entertainment, their work constantly revived for younger generations to enjoy, but the soccer stars who were famous when Bogart and Presley were at their peak are now largely forgotten, except by the older supporters. The names of the greatest of them may be vaguely familiar to the young fans, but they are no longer idolized. The hero worship of the Soccer Tribe is a fickle, fleeting thing.

Even at small amateur clubs (right) there are heroes to be championed, in this case on the sweater of an ardent supporter. For one baby girl (far right) hero worship was taken to unusual extremes that she will remember for the rest of her life. Her father, a fanatical Liverpool supporter, named her after the entire Liverpool team and coaching staff. Her full name, on her birth certificate, reads: Paula St John Lawrence Lawler Byrne Strong Yeats Stevenson Callaghan Hunt Milne Smith Thompson Shankly Bennett Paisley O'Sullivan.

The fruits of fame and the hazards of hero-worship – players besieged by autograph hunters (left), ecstatic fans (below) and press cameramen (right).

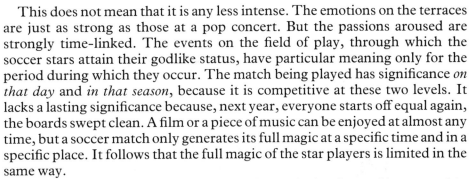

This does not mean that it is any less intense. The emotions on the terraces are just as strong as those at a pop concert. But the passions aroused are strongly time-linked. The events on the field of play, through which the soccer stars attain their godlike status, have particular meaning only for the period during which they occur. The match being played has significance *on that day* and *in that season*, because it is competitive at these two levels. It lacks a lasting significance because, next year, everyone starts off equal again, the boards swept clean. A film or a piece of music can be enjoyed at almost any time, but a soccer match only generates its full magic at a specific time and in a specific place. It follows that the full magic of the star players is limited in the same way.

Two other factors work against a faithful, enduring form of hero worship amongst the Soccer Followers: teams and transfers. The idolized player is a member of a team which represents a club. His individual merit may be immense and he may stand out from his team-mates like a great star with a supporting cast, but whereas a famous cinema star can virtually carry a whole film, no one player can carry a whole match. His skills are far more interlocked with those of his colleagues. They may lack his glamour or charisma, but their talents are so vital to his success that he can never be elevated very far above them in the adoration of the fans.

The transfer market causes further damage to his godlike role. Enduring fan-worship involves an act of great loyalty to the idolized figure. It is difficult for even the most besotted fan to retain this loyalty following the transfer of a star performer to another club. It is not merely the fact that the Great One has abandoned the tribal home; more important is that he is now actively displaying his talents at the home of a potential rival. In making the transfer, he is not merely *dis*loyal, he is *anti*-loyal. And even while the star is still with a particular club, his devoted followers know, at the back of their minds, that one day he may suddenly announce that he is leaving to join an enemy team, so they are always, in a sense, anticipating his defection. This, more than anything else, destroys any hope of long-term hero worship and limits it to the immediate present.

No such feelings would affect the fans of a great film star. If he 'transferred' from Warner Brothers to MGM it would make not the slightest difference to them because they feel no allegiance to any particular studio. Their emotions

are linked entirely to the end-product, the film itself. But for the soccer fan the 'film and the studio', that is, the match and the club, are inseparable. So, unless all soccer teams are in future restricted to local players and all transfers forbidden, the hero worship of the soccer world will undoubtedly retain its present transient form.

This said, it is worth recording that there are a few exceptions to the general rule. While most soccer stars are 'club heroes', or perhaps no more than 'heroes of the moment' in one particular match, there are a few extraordinary individuals who transcend all barriers and become true world stars, beyond club, beyond country, beyond all restrictions and local loyalties. These godlike figures are revered wherever they go, but there are few enough of them to be numbered on the fingers of two hands. They are the men like Pelé, Keegan, Cruyff, Beckenbauer, Bettega, Best and Kempes and they belong in a class of their own. Wherever they play, the hero worship of the fans can be seen at its most extreme. There are countless autograph books to be signed, hundreds of cameras constantly clicking, and repeated attempts to reach out and touch their sacred bodies. Sometimes the urge to touch the Great Ones becomes so strong that they are mobbed to the point of physical injury. One Brazilian star, after a brilliant performance in which he scored five goals, was so badly mobbed that his jaw was broken and he ended the day in hospital.

One of the greatest heroes of yesterday, Stanley Matthews, produced reactions so intense in those who witnessed his wizardry, that they were even inspired to write poems for him, one of which ended: 'Expressionless enchanter, weaving as on strings/Conceptual patterns to a private music, heard/Only by him, to whose slowly emerging theme/He rehearses steps, soloist in compulsions of a dream.'

The average fan is more likely to say of his idol 'he's magic', and leave his verbal praise at that, but his inner feelings may not be so very different.

39 Tribal Souvenirs

PENNANTS AND PROGRAMMES, STICKERS AND STAMPS

When the Soccer Tribesman withdraws from the nerve-centre of tribal life – the stadium – and wends his way home to the privacy of his room, he feels temporarily cut off from the climate of excitement. This is something a native tribesman would not experience, as his hut would be one of the cluster that makes up the heart of the tribal village. He would require no reminder of his tribal affiliation. But the Soccer Tribesmen's homes are scattered far and wide through the city, often several miles from the stadium, and this gives rise to a special need – a need for souvenirs.

By covering the walls and shelves of his private room with mementoes, he can re-create the atmosphere of the Tribal Gatherings, can relive the moments of shared elation. To do this he has to forage for tribal bric-à-brac, collecting and hoarding anything that has associations with his particular team or club.

The most precious souvenirs are those that are unique to him, personal mementoes of particular incidents – a programme autographed by one of his heroes, a discarded shinpad stolen from the edge of the pitch, or a banner he made himself for a vital match. Sometimes these special souvenirs are obtained under extraordinary circumstances. Once, long ago, when an

After a Scottish victory at Wembley, a great tartan army swarmed on to the pitch, smashed the goals and carried off bits of them as souvenirs (above). They also dug up pieces of the sacred turf to take home as mementoes of the English defeat. Despite bellows of rage from the authorities, the Scotsmen defiantly celebrated the event by printing special T-shirts proudly proclaiming their actions (above right).

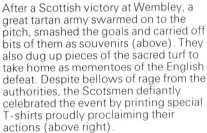

Even when the team is out of sight it need not be out of mind. The most fanatical followers take their obsession home with them in the shape of countless club souvenirs. In this case (left) an ardent Everton supporter has completely covered his bedroom walls with photographs, posters, emblems and bric-à-brac.

English team was playing at the town of Wageningen in Holland, a shot at goal was struck so forcibly that the crossbar broke in two. The spectators surged on to the field and, dragging the shattered timber to one side, took out their pen-knives and began cutting splinters from it to take home as precious relics, as if they were fragments of a holy cross. An observer recorded later that, 'Some of those small chunks carved out of that crossbar are to be found today in glass cases treasured in the neat little homes of Wageningen.'

A similar, but more destructive incident occurred following a Scottish victory over England at Wembley in 1977. As the final whistle blew, the Scottish supporters swarmed across the pitch and clambered in large numbers on to the goals, until the crossbars broke under the strain. They tore at the bars and the goal-netting in their urgent quest for souvenirs of their great day of triumph over the hated southerners, and some used their knives to hack out lumps from the sacred turf of the pitch itself. This particular foray for mementoes caused damage estimated at £18,000.

In an attempt to satisfy this collecting urge in a way that avoids theft and pillage, clubs have for many years sold a variety of official souvenirs in 'club shops'. Although these lack the personal magic of the unique souvenirs, and despite the fact that they are usually mass-produced by large firms rather than made at the club headquarters, they are nevertheless acceptable to many tribesmen. With particularly successful clubs, the demand becomes almost insatiable and the firms that market them have to strain their imaginations to devise a wide enough variety of objects to offer for sale.

In addition to the usual coloured scarves and flags, badges and stickers, rosettes and pennants, clothing-patches and ties, photos and posters, it is now possible to obtain glasses embossed with the club emblem, mugs decorated with the faces of the team complete with replica signatures, fancy hats in the team colours, emblematic tie-pins, and ornate mirrors overprinted with the club insignia and records of their cup triumphs. Then there are club annuals and record-books, club-coloured carrying bags, club T-shirts, club fountain-pens, animal mascots, and even 'Team Names Ceramic Door Tiles with Illustrated Emblem' which the fanatical tribesman can fix to the door of his private room, announcing his allegiance to all visitors and making his den somehow more a part of the club centre. Even when he retires to bed, his team

need not be forgotten, because he can now buy a 'Machine Washable Easy Care Polyester Viscose Fast Colour Football Club Bedspread'.

If his obsession drives him still further, there is a third category of souvenir in which he can indulge. This type is neither personal nor linked to his own club, but is concerned instead with the sport in general. He may branch out into the world of football cigarette cards, now a specialized and expensive hobby, or the equally costly business of assembling a collection of soccer postage stamps, of which hundreds are available. And a thriving business is developing around the mania for collecting match programmes of all clubs and from all periods. So many dealers are now operating in this field that regular 'programme fairs' are organized, where the experts sift and sort and try to ferret out a particularly rare and elusive item.

In these many different ways, the soccer enthusiast expresses his devotion to his tribe and fills his home with visible and tangible reminders of his passion and his intense loyalty. Surrounded by all the paraphernalia of his club, he need never have his beloved team out of his mind for a moment. His retreat becomes a virtual shrine to soccer.

(previous pages) Many Tribal Followers, both young and old, collect club badges in large numbers and their clothes are often so covered in these that they appear to be wearing a kind of decorative armour. These and other ornaments are purchased from special supporters' shops found at most stadia, or from souvenir-sellers outside the ground. For the insatiable collector there are also soccer stamps, cigarette cards, programmes and a wide variety of mail order items obtainable through soccer magazines.

40 Tribal Mascots

TEDDY BEARS AND TOYS, SMALL BOYS AND OLD MEN

Like the players, the Tribal Followers are deeply superstitious and employ many magic rituals to bring their teams good luck on the field. They dress in lucky garments, carry lucky charms and perform special actions which they hope will influence the outcome of the match. As with the players, most of the precautions are taken privately, even secretly, as if to broadcast them would somehow reduce their effectiveness. But in one particular respect, the good luck magic is performed openly and publicly, with the bold display of a conspicuous club mascot. This figure, human or animal, acts as the embodiment of the club's good luck wishes for their team.

The mascots take many forms. Frequently they are animal toys or images based on the creatures that appear on the official club emblems, often a lion, a horse, or a bird of some kind. In the case of Carlisle, for instance, where a fox's face is depicted in the centre of the club crest, an ardent supporter regularly carries a stuffed fox with him to matches to ensure that fortune smiles on his home team. Other fanatical fans dress themselves up in complete animal costumes for important games, bringing their totemic animals to life to increase the power of their magic.

Men dressed as animals are particularly popular at North American soccer matches, but their status is rather different. Whereas the European animal-man is an unofficial mascot, part of the crowd, the American counterpart is always a member of the official warm-up parade and usually accompanies the troupe of cheer-leaders on to the field, remaining on the perimeter throughout the match as an additional crowd-rouser. The New York Cosmos, for example, being run by Warner Communications, employ an animal-man mascot dressed as the star of the Warner Brothers cinema

Carlisle's lucky mascot, a stuffed fox, has been ceremonially placed on the centre spot of the pitch before every home match for over twenty years by this devoted supporter (below). The mascot of the New York Cosmos team, Bugs Bunny (below right), was adopted from the Warner Brothers cartoon.

(opposite) The most popular toy mascot is the teddy bear, taken as a good luck charm to many matches, despite the fact that it usually has no connection with the clubs' official emblems.

cartoons, Bugs Bunny. The giant rabbit, complete with outsize carrot, entertains the spectators before the kick-off and then stays to wave on his team from the touch-line.

Nothing quite so obtrusive appears on European touch-lines during the actual match, but in earlier days it was a common practice for one particular, brightly clad, unofficially 'official' human mascot to parade around the edge of the pitch before the start of the game, dressed in the team's colours. This seems to have faded out in recent years, although for many seasons an England mascot in the colourful shape of Mr Ken Bailey has accompanied the national side whenever it travels abroad. Clad in immaculate red tailcoat and black top hat, with a Union Jack waistcoat and carrying a flag and shield, he has become a familiar and popular figure in many countries. So impressive is his appearance that even the usually hostile local fans treat him in a friendly and respectful way.

Perhaps the most surprising choice for a lucky soccer mascot is the teddy bear. It is surprising for three reasons. First, it is basically a child's toy and therefore, in theory, lacks the dramatic impact of a more heraldic image. Second, it represents a cuddly bear-cub and not a fierce, awe-inspiring, adult bear. Third, it has nothing to do with the official emblems of the clubs where it appears so often as a mascot figure. There are, for example, Arsenal teddy bears and West Ham teddy bears, although Arsenal's emblematic image is a cannon and West Ham's is a giant hammer. But despite its apparent lack of connection with the Soccer Tribe, and despite the way in which it clashes with official club images, the teddy bear crops up over and over again, on the terraces, in the supporters' buses and outside their decorated homes.

How the teddy bear managed to make such a successful invasion of the soccer world is a mystery. It began life in the United States in 1902 as a result of a hunting trip undertaken by the American President, Teddy Roosevelt.

Rival human mascots used to parade together around the touch-line before important matches in England (above). The custom has faded in recent years, but a few human mascots still accompany their national teams, including the much-travelled Serafino of Italy (below) and Ken Bailey of England (below right).

A number of teams have developed the ritual of taking small boys, dressed in playing kit, on to the field for the pre-match warm-up.

He sportingly refused to shoot a small bear because he claimed that it was little more than a cub. The story quickly spread and became a favourite theme for political cartoonists, who used the incident to depict the President as the defender of the weak. The animal became known as 'Teddy's bear' and later, as toys were made based on the cartoonists' drawings, this was shortened to 'Teddy bear'. So the original significance of the now immensely popular teddy bear was that it symbolized 'a creature spared from disaster'. Children who cuddle their friendly 'teddies' today have no idea of this meaning and it seems far-fetched to suppose that early soccer fans saw the bear as a magic charm that would spare them disaster. There is a faint possibility that they adopted this piece of symbolism deliberately, but it seems more likely that the small children of fans sometimes took their favourite toy with them to matches and, when their fathers' teams were successful, the bear became instantly linked with good fortune. After that it would be dangerous to leave it at home and, later on, special giant teddy bears would have to be made, not for the children but for the serious adult fans, as part of their superstitious rituals. But even if this simpler explanation is the correct one, it remains a happy coincidence that the mascot which sits defiantly on the terraces behind the home team's goalmouth began life as something at which a great man was unable to shoot.

Finally, there is a totally distinct form of mascot which is now becoming increasingly popular at many clubs – the boy player. As a special honour at each home game, a small boy, dressed in the colours and football kit of his club, is allowed to accompany the players as they run out through the tunnel for the pre-match kick-about. He joins them on the sacred turf for this warm-up period, kicking the practice balls back and forth with his heroes. Then, when the referee and linesmen arrive and take up their places on the centre spot, he runs over, shakes hands with them and runs off to the applause of the home crowd. From such simple ceremonies, future fanatics are born.

41 Tribal Exhibitionists

LOONIES, STREAKERS AND MOONERS

There is a general tendency for people to behave in a more restrained way in public than in private. Out and about among strangers, in the streets and shops, restaurants and offices, at public meetings and places of entertainment, we inhibit our actions. Many of the things we do in the privacy of our homes become taboo. We are more careful of our appearance. We observe the formalities.

In the early days of soccer the Tribal Followers obeyed this code. They put on their best clothes to attend matches. They clapped and cheered politely. But as the years passed, the mood changed. As amateurs gave way to professionals on the field, and the crowds grew bigger and more passionate in their loyalties, the usual social inhibitions began to break down. Eccentric and brightly hued costumes started to appear. The more ardent supporters blossomed into full display plumage, boldly presenting to the world their tribal colours. In language and dress they became increasingly uninhibited.

Despite this sense of freedom, the vast majority of supporters today still recognize certain limits beyond which they will not go. For a few eccentrics, however, the mood of bold display becomes so stimulating that they are driven past these limits to perform some extreme act of exhibitionism. They fall into three groups: the Loonies, the Streakers and the Mooners.

The Loonies simulate some kind of madness. They are, of course, perfectly sane, but for a while they enjoy the total release of wild, pretended craziness. One of them may dress in completely bizarre clothing, far beyond the usual display costume; another may wander around in the middle of the street, waving, weaving in and out of traffic and singing at the top of his voice; another may climb to some high point and sway or teeter as if about to crash to his death; and another may set off on a meandering solo run across the sacred turf of the pitch, as if, in his dreaming head, he has magically become one of his own great Tribal Heroes.

The usual explanation offered for such behaviour is that the men were uncontrollably drunk. But this is only a partial truth. Had they been equally drunk in some other social context, they would not have acted in quite the same way. Alcohol may well have contributed to their abandoned displays, but the special mood of the tribal assembly was also important. Like tribal warriors worked up into a frenzy of activity by war-dances and chants, or religious fanatics driven into a state of ecstasy by magical rites and incantations, they are men possessed. Momentarily they are on another plane, boosted out of orbit by the mass of excited fans around them.

Sadly, because they often cause too much of a disturbance, they are sometimes treated as if they are aggro-thugs and are strong-armed away by the police. More experienced policemen recognize them for what they are and handle them more gently, as harmless eccentrics. Only the more pompous and puritanical of tribesmen become seriously offended. The majority smile on them with tolerance, seeing them as an extreme caricature of their own state of mounting excitement.

A rare but distinct type of exhibitionist is the Streaker. This form of eccentricity involves performing a highly private act in a highly public place – namely, making a conspicuous run, stark naked, in front of a large crowd of onlookers. It seems to have first appeared at the beginning of the 1970s. The earliest examples were probably the result of dares and wagers, but then it became contagious and naked bodies, sprinting defiantly along, startled the unprepared crowds at a number of public events. Inevitably, soccer spectators were soon to be treated to this new form of exhibitionism. Their

The Streaker is a comparative newcomer to the rich variety of extroverts inhabiting the Soccer Tribe. The most adventurous, like this Dutchman at a match in Utrecht (below), reveal all from the top of one of the floodlight pylons, but this is a rare feat. Most Streakers content themselves with a lightning dash across the pitch, clutching their clothes in a carrier-bag (bottom).

Mooners are less extreme than Streakers, exposing only their buttocks. Sometimes this is done boldly from the centre spot, with the naked behind displayed to each of the four grandstands in turn (above, in England), and sometimes from the windows of a passing car outside the stadium (below, in Italy).

reaction, far from outrage, was one of surprised amusement, and the valiant Streaker was usually cheered on as he rushed away, chased by slightly embarrassed policemen, who presumably did not relish the thought of being photographed in hot pursuit of a naked man.

The Streaker's display is a curious one. It involves quietly stripping without drawing attention and then setting off on a run that must suddenly become as conspicuous as possible. Finally, it requires a vanishing act as unobtrusive as the original undressing, to avoid arrest for 'indecent exposure'. Its purpose is one of simple, bold shock. Unlike the act of 'flashing', in which a man in hiding leaps out on unsuspecting women and exposes his genitals to their gaze, the act of streaking has no sexual significance. Its aim is to startle, not disgust. For the soccer Streaker, it poses one special problem – namely, how to regain one's clothing. The chances of being able to run a looping path and end the streak where it began, are remote, so the performer must either risk ending up vulnerably naked, or must adopt the rather ludicrous procedure of carrying his clothes with him in a small bag. The latter solution seems to have been the one most favoured, further heightening the crowd's amusement at this unexpected form of extra entertainment.

The third type of exhibitionist is the Mooner. According to a *Guardian* report in 1974, the Mooner was a less extreme forerunner of the Streaker: 'Streaking ... seems to be the mainly male equivalent of the mainly female practice that cropped up in campuses across the United States in the late fifties and early sixties. This was known as "mooning". Mooning consisted ... of exposing the bottom in the general direction of whoever the mooner wanted to impress, protest to, or affront.' The suggestion that female American students were the originators of this form of taunt is misleading. They may have made a new fad out of it and given it a new name, but the act of 'showing one's arse' as a gross insult is centuries old. Phrases such as 'kiss my arse' and 'arseholes to you' are well known from earlier times.

The essential message of the act of mooning is not, as some have supposed, sexual. Basically, one might say fundamentally, it is a symbolic act of defecation on the victims at which it is aimed. As a result, when performed by male soccer exhibitionists, it sometimes causes a more powerful reaction than the less hostile act of streaking.

Two examples serve to illustrate this. In 1980 a bus carrying Grimsby supporters home after an away match was being followed in heavy traffic by a family saloon. The five young fans in the rear seat of the bus dropped their trousers and pressed their buttocks against the rear window, presenting a dramatic multi-moon to the mother, father and children in the car. The father was so outraged that his young daughters should be offered such a view that he made angry signs to the offenders. This, in turn, annoyed them and, when the bus was halted at a red light, they leapt from the bus and began kicking the car and threatening the occupants. The father struggled out of his door to stop them and a fight ensued. His twelve-year-old daughter went to his rescue and both received head wounds that required hospital treatment and stitches. Had he merely smiled at the Mooners, trouble would have been avoided, but the insult carried by the display was too strong for him to ignore.

The same was true of an incident that occurred at Arsenal's Highbury ground the year before. Once again an act of mooning caused outrage, this time on the part of the authorities. The scene was set in the following way: Arsenal were hosts to Coventry; the home team had failed to score, but the visitors had managed to sneak in a goal, apparently deflected off Arsenal defender Sammy Nelson. Although he was a full-back, Nelson was so determined to make amends that during the second half he stormed up the field and succeeded in scoring the equalizer. Instead of waving to the crowd in the usual way, he turned towards them and dropped his shorts, exposing his buttocks as if to say, 'So much for any bad thoughts you were having about me.' The crowd were happy enough about his triumph to take the joking rebuke in good part, but the Tribal Elders were far from amused. They overreacted wildly, claiming that he had brought the game into disrepute. Fuel was added to the fire by some journalists who, starved of controversy for their columns, demanded that he should never be allowed to play for Arsenal again.

In his autobiography, Nelson's friend and team-mate Liam Brady strongly attacked the way the incident was handled: 'Sammy, a natural prankster, dropped his shorts as nothing more than a fun gesture ... But not only was Sammy fined and suspended by Arsenal, he received an even heavier dose of punishment from the [FA] authorities. Which just about sums them up. These people come down hard on silly, stupid and trivial matters yet rarely appear to be so sharp when it comes to players on the field who kick their way through one game after another.'

Mooning is by no means confined to the English-speaking world. When British photographers were in Italy in 1980 to cover international matches being played there, one of them spotted a car-load of Italian fans cruising towards him and took pictures of them as they passed by. He was slightly alarmed to see the car make a sudden U-turn and head slowly back towards him, wondering whether they had taken offence and were about to leap out and threaten him. Instead he was amazed to see pairs of naked buttocks protruding from the open windows and cheerfully recorded the display for posterity.

The famous Sammy Nelson incident at (appropriately named) Arsenal, when the player jokingly rebuked his fans by dropping his shorts in front of them. Both the Arsenal officials and the FA authorities brought ridicule on themselves by overreacting wildly to this mild escapade. Nelson was severely punished for his light-hearted indiscretion, despite the fact that the fans were obviously amused by it.

The Tribal Tongue

The Soccer Tribe has its own private language, made up of traditional phrases, technical cant, slang words, chants and slogans. With the liberal use of these a conversation in soccerese can take place in what appears to be the national tongue of the speakers, but which is nevertheless incomprehensible to anyone from outside the soccer world.

The development of specialized jargon irritates many people. They feel that it should be replaced by simple, plain English that everyone can understand. They also accuse the soccer speakers of being cliché-ridden and inarticulate. But they are overlooking three important points. First, the actions most commonly discussed are difficult to translate into verbal expression. The subtle differences in body movement and tactical skill are noted with great sensitivity by the watching eyes of both spectators and players, but they defy simple definition. This is true of many physical performances. The audience at a ballet, for example, may boast a more scholarly background than the crowds on the soccer terrace, but they find it equally difficult to describe in words what it is that makes the movements of one dancer slightly more satisfying than another. Superficially their descriptions may sound more articulate because they employ longer words, but a careful analysis of precisely what they are saying soon reveals that they are as unsuccessful as the soccer fan when it comes to pinning down the features of a virtuoso performance. In general, our vocabulary for dealing with the details of skilful or athletic body movements is woefully inadequate. As a result, clichés abound.

(below and right) Wherever there are unprotected walls, doors or fences, the soccer fanatic is liable to leave his mark – either extolling the virtues of his own team or threatening the survival of his enemies.

Second, many of the actions and sequences of play are unique to the soccer field and are not found in other aspects of our social life. There are no plain English words to describe them. Technical terms have to be invented. As a result, jargon words abound.

Third, there is always a desire in tribal groups that club together, to demonstrate verbally their difference from the rest of mankind. By deliberately using words which outsiders cannot understand, they set themselves apart and emphasize their distinct identity. They display their expertise by their knowledge of the 'secret language' of the tribe. As a result, slang expressions abound.

With these three influences at work it is not surprising that a soccer star, interviewed on television after a match, sounds decidedly odd to non-tribal ears. But the truth is that, if a great poet or author were persuaded to play a game of soccer and immediately afterwards had a microphone thrust under his nose, he would probably find himself equally at a loss for eloquent words and telling phrases. Consider this quotation: 'One wondered if a goal would ever come. White missed an easy chance in the opening minutes; just before half-time Jones had what seemed a good goal disallowed for off-side; Allen and Dyson missed open goals in the second half. It was not until the last quarter of the game that Smith, the centre-forward, beat a Leicester defender skilfully on the turn and scored with a shot which the goalkeeper had no chance to save.' Hardly singing prose; certainly lacking in poetic imagination, and without any signs of originality of thought or verbal interpretation. In short, it reads like any other post-match summing-up by a journalist, a manager, or even a player. And yet this quote comes from an article written for the *New Statesman* by one of the world's greatest living philosophers, A. J. Ayer, who also happens to be a lifelong soccer enthusiast. Faced with the task of writing about a match, his verbally brilliant mind was quickly reduced to much the same level as any other soccer fan. This is worth recalling when wincing at yet another predictable and seemingly thick-skulled answer to an interviewer's question, as a player of genius fumbles for his words shortly after completing a majestic tour-de-force on the pitch.

We would do well to ignore the mumbled inanities and remember only the game, but the problem is that, when a soccer player is interviewed, we see his face in close-up and he becomes suddenly more of an individual – more intimate. We have watched his distant figure on the field during the game,

but now we observe his facial expressions as he talks and we pay more attention to him as a person, rather than as a member of a team. The result is that, as we listen to him clumsily describing his feelings and his tactics, we give his words too much importance. It is hard not to come away with the idea that he is a dull-minded individual, despite the fact that minutes earlier we were marvelling at the skilful artistry of his physical actions, which were clearly both sensitive and imaginatively creative.

Perhaps the answer is that top sportsmen should refuse to give interviews, on the grounds that top writers are not expected to explain the significance of their new books by leaping about on a sports field. A golden silence would force their critics to accept the players on their own terms.

These comments apply, however, only to attempts to describe the game itself and the subtleties of play. In other social contexts the Soccer Tribesmen, including the players and managers, display a capacity for rapid verbal riposte that mirrors more closely the lightning moves on the field. This reveals itself most clearly in the sphere of tribal humour. The quick-fire back-chat of teams of players relaxing together away from the stadium is full of the tricks and feints, the trips and traps, with which their minds are so preoccupied during the game. They are for ever trying to catch one another out in some playfully insulting way – to leave a friend verbally stranded in the same manner that they leave an opponent physically stranded on the pitch.

It is impossible to translate these verbal moments into general comments.

ALLEY
WIJ GAAN NAAR ROME NU JULLIE NOG !!!
HOLLAND
Holland eindig B

At important matches, home-made slogans appear, either hung over barriers (above) or held high as a sea of waving banners (opposite). Occasionally, outsiders infiltrate the crowds to display their own rival slogans – sometimes political and sometimes religious (below).

JESUS TOOK THE PENALTY

To quote them is to destroy their quality. They are highly dependent on their contexts. The nearest one can get to describing the sharp, acid humour of the Soccer Tribe is to turn from the players to the supporters and to a special type of verbal joke – the slogan.

At an important match – a cup final, an international, a promotion battle, or a local derby – the verbal oddities and preoccupations of the tribe are displayed in a special, encapsulated form as sayings on banners, placards, flags and notices. These carefully chosen words are carried high in processions of followers converging on the great stadium, waved from cars, stuck on to clothing, scrawled as graffiti on walls, and finally held aloft in a massive terrace display inside the ground during the warm-up to the match.

These slogans fall into two main groups – those that are hostile and abusive to the enemy and those that are loyal and full of praise for the heroes. Some of the simplest banners do little more than announce the name of the club or team, but the majority attempt a full slogan, with a touch of tribal humour. Sometimes, with graffiti, a simple message is embellished by another hand. For example, a scrawled message on a London wall read CHELSEA ARE MAGIC and beneath it someone else had written WATCH THEM DISAPPEAR FROM THE FIRST DIVISION. This is typical of the 'come-back' or 'put-down' of the off-duty humour of the players themselves, and occurs over and over again. Beneath a religious poster announcing JESUS SAVES someone had daubed the words BUT PEARSON NETS THE REBOUNDS.

Once a saying like this has been invented it begins to appear repeatedly, with minor variations. JESUS SAVES BUT SMITH NETS THE REBOUNDS is written out as a complete banner, to be paraded around the ground on the morning of the match. An amusing sidelight on this raiding of the religious sphere was observed in the late 1970s, when groups of young Christians mingled with the gathering soccer fans at Wembley, carrying their own banners. Their slogans retaliated by raiding soccer for religious catch-phrases, such as JESUS TOOK THE PENALTY and CHRIST IS MY SUBSTITUTE.

Many soccer slogans follow this principle of playing on the double meaning of a word – one general and one special to the sport. A typical example is JOE JORDAN STRIKES FASTER THAN BRITISH LEYLAND. Sometimes the names of the teams lend themselves to this kind of treatment. When

Wolverhampton Wanderers met Nottingham Forest in a cup final, the slogan writers had a field day, with banners proclaiming such things as: WOLVES WILL DESTROY THE FOREST QUICKER THAN DUTCH ELM DISEASE, or WOLVES ARE THE LORDS OF THE FOREST.

Dwelt on separately, these slogans may not amount to much, but seen passing by on the occasion of an emotional match-day encounter, or brandished in great numbers as a massed display on the terraces, they add an attractive verbal footnote to the passions of the day. The fact that, like many of the exotic costumes, the banners and placards are privately manufactured by the fans themselves, rather than mass-produced, helps to intensify the atmosphere of quasi-religious fervour conjured up by these great occasions.

Many tribal sayings do not graduate to banner-display. They exist as favourite maxims or retorts rather than specific slogans. Passed on from one club to the next by word of mouth, they spread through the tribal network until they become part of the general soccer folklore. Spawned by verbally inventive individuals, they gradually become common property, and the Soccer Tribe has one for almost every occasion:

Manager to beaten players: 'If the meek are going to inherit the earth, you lot are going to be property millionaires.'

Trainer to exhausted players: 'If you drop dead tomorrow, at least you'll know you died in good health.'

Defeated manager to press: 'Even Napoleon had his Watergate.'

Supporter to expensive transfer: 'Hit him with your wallet.'

Players returning from foreign tour, about to meet their wives after a long absence: 'OK you guys, look horny.'

Manager on how to handle directors: 'Treat them like mushrooms. Keep them in the dark and throw manure over them at regular intervals.'

Pessimistic fans: Q. 'Are you going to watch United this week?' A. 'Why should I, they didn't come to see me when I was bad.'

Soccer slogans can now be seen all over the world, not only in traditional European strongholds of the game (below) but also in new territories such as Florida (below right).

Sexual jokes often figure in tribal humour and frequently appear on banners and placards at cup finals. Here, two rival comments from opposing fans play on the double meaning of the name of one of the star players.

Manager on press relations: 'I've always said there's a place for the press but they haven't dug it yet.'

The heaviest criticisms of the Tribal Language are reserved, not for the players and fans, but for the commentators and reporters on radio and television. These unfortunate men, burdened with long minutes of air-time to fill before and after bouts of play, face the most difficult verbal task of all. Like everyone else they would be happier merely to watch the game itself but, because of some curious official dictum, they are forced to indulge in interminable, analytical discussions. It is fondly imagined that such debates give extra significance to the events of the day, when in reality they diminish them. For the reasons given earlier, there is little of value that can be added, especially by people who have not been involved in the game, and the overall effect of prolonged match analysis is to alienate people who might otherwise be drawn into the tribal sphere by the excitements of the match itself. Television critic Clive James sums up the typical reaction with these comments: 'Television has caught football the way Europe used to catch the bubonic plague ... If all we saw was the matches themselves then things would not be so bad, but there are hours of uninspired chat to listen to as well. "Very sharp ... very quick ... like Ian says ... tremendous power ... tremendous ability to find the man ... tremendous second half ... certainly a willing worker ... never stops running ... showing his skills ... tremendous."' James concludes caustically: 'I scooped most of that up off the floor during ITV's coverage of the Italy v Spain match. It had drivelled out of the set and piled up like spume.'

The message is clear enough: the Tribal Language should be kept where it belongs – inside the tribal sphere itself. There, it can serve the function of exchanging technical information between experts and of providing a vehicle for tribal humour, banter and chit-chat. Elevated to the level of nationally transmitted debate it is in danger of becoming as tiresome as the hollow phrases of Party Political Broadcasts.

43 Tribal Chants

SONGS OF PRAISE AND HYMNS OF HATE

One of the most striking features of the modern soccer match in Britain is the massed chanting of the Tribal Followers after they have assembled on the terraces. Some form of chanting occurs at matches all over the world, but nowhere does it reach the complexity or intensity of the performance at British clubs, where the ritual singing of the tightly packed supporters has reached the level of something approaching a local art form.

A complete stranger to the game, passing by a crowded British stadium on match-day, might be forgiven for imagining that the event taking place inside was a sacred festival of some kind, or at the very least an international song contest, rather than a serious sporting encounter. He would find it hard to accept that the tough, heavy-booted fans who, moments before, had been pushing through the turnstiles, could suddenly become converted into melodious choirboys. Yet his ears would insist that this was indeed the case.

If he entered the stadium he would see, at each end, a huge cluster of singing heads, their actions synchronized as if by some unseen tribal choirmaster. As he listened he would hear chant after chant rise, pass through a series of rhythmic repetitions and then die. Sometimes the message of a particular song would be crystal clear, even to an outsider; sometimes, it would be obscure and puzzling. Even more perplexing would be the way the chanting continued after the game had begun, interspersed with cheers and roars, groans and boos, as the play ebbed and flowed. At certain moments the singing would seem to dominate the crowd's attention to the exclusion of the game itself. The inescapable conclusion would be that there were two contests taking place at the same time – a physical one between two teams of players and a vocal one between two choirs of supporters.

How has this British song-battle arisen? There appear to be several sources. Long ago there was a Victorian tradition of community hymn-singing before sporting events. It was rather formal, occasionally backed by music and usually fronted by a conductor on a small rostrum. Remnants of this practice still survive, such as the singing of 'Abide with Me' at Wembley, before the FA Cup Final, but as an organized event it has largely vanished. As a tribal memory, however, its influence was undoubtedly present when the fans on the terraces took matters into their own hands, somewhere around the middle of the twentieth century.

With the dramatic increase of post-war air travel and the stepping up of international soccer contests, the 1950s and 1960s saw the mixing together of a number of different 'fan-customs'. This was to provide a second major source. Mediterranean and South American fans were already drumming and clapping their heroes in a frenzy of devotion and encouragement, and these sounds found their way to British ears. Experts differ on the exact route taken. According to Stanley Reynolds, 'Chanting, banner-waving fans came first out of Italy.' Brian Glanville has another view. Prior to the 1966 World Cup in England, he claims, the English crowds at Wembley had 'been notorious for their cool, quiet indifference. But the World Cup had galvanized them, and they employed the hand-clapping chants which had come to Britain from Brazil via Chile in the 1962 World Cup, to be reworked on the Spion Kop terraces of the Liverpool ground.'

This mention of Liverpool introduces a third major influence. During the 1960s, when the chanting rituals first grew to epic proportions, the world of pop music was exploding in the cellars and clubs of Liverpool. The epoch of the Beatles had arrived and Merseyside awoke to find itself a centre of popular culture. The young fans of the Liverpool soccer terraces proudly

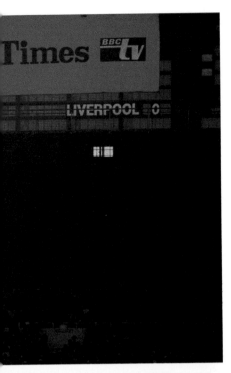

Community singing, with an official leader, before great contests (top) was a regular pre-match ritual in earlier days. Although it has now virtually disappeared, its influence remains in the informal, spontaneous chanting of the fans on the terraces (above).

took their new songs with them to the matches and gave mass renditions of them before the games, as a way of saying '*We* are the focus of today's music.'

With this musical development, the scene was set for a merging of the different influences: the Victorian hymn-singing, the Italian chanting, the South American clapping and shouting, and finally Beatlemania. They all came together on the sloping terraces of Liverpool's famous Spion Kop, and there a new tribal ritual was born, one which was to spread like wildfire from club to club across the land.

Before following its progress, a word is needed about the Kop itself. This stand at one end of the Liverpool stadium, originally a huge open slope, has become famous, even notorious, throughout the Soccer Tribes of the world. It has acquired the aura of a Mother Temple, a Holy Mecca, a Sacred Place where only the true initiates may set foot. To arrive there wearing, for example, a blue scarf would be the act of a lunatic or a potential suicide.

The Kop acquired its name in an unusual way. On the night of January 22nd 1900, British troops fighting the Boer War in South Africa engaged in a bloody battle that cost many lives. In their attempt to relieve their comrades at Ladysmith they were faced with an awesome obstacle – a defended hill called Spion Kop. The battle for the hill went on all night and by dawn, when the crest had been taken, the blood of two thousand men stained its surface. The victory was short-lived, however, the British commander being forced to withdraw to avoid further carnage, and the Spion Kop was reoccupied the next day by the Boers. Nothing had been gained, but great courage had been shown and it was the memory of this courage that the survivors took home to England. Some were Liverpool men and when they came back as heroes to their home town they brought with them the stirring tale of the bloodstained night of valour standing on the Spion Kop. Before long they found themselves standing on another slope – the great bank at one end of Liverpool's Anfield ground – watching their local team do battle in their own way on the field below, and they named the bank after their other battleground in South Africa. Years later, in the 1928–9 season, a covered stand was built over the Anfield Kop and it remains there to this day.

In the early 1960s the proud Kopites not only sang the latest Liverpool songs, but they began to adapt them to the mood of the moment. They invented new words for the tunes, relating their comments to the local players, their rivals, and special incidents in the game. When visiting fans at the other end of the ground heard this, they soon started to imitate the Kopite chants, changing the words yet again to suit their own grounds and players. In this way, like a chain-letter, the habit of inventing or adapting chants spread from club to club until it covered the entire country. Many of the singing fans now had no idea how or where their favourite chants had begun. But that mattered little. A major ritual had been established and it quickly expanded to include, not only the warm-up period before the match, but the ninety minutes of play as well.

Perhaps the most famous of all the chants is YOU'LL NEVER WALK ALONE, usually performed in moments of triumph with all the coloured scarves of the chanters stretched out horizontally to make a great quilt of tribal colour. Like so many of the ritual songs, this was first heard at the Kop in the early 1960s and owes its origin to the fact that a local pop star, Gerry Marsden, had a recording of it in the Top Ten of the day. His group, Gerry and the Pacemakers, has long since vanished from the charts and is largely forgotten, but remains anonymously immortalized by the Soccer Tribe's adoption of that one song.

Another chant, WHEN THE SAINTS GO MARCHING IN, based on an old jazz tune, was introduced by the Kop to honour one of their star players, Ian St John. It is now employed up and down the country with minor variations, but again its source is unknown to almost all who sing it.

It would be wrong to suggest that other clubs were not involved in introducing chants of their own. Tottenham had its GLORY GLORY HALLELUJAH, THE SPURS GO MARCHING ON and West Ham rejoiced with its WE'RE FOREVER BLOWING BUBBLES, to mention but two. And as the chanting habit spread, it became almost impossible to keep track of which chant began where. Eventually they all became inextricably mixed together – common tribal property to be used by all true supporters of any club.

That is the position today and the overall repertoire has become staggeringly complex, awaiting some folklore scholar to unravel it. As a step in that direction I arranged for recordings to be made at a number of matches in England during the 1978–9 season. A minute-by-minute analysis of these recordings has provided some interesting facts:

1 A study of four First Division clubs revealed a remarkable consistency in the rate of chanting. The total number of chantings per match varied only between 138 and 160, giving an average of 147.

2 The repertoire size of these four clubs (the number of different chants per match) varied between 44 and 68, the average being 57.

3 There was considerable overlap in the chants used from one club to another.

4 There were more chants in the period before the half-time whistle than in the period after it (three-fifths to two-fifths).

5 When a more detailed study was made of one Third Division club (Oxford United), involving a complete analysis of 15 home games during one season, it emerged that there were few differences between this and the First Division clubs, despite the much smaller size of the 'choir'. The total number of Oxford chantings per match was between 106 and 189, giving an average of 145 per game – surprisingly close to the figure of 147 obtained from the four First Division games.

6 The repertoire size of the 15 Oxford games was between 49 and 86 chants per match, giving an average of 67, slightly higher than the First Division clubs.

7 As before, there were more chants before the half-time whistle than after it (again, three-fifths to two-fifths).

These rather surprising results reveal that there is a typical level of chanting at English soccer matches, almost as if the singers have just so much to give, no more and no less, regardless of what is happening on the field, or how important the game may be. It is as though they attend a match to 'fulfil a singing engagement', complete their programme, and then leave. This suggests that many of the chants are independent of moment-by-moment incidents on the pitch, and are triggered off instead by some kind of 'internal display energy' from the terraces themselves.

To test this idea, four of the Oxford matches were studied to see how many of the individual chantings were 'event-timed' and how many were not. For example, if BRING ON THE CHAMPIONS is sung just before the home team emerges from the tunnel, or if THE REFEREE IS A BASTARD is chanted immediately after he has given a penalty to the enemy, such cases are said to be 'event-timed'. If songs erupt suddenly, seemingly of their own accord, when nothing special is occurring on the field, then they are said to be 'independent' chants:

> Average number of chantings per match, *event-timed*: 57
> *independent*: 98

This means that roughly 60 per cent of all chantings are unrelated to influences from the game. They belong to the separate world of the terrace culture. All the game has to do to trigger them off is to be *there*.

Some clubs have their own 'signature tunes'. At West Ham, where their theme song is 'I'm forever blowing bubbles', the words are sometimes brought to life with real bubbles.

One type of song that illustrates the need for a certain level of 'chant-output' is the boredom chorus. If a game lacks excitement, so that the mood of the crowd loses its tension, the terraces may fall silent for a while. Eventually, however, the chanters will feel a mounting need to express themselves, even though the style of play does not encourage it. They then sing deliberately irrelevant songs. Even the Kopites have been known to assail their beloved Liverpool team in this way. One Anfield match report commented: 'Liverpool's display . . . drew the ultimate insult from the Kop – a resounding chorus of "We all agree, *Tiswas* is better than *Swap Shop*".' *Tiswas* and *Swap Shop* are two rival children's television programmes that pointedly have nothing whatever to do with football. Clearly, the urge to chant has developed its own momentum and nothing, not even a poor game, can stop it, now that it has become a tribal ritual in its own right.

Another curious aspect of the independence of the chant-ritual is the way in which the tone of the songs often has no relation to the mood of the message. The fans may sing savage threats or gross insults in a tone of voice which is joyous, friendly, or even sentimental, according to the tune on which it is based. There is frequently no attempt to make loyal songs stirring, or hostile songs vicious and snarling. This contrast between style and content, in which sweet ballads are sometimes employed to convey a message of death and mutilation to the enemy, adds considerably to the formalized nature of the whole performance and enhances its ritual atmosphere.

To study the messages of the chants more closely, the fifteen Oxford United home matches were analysed chant by chant. Altogether there were 2,179 separate chantings, made up of 251 different chants. The basic messages of the chants fell into a number of distinct categories:

Confidence and Optimism
There were fifteen different chants in this category. Ten of them were bold assurances of future success:

1 WE WILL WIN, WE WILL WIN, WE WILL WIN . . . (repeat)
2 WE'RE GOING UP THE LEAGUE, TRA LA LA LA LA
3 WE'RE GOING UP, WE'RE GOING UP, EE AYE ADIO, WE'RE GOING UP . . . (repeat)
4 UPWARD BOUND, LA LA LA, UPWARD BOUND, LA LA LA
5 WE'RE GOING TO WIN DIVISION THREE AGAIN (followed by clapping)
6 WE'RE GONNA WIN THE CUP, WE'RE GONNA WIN THE CUP,
   AND NOW YOU'RE GONNA BELIEVE US AND NOW YOU'RE GONNA BELIEVE US,
   AND NOW YOU'RE GONNA BELIEVE US, WE'RE GONNA WIN THE CUP
7 WHATEVER WILL BE, WILL BE, WE'RE GOING TO WEM-BER-LEE, CHE SARA, SARA . . . (repeat)
8 WEM-BER-LEE, WEM-BER-LEE, WE'RE ALL DRESSED UP AND READY FOR WEM-BER-LEE
9 WE SHALL NOT BE MOVED, WE SHALL NOT, WE SHALL NOT BE MOVED, WE
   SHALL NOT, WE SHALL NOT BE MOVED,
   WE'RE GONNA WIN THE FA CUP, WE SHALL NOT BE MOVED
10 WE SHALL NOT BE MOVED, WE SHALL NOT, WE SHALL NOT BE MOVED,
   WE SHALL NOT, WE SHALL NOT BE MOVED,
   JUST LIKE A TEAM THAT'S GONNA WIN THE FA CUP,
   WE SHALL NOT BE MOVED

The subtle difference between chants nine and ten is amusing. When number ten was being sung, Oxford had already been knocked out of the FA cup competition, but the fans refused to allow this set-back to eliminate the 'we shall not be moved' song from their repertoire. They simply inserted the words 'just like a team that's' in place of 'we're'.

The other chants in this general category were references to team invincibility, such as BRING ON THE CHAMPIONS, or the straightforward songs

Chanting is a predominantly British soccer ritual, but it has already spread to other countries, as here with these North American fans of the Vancouver Whitecaps.

of joy and triumph, such as OH COME ALL YE FAITHFUL, JOYFUL AND TRIUMPHANT, or WHEN YOU'RE SMILING, or ALL THINGS BRIGHT AND BEAUTIFUL.

Encouragement
There were eleven chants in this category, asking or demanding more effort from their team. The most popular were:
1 COME ON OXFORD, COME ON OXFORD . . . (repeat)
2 COME ON YOU YELLOWS, COME ON YOU YELLOWS . . . (repeat)
3 COME ON YOU US, COME ON YOU US . . . (repeat)
4 GET INTO 'EM, GET INTO 'EM . . . (repeat)
5 ALL WE ARE SAYING IS GIVE US A GOAL . . . (repeat)
  To the tune of John Lennon's song 'Give peace a chance'
6 SHOOT, SHOOT, SHOOT, SHOOT . . . (repeat)
7 FIGHT, FIGHT, FIGHT, FIGHT . . . (repeat)
8 ATTACK ATTACK ATTACK ATTACK . . . (repeat)

Praise
There were eighteen chants in this category, either praising the whole team with such songs as WE ALL AGREE, OXFORD UNITED ARE MAGIC, or praising the individual players, usually immediately after they had performed a successful move on the field. Twelve different song rhythms were employed in these cases. Some rhythms only suited one particular name; others were used for a variety of names, but only one example of each is given here:
1 HUGHIE, HUGHIE, I'D WALK A MILLION MILES FOR ONE OF YOUR GOALS,
  OH HUGHIE, LA LA LA, HUGHIE, LA LA LA, HUGHIE,
  I'D WALK A MILLION MILES FOR ONE OF YOUR GOALS, OH HUGHIE
2 NICE ONE DAVID, NICE ONE SON, NICE ONE DAVID,
  LET'S HAVE ANOTHER ONE
3 PETER FOLEY WALKS ON WATER, TRA LA LA LA LA, LA LA, LA LA
4 GRAYDON GRAYDON GRAYDON GRAYDON,
  BORN IS THE KING OF OXFORD TOWN
5 DUNCAN IS BACK, DUNCAN IS BACK, OH-OH, OH-OH
6 ONE JASON SEACOLE, THERE'S ONLY ONE JASON SEACOLE . . . (repeat)
7 BURTON FOR ENGLAND, BURTON FOR ENGLAND . . . (repeat)
8 WE WANT CURRAN, WE WANT CURRAN . . . (repeat)
  A call to bring on the substitute
9 GORDON-GORDON HODGSON, GORDON-GORDON HODGSON . . . (repeat)
10 OH ARCHIE-ARCHIE, ARCHIE-ARCHIE-ARCHIE-ARCHIE-ARCHIE WHITE
11 LES TAY-LOR, LES TAY-LOR . . . (repeat)
  Long-drawn-out words
12 SUPERMAC, SUPERMAC . . . (repeat)
  Most of these rhythms are used at all clubs, adapted to the names of their own players. The repertoire listed here permits almost any name to be fitted in to one chant rhythm or another.

Loyalty and Pride
There were twenty-nine chants in this category, expressing pride at being supporters of Oxford United and loyalty to the club. Most mentioned the name of the club itself, but a few, such as YOU'LL NEVER WALK ALONE, or LOY-AL SUPPORTERS, LOY-AL SUPPORTERS, or WE'LL BE HERE, WE'LL BE HERE, WE'LL BE HERE ON SATURDAY, were less specific in their wording. Among those using the club's name, the most popular were:
1 YOU ARE MY OXFORD, MY ONLY OXFORD, YOU MAKE ME HAPPY,
  WHEN SKIES ARE GREY, IF YOU ONLY KNEW HOW MUCH I LOVE YOU . . .
2 AND IT'S OXFORD UNITED, OXFORD UNITED FC,
  WE'RE BY FAR THE GREATEST TEAM THE WORLD HAS EVER SEEN,

There are special chants for individual players. During the warm-up period, the aim is to provoke an acknowledging wave from a particular favourite.

AND IT'S *OX*FORD UNITED, OXFORD UNITED FC,
WE'RE THE GREATEST TEAM

3 OH WE ARE THE OXFORD BOYS, OH WE ARE THE OXFORD BOYS,
WE WILL FOLLOW UNITED, OH WE ARE THE OXFORD BOYS

4 YES WE ARE THE US, OH-OH, YES, WE ARE THE US, OH-OH, YES WE ARE THE US,
O . . . X . . . F . . . O . . . R . . . D, OXFORD, OXFORD, OXFORD

5 SHE WHEELS HER WHEELBARROW THROUGH STREETS BROAD AND NARROW,
SINGING . . . OXFORD, OXFORD, OXFORD

6 WE HATE NOTTINGHAM FOREST, WE HATE SWINDON TOO,
WE HATE NOTTINGHAM FOREST, BUT OXFORD WE LOVE YOU

7 WE'RE THE BARMY OXFORD ARMY, TRA-LA-LA-LA-LA . . . (repeat)

8 WE ARE THE FAMOUS, THE FAMOUS OX-FORD

9 GOOD OLD OXFORD, GOOD OLD OXFORD, WE'LL SUPPORT YOU EVERMORE

10 OH-OH, OXFORD BOYS WE ARE HERE, OH-OH,
OXFORD BOYS WE ARE HERE, OH-OH, UNITED BOYS WE ARE HERE . . .

11 OXFORD *ARE* BACK, OH-OH, OH-OH, OXFORD *ARE* BACK, OH-OH . . .

12 JINGLE BELLS, JINGLE BELLS, JINGLE ALL THE WAY,
OH WHAT FUN IT IS TO SEE OXFORD WIN AWAY

13 OX-FORD, OX-FORD, OX-FORD . . . (repeat)

14 O–O . . . X–X . . . F–F . . . O–O . . . R–R . . . D–D OXFORD!
(chant leader sings each letter and chorus replies)

15 O . . . X . . . F . . . O . . . R . . . D . . . WHAT HAVE YOU GOT? OXFORD! OXFORD!

16 OXFORD!   (clap/clap/clap-clap-clap/clap-clap-clap-clap/clap/clap)
(repeat)

17 UNITED! (clap-clap-clap) UNITED! (clap-clap-clap) . . . (repeat)

18 OH WHEN THE US . . . (reply) OH WHEN THE US,
GO MARCHING IN . . . (reply) GO MARCHING IN,
OH WHEN THE US GO MARCHING IN,
I WANT TO BE IN THAT NUMBER, WHEN THE US GO MARCHING IN

19 YOU'LL NEVER TAKE THE MANOR . . . (repeat)
Refers to the name of the home ground

20 WE ARE THE LONDON ROAD, OH WE ARE THE LONDON ROAD . . . (repeat)
Refers to the home fans' end of the ground

In addition there are special loyalty chants that relate to travelling to away games. Only a section of the fans are sufficiently loyal to undertake this expensive and sometimes hazardous business, and they are at pains to chant out from time to time:

IF YOU'RE ALL GOING TO (BLACKPOOL) CLAP YOUR HANDS,
IF YOU'RE ALL GOING TO (BLACKPOOL) CLAP YOUR HANDS,
IF YOU'RE ALL GOING TO (BLACKPOOL), ALL GOING TO (BLACKPOOL),
ALL GOING TO (BLACKPOOL) CLAP YOUR HANDS . . .

This is then followed by fast hand-clapping to indicate that they are all determined to follow the team, wherever they may go. Sometimes there is a variant of this: IF YOU ALL WENT TO (BLACKPOOL) CLAP YOUR HANDS . . . Or alternatively, WHERE WERE YOU, WHERE WERE YOU, WHERE WERE YOU AT (BLACKPOOL), WHERE WERE YOU AT (BLACKPOOL). The name of the away club is changed each week and these loyalty chants are of high frequency.

Criticism of Home Club

In stark contrast to the songs of loyalty are those of criticism and sarcasm. These are nearly always reserved for the enemy, but when the home team is playing particularly badly, or has been having a run of poor results, the home crowd begin to aim their hostility at them. There are twenty-three chants in this category. Some of these are insults directed at particular players, but others are more general. Popular examples include:

1 WHAT A LOAD OF RUBBISH, WHAT A LOAD OF RUBBISH . . . (repeat)
2 WE WANT A MANAGER, WE WANT A MANAGER . . . (repeat)

Synchro-clapping, with the hands held high above the head, often accompanies the chanting of the fans, adding special rhythms to the singing.

3 BRING ON THE FIRST TEAM, BRING ON THE FIRST TEAM
  Implies that the manager must be playing the reserves by mistake
4 IF YOU'RE *NOT* GOING TO (BLACKPOOL) CLAP YOUR HANDS
  A sarcastic version of the loyalty song
5 IT'S THE SAME THE WHOLE WORLD OVER, IT'S THE POOR WHAT GETS THE PAIN
6 WE ALL AGREE, OXFORD CITY ARE BETTER
  Refers to a small local, non-League club
7 TIME TO GO HOME, TIME TO GO HOME . . . (repeat)
  Sung just before the half-time whistle
8 WE ARE BORED, WE ARE BORED
9 HUGHIE FOR MANAGER, HUGHIE FOR MANAGER
  Suggests that one of the players would make a better manager
10 LIVERPOOL, LIVERPOOL
  Implies that their local loyalty is waning
11 WE WON THE BOAT RACE, WE WON THE BOAT RACE
  Makes an irrelevant point to underline the boredom of the game
12 BACK TO SCHOOL ON MONDAY, BACK TO SCHOOL ON MONDAY

Comments for the Referee
Rather surprisingly, there are only eight chants in this category. The reason seems to be that there is one dominant chant that is given almost automatically to any (supposed) bad decision by the referee:

  THE REFEREE IS A BASTARD, AND SO SAY ALL OF US,
  AND SO SAY ALL OF US, THE REFEREE IS A BASTARD,
  THE REFEREE IS A BASTARD, THE REFEREE IS A BASTARD,
  AND SO SAY ALL OF US, AND SO SAY ALL OF US . . .

There appear to be only three alternative ways of hurling abuse at this unfortunate official, apart from general yelling and booing. They are: EE AYE ADIO, WE WANT A REF, WE WANT A REF, WE WANT A REF, EE AYE ADIO, WE WANT A REF. And the more vicious one: REFEREE, REFEREE, YOUR OLD LADY IS A WHORE, YOUR OLD LADY IS A WHORE. Also, a curious shout in which a long-drawn-out OOOOOOOOOOOOOH! ends with the spitting out of BASTARD! BASTARD!

Apart from these, there are various requests such as GET HIM OFF, GET HIM OFF, GET HIM OFF, or the simpler OFF-OFF-OFF-OFF-OFF, when an enemy player has committed a foul. Also, WHY ARE WE WAITING when an opponent's injury is holding up the game, and HANDBALL! when the fans consider that the referee has not recognized the fact that an enemy player has deliberately handled the ball.

Comments for the Police
There were fifteen chants in this category, some indicating simple hatred, others more jokingly insulting. Examples include:
1 IF YOU ALL HATE COPPERS CLAP YOUR HANDS,
  IF YOU ALL HATE COPPERS CLAP YOUR HANDS,
  IF YOU ALL HATE COPPERS, ALL HATE COPPERS,
  ALL HATE COPPERS CLAP YOUR HANDS (followed by much clapping)
2 WE ALL HATE PIGS AND PIGS AND PIGS AND PIGS AND PIGS, PIGS . . . WE ALL HATE PIGS AND PIGS AND PIGS
3 WE CALL ON THE COPPERS TO GIVE US A SONG,
  SO SING YOU BASTARDS, SING
4 BRING ON THE COPPERS, BRING ON THE COPPERS
5 OLD MACDONALD HAD A FARM, E–I, E–I, O,
  AND ON THAT FARM HE HAD SOME PIGS, E–I, E–I, O,
  WITH A NICK-NICK HERE AND A NICK-NICK THERE,
  HERE A NICK, THERE A NICK, EVERYWHERE A NICK-NICK,
  OLD MACDONALD HAD A FARM, E–I, E–I, O
6 DOODAH, DOODAH, WHO'S THAT COPPER WITH HIS HAT ON HIS HEAD, DOODAH DOODAH DAY

Overhead clapping, performed here by West German fans (right), is now widespread as a chant accompaniment.

Several of the most popular chants involve the joyous singing of obscenities. This offends the sensitive ears of the more puritanical Tribal Elders and a number of unsuccessful attempts have been made to eliminate the taboo words. This appeal (below) from team manager Brian Clough is a recent plea for 'cleaner chants', but, as the tattered poster (below right) at an old, derelict football ground testifies, the problem is by no means a new one.

GENTLEMEN NO SWEARING PLEASE!

7 CAN YOU HEAR THE COPPERS SING, NO-OH, NO-OH . . .

8 LA LA LA, NICK NICK NICK NICK, LA LA LA, NICK NICK NICK, LA LA LA

Insults Aimed at the Opponents

This is by far the most popular form of chanting and includes no fewer than sixty different examples. Many include extreme obscenities, which are sung with great gusto across the stadium, much to the distress of the more genteel visitors in the expensive seats. Many are also slanderous and would become libellous if written down here. Nothing is too vicious for the cheerful bands of chanters, from implications of sexual inadequacy or abnormality, to suggestions of lunacy and advanced alcoholism. If any opposing player, manager, or even director is known to have some personal problem or human weakness it is ruthlessly exploited in song after song. If no such weaknesses exist, they are happily invented.

The object of these chants is to unnerve the enemy to such an extent that they lose their concentration and give away a goal. Paradoxically, although the insults are highly personal, implying for example that one player is senile, another is a homosexual, another a cuckold, and another a transvestite, they are not really aimed at the man as an individual. He is being attacked only as a member of a team. If he left the enemy team and was bought by the home team, he would immediately become the hero of the praising chants and his real or imagined defects would be forgotten.

This paradox was underlined recently when an England player was involved in a sexual scandal. Playing for his own club in a League match shortly afterwards he was the butt of endless ridicule in chant after chant, but once the game was over and he was leaving the field, the enemy chanters immediately switched to songs of praise for him. There was now no point in trying to unnerve him, since the final whistle had gone and he was no longer a threat to their own team. In an instant, he became their 'England hero' once more and was serenaded accordingly. Nevertheless, he was so upset by the obscenity of the chants against him during this and other matches that he has threatened to leave England altogether and play abroad. The chants clearly have considerable impact.

The most popular general insults include the following:

1 WHAT'S IT LIKE TO BE OUTCLASSED, WHAT'S IT LIKE TO BE OUTCLASSED, WHAT'S IT LIKE, WHAT'S IT LIKE, WHAT'S IT LIKE TO BE OUTCLASSED?

2 YOU'RE NOT FIT TO WIPE MY ARSE, YOU'RE NOT FIT TO WIPE MY ARSE

3 IN THE (SWANSEA) SLUMS, IN THE (SWANSEA) SLUMS,
   THEY LOOK IN A DUSTBIN FOR SOMETHING TO EAT,
   FIND A DEAD CAT AND THINK IT'S A TREAT,
   IN THE (SWANSEA) SLUMS
   Originally applied to clubs from the poorer districts of London, but now used as a 'poverty' insult towards any city, whether it has bad slums or not

4 DOES YOUR MUMMY, DOES YOUR MUMMY, DOES YOUR MUMMY KNOW YOU'RE HERE, DOES YOUR MUMMY KNOW YOU'RE HERE?
   The implication is that the opposing fans are infantile

5 TWO-ONE, TWO-ONE, TWO-ONE . . . (repeat)
   The popular score-taunt when the enemy are losing

6 WHAT DO YOU THINK OF (SWINDON)? (lone voice)
   SHIT, SHIT, SHIT! (chorus)
   (SWINDON) (voice) SHIT! (chorus) (SWINDON) (voice) SHIT! (chorus)
   (SWINDON, SWINDON, SWINDON) (voice) SHIT SHIT SHIT! (chorus)
   An increasingly popular and widespread insult that has caused much consternation among soccer authorities in Britain, although it is mild compared with some others

7 SIT DOWN YOU BUMS, SIT DOWN YOU BUMS . . . (repeat)
   Chanted when opposing fans rise to applaud their players

8 YOU DIRTY (WALSALL) BASTARD, YOU DIRTY (WALSALL) BASTARD . . . (repeat)
Sung, with the appropriate enemy team name inserted, when an opponent has committed a foul that has injured a home player

9 OH LUCKY-LUCKY, LUCKY-LUCKY-LUCKY-LUCKY-LUCKY (BURY) . . . (repeat)
Sung when a home shot at goal narrowly misses, implying that it was not skill that saved the enemy, but merely chance

10 IF YOU ALL HATE (GILLINGHAM), CLAP YOUR HANDS . . . (repeat)

11 WE HATE SWINDON, WE HATE SWINDON, WE HATE SWINDON . . . (repeat)
A chant reserved exclusively for the local League rivals

12 WHITES AND WHITES AND WHITES AND WHITES AND WHITES,
WE ALL HATE WHITES, WE ALL HATE WHITES,
AND WHITES AND WHITES AND WHITES . . .
Sung against a visiting team that wears white shirts

In addition to these general insults there are also the specifically sexual taunts. The vast majority of these are based on the idea that the enemy players, managers or supporters are forced to find sexual outlet through masturbation. In other words, that they are too ineffectual to obtain a sexual partner. There are no fewer than seven different masturbation chants. The most popular is SO-AND-SO'S A WANKER, SO-AND-SO'S A WANKER, when an enemy player fails to succeed with a shot at goal or a difficult move on the field. The whole team may be greeted by BRING ON THE WANKERS at the start of the match, in contrast to the home team's welcome of BRING ON THE CHAMPIONS. The visitors may also be sneered at with YOU'RE JUST A BUNCH OF WANKERS when their efforts to score are collapsing. Various other rhythms are also employed, such as (MANCHESTER), WANK WANK WANK, (MANCHESTER), WANK WANK WANK . . . or WE ALL AGREE, SO-AND-SO IS A WANKER.

Implications of homosexuality are also common: (TRANMERE) BOYS, THEY ARE QUEER, (TRANMERE) BOYS, THEY ARE QUEER or OH WHAT A LOT OF SODS, SING, WHAT A LOT OF SODS, SING, WHAT A LOT OF SODS.

Anyone with a drinking problem is greeted with SO-AND-SO IS A WINO, SO-AND-SO IS A WINO, LA LA LA LA. Alternatively, SO-AND-SO WALKS ON CIDER, TRA LA LA LA LA LA LA, as a contrast with the WALKS ON WATER chant reserved for home players.

A special group of insults is hurled at the opposing supporters who form the rival 'choir'. The most popular is CAN YOU HEAR (CARDIFF) SING, NO-OH, NO-OH, when the enemy camp has fallen silent because they are losing or doing badly. Alternatives include SING UP YOU BUMS, SING UP YOU BUMS, SING UP YOU BUMS, SING UP, to the tune of 'Auld Lang Syne', or IT'S ALL GONE QUIET OVER THERE, AND IT'S ALL GONE QUIET, ALL GONE QUIET, ALL GONE QUIET OVER THERE, or SING UP (CARDIFF), SING UP (CARDIFF), or (WALSALL), SING US A SONG, (WALSALL), SING US A SONG, or (SHREWSBURY), WHERE ARE YOU, (SHREWSBURY), WHERE ARE YOU? If there are no visiting fans to support the enemy team, the taunt goes instead to the players themselves, with (COLCHESTER), (COLCHESTER), WHAT'S IT LIKE TO HAVE NO FANS?

Specific insults aimed at individual players include the popular 'reject' taunt: (CHELSEA) RE-JECT, (CHELSEA) RE-JECT, OH-OH. This is directed at a player recently sold by a particular club. Even if he has been sold for a very high transfer fee, he is still assailed by a chant implying that his old club no longer wanted him.

If a player makes an accidentally funny fall, he is regaled with NORMAN NORMAN WISDOM, NORMAN NORMAN WISDOM, referring to the comedian who specializes in comic falls and trips. If another player is caught napping by a fast ball, the chant becomes SO-AND-SO IS A STROLLER. If a manager is heard calling out to the rival team, he is bombarded with SO-AND-SO, SHUT YOUR MOUTH, SO-AND-SO, SHUT YOUR MOUTH, until he quietens down.

Insults aimed at nobody in particular include the famous distortion of the West Ham 'club song', which goes:

Soccer songsheet

I'M FOREVER BLOWING BUBBLES, PRETTY BUBBLES IN THE AIR,
THEY FLY SO HIGH, THEY REACH THE SKY,
THEN LIKE WEST HAM, THEY FADE AND DIE.

This insult verse may be sung in a match which does not involve West Ham and in a division where West Ham does not even play. It presumably appeals to the followers of lower division clubs simply because it is rude about a higher level club.

Finally, there is an ancient group of insults directed at the local occupations of the inhabitants of the rival town or city. Clubs from South Wales will be offered the chant COAL-MINERS, COAL-MINERS, for example. These taunts go back to the days when factory workers in one area would look down their noses at the occupations of workers in other regions, usually because they were less well paid or dirtier jobs.

Threats to the Opponents

This, the most violent category, includes twenty-four different chants. Most of them promise injury or death at some point in the future. There is a special rise in frequency of these threats just after a rival goal has been scored and also near the end of the match. The most commonly used threats are:

1 YOU'RE GONNA GET YOUR FUCKING HEADS KICKED IN
2 HIT HIM ON THE HEAD, HIT HIM ON THE HEAD,
   HIT HIM ON THE HEAD WITH A BASEBALL BAT
3 OXFORD AGGRO, OXFORD AGGRO, OH-OH
4 OXFORD BOYS'LL COME AND GET YOU
   AND WRAP A CHAIN AROUND YOUR NECKS
5 WE'RE ALL BOBBING ALONG . . . SHOOT THE BASTARDS, SHOOT THE BASTARDS
6 WE ARE EVIL, WE ARE EVIL . . . (repeat)
7 SHOW ME A (WATFORD) FAN LA LA LA LA LA LA,
   SHOW ME A (WATFORD) FAN LA LA LA LA LA, I SHOW YOU A DEAD ONE
8 OH-OH, OH-OH, WE ARE THE OXFORD BOYS,
   OH-OH, OH-OH, WE ARE THE OXFORD BOYS,
   AND IF YOU ARE A (CARDIFF) FAN SURRENDER OR YOU'LL DIE,
   WE WILL FOLLOW UNITED
9 YOU WILL DIE, YOU WILL DIE . . . (repeat)
10 KNEES UP MOTHER BROWN, KNEES UP MOTHER BROWN,
   ON THE TABLE YOU MUST GO, E-I-E-I-O,
   IF I CATCH YOU BENDING I'LL SAW YOUR LEGS RIGHT OFF,
   E-I-E-I-O, KNEES UP MOTHER BROWN

In addition, there are the special 'end of match' threats chanted mostly during the last five minutes of the game:

1 WE'LL SEE YOU ALL OUTSIDE, WE'LL SEE YOU ALL OUTSIDE . . . (repeat)
2 IT'S TIME FOR YOU TO RUN, IT'S TIME FOR YOU TO RUN . . . (repeat)
3 YOU'RE GOING HOME BY AMBULANCE, YOU'RE GOING HOME BY AMBULANCE . . .
   (repeat)
4 YOU'LL NEVER MAKE THE COACHES, YOU'LL NEVER MAKE THE COACHES . . .
   (repeat)
5 ON THE PITCH, ON THE PITCH . . . (repeat)
   Asking for a pitch invasion and a hand-to-hand battle of rival fans
6 COME AND JOIN US, COME AND JOIN US, COME AND JOIN US OVER HERE

Finally, there is a group of threats aimed at future rivals, in matches arranged for the weeks to come, including:

1 (SWINDON) DIE ON MONDAY, (SWINDON) DIE ON MONDAY, LA LA LA LA LA LA
2 WE'RE GOING (SWANSEA)-BASHING, LA LA LA LA LA LA
3 (WALSALL) (WALSALL) YOU ARE NEXT, (WALSALL) YOU ARE NEXT
4 WE'RE GONNA TAKE (SWINDON), WE'RE GONNA TAKE (SWINDON) . . . (repeat)
5 (COUNTY) (COUNTY) HERE WE COME, (COUNTY), HERE WE COME . . . (repeat)
6 MY OLD MAN SAID, BE AN OXFORD FAN AND DON'T DILLY DALLY ON THE WAY

WE'LL TAKE (SWINDON) AND ALL THAT CITY,
WE'LL TAKE (SWINDON) IN HALF A MINUTE,
WITH HATCHETS AND HAMMERS, AND HALF A DOZEN SPANNERS . . .

Needless to say, the bloodthirsty tone of these chants is seldom matched by reality. After the cheerful singing, there is little or no bloodshed. Just occasionally, however, there is a real fight and, although an extremely rare event, it is enough to give an 'edge' to the threat-chants that lasts for many weeks, or even months.

Celebration of Disruption

There were eight chants in this category, occurring when there had been some form of disturbance or disruption of play. On one occasion, for example, the Oxford fans lit a fire on their terrace and chanted WE'VE GOT A FIRE, WE'VE GOT A FIRE, EE AYE ADIO, WE'VE GOT A FIRE. As the fire grew in size, they boomed out with THE LONDON ROAD IS BURNING DOWN, BURNING DOWN, BURNING DOWN, THE LONDON ROAD IS BURNING DOWN, POOR OLD LONDON.

When an announcement was made over the loudspeakers asking a 'phantom whistler' in the crowd to keep quiet, the fans answered with a chant of WE'VE GOT THE WHISTLE, WE'VE GOT THE WHISTLE. When the ball was accidentally kicked into their stand, they refused to give it up, chanting WE'VE GOT THE BALL, WE'VE GOT THE BALL, EE AYE ADIO, WE'VE GOT THE BALL. And when some of their members fell over and were carried off by the police, they sang out WE ARE UNITED, WE ARE UNITED, WE ARE UNITED AND WE'RE DRUNK. Chants of this type are essentially protests against a boring game. The fans must make their own entertainment and celebrate the fact in song. The next category consists exclusively of 'boredom chants' of this type:

Insider Rivalry

No fewer than twenty-eight different chants were aimed by home fans at other home fans. They were mock-insults, invented to pass the time, or pseudo-rivalries set up to provide some excitement on a dull afternoon. The main basis for this chanting was the division of the fans' stand into two halves, the right side and the left side. The stand is, in fact, separated by a central fence, so that 'left-siders' and 'right-siders' could pretend to be enemies. This only happened when the visiting team brought no supporters with it, thereby offering no vocal opposition. Popular chants included:

1 YOU'LL NEVER TAKE THE LEFT SIDE, YOU'LL NEVER TAKE THE LEFT SIDE, THE LEFT SIDE
2 LA LA LA LA, LA LA LA LA, LEFT SIDE ARE THE CHAMPIONS, LEFT SIDE ARE THE CHAMPIONS . . .
3 LEFT SIDE, LEFT SIDE, WHO ARE YOU? LEFT SIDE, WHO ARE YOU?
4 WE ARE THE RIGHT SIDE, WE ARE THE RIGHT SIDE, WE ARE THE RIGHT SIDE, LONDON ROAD

There were ten such chants altogether. In addition, there were many songs both praising and attacking the fans from the various districts around Oxford. Supporters travel into the city from these villages or suburbs on match-day, and can therefore set up a friendly rivalry to keep themselves amused: ABINGDON, WHERE ARE YOU? or WE ARE THE THAME BOYS, WE ARE THE THAME BOYS, or BLACKBIRD BLACKBIRD BLACKBIRD LEYS, BLACKBIRD LEYS.

The most extreme example of this false-rivalry came in a match where it appeared that a group of rival fans had sneaked into the sacred home territory, the London Road stand. They set up a series of chants supporting the enemy team and were quickly threatened by home fans. The police rushed in to protect them and formed a dense guard around them, little realizing that they were ordinary Oxford fans, deliberately stirring up trouble to provide a side-show at a boring match. Such incidents do not occur when the home team are doing exceptionally well. They crop up almost as a

In the Score-taunt, the hands are rhythmically thrust towards the enemy, with the extended fingers triumphantly signalling the score to remind the losing supporters of their plight. To emphasize their message, the gestures are accompanied by loud synchronized chants, repeating the scoreline over and over again.

way of distracting the supporters from the thought of how badly their team are doing on the field.

Atmospheric Chants

In this final group there are five chants concerned with creating an atmosphere of excitement, but without any specific message being transmitted. They are as follows:

1 ATMOSPHERE, TRA LA LA, ATMOSPHERE, TRA LA LA
2 LA LA LA LA LA LA LA, LA LA LA LA LA LA . . .
  Sung to 'The Yellow Rose of Texas'
3 GIVE US AN OOH! GIVE US AN ARGH! WHAT HAVE YOU GOT? OOH-ARGH!
4 OOOOOOOOOOH . . .
  A long-drawn-out sound, taken up by more and more voices
5 ARRRRRRRRRRGH . . . A long-drawn-out nasal snarl

Apart from four unidentifiable chants, that completes the repertoire of the Oxford United fans. Their 251 chants are nearly always short and simple, permitting endless repetition. This is important, because it allows more and more fans to join in, as the rhythm builds up and the noise reaches a crescendo.

Each chant has a 'typical intensity'. In other words, it has a typical number of times that the basic phrase is repeated, before the chanting dies away. The most common of all the 251 chants at Oxford was U-NI-TED (clap/clap/clap), U-NI-TED (clap/clap/clap) . . . and so on. It occurred no fewer than 286 times during the fifteen games in question and when each instance is examined, it emerges that the most common number of 'repeats' was three (below left). This makes it a chant with a 'typical intensity' of three units.

Different chants have different 'profiles', some of them characteristically with a very large number of repeats, some with a very small number. It is as though each time a chant is set up it takes control of the fans like a 'fixed vocal emblem', generating its own power and making its own demands, almost as if it is a mystical incantation inducing a form of mass hypnosis. But this is only an illusion, for the fans are always acutely tuned in to the world around them and ready to invent new variations to fit any occasion.

For some reason, this chant-ritual has remained a largely British affair. In other countries, it is possible to hear the basic chant of the name of the local club: A-VEL-LI-NO, A-VEL-LI-NO in Italy, for example, or ALLEZ-NICE, ALLEZ-NICE, in France. But nowhere is there the extraordinary richness and variety to be heard emanating from the crowded British terraces. Part of the reason for this is that continental and South American matches are played out to an almost non-stop deafening roar of massed drummers and hooters in the crowd. Few such instruments are taken into a British stadium, so there is less background noise and more possibility for singing to be heard effectively.

In the United States, simple chanting from the crowd has already begun. In New York it is now possible to hear COS-MOS COS-MOS rising from the grandstand, not because it has been imposed externally by high-kicking cheer-leaders, but because it has started to grow naturally as a genuine expression of club loyalty from the supporters themselves. Unfortunately, American sports organizers are so used to spoon-feeding their audiences with appropriate chants and songs that their first reaction on hearing the new, spontaneously occurring chant was to flash up requests for it on their giant scoreboard. Instead of increasing the chant this had the opposite effect, irritating the chanters, who had developed something of their own. As a result, steps were taken to avoid scoreboard interference, and it is now likely that true, indigenous chanting will spread of its own accord.

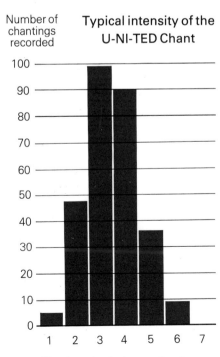

Number of chantings recorded

Typical intensity of the U-NI-TED Chant

Number of units in one chanting

44 Conclusion

In describing the curious world of the ritual-laden, male-dominated Soccer Tribe I have tried to remain as objective as possible. It is not the task of a scientific observer, visiting a strange tribe, to lay down the law or even offer advice as to how the tribesmen should behave. It is his job to record the culture as he finds it and leave it to others to make judgments.

In dealing with the controversies that rage within the tribe I have attempted to present both sides of the picture in each case. To the biased mind, the players can be viewed either as illiterate, mercenary, vicious, temperamental ego-maniacs or as brilliant, loyal, courageous, ill-treated heroes; the managers can be seen as unnecessary, self-important, publicity-seeking martinets or as essential, dedicated, insecure executives, callously treated by their employers; the directors can be described as pig-headed, senile, autocratic, bungling amateurs seeking only power and glory or as caring, thoughtful, passionately devoted enthusiasts sacrificing both time and money to promote the game they love; the young fans can be depicted as brutish, cowardly, violent, mindless louts causing nothing but trouble or as long-suffering, brave, tough, colourful supporters keeping the excitement of the game alive.

Most authors when writing about the sport have stressed only its positive qualities; the few exceptions have chosen to launch all-out attacks. I have tried to avoid both these extremes, presenting not only the tribe's virtues but also its vices. The balance between the two which emerges when this is done is not unflattering. Examined 'warts and all', the face of the Soccer Tribe is somehow more sympathetic and appealing than when it is given the rather phoney, cosmetic treatment usually handed out by 'official' sports writers. They, and the Tribal Elders generally, seem so fearful that critical comments may 'bring the game into disrepute' that they feel obliged to present the sport as God's gift to human health, happiness and the pursuit of international harmony and goodwill. Since it is patently obvious that it is also capable of providing its share of human injury, stress and international ill-feeling, their remarks inevitably sound naive and one-sided to any outsider. There is no need for them to be so defensive. All major human preoccupations – not only sport, but also religion, science, art, politics and the rest – carry within them the potentials for both good and ill, for both ecstasy and agony. It is what we make of *them* that matters, not what they make of us.

Perhaps the greatest dilemma facing the Soccer Tribe today is the question of whether its main activity is a sacred ritual or a social entertainment. Should attending a soccer match be a passionate, manly ordeal or a light-hearted family outing? Should the ancient traditions of spartan suffering give way to theatre comforts and modern razzmatazz?

The traditionalists believe that any softening of the ritual will inevitably rob it of its intensity and its significance; the modernists insist that without showbiz glamour and improved amenities the tribesmen will drift away and the sport will die. Soccer has been described as a pseudo-religion, and a similar conflict of opinion exists in the church itself, with those priests favouring high ritual clashing repeatedly with modernists who wish to bring religious practices up to date and more into line with twentieth-century attitudes and lifestyles. If their world is any guide and a parallel can be drawn, then the immense success of Papal pomp and ceremonial display in recent years would seem to favour the soccer traditionalists. Guitar-playing vicars who scorn difficult ritual have proved a singular failure. Perhaps if the soccer match becomes 'fun for all the family' it will lose the very quality which has enabled it to spread around the world and attract larger, more devoted audiences than any other human pastime – the quality of a sternly fought contest. At its most ritualistic this contest contains within it so many symbolic echoes from our primeval past – when we were brave hunters pursuing dangerous prey – that to tamper with it too much may prove disastrous. To turn this symbolic event into Disneyland fun may be to destroy its essential dignity. To succeed, it may always have to be an intensely serious and male-dominated activity.

Perhaps, in the end, it will be possible to have the best of both worlds. Perhaps the reformers who wish to provide modern comforts and efficient organization for the sport will be able to do so without damaging the ceremonial drama of the game. Adequate car-parking, good food and drink, attractive displays before the kick-off and dry, comfortable seating may not, after all, weaken the sense of fanatical loyalty and tribal fervour. This remains to be seen. Only a fool would attempt a confident prediction. One thing seems certain, however: whether the Soccer Tribe remains stubbornly traditional or becomes daringly modernistic, or whether it manages a magic blend of the two, it will be around for many years. Unlike so many tribal societies now teetering on the brink of extinction, it is a vigorous, widespread and thriving community. In countries where it is beset with temporary troubles – violence, corruption or falling attendances – the cry goes up that there is a tribal 'crisis'. Anxiety-makers pound their typewriters and imminent doom and disaster are forecast. Viewed on a global scale, nothing could be further from the truth. The local troubles soon pass. Even as they occur, somewhere else the tribe is expanding and celebrating new peaks of success.

For a simple, child-like ball-game, soccer has come a very long way . . . and it shows no sign of retreating to the playroom shelter of its humble origins. As long as the human race is able to concern itself with more than mere survival, the Soccer Tribe will have its place.

Bibliography

Alcock, C.W. 1874. *Football, Our Winter Game.* London.

Alcock, C.W. 1890. *Football, The Association Game.* G. Bell and Sons, London.

Alcock, C.W. 1906. *The Book of Football.*

Allison, M. 1967. *Soccer for Thinkers.* Pelham Books, London.

Anon. 1901. *The Football Who's Who. Season 1900–1901.* Arthur Pearson, London.

Anon. 1936. *The Football Association Coaching Manual.* Evans Brothers, London. (Rev. edn, 1949.)

Archer, M., *et al.* 1977. *The Hamlyn International Book of Soccer.* Hamlyn, London.

Ateyo, D. 1979. *Blood and Guts. Violence in Sports.* Paddington Press, London.

Ball, D. W., and Loy, J.W. 1975. *Sport and Social Order. Contributions to the Sociology of Sport.* Addison-Wesley, Reading, Massachusetts.

Barrett, N.S. 1978. *Purnell's New Encyclopedia of Association Football.* Purnell, London.

Becker, J. 1975. 'Superstition in sport.' *Internat. J. Sport Psychol.*, 6, 3. pp. 148–52.

Beltrami, A. 1978. *Almanacco Illustrato del Calcio.* Edizioni Panini, Modena.

Brady, L. 1980. *So Far So Good ...* Stanley Paul, London.

Brasch, R. 1972. *How Did Sports Begin? A Look into the Origins of Man at Play.* Longman, London.

Brazier, C. 1978. 'Terrace culture.' *Melody Maker.* April 22nd 1978. pp. 39–42.

Brody, M.K. 1979. 'Institutionalized sport as quasi-religion: preliminary considerations.' *J. Sport and Social Issues*, 3(2). pp. 17–27.

Budd, A., and Fry, C.B. 1897. *Football.* Lawrence and Bullen, London.

Butt, D.S. 1976. *Psychology of Sport.* Van Nostrand Reinhold, New York.

Cameron, J. 1909. *Association Football.*

Carter, F.W., and Capel-Kirby, W. 1933. *The Mighty Kick.* Jarrolds, London.

Catton, J.A.H. 1900. *The Real Football.* Sands, London.

Chester, N. 1968. *Report of the Committee on Football.* (The Chester Report.) Department of Education and Science, HMSO, London.

Coles, R.W. 1975. 'Football as a surrogate religion?' in M. Hill (ed.), *A Sociological Yearbook of Religion in Britain*, No. 6.

Corbett, B.O. 1901. *Football.* London.

Cottrell, J. 1970. *A Century of Great Soccer Drama.* Hart-Davis, London.

Csanádi, A. 1978. *Soccer. Technique – Tactics – Coaching.* Corvina Kiadó, Budapest.

Davies, H. 1972. *The Glory Game.* Weidenfeld and Nicolson, London.

Delaney, T. 1963. *A Century of Soccer.* Heinemann, London.

Delaney, T. 1963. *The Footballer's Fireside Book.* Heinemann, London.

Dunning, E. (ed.) 1972. *The Sociology of Sport: A Selection of Readings.* University of Toronto Press, Toronto and Buffalo.

Dunning, E. 1975. 'Industrialisation and the incipient modernisation of football.' *Stadion* 1, no. 1.

Dunphy, E. 1976. *Only a Game? The Diary of a Professional Footballer.* Kestrel Books, London.

Edgell, S., and Jary, D. 1973. 'Football: a sociological eulogy', in M. Smith, C. Parker and C. Smith (eds), *Leisure and Society in Britain.* Allen Lane, London.

Edwards, C. 1892. 'The new football mania.' *The Nineteenth Century*, 32.

Ellis, A. 1962. *The Final Whistle.* Stanley Paul, London.

Ensor, E. 1898. 'The football madness.' *Contemporary Review*, 74.

Fabian, A.H., and Green, G. 1960. *Association Football* (4 vols). Caxton Press, London.

Frewin, L. (ed.) 1967. *The Saturday Men.* Macdonald, London.

Fry, C.B. 1895. 'Football.' *Badminton Library of Sports and Pastimes.* I.

Ghirelli, A. 1954. *Storia del Calcio in Italia.* Einaudi, Turin.

Gibson, A., and Pickford, W. 1906. *Association Football and the Men Who Made It.* Caxton Press, London.

Glanville, B. 1962. *The Footballer's Companion.* Eyre and Spottiswoode, London.

Glanville, B. 1968. *Soccer. A Panorama.* Eyre and Spottiswoode, London.

Glanville, B. 1980. *The History of the World Cup.* Faber and Faber, London.

Golesworthy, M. 1972. *We are the Champions.* Pelham Books, London.

Golesworthy, M. 1973. *The Encyclopedia of Association Football.* Robert Hale, London. (The first of many editions appeared in 1956.)

Golesworthy, M., and Macdonald, R. 1966. *The AB–Z of World Football.* Pelham Books, London.

Goodall, J. 1898. *Association Football.* W. Blackwood and Sons, Edinburgh and London.

Gray, M. 1980. *Football Injuries.* Offox Press, Oxford.

Greaves, J. 1966. *Soccer Techniques and Tactics.* Pelham Books, London.

Greaves, J., and Gutteridge, R. 1972. *Let's Be Honest.* Pelham Books, London.

Green, G. 1949. *The Official History of the F.A. Cup.* Heinemann, London.

Green, G. 1953. *The History of the Football Association.* Naldrett Press, London.

Green, G. 1953. *Soccer, The World Game.* Phoenix House, London.

Green, J., and Ateyo, D. 1979. *The Book of Sports Quotes.* Omnibus Press, London.

Hall, W., and Parkinson, M. 1973. *Football Report.* Pelham Books, London.

Harris, H.A. 1972. *Sport in Greece and Rome.* Thames and Hudson, London.

Harvey, C. 1959. *Encyclopaedia of Sport.* Sampson, Low, Marston and Co., London.

Heighway, S. 1977. *Liverpool: My Team.* Souvenir Press, London.

Herbin, R., and Rethacker, J.P. 1978. *Soccer. The Way the Pros Play.* Sterling Publishing, New York.

Hill, J. 1961. *Striking for Soccer.* Peter Davies, London.

Hole, C. 1949. *English Sports and Pastimes.* Batsford, London.

Hopcraft, A. 1968. *The Football Man. People and Passions in Soccer.* Collins, London.

Howell, D. 1968. *Soccer Refereeing.* Pelham Books, London.

Hughes, C.F.C. 1973. *Tactics and Teamwork.* E.P. Publishing, Wakefield, Yorkshire.

Ingham, R., Hall, S., Clarke, J., Marsh, P., and Donovan, J. 1978. *Football Hooliganism. The Wider Context.* Inter-Action Imprint, London.

Jackson, N.L. 1895. *The Association Football Handbook* (1894–5).

Jackson, N.L. 1900. *Association Football.* George Newnes, London.

James, B. (ed.) 1971–3. *Book of Football.* (In 75 parts.) Marshall Cavendish, London.

Jeffery, G. 1963. *European International Football.* Nicholas Kaye, London.

Jewell, B. 1977. *Sports and Games. History and Origins.* Midas Books, Tunbridge Wells, Kent.

Johnston, F. (ed.) 1934. *The Football Encyclopedia.* Associated Sporting Press, London.

Johnston, F. (ed.) 1935. *The Football Who's Who.* London.

Jones, J.H. 1904. *Association Football.*

Keegan, K. 1979. *Against the World.* Sidgwick and Jackson, London.

Keeton, G.W. 1972. *The Football Revolution.* David and Charles, Newton Abbot.

Koppehel, C. 1954. *Geschichte des Deutschen Fussball-sports.* Frankfurt.

Laschke, I. 1980. *Rothman's Book of Football League Records 1888–89 to 1978–79.* Macdonald and Jane's, London.

Lefebre, L.M., and Cunningham, J.D. 1977. 'The successful football team: effects of coaching on team cohesiveness.' *Internat. J. Sport Psychol.* 8, 1. pp. 29–41.

Lightbown, C. 1971. 'Football gangs.' *Time Out.* April 28th 1971.

Macdonald, R. 1977. *Soccer. A Pictorial History.* Collins, London.

McMenemy, L. 1979. *The Diary of a Season.* Arthur Barker, London.

Magoun, F.P. 1930. 'Football in Medieval England and in Middle English Literature.' *American Historical Review*, 25.

Magoun, F.P. 1938. *History of Football. From the Beginnings to 1871.* Kölner Anglistische Arbeiten. Band 31.

Marples, M. 1954. *A History of Football.* Secker and Warburg, London.

Marsh, P. 1978. *Aggro. The Illusion of Violence.* Dent, London.

Marsh, P., and Harré, R. 1978. 'The world of football hooligans.' *Human Nature*, 1 (10). pp. 62–9.

Marsh, P., Rosser, E., and Harré, R. 1978. *The Rules of Disorder.* Routledge and Kegan Paul, London.

Mason, T. 1980. *Association Football and English Society, 1863–1915.* Harvester Press, Sussex.

Matthews, S. 1948. *Feet First.* Ewen and Dale, London.

Meisl, W. 1955. *Soccer Revolution.* Phoenix House, London.

Mercier, J. 1966. *Le Football.* Paris.

Moir, I. 1972. *Association Football: The Evolution of the Laws of the Game.* University of Birmingham, M.A. thesis.

Moore, B., and Tyler, M. 1980. *The Big Matches. A Decade of World Soccer.* Queen Anne Press, Macdonald and Jane's, London.

Morris, D. 1979. 'Violence in the stands.' *Britannica Book of the Year 1979.* Encyclopaedia Britannica, Inc., Chicago.

Moynihan, J. 1966. *The Soccer Syndrome.* MacGibbon and Kee, London.

Moynihan, J. 1974. *Football Fever.* Quartet Books, London.

Needham, E. 1900. *Association Football.* Skeffington and Son, London.

Parkinson, M. 1975. *Best. An Intimate Biography.* Arrow Books, London.

Parkinson, M., and Hall, W. 1975. *Football Final.* Pelham Books, London.

Pawson, T. 1972. *100 Years of the F.A. Cup.* Heinemann, London.

Pawson, T. 1973. *The Football Managers.* Eyre Methuen, London.

Pelé, and Fish, R.L. 1977. *Pelé: My Life and the Beautiful Game.* Doubleday, New York.

Pickford, R.W. 1941. 'The Psychology of the history and organization of football.' *British Journal of Psychology*, 30–1.

Rollin, J. 1978. *The Guinness Book of Soccer Facts and Feats.* Guinness Superlatives, London.

Rote, K. 1978. *Complete Book of Soccer.* Simon and Schuster, New York.

Schidrowitz, L. 1951. *Geschichte des Fussballsports in Österreich.* Vienna.

Shearman, M., and Vincent, J. 1885. *Football: Its History for Five Centuries.* Field and Tuer, London.

Shearman, M., *et al.* 1901. *Football.* Longmans, Green and Co., London.

Soar, P. 1978. *World Cup 1978.* Marshall Cavendish, London.

Soar, P., and Tyler, M. 1978. *Soccer, The World Game.* Marshall Cavendish, London.

Soar, P., and Tyler, M. 1979. *Encyclopedia of British Football.* Marshall Cavendish, London.

Strutt, J. 1801. *The Sports and Pastimes of the People of England.* (Enlarged edition published 1903 and reissued 1969 by Firecrest Publishing, Bath.)

Sturdee, R.J. 1903. 'The ethics of football.' *Westminster Review*, 159.

Taylor, I. 1969. 'Hooligans: Soccer's resistance movement.' *New Society.* August 7th 1969. p. 204.

Taylor, I. 1971. 'Soccer consciousness and soccer hooliganism', in Cohen, S. (ed.), *Images of Deviancy.* Penguin, Harmondsworth.

Thomas, V. 1978. 'The hunt for the X factor. Are sportsmen born or made.' *New Psychologist*, 1, 4. pp. 10–12.

Trevillion, P. 1971. *King Pelé.* Stanley Paul, London.

Tyler, M. 1978. *The Story of Football.* Marshall Cavendish, London.

Vernon, L., and Rollin, J. 1980. *Rothman's Football Yearbook.* Queen Anne Press, London. (And earlier volumes, published throughout the 1970s.)

Vinnai, G. 1973. *Football Mania.* Ocean Books, London.

Walvin, J. 1975. *The People's Game. The Social History of British Football.* Allen Lane, London.

Whiting, H.T.A. 1972. *Readings in Sports Psychology.* Henry Kimpton, London.

Whiting, H.T.A., and Masterson, D.W. 1974. *Readings in the Aesthetics of Sport.* Lepus, London.

Widdows, R. 1978. *Football Handbook.* (In weekly parts.) Marshall Cavendish, London.

Winterbottom, W. 1960. *Training for Soccer. An Official Coaching Manual of the Football Association.* Heinemann, London.

Wooldridge, I. 1973. 'The language of the game.' *Football Monthly.* January 1973.

Yaffé, M. 1975. 'Stress and the soccer stars.' *Psychology Today*, 1 (3), (June). pp. 26–31.

Young, P. 1968. *A History of British Football.* Stanley Paul, London.

Index

Acknowledgments

The production of this book would have been impossible without the help of many people. In particular I would like to express my debt to my wife Ramona who has carried out extensive library research and has assisted in every stage of the book's preparation. I would also like to pay special tribute to the work of Nigel Tattersfield who painstakingly obtained many hours of field recordings for me; to Lynda Poley for her picture research; to the book's designer, Ian Craig of Jonathan Cape; and to its chief photographer, Eamonn McCabe of the *Observer*.

In addition I would like to thank the following for valuable assistance of many different kinds while I have been researching and writing the book: Brian Aldiss, Sherry Arden, Bill Asprey, Roy Barry, Les Bateman, John Bay, Mick Brown, Peter Collett, Geoff Coppock, Mike Cuerden, Michael Desebrock, Gerald Edelshain, Marilyn Edwards, Ken Fish, Fred Ford, Rita Francis, Tom Goodway, Ian Greaves, Geoffrey Green, Jim Hunt, Russell Kempson, Harold Kimber, Tom Lees, Crispin Leyser, Lawrie McMenemy, Peter Marsh, Tom Maschler, Tony Mason, Jason Morris, Bob Oakes, John O'Callaghan, Glyn Pritchard, Bill Reeves, Paul Reeves, Dick Richardson, Robert Rolontz, Tony Rosser, Deborah Shepherd, Brooke Snell, Lee Strange, Tom Swan and Maurice Yaffé. I would also like to record my gratitude to the Harry Frank Guggenheim Foundation for its support of the research project from which this book developed.

Finally, a particular word of thanks to the players and supporters of Oxford United Football Club where many of my observations were carried out, and where I learned what it was like to become a member of the Soccer Tribe.

The author and the publishers wish to thank Grundy and Northedge for the artwork, and the following sources for contributing illustrations (unless otherwise stated, all the illustrations on a given page are credited to the same source): Adidas, 191 top right, centre right, 195 centre left and right, bottom left and right; Aerofilms, 41 top; All-Sport, 7 left, 14 bottom, 16 right, 19, 24 top, 27 left, 35, 43 top left, 45, 78, 81, 88 top and bottom left, 89 top right, 92 left and top right, 115 top, 117, 118, 122, 123 left, 127, 173, 174 left, 176 centre and bottom left, 178 bottom right, 210 right, 213 bottom left and right, 220 bottom right, 225 top left, 229 top centre, bottom left, bottom centre, bottom right, 233, 234, 241 bottom right, 242, 243 right, 282 top right, bottom left and right, 287 bottom left, 293 bottom, 302 right, 303 left; Ardea, 9; *Ashbourne News Telegraph*, 192; Associated Newspapers, 267; BBC Hulton Picture Library, 32, 37 bottom centre, bottom right, 194 right, 195 top left, 206 top, 244 bottom, 272; I. N. Bild/Bader, 48 right; British Museum, 187; Capital Press/Mick Alexander, 90 top, 134 right; Bruce Coleman (UK), 205; Peter Collett, 14 top, centre; Colorsport, 8 top left, 13 bottom, 20, 23, 24 bottom, 49 top left and right, 50 right, 54, 63 top right, bottom, 75, 82 top, 87 bottom, 89 top left, 109 top, 110 bottom, 111, 112 right, 120 top right, 136, 138 bottom left, 141, 158, 161 top left, 162, 167 top centre, bottom, 176 top right, 178 top right, 206 bottom left, 214 bottom right, 225 top centre, top right, bottom left, 241 right, 245 bottom left, 248 top left, 254 top, 257, 260, 266, 268, 269 bottom right, 279 top right, 282 centre left, 284 top, 285 left, centre, 290 bottom left; Gerry Cranham, 2, 31, 83, 236 bottom, 248 top centre, 290 bottom right, 291 top left; *Daily Telegraph* Colour Library, 134 left, 179 right; Fox Photos, 155, 214 left, 244 top, 281 top left, 290 top; Gola, 197 right; Ray Green, 21, 22 left, 26, 29, 41 bottom, 47, 51 top right, bottom left, 52 top left and right, 53, 60, 61, 86, 89 top centre, 90 bottom, 115 bottom right, 116, 120 top left, bottom left and right, 139, 142 top, 143, 144, 146 left, 154 top, 157, 159 top left and right, 161 centre, centre right, bottom left, bottom centre, 163, 167 top right, 169 right, 170 bottom, 172 top, 182 top and bottom left, 184 bottom, 194 left, 204 bottom, 212, 216, 218 left, 225 centre, bottom centre, 229 top right, centre left, centre, 232 right, 235, 237, 243 left, 245 top, 246 centre, 254 bottom right, 258 top, 259 top, 265, 269 centre left, bottom left, 277 top, 280 right, 289 left, 291 bottom left, 300 bottom, 302 left, 304/5, 308, 311 bottom, 314; Hamlyn Group, 37 top right; Robert Harding, 11; Tommy Hindley/Tottenham Hotspur, 221; Alan Hutchinson, 15 top, 16 left; *Illustrated London News* Picture Library, 160; Keystone Press Agency, 32 top, 65, 274, 276, 278, 279 bottom; Kishimoto, 88 right, 105 bottom, 106 left; LFI, 220 top right; Jerry Liebman/Cosmos, 289 right;

Chris Lightbown, 219; Eamonn McCabe, 12 top, 15 bottom, 39, 43 upper top right, centre top right, 44 top, 48 left, 49 centre left and right, bottom left and right, 51 top left, 52 bottom left, 57, 58 bottom, 84, 85, 87 top, 89 bottom, 93, 102, 103, 106 right, 107, 110 top, 119, 124, 128, 131, 140 right, 142 bottom, 147 top, 148 top, 150, 154 bottom, 156, 159 bottom, 161 top centre, top right, 165, 166, 172 bottom, 175 right, 176 top left, 177, 178 left, 195 top centre, 198 top, 207, 211 left, 222 top, 225 centre right, bottom right, 227, 229 top left, centre right, 230, 236 top, 241 top left, bottom left, 245 bottom right, 246 bottom, 247, 248 top right, bottom, 249, 253 right, 261 bottom, 262, 263, 264, 269 top left and right, 270, 279 top left, 286, 287 top, centre left, bottom right, 291 top right, 292, 294 bottom, 295, 297, 298, 299, 300 top, 301, 303 right, 306, 309, 311 top; Mansell Collection, 71 bottom; Peter Marsh, 251; Leo Mason, 80, 161 bottom right, 169 left, 269 centre right; Minerva, 191 top left, centre left, bottom right; Miroir Sport, 97 bottom; Mondadori, 261 top; Desmond Morris, 4 top, 7 right, 8 top right, 37 top centre, 100, 188, 193 top, 195 top right, 226 bottom; Peter Myers, 189, 288; National Archaeological Museum, Athens, 12 bottom; Popperfoto, 72 top, 108 bottom, 151, 153, 174/5, 226 top, 271, 277 bottom; Press Association, 27 right; Presse Sports, 171, 195 bottom; Private Collection, 25; Rex Features, 203, 255; G. Reszeter, 51 bottom right, 82 bottom left, 140 left; Peter Robinson/Mick Alexander, 18, 30 left, 40, 43 bottom, 58 top, 63 top left, 77 top, 79, 95, 97 left, 98, 99, 109 bottom, 120 top centre, 147 bottom, 152, 183 bottom, 186, 190, 201, 204 top, centre, 206 right, 213 top left, centre and right, 215, 223, 232 left, 246 top, 253 left, 254 bottom left, 282 centre right, 307, 317; Roy of the Rovers © IPC Magazines, 67, 218 right; Sport and General, 273; Scala, 13 top; Phil Shaw (supplied programme), 288; Frank Spooner Pictures, 112 left, 185; Sporting Pictures (UK), 82 bottom right, 108 top, 113, 135, 161 centre left, 167 top left, 170 top, 179 left, centre, 180 bottom, 181 top right, 183 top, 191 bottom left, 195 top right, 198 bottom, 211 right, 213 bottom centre, 214 centre, 225 centre left, 231, 280 left, 281 bottom, 282 top left, 283; *Sunday Times*, 220 left; Syndication International, 104 top, 105 top, 115 bottom left and centre, 121, 123 right, 146 right, 148 bottom, 180 top, 181 bottom left, centre and right, 182 right, 193 bottom, 250, 281 top right, 284 right, 285 right, 291 bottom right, 296, 310, 320; Bill Tidy, 222 bottom; John Topham Picture Library, 195 top left, 197 left; Nicholas Treadwell, 30 right, 184 top, 238; UPI, 92 bottom right; Voetbal International, 77 bottom, 258/9, 293 top; World Sport, 125; Zefa UK, 8 bottom left, 15 upper and lower centre, 22 right, 28, 38, 44 bottom, 50 left, 69, 91.